640
H

The Homesteader's manual

DATE			
4-30			
9-25			
1-29			
3-15-11			

© THE BAKER & TAYLOR CO.

Bismarck Public Library

No. 1629
$19.95

THE HOMESTEADER'S MANUAL

BY THE EDITORS OF FARMSTEAD MAGAZINE

TAB BOOKS Inc.
BLUE RIDGE SUMMIT, PA. 17214

FIRST EDITION

THIRD PRINTING

Printed in the United States of America

Reproduction or publication of the content in any manner, without express permission of the publisher, is prohibited. No liability is assumed with respect to the use of the information herein.

Copyright © 1983 by TAB BOOKS Inc.

Library of Congress Cataloging in Publication Data

Main entry under title:

The Homesteader's manual.

    1. Home economics, Rural. I. Farmstead magazine.
TX147.H755   1983   640   83-4978
ISBN 0-8306-0629-7
ISBN 0-8306-1629-2 (pbk.)

Contents

	Introduction	v
1	**Land** Removing Stumps—Raking—Wildlife and Land Management	1
2	**Insurance** Medical Insurance—Fire and Homeowner's Insurance—Auto Insurance—Other Coverages	11
3	**Building a Log Cabin** Tools—Trees—Foundation—Sill Logs—First Cross Logs—Floor—Door and Windows—Loft—Roof—Porch—Chinking—Extra Room—Cost per Room—Final Note	18
4	**Water** Dowsing—Farm Pond—Natural Cooler	30
5	**Plumbing** Shallow Trap Toilet—One-Piece Toilet—Automatic Slop Toilet—Pressurized Flush Toilet—Oil Flush and Vacuum Toilets—Composting Toilet—Biological Toilet—Other Alternatives—Waste Water Toilet	49
6	**Heating** Active Solar Heating System—Passive Solar Heating System—Heating with Wood—Buying a Wood Stove—Wood Stove Safety—Barrel Stove—Making Charcoal	59
7	**Energy-Saving Ideas** Heat Flow—Windows—Infiltration—Adding Insulation—Fireplaces—Homesteader's Guide to Insulation	94

8 Wood — 121
Forest Management—Forest Types—Growth Rate and Access—Criteria for Selecting Trees to Cut—Drying Wood—Felling a Tree—Splitting Wood—Recycling Lumber

9 Tools — 149
Hand Tools—Power Tools—Hammers—Chain Saws—Shovels

10 Construction Projects — 175
Woodshed—Chimneys—Fence—Modular Cold Frame—Hotbed—Honey Extractor—Electric Seedling Machine—Snowshoes—Carving Spoons

11 Crafts — 224
Sewing—Treadle Sewing Machines—The Art of Quilting—Quilting Projects—Crazy Quilt—Spinning and Weaving Flax and Wool—Mittens—Socks—Rugmaking

12 Gardening — 268
Spring and Summer Flower Gardening—Easy-to-Grow Flowers—Garden in the Pantry—Indoor Gardening in Winter

13 Food Preservation — 283
Food Storage—Storing Fruits and Vegetables—Canning Fruits and Vegetables—Making Jams and Jellies—Making Low-Sugar Jams and Jellies

14 Cooking — 309
Apple Recipes—Honey Recipes—Parsley Recipes—Spinach Recipes—Beet Recipes

Index — 325

Introduction

Homesteaders are always looking for ways to become more self-sufficient. They are interested in saving time, energy, and money.

This book has information on land, insurance, building a log cabin, water, plumbing, heating, wood, tools, construction projects, crafts, gardening, food preservation, and cooking. There are practical suggestions for people who want to go back to the basics.

All of the material in this book has been made available by the editors of *Farmstead Magazine*. Without their efforts and cooperation, this book would have been impossible.

Chapter 1

Land

If you're expanding or reclaiming an old farm or if you're starting fresh in the woods, then it's likely that you're going to clear land. The urge to push back the jungle is in us all. Common sense tells us that the first step in clearing land is to cut and remove the trees and large bushes. At first you might do this to open up a fine view or just to give more open space. Experience soon teaches us that we must do more if we are really going to clear the land. If the trees you've cut include such broadleaf varieties as ash, aspen, apple, alders, locust, or cherry, then these trees will soon sprout again if their stumps are not removed. Furthermore, after two years the tangle of new growth from the original stump will be harder to remove than the original tree. Clearing the land means removing what was on it and replacing it with something that is more manageable. The land is never empty; like a cleared table in a busy house, things fill it as soon as you turn your back.

REMOVING STUMPS

Once your usable wood is removed, and the slash is piled in cleared areas for burning, or piled in low areas for fill, you face the age-old problem of removing stumps. In countries where labor is cheap, stumps of trees that grow back again are removed by hand. A pit is dug around the stump, and the stump is chopped until there is no more stump in the pit. Then the pit is filled with dirt. It takes a while for the roots that are still in the ground to send up new sprouts.

Another way to pull stumps is with a tractor. Tractors are better than trucks, but a strong old 2-ton truck can pull stumps—not with straight constant pressure but with continued jerks. This method is hard on your vehicle and takes a long time. It can be facilitated by cutting the tree several feet above the ground to act as a lever rather than cutting just above ground level. Stumps can also be removed by using explosives.

The only sensible way to pull stumps is to hire a backhoe. A backhoe clears stumps faster than any of the above mentioned techniques and does so for a reasonable price. If you're a farmsteader and you're not acquainted with backhoes, you can't be an efficient farmsteader. A backhoe can get more done in an hour than you alone can do in a week.

There is a definite technique to clearing land with a backhoe (Fig. 1-1). First you pull out the large stumps. You won't believe the strength of that one arm claw. Then you stick the arm out with the bucket held like a rake and make wide sweeping arcs skimming through, but not removing the top 3 inches of soil. This loosens the little stumps and detects hidden obstacles such as boulders that should be removed, too. This second step is as important as the first, but you might have to make a special request for it as it differs from merely extracting stumps.

Now what do you do with the stumps and boulders? Stumps can ultimately be burned either in your stove or in the garden for the ashes. A stump fence also is useful even if not particularly beautiful. Deer think twice about jumping over the tangle of fence made of several layers of stumps. Have the backhoe operator build this fence if you're going to have one, and you don't have your own front-end loader. The stump and large roots of an ash 7 inches in diameter weigh more than you think. Be careful cutting the roots of a stump. The rocks and gravel attached to them will be hard on your cutting tools, although several seasons of rain may remove some of this grit.

The stones also have uses. Besides their value in building foundations, chimneys, wells, and walls, you might think of leaving a few just to sit on or make a pile for kids (goats and/or people) to climb on. Anyway, the backhoe can move these large rocks with ease, so have plans for some large rocks before the backhoe arrives.

RAKING

The backhoe has come and gone, and you have land that now

Fig. 1-1. An efficient farmsteader needs a backhoe for clearing land.

looks like it's been chewed up by a monster. The land is covered with debris; many roots are still in the ground that have only been loosened. More work is necessary before the land can be considered cleared. This mess can be removed in three ways. First, you can bring in pigs to clean it up. Second, you can carry off the larger stuff and hire a plow or tractor-pulled tiller to bury the smaller stuff. Third, you can do a slow but very clean and complete job by hand. It all depends on how much time you have and how much land you're clearing. The last method seems best and is the only one we'll explain in detail here.

After you've hauled away the branches, you've got to make piles of the smaller stuff. A potato rake, a clam hoe with a long handle, is the best tool for this. It rakes deeper than an ordinary rake, makes a smaller swath, and seems to work more easily and better than a rake. If the ground is dust dry, as in August, then the stones and old sticks and roots will rake out more easily than if the soil is wetter. If the ground is wet, you'll have to either throw away a lot of good soil or screen the soil out. The mess you're raking and screening out is just about useless except for fill, although perhaps the organic matter will burn in the intense brush fire you'll be making in the first snow from the limbs of those trees.

You now have a thin layer of productive soil. What are you going to plant so that you can manage this space and say that you've really cleared it? Remember nature wants to cover everything; it must be directed. If you have no specific plans, then how about a vegetable garden, a flower garden, a berry patch, an orchard, or a windbreak? If you have no other use for the land you must manage, grass (animal cropped or people mowed) is better than the locust and cherry weeds that will sprout naturally.

WILDLIFE AND LAND MANAGEMENT

Variety is the spice of wildlife. Variety in plants and land forms generally ensures variety in wildlife. What is variety within the 100- to 200-acre home range for a doe is not variety for the small home range of a deer mouse. Generally, the more diversity within a small area, the better the habitat for wildlife. Each animal must have all of its necessities for life within its home range.

Many species of wildlife are found in rural areas throughout most of the United States (Fig. 1-2). The white-tailed deer is the most common large species; black bear and moose are less common. Smaller mammals such as foxes, raccoons, and skunks are abundant, as are squirrels, rabbits, and snowshoe hares. Muskrats,

Fig. 1-2. Many species of wildlife are found in rural areas.

chipmunks, mice, and voles are found in many habitats. Warblers, woodpeckers, finches, birds of prey, and many other birds frequent dry and moist sites, while waterfowl and wading birds utilize wet areas.

Many animals are self-regulating and will limit their own numbers. Song birds are territorial during breeding season and generally will not overpopulate. Most small rodents and deer are not in this category and will overpopulate to the detriment of their habitat and welfare, and to that of mankind. You cannot stockpile wild animals like grain. If not naturally regulated, their numbers will have to be controlled artificially.

Like any crop, wildlife is a product of the land, and the landowner can increase or decrease the number and variety of wild animals on his land by the way he manages it. Most management practices will increase the number of some animal species and at the same time decrease others. By ignoring management, the landowner has no guarantee that all species of animals will increase; many animals will decrease without man's modification of the land. Plant variety often occurs naturally where different landforms meet. Where the swamp meets the hillside, vegetation changes from an herbaceous swamp grass and cattail plant community to a shrubby dogwood-alder community of the edge and then to a woody plant community on the hillside. Capitalize on this natural dispersion. If the hillside is eroded pasture, let it convert to woodland. Given a little time it will convert naturally, but you can hasten the process by planting. If all of your pasture converts to woodland, you have lost variety, so keep some pasture brush-free by mowing or burning. Don't worry about the low, wet swales; you're fighting an uphill battle in those places. Concentrate on the drier areas. Try to retain a sod of mixed pasture grass and the broadleaf forbs often associated with the grasses.

Woodlands

Most Northeastern farms have some woodland. It may only be a small corner, or the entire area may be covered by trees. If there is only a small patch, little can be done for wildlife except to ensure that the wooded cover is kept, but many management alternatives and their impacts on wildlife can be considered for larger tracts.

Wood products may be harvested in several ways to benefit wildlife. On larger ownerships you may want to consider clearcutting 5- to 10-acre patches. With this system, all trees on the area are cut, and natural regeneration is counted on to restock the area. Complete removal of the overstory greatly stimulates the growth of understory plants. Many of these plants provide substantially more food for wildlife than was present before the cutting. Deer, rabbits, some small rodents, and several species of birds are attracted to these areas the first few years after cutting. Different birds will occupy the area as the new trees begin to form a closed canopy and increase in height. At the same time, low-growing plants will receive less sunlight and decrease in vigor and abundance. Animals dependent upon these plants will have less food. If there is a pattern of small areas cut at 5- or 10-year intervals, a diversity of forest habitats will be available. Animals will be able to move to these nearby areas. Thus, variety can be created by management of the land.

If your ownership is too small to create variety with small clearcuts, you can harvest trees by group selection, cutting as few as three trees in a group or cutting all trees on ½ to 1 acre. These smaller openings will also stimulate growth of the understory and provide plant variety. Scattered cuttings will create variety over your ownership. Woodlands with small openings will retain those species of birds that prefer a complete canopy, such as nuthatches and kinglets, and still include those species that depend on brushy openings, such as the white-throated sparrow. Many other wild species will benefit from the increase in plant variety.

Cutting single trees or cutting smaller trees that do not form part of the canopy generally will not affect stand variety or cause much change in animal numbers or variety unless the cutting is done to eliminate the few hardwoods in a conifer stand or conifers in a hardwood stand. This practice might well reduce numbers and variety of wildlife. Encourage a mix of evergreen and broadleaf trees. Do not remove all dead or dying trees. Many species of wildlife depend on them for hiding and nesting cavities, and insects found in decaying wood provide food for many birds.

Deer are dependent on dense conifer stands for protection during winter. These areas are critical and require special treatment. If you have a conifer stand that receives intensive deer use through the winter, check with the state wildlife agency for advice. They can tell you if you own part of an important deer wintering area and the best land management methods to ensure that the area remains good winter habitat. The farther north they are, the more important are these wintering areas.

Open Land

Wild animals obtain considerable food from cropland, whether we like it or not. Crop areas scattered throughout woodland, brushland, or pastureland provide food for wildlife with cover nearby— almost ideal conditions for wildlife. You can plant enough for yourself and wildlife, try using wildlife repellents, or (if your land is exceptional for New England) eliminate cover and establish crops over the entire ownership. This will lessen crop loss from wild animals, but will decrease the wildlife population.

Many landowners plant a little extra food and accept the crop loss to wildlife because they enjoy the benefits that the animals provide. Others try commercial or noncommercial repellents. The effectiveness of chemical and physical repellents varies by area, season, the species of animal to be repelled, and by other factors not fully understood. The old preventative of human urine applied to a rag on a stake near the garden may help protect small plots. Dogs confined near the garden may also be helpful on small areas. Your county agent or state wildlife agency can give you more advice on repellents. You may have to fence your garden as a last resort.

Control of small rodents can be enhanced by mowing grass or weed patches near areas you want to protect. Owls, foxes, and hawks will do a good job of controlling harmful rodents if you give them a little help (Fig. 1-3). If a fox tries to get into your house or barn or acts abnormally in other ways, its behavior is suspect and you should part company, as it might be rabid.

Woody fence rows between fields have considerable value for almost all wildlife. Wide rows provide nesting and brood cover for many species of birds, such as robins, wrens, and bluebirds—effective predators of insects harmful to crops. Foxes and other predators use these protected travel lands. Deer use brushy fence rows for cover and as a source of food. When you plow or mow, stay away from the fence. Brushy plants will come in naturally. If trees in the row become so tall that they shade too much crop area, cut them and allow shrubby vegetation to reassert itself.

Abandoned crop and pasture lands will eventually revert to woodland. These areas have considerable value for wildlife, particularly in the first few years after their abandonment. At this time herbaceous plants are intermixed with small woody plants and variety is great. As these areas age, woody plants begin to shade out the lower growing herbaceous plants and variety decreases. As tree species grow taller and their crowns form a continuous canopy, even the shrubby vegetation decreases and plant variety is substantially limited. Opening the canopy will benefit wildlife by increasing variety and numbers. Opening the canopy requires a substantial operation: cutting, bulldozing, chemical silvicides, or fire. An easier way is to preserve a scattering of open areas by mowing or disking about every other year. Such planned abandonment is not always possible, but where it is, quality habitat can be maintained.

Man and wildlife still compete for the same foods—witness deer in gardens. Mice, voles and other rodents, if not kept in bounds by natural controls, can be very destructive. Small rodents eat the inner bark and kill the trees. Through land management practices, you can help nature control the small gnawers.

In the past, animals provided man food and also protection from the elements through clothing, furnishings, and shelter. They still can. Gloves or a jacket can be made from deer hide. A bear's hide can provide a warm spot for sitting on a cold living room floor.

Perhaps the greatest value of wild animals accrues from just

Fig. 1-3. An immature goshawk.

knowing they are there on your own land. They serve to tie you to nature. Many small landowners appreciate the wild animals that inhabit their land and want to encourage their numbers, whether they want to observe and study nature or appreciate bear stew along with nature study.

If you think about plant and landform variety as you manage your farm, you won't have to worry about having enough wildlife. It will be there.

Additional information on managing land for wildlife may be obtained from the Soil Conservation Service, U.S. Department of Agriculture, the Extension Service of your state university, and your state wildlife agency.

Chapter 2

Insurance

One of the major dollar considerations facing the would-be farmer or homesteader is the insurance coverages he may or may not need. For the large, profit-oriented, heavily-equipped farm operation, the need for most coverages is clear and is taken on as a business expense. The farmsteader, trying to avoid the money economy as much as possible, may gamble on dropping all coverages and find himself in real trouble.

The average person generally thinks of insurance as a huge expense and ongoing annoyance. He feels resentment toward some insurance companies and rightfully so, because their fancy buildings and expensive ad campaigns come out of his pocket. Insurance company extravagances are an unnecessary violation of the true principles of insurance, for insurance was one of the first and most successful of communal activities—the sharing of risk among a large number of people. You're not altogether at the mercy of these companies, however, for an independent insurance agent can pick and choose among them to provide you with the best available coverages.

To some extent, the small farmer is already a gambler, having opted for self-sufficiency and the rural life over the security of a desk job and pension in the city. The wise homesteader plans ahead, and some insurance questions must be part of his considerations. Should he carry medical insurance, and if so, what kind and to what extent? What about fire insurance on his house and barn, insurance for wind and water damage, and the like? If he has a roadside stand, should he carry liability insurance, and what about liability protection (or *workmen's compensation* requirements) for seasonal or full-time hired hands?

Then there's auto insurance, which includes liability for bodily injury and property damage, physical damage, comprehensive (fire, theft of the auto, etc.) and collision, as well as protection against uninsured motorists. Does auto insurance provide coverage for tractor accidents as well?

A few farmsteaders are concerned enough about geologic fault to inquire about earthquake insurance. Those in low-lying areas may want flood insurance (which is now available for qualified areas).

Then there's life insurance, disability income insurance, insurance on crops, livestock, and woodlots. This list is virtually endless. So where do you begin?

MEDICAL INSURANCE

Let's begin by considering the aspirations and the dangers that confront the small farmer. The small farmer to a great extent relies on his health for his success, yet he is exposed to more dangers than workers in nearly any other field. Indeed, of all occupations in this country, farming is the third most hazardous, preceded only by logging and mining. The small farmer is a jack of all trades, working with tractors, tillers, chain saws, trucks, horses and cattle. He works, not from nine-to-five, but from sunrise to sunset, and he's often tempted to take unwarranted chances with old equipment or too heavy loads.

The best insurance is maintenance of equipment and care in its use. The extremely high risk of accidents on the farm, coupled with the increased chances of infection and disease, warrant serious consideration of medical insurance. This is extremely unfortunate, because medical insurance is perhaps the most expensive coverage you can carry, due to the high costs of health care in this country.

Let's pause for a minute to consider the concept of "self-insurance" and deductibles. One hundred percent insurance protection is the most expensive and least desirable coverage you can buy. Why pay $1,200 a year to an insurance company when you could bank, say, $800 of it in a savings account and collect interest on it until you need it to pay a medical bill? The amount you can afford to bank (without counting on using it for something else) is the degree to which you can be self-insured. This is true for many kinds of insurance, but it pays off most heavily in medical insurance savings. If you can assume responsibility for, say, the first $1,000 of medical bills, you can obtain *major medical* coverage at far more reasonable rates and be protected for the next $10,000 (or more) of expense. In looking at various plans, be realistic about what amounts you can self-insure for, and then set that money aside. Self-insurance hinges on your own bankbook.

In considering what insurance companies to approach remember that Blue Cross and Blue Shield, being nonprofit, have an operating expense advantage over most other companies. Get a quote from "the Blues" and take it to an insurance agent to see if one of the companies he represents can offer you a better deal. Sometimes they can, depending on the coverage you need.

FIRE AND HOMEOWNER'S INSURANCE

Second to your health, your farm is probably your most valuable resource. Being a farm, it is also one of the trickiest and most expensive of properties to insure. This is again because of the exposures involved—the storage of hay, the storage of oil and gasoline, the generally older age of farmhouses and barns, and the high expense of replacing them with new buildings of a similar size.

The owner-built, one-room cabin with an adjoining shed for animals probably does not require fire insurance. If its construction costs were low, the owner can simply build another one should it burn. (He may wish to insure the contents, however.) A 10-room 100-year-old farmhouse is another matter altogether. First, if the farm was bought on a mortgage, the bank will require enough insurance to cover the outstanding mortgage loan. If you bought the farm cheap and have spent considerable energy and expense in its repair, however, you will want to insure it not for its purchase price, but for something approaching its market value or replacement cost. (Note that we are speaking of the value of the building alone; don't include the value of the land it sits on.) With an 80 percent coinsurance clause in your fire policy, you must be insured for at least 80 percent of the replacement cost of the structure at current prices to collect the face amount of the policy. If the house is a veritable mansion—one that would cost $100,000 to replace—and you paid $5,000 for it, then it would be ridiculous to try to insure it for 80 percent of its replacement cost. Insure for that proportion of replacement cost that will provide you with what you could get by on should your home be partially or completely destroyed. (*Flat rate* fire insurance accomplishes this.) Your insurance agent can help you figure out what is best for you.

When is a farm a farm? This is a terribly important question to the insurer and the insured, and especially so since the development of the preferred-rate package known as "homeowner's" insurance. For if you can qualify for homeowner's insurance, your insurance coverage will be far more extensive and will cost you less than if your house is rated as a farm. This is especially true in so-called "unprotected" areas, i.e., rural areas where hydrants and fire stations aren't immediately available.

Many people do not realize that there are different homeowner's coverages as well, known as HO-1, HO-2, and HO-3 policies. Understandably, there are considerably different rates for each kind of coverage. The homeowner should weigh the risks against the rates and insure accordingly. Incidentally, there is a package policy for farms known as a Farmowner's Policy, but not many companies offer it, and it tends to be more expensive than homeowners.

The technical definition of a *farm* is a property where five or more head of livestock are maintained, or a flock of more than 300 birds is kept. Some companies, such as Allstate, stick strictly to this definition and refuse to write homeowner's insurance for the small farmer. Some other companies take a more liberal view, as long as the farm operation doesn't increase the danger of loss. For example, a house with an attached barn where hay is stored has a much greater chance of burning than one whose barn is more than 50 feet away. Along these same lines, a house with a central heating system (an oil, gas, electric, or wood furnace in the basement or electric baseboard heat) is exposed to less risk than one heated solely with wood stoves on combustible floors. That's not to say, however, that you can't supplement your central heating with wood stoves, so long as your chimneys meet minimum requirements. The difference in your insurance rates between a homeowner's and separate fire, extended coverage, and liability policies could be enough over a few years to pay for the installation of a central heating system.

The small farmer or homesteader who is planning to remodel or build might well consider reviewing the farm fire rating manual and the requirements for homeowner's insurance before starting to work. The rules, though seemingly arbitrary, do indicate the collective experience of insured farms over the years; they can provide some guidelines for the safest design, construction, and space between farm buildings.

AUTO INSURANCE

The next area of concern to the homesteading farmer should be his auto insurance. Fortunately, the farmer, rather than being penalized, is actually given a better rate if his vehicle is kept primarily on a farm, for his exposure to liability or collision loss is reduced. Furthermore, most business uses for your family auto generally push your auto insurance into a more expensive rating, but not farm business. The family policy covers autos and panel and pickup trucks (up to ¾ ton) used on the family farm. Moreover, the family policy covers farm wagons or machinery while being towed by a farm utility automobile.

Though tractors and other mobile farm machinery cannot be covered under your family auto policy, the kinds of coverage you may want—liability, comprehensive (fire, theft), or collision—can be had on what is known as an *inland marine floater*. One legitimate way you can save money on your insurance premiums is to suspend coverage on vehicles or equipment used seasonally. If you have a truck that is used only in the fall to deliver produce to market, or a tractor used only in the spring and fall, there is no good reason to carry full coverage all year round. (You should maintain your comprehensive coverage, however, to guard against fire or theft of the stored vehicle.)

As with other kinds of coverages, check to see if the savings make taking a higher deductible worthwhile. Generally speaking, it's worth having full comprehensive coverage on the family auto, but a $100 deductible on collision insurance might make sense. If you have an older car or truck, it may make even more sense not to carry any collision coverage (which only pays for repairs to your car up to its market value).

One last word on auto insurance. There are a tremendous number of variables involved in auto insurance rates, including your age, marital status, location, number of young drivers in the family, number of vehicles insured, record of accidents and violation convictions, where you live, how far you drive to work, etc. Different companies offer different advantages for different situations, so it pays to shop around.

OTHER COVERAGES

Let's look briefly at some other types of coverages.

Liability. There are many areas where a farmer can be held liable, but be realistic about the chances of some things ever happening (such as being sued for selling produce that made the buyer sick). On the other hand, the chances of an employee being injured on the job are fairly good, and this is an area where the employer should have coverage or is required (under the workmen's compensation law) to have coverage. If you are a seasonal or full-time employer, call your insurance agent and find out what your responsibilities really are. A "farmer's comprehensive personal liability policy" (FCPL) is designed to protect a farmer for his personal activities and farming operations. It comes automatically as Section II of the Farmowner's Policy or can be purchased separately. For a nominal additional charge, animal collision coverage can be added to provide reimbursement to the insured if one of his animals is struck by a vehicle. An FCPL is not "comprehensive," however, despite its name, so be sure to read what's excluded before you buy it.

Protection for Animals. The inland marine floater mentioned earlier can be written for livestock, too. You might well wish to insure horses and cattle against loss by fire, even if you choose not to insure the barn they're kept in. Coverage for crops, hay, and even woodlots is also available, though it's seldom considered by the small farmer.

Life. Excessive life insurance is a sorry second choice to making sure that every adult member of the family could support him/herself if another died. Nevertheless, deaths change plans, expectations, and possibilities; what was a viable family farm may not be manageable by the wife or husband alone. There may be a mortgage, large bills, or inheritance taxes that would force the survivor to sell their farmstead. It's the proper role of life insurance to protect your mate from this situation, and the least expensive way of doing this is with decreasing term life insurance. The big expenses of your life—raising children, paying off a mortgage—are incurred early, and your death at an early age requires more dollars for a longer time. If you're a young father with young children and a 20-year mortgage, then it would make sense to carry a 20-year decreasing term policy for an initial face value of at least $25,000 or $30,000. As you get older the coverage decreases, but so does your mortgage and the number of years your children need to be supported. This type of coverage is really cheap for the protection it provides.

In planning your life in the country, be realistic. If you're deep in the woods, that volunteer fire department 10 miles away probably won't be able to do a thing for your chimney fire. Keep your chimneys clean and in good repair by keeping several dry chemical fire extinguishers handy, an alternate second-story escape route planned, and adequate insurance coverage. The same attitude and care must be taken with your other daily risks, too. Preventive maintenance on your car, chain saw, and tractor are critical if you anticipate a long and happy life on your farmstead. Good experience often means lower insurance rates on your various coverages as well, so you will be doubly rewarded by running a shipshape, low-hazard farm.

Chapter 3

Building a Log Cabin

If wild greens and Euell Gibbons turn you on, you can harvest the ultimate wild bounty—your very own log cabin. If you have 100 softwood trees, a few hundred dollars, and love invigorating work, you're ready to go. Here's how David VanderZwaag and his wife built a cozy lodge, without previous experience, on McLeod's Island off the Atlantic coast of Nova Scotia (Figs. 3-1 and 3-2).

TOOLS

A chain saw certainly saves time and effort. The VanderZwaags decided in favor of a bow saw: first, to save over $100 on a saw purchase; second, so as not to disturb wildlife, especially a rookery of blue herons nearby; third, they were so far away from a doctor or hospital in case of a serious accident, which seemed more likely with a power saw. Their other equipment included an ax, hammer, chisel, level, ruler, and screwdriver.

TREES

Straight trees without much taper from trunk to crown make the best building blocks. Thinking big, the VanderZwaags chopped like industrious beavers at a 3-foot diameter spruce tree. As the giant crashed, David suddenly realized that not even four harnessed whales could tote such a tree out of the woods. Then insight struck. The VanderZwaags had to build with smaller trees which they could

Fig. 3-1. The VanderZwaags' cabin is located on McLeod's Island off Nova Scotia (photo by David VanderZwaag).

Fig. 3-2. The cabin is made out of softwood trees (photo by David VanderZwaag).

carry, about 6 inches in diameter, and thus reduce the cabin size to a snug 16 feet by 12 feet. Therefore, they cut the trees into 14-foot and 18-foot lengths to allow for a 1-foot overhang at each cabin corner.

To beat a fast approaching winter, the VanderZwaags built with green wood. Seasoned trees would have been much lighter.

Stripping the bark off the trees was necessary to prevent insect attack and was easily done with nothing but an ax. Bark almost falls off during spring and summer when the sap runs freely.

Their work plan was to cut and strip four trees a day and to notch four into place. Figuring on about 100 trees a room, it took them approximately 30 days to complete the task.

FOUNDATION

Neither time nor muscle allowed the VanderZwaags to build a conventional foundation. Cement was out of the question as 100-pound bags would surely sink their kayak. Yet they wanted a foundation that would not heave with winter frost—in their area about 3 feet below ground.

Their solution was to dig a 3-foot hole at each cabin corner. They then piled flat beach rocks in each hole to make four support piers. Each pier projected 18 inches above ground level to provide a moistureproof base. Although somewhat wobbly at first, the piers stabilized with the added pressure of logs.

After the cabin was completed, the VanderZwaags filled in the space between piers with additional rocks for looks, extra support, and additional insulation.

Fig. 3-3. The log ends were grooved where they would lay on the piers (drawing by David VanderZwaag).

Fig. 3-4. Procedure used for notching in the first cross logs (drawing by David VanderZwaag).

SILL LOGS

The biggest trees naturally became the bottom logs, not only for a look of solidarity but to save the backs as well.

To prevent the sill logs from rolling off the foundation, the VanderZwaags grooved the log ends where they would lay on the piers (Fig. 3-3). The VanderZwaags then brushed on creosote preservative over sills, as they are most prone to rot and insect attack. To counteract the tapering effect of trees, the front sill ran thick end to thin end while the rear sill ran thin end to thick end (Fig. 3-3).

A cardinal rule they followed in placing on subsequent logs was a slender end of a tree goes on top of a thick end and vice versa. This formula assured that all walls would end up close to equal in height.

FIRST CROSS LOGS

The VanderZwaags chose to use the popular and easy saddle notch. To notch in the first cross logs, they first placed them on top of the sill logs. With a pencil they marked three dots near each cross log end, both inside and out (Fig. 3-4). The lower dots were spaced to match the width of the sill log below while the upper dot was placed approximately at the cross log's midsection. Next, they connected the dots forming a rough arc near each log end, both inside and out (Fig. 3-4).

Positioning the cross logs on the ground, marked side up, the VanderZwaags then hollowed out all the wood inside their lines with an ax and chisel (Fig. 3-4).

The same procedure was repeated for all subsequent layers of logs. If gaps between logs were greater than 1 inch, they would hollow notches deeper than original lines. If some logs rubbed together due to crooks, they would hew down the problem spots with an ax.

FLOOR

To assure stable and longlasting floor joists, the VanderZwaags notched their sawmill 2×4s directly into the sills instead of using spikes. The process involved two main steps; first they chiseled 12 equidistant 2×3×3-inch grooves along the inner edge of each sill log (Fig. 3-5). Next they notched 12 2×4s per Fig. 3-6 and set them (A side up) into the sill grooves.

The joists were further stabilized by nailing scrap 2×4s between all joists (Fig. 3-6). For underflooring, they tacked 4×8-foot panels on ¼-inch exterior plywood to the underside of floor joists. For floor insulation, the VanderZwaags stuffed armloads of dry eelgrass, a ribbonlike seaweed tossed up by tons in shallow island coves, between all joists.

Sphagnum moss, however, would have supplied an excellent alternative. For overlay, 1×5-inch spruce planking, planed on the top side, furnished the final rustic look.

DOOR AND WINDOWS

Unlike many cabin builders who cut out window and door

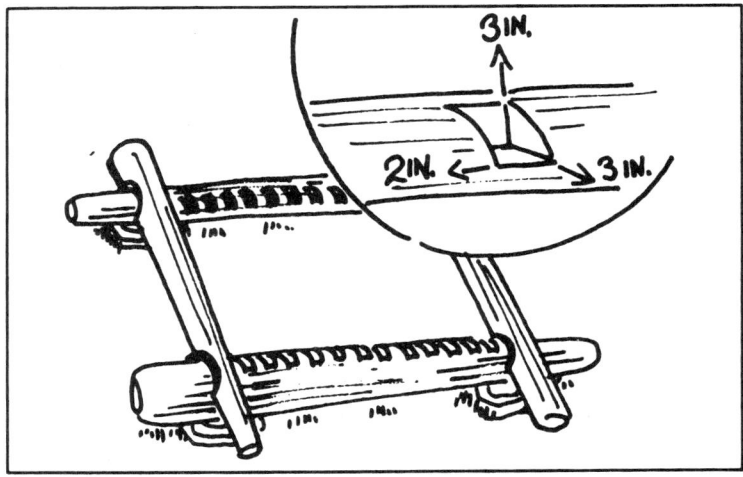

Fig. 3-5. Twelve equidistant 2×3×3-inch grooves were chiseled along the inner edge of each sill log (drawing by David VanderZwaag).

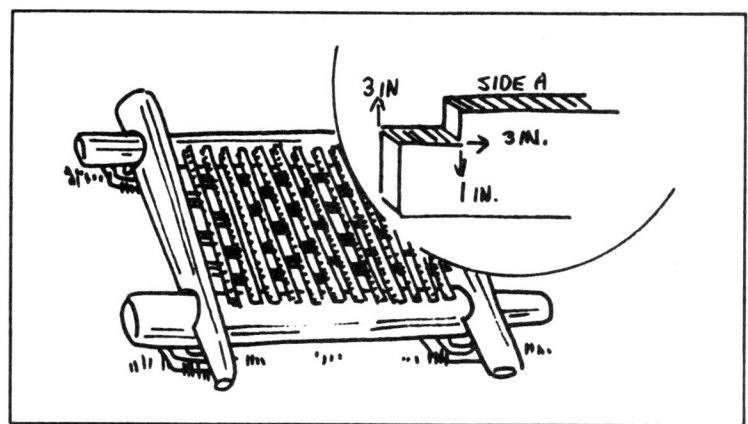

Fig. 3-6. Twelve 2×4s were notched and set into the sill grooves. Scrap 2×4s were nailed between all joists (drawing by David VanderZwaag).

openings when all walls are complete, the VanderZwaags chose to notch and spike the frames into place while raising the walls. This not only permitted convenient access to the cabin interior, but also allowed the use of shorter trees where frames were inset.

All frames were constructed of 2×6-inch lumber which providentially washed up after a violent gale. The door and windows, meanwhile, were salvaged from a quaint fishing cottage on the mainland.

The door frame was notched into the first cross log as follows; first, the frame width was marked onto the cross log. Then 1-inch cuts with the bow saw were made at 6-inch intervals (Fig. 3-7) that permitted the VanderZwaags to easily chip out a uniform groove with the ax. They then set and spiked the door frame into the groove (Fig. 3-7). Subsequent logs around the door were cut into 2-foot and 9½-foot lengths. Outer log ends were saddle notched as usual while inner log ends were spiked to the door frame (Fig. 3-8). The log above the door frame had to be grooved on the underside to complete the framing in process. Window frames were grooved and spiked into place with the same procedure.

LOFT

Besides giving extra storage space, the loft permits the VanderZwaags to sleep in the warmest area of the cabin, a factor greatly appreciated when icy January winds blow through cabin chinking.

When the cabin walls stood about 7 feet high, they notched in six old barn beams in the same way the floor joists were notched into

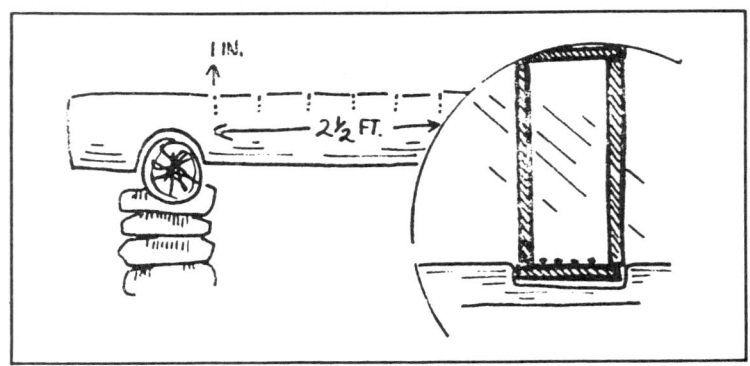

Fig. 3-7. One-inch cuts were made with a bow saw at 6-inch intervals, and an ax was used to chip out a uniform groove. Then the door frame was set and spiked into the groove (drawing by David VanderZwaag).

the sill logs, except beams were spaced about 1½ feet apart and extended over just half the cabin area.

Rough barnboards made an impressive flooring while four more tiers of cabin logs (the last being lengthwise) completed the lofty walls.

ROOF

Like many an amateur, the VanderZwaags quaked at the prospect of performing acrobatic saw tricks 15 feet above rocks and

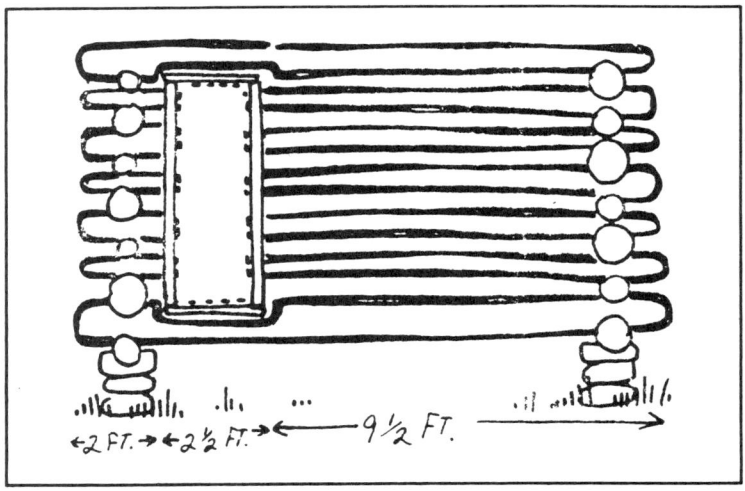

Fig. 3-8. Outer log ends were saddle notched, and inner log ends were spiked to the door frame (drawing by David VanderZwaag).

shale in an attempt to roof the cabin. Even more, they trembled at the idea of having to repeatedly hoist 200-pound timbers high above their heads. Again insight struck. By stationing the final log tier as a temporary foundation on the ground, they could easily "prefab" the roof on firm earth per Fig. 3-9.

All roof notches were cut in tops of logs (rather than on undersides). Therefore, they notched top sides of A_1 and A_2 to hold log #1, they notched top side of #1 to hold B_1 and B_2 and so forth. Numbers 1, 2, 3, etc., were their gable logs and had to be tapered at each end to approximate the roof slope. Letters A_1, A_2, B_1, B_2, etc., were poles running the length of the cabin.

When all roof pieces were in place and numbered, they disassembled the structure and, in a matter of a few hours, hoisted and snapped all the prefitted logs atop the cabin. Rough 1×5-inch planks, nailed to the roof poles, completed the woodsy rooftop.

Since wooden shingles would have posed a possible fire risk, they chose to waterproof the roof with asphalt shingles.

PORCH

By cutting the roof poles an extra 4 feet in length (22 feet), the VanderZwaags easily extended the roof beyond the gables to form a protected veranda. Upright poles were spiked to the ridgepole and bottom roof logs to support the overhang.

CHINKING

Because sphagnum moss chinking would harbor insects and because mortar chinking would crumble as unseasoned logs gradually shrunk in diameter, the VanderZwaags settled on oakum, a ropelike caulking (available at most hardware stores) used by plumbers and seamen to plug leaky seams.

With a screwdriver they tightly packed the oakum strands between all log gaps, being careful not to allow oakum to bulge beyond the log exteriors (Fig. 3-10). Protruding oakum would absorb rain that would likely facilitate the rotting of logs.

EXTRA ROOM

Although constructing a second room concurrently with the first room would have been more structurally sound, the VanderZwaags waited until a year later to add their comfortable 10×14-foot workroom, for hundreds of chores like clearing a garden and digging a well pleaded to be done first.

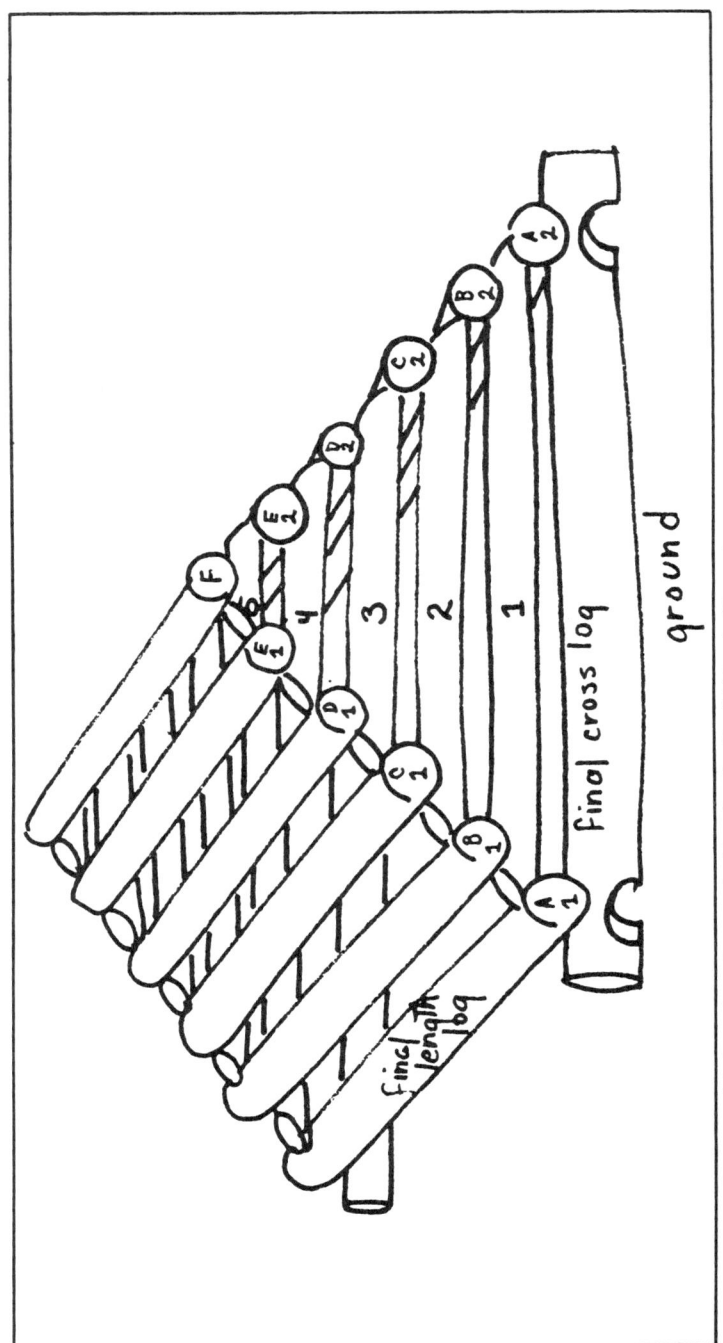

Fig. 3-9. The roof was prefabricated on firm earth (drawing by David VanderZwaag).

Fig. 3-10. The oakum strands were tightly packed between all log gaps. The oakum could not be allowed to bulge beyond the log exteriors (drawing by David VanderZwaag).

Erection of the spare room followed their previous procedures, except a few innovations became necessary to couple onto the original cabin:

- Two upright poles about 7 feet in height were spiked onto the cabin exterior (A, B, of Fig. 3-11) with each upright supported by a pier of rocks.
- Wall logs of the extra room were then grooved on one end per Fig. 3-12 and spiked to the uprights. Outer log ends were saddle notched as usual.
- Three poles were nailed in triangular fashion (with vertical braces) above the uprights to support the roof poles (Fig. 3-11,C).
- Roof poles were supported by gable logs on outer wall (just like Fig. 3-9) but spiked onto the roof support (C, Fig. 3-11) on the inner wall.
- The window opening was enlarged into a doorway for the new room.

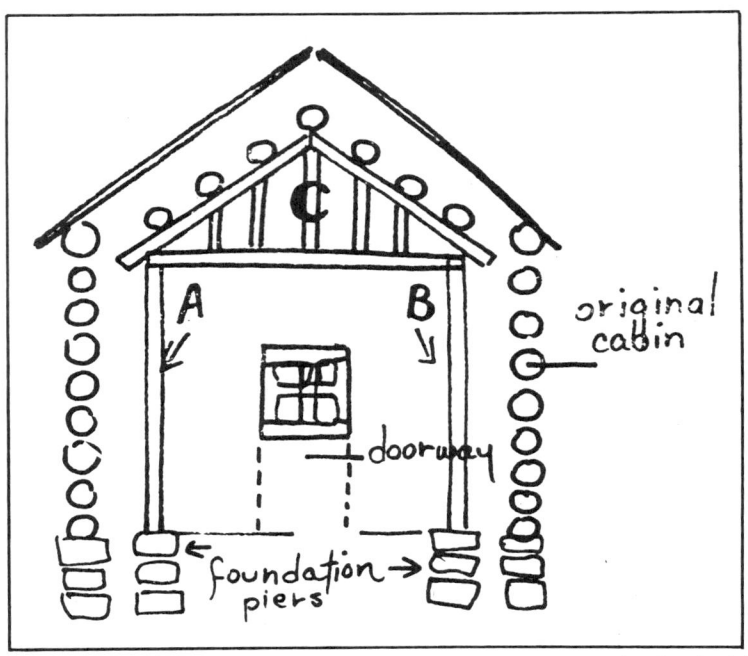

Fig. 3-11. Procedure used to construct the spare room (drawing by David VanderZwaag).

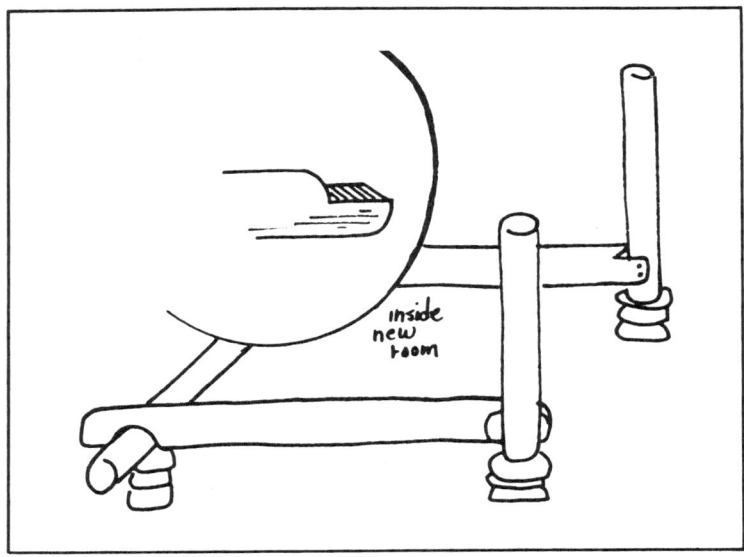

Fig. 3-12. Wall logs of the extra room were grooved on one end and spiked to the uprights (drawing by David VanderZwaag).

COST PER ROOM

12	2×4s (12-foot lengths) for floor joists	$ 12.00
6	¼-inch exterior plywood (4×8-foot sheets) for underflooring	$ 60.00
39	1×5-inch spruce planks (12-foot lengths) planed one side for flooring	$ 43.00
39	1×5-inch rough spruce for roofing (14-foot lengths)	$ 47.00
90	pounds of plumber's oakum	$ 72.00
	Roofing: shingles, asphalt felt, plastic cement	$ 75.00
Nails		$ 15.00
Total cost:		$324.00

Prices are bound to vary from area to area, but shopping around definitely pays.

By searching out a backwoods sawmill, the VanderZwaags saved more than $100 on lumber, avoided a middleman, and gave a boost to the "little guy." Some sawmills will even work out swaps. You bring in 50 trees, and they cut 25 into planking and keep 25 trees for payment.

FINAL NOTE

Cabin building has so many variations and so much leeway for error that one oldtimer recently uttered. "The only man who can't put up a log cabin is either darn lazy or dead." So pick up your ax and give it a try. You'll be surprised at the results.

Chapter 4

Water

Water is one of the elements without which no life as man knows it could exist. Few of us pause to consider how precious an element water is and how basic it is to our daily life. We seldom consider how many ways Mother Nature has of supplying her Earth with water. There are many—from the tiny springhead giving out its clear, refreshing trickle, to mighty rivers.

Locating a water supply is probably the most important aspect of locating a homestead. If people have lived on the place before, there must be a water supply. If it is a new place, locate water first, then plan for locating your dwelling, barn, and so on, accordingly. You'll save yourself a great deal of trouble and expense if you do it that way.

There are many sources of homestead water, from springs and seeps that can be developed into an inexpensive gravity-feed water system, to deep underground water that must be drilled for at no small expense. Most of the Northeast is blessed with abundant, good water, and shallow, dug wells from 8 to 30 feet deep provide sufficient water.

Contrary to popular belief, water veins aren't subterranean brooks, nor do they seem to be like underground "water pipes." These last are very rare. Water does flow in some of these water veins, but it does not flow in any relation to the surface contours of the ground.

What you'll usually find will be a layer of earth that is porous through which water trickles or seeps constantly. The place may be but a few inches in diameter, or 2 feet, or more, when ground is cut cross-sectionally. Surrounding earth may be damp, moist, or even dry. That is why a water vein can be easily missed in digging.

Most water veins trickle through sandy gravel, or just sand, and the place looks like pencil-sized holes that dribble. The water volume can be amazing. If properly handled, it will supply enough water for average homestead needs of people, animals, and poultry the year round.

A gravel pit, such as those dug by highway departments or construction companies, is an excellent way to see the land in your vicinity in cross section. There you can see the character of the gravels, sands, and other soils present, and the rocks to be found in the region. Take a look at the other "diggin's" that may be about, and don't hesitate to ask questions of others (who may become neighbors)—especially any who recently dug water wells, springs, and well springs within five years or so. Also, ask people who have lived in the region for many years. From such sources you can obtain more specialized information than in any other way. Older residents know how water supplies held out during droughts. Wells get low during droughts; some even go dry. Some, though they do get low, never are known to go dry. The depth of the well has little to do with how it holds out. Some natural springs and well springs have never been known to go dry.

A nature student knows that certain kinds of vegetation are sure to grow where the water table is high and will be sparse or lacking where the ground water level is lower. Some kinds of shrubbery and grasses (willows, alders, marsh grass, etc.) cannot exist at all in places with the water table more than 6 feet below the surface. Others will tolerate lower levels. Examine vegetation carefully if you intend to have a cellar under your house or an outside root cellar, or you just might end up with a water hole instead—seasonally if not all of the time.

DOWSING

Dowsing can find a place to dig, and a good water well results, provided the digger digs on the place marked. If he doesn't, he isn't apt to get water. It doesn't take much of a mistake at this point to miss the water altogether or get only a seep, or even no water at all.

There are those who use their ability in a practical way to find needed water, and there are those who like to impress others with a great deal of hocus-pocus, shroud the whole thing in deep mystery, perform mysterious rites, and otherwise show off. Some even make claims for their prowess and try to turn dowsing into a money-making scheme. These are best avoided, for after all, the homesteader needing to locate a reliable water source isn't interested in hocus-pocus, mysterious rites, and showing off (Fig. 4-1). He wants water.

It's a good idea to try it yourself. You may be one of those who can find water and not be aware of it. The forked stick, or dowsing stick, doesn't have to be from some particular hardwood tree or shrub, though some do better than others. Its use doesn't involve any magic words mumbled during selection, preparation, or use. You can select and cut a stick at the site and trim it neatly with a pocketknife.

Maple, willow, hazel, and several others found growing where the ground is moist are all good to use. Select one that, when trimmed, is shaped somewhat like the wishbone of a chicken, with its two prongs as nearly equal in size as possible, and a little thicker than a pen barrel. Such a stick is responsive, yet doesn't break easily, and is prepared with an ordinary jackknife such as every outdoorsman carries. A 2-foot length is about right. Trim away smoothly all twigs and nodes where new twigs are about to grow.

Holding the arms at elbow height, turn extended hands palms upward, thumbs pointing outward. Grasp the two prongs of the stick firmly about a third of the distance from tips to the point where they join. Spread the hands apart until you feel a little tension on the stick. Now slowly walk forward, keeping the stick's point at the level of your elbows. If there's water down below, and you are capable of dowsing, you'll feel a downward pull of the stick's point as you approach the place where there's a water vein below. With your hands, resist the pull. When you just can't keep the stick up to the horizontal plane where it's to be held when in use, and it goes down anyway, you're standing over the water. The more water down there and the nearer the ground surface, the stronger you'll feel the pull. It helps you to estimate the distance below the surface where the water vein flows. Experience and your own degree of sensitivity will help you become accurate on depth.

To test yourself, try dowsing around a place where there is already a water well or a natural spring. If nothing happens, you're a person who can't dowse and just forget doing it yourself. Find someone else who can. If you can dowse, practice around places where the well depths are definitely known to get the feel of it. Then try it on your own homestead.

Fig. 4-1. The homesteader isn't interested in hocus-pocus when trying to locate a water source.

A good procedure is to supply yourself with an armful of little marker sticks and a hammer to drive them into the soil. Place the first marker at the exact spot where you get your first really hard pull-down. Walk in widening circles until at least three markers have been placed, which will give you some idea as to the direction the water vein is traveling. Water veins don't travel in straight lines any more than do brooks, so your markers aren't apt to be in straight lines. You'll find main lines (where you get the strongest pull-downs) and side lines that cross them. These have less pull and are feeders. These may be on or near the same level as the main lines, above or below them. A junction of main line and one or more feeders is a good place to dig. If you work seriously and carefully, it's a good plan to color code your markers. One color for the main line, and a different color for feeders, using any little strings of cloth you happen to have handy. Once the point to dig has been chosen, mark this one with a fence stake driven in to stay put. That way, it doesn't get accidentally misplaced or lost, for this spot is to be the center of the hole to be dug to reach the water.

An honest dowser welcomes checking. Though as far as we know, science, as such, hasn't yet any established proofs about dowsing for water, those among them who can do it are puzzled, and those who can't scoff.

It has something to do with static electricity. Some people seem to have a good deal in their bodies, regardless of the person's size, and others have very little or possibly none. Of these last, we've yet to know of one who can dowse for water. The stick just won't do anything. The others get response in varying degrees.

Static electricity is attracted by water, as we know is true of lightning, one form of static. While dowsers aren't miniature lightning bolts, they do have enough in their bodies to make the stick work (Fig. 4-2). They also soon magnetize a watch, particularly a wristwatch, unless it's an expensive antimagnetic one.

Dowsing for a well quite often attracts onlookers who watch with interest or come to scoff. Invite these people to try it themselves. To their utter astonishment, some discover that it works for them.

To dowse together, have your partner stand beside you, either side. Position the stick in his hands properly. Grasp the other prong yourself and take his free hand in your own free hand and begin walking. As the water vein is approached, he begins to feel the pull, and his face is a study. Tell him not to let the stick turn down. He struggles but it goes down anyway. If he's scientific, he's greatly

Fig. 4-2. A person with a lot of static electricity in his body may be a good dowserman.

puzzled, but can't explain why it works. If he's superstitious, he's sure that "the old scratch" himself has reached up from below with invisible hands and pulled down the stick.

It's a good laugh, anyway. In olden times, the whole thing was linked, in people's minds, with the supernatural. It wasn't and isn't, and the explanation will someday come with more knowledge about

35

static electricity. In the meantime, it will continue as a means of finding a place to get water, as it has for centuries in the past.

FARM POND

The demand for water has increased so greatly that private land users have built more than 2 million farm ponds in the United States since 1940. The farm pond is the most reliable and economical source of water, and when properly constructed it can be used for many purposes (Fig. 4-3). Livestock watering, irrigation, fish production, fire protection, reaction, and providing habitat for wildlife are some of the more common uses (Fig. 4-4).

There are basically two kinds of ponds—the *embankment* and the *excavated*. An embankment pond is made by building an embankment or dam across a stream or watercourse. These ponds are usually built where the natural drainage ways or gentle valleys flow

Fig. 4-3. The farm pond is the most reliable and economical source of water (drawing by Joe Burns).

Fig. 4-4. This pond is used for wildlife attraction. The wood duck box shows a ladder for the convenience of a lame pet duck (courtesy of the Soil and Water Conservation Service).

to a larger drain area downstream. Embankment ponds should be built where 8 or more feet of water can be impounded.

Excavated ponds are the simplest to build in relatively flat terrain, and their size is limited generally to ½ acre and smaller. They are best suited to locations where the water demand is small. There are two kinds of excavated ponds. One is fed by surface runoff and the other by ground water aquifers, or what we refer to as the water table.

Selection of the pond site is most important. The low point of a silty, clay type soil in a natural depression is often a good location. One can see where an ideal location for a ¼ to ½ acre pond, which is approximately 100 feet long by 100 feet wide and graded to a center bottom depth of 10 to 12 feet, would be in a low spot in a gentle rolling field. The surface area draining to the pond site should be less than 5 surface areas and the soil a heavy silt loam or clay loam. (Site inspection assistance is available from county Soil and Water Conservation District offices.) The water table in this low depression area should be at or within 1 to 3 feet of the surface.

Suitability of the site depends on the capacity of the soils in the reservoir area to hold water. The soils should contain a layer of material that is impervious and thick enough to prevent excessive seepage. Again, clays and silty clay loams are excellent for this purpose. Course-textured sands and sand-gravel mixtures are highly pervious and therefore usually unsuitable.

Avoid potential pollution of pond water by selecting a location where drainage from barns, feed lots, and sewage lines cannot reach the pond.

Do not locate your pond where failure of the dam could cause loss of life, injury to persons or livestock, damage to residences, highways, or interrupted use or service of public utilities.

Be sure that no buried pipelines or cables cross a proposed pond site. They could be broken or punctured by the excavating equipment, which may result not only in damage to the utility but also in injury to the operator of the equipment. If it is necessary to use a site crossed by pipelines or cables, notify the utility company before starting construction. Avoid sites under power lines. The wires may be within reach of a fishing rod held by someone fishing from the top of the dam.

For an economic viewpoint, locate the pond where the largest storage volume can be obtained with the least amount of earth fill. Avoid large areas of shallow water; it results in excessive evaporation and the growth of noxious aquatic plants.

The physical characteristics that directly affect the yield of water are relief, soil infiltration, plant cover, and surface storage. Storm characteristics such as amount, intensity, and duration of rainfall also affect water yield. These characteristics must be considered before determining the watershed area requirements for a particular pond site. The hydrological studies can also be accomplished by the Soil and Water Conservation office.

You may wish to use the water in your pond for more than one purpose. For example, you may wish to provide water for livestock, fish production, and irrigating your field crops. If so, additional factors must be considered. In estimating your water requirements you must total the needs for each purpose. Be sure that you provide a supply adequate for all the intended uses. Make sure that the purposes for which the water is to be used are compatible. If you built a pond for irrigation, you would probably use most of the water during the irrigation season, making swimming impractical.

If farm ponds are used to water livestock, make one available in or near each pasture or other grazing area. Water is as important as forage in the production of livestock. Since forcing livestock to travel long distances to water is detrimental to both the livestock and the grazing area, the distance between ponds is important.

Development of enough livestock watering places helps in establishing beneficial soil and water conservation practices on farm land. Enough well-spaced watering places in pastures encourage more uniform grazing, facilitate pasture improvement practices and grassland management, and retard erosion.

An understanding of stock water requirements helps you plan a pond large enough to meet the needs of the stock using the surrounding grazing area. Table 4-1 shows the average daily consumption of water by different kinds of livestock and is a guide for estimating your water needs.

Once you determine the probable location of the pond, make engineering surveys to plan the dam, spillway, and other features (Fig. 4-5). Good construction is important regardless of size, and the cost is usually little more than that for dams built carelessly.

When building the pond, clear the pond site, including areas on which waste material is to be placed, of all vegetation. Clear all trees and brush and grub stumps and large roots from the foundation area.

All material cleared and grubbed from the pond site, from the spillway and borrow areas, and from the site of the dam itself should be disposed of downstream. It should be properly covered and seeded for erosion control.

The kind of excavating equipment used depends on the climatic and physical conditions at the site and on what equipment is available. Bulldozers can only push the excavated material, not carry it. If you use a dragline excavator, you usually need other kinds of equipment to stack or spread the waste material uniformly. Most district offices maintain lists of conservation contractors who have agreed to do conservation work.

To insure a permanent water supply, the water must be deep enough to meet the intended use requirements and to offset probable seepage and evaporate losses during periods of no rainfall. An adequate pond depth is generally 10 to 12 feet at the deepest part.

Construction of your pond is not complete until you have provided protection against erosion and any other source of damage. Ponds without this protection may be short-lived and the cost of maintenance high.

Table 4-1. Average Daily Consumption of Water by Different Kinds of Livestock.

Kind of livestock	Gallons per head per day
Beef cattle and horses	12 to 15
Dairy cows (drinking only)	15
Dairy cows (drinking and barn needs)	35
Hogs	4
Sheep	2

Fig. 4-5. This is a concrete spillway for a small dug pond. The flash boards allow for control of the water level (courtesy of the Soil and Water Conservation Service).

A pond, no matter how well planned and built, must be adequately maintained if its intended purposes are to be realized throughout its anticipated life. Most county Soil and Water Conservation Districts will include as a part of the pond design information on maintenance required for a quality pond.

To maintain the required depth and capacity of a pond, the inflow must be reasonably free of silt. If an eroding or inadequately protected watershed must be used to supply pond water, delay pond construction until conservation practices are established to stabilize the watershed area.

In most areas the exposed surfaces of the dam, the spillway, borrow areas, and other disturbed surfaces can be protected by establishing a good cover of sod-forming grasses. As soon after construction as practicable, prepare a seedbed. Disk and harrow seed mixtures of perennial grasses and legumes adapted to local soil and climatic conditions and fertilize. Irrigate these soils to ensure prompt germination and continued growth. Mulching with a thin layer of straw, fodder, old hay, or one of several commercially manufactured materials available may be desirable. Mulching not only protects the newly prepared seedbed, seeds, or small plants from rainfall damage but also conserves moisture and provides conditions favorable for germination and growth. The best protection is adequate erosion control on the contributing drainage area. Land under permanent cover of trees or grasses is the most desirable drainage area.

If the pond is to be used for irrigation, the requirements are greater than those for any other purpose. The area irrigated from a farm pond is limited by the amount of water available throughout the growing season. Pond capacity must be adequate to meet crop requirements and to overcome unavoidable water losses. For example, a 3-inch application of water on 1 acre requires 81,462 gallons.

The required storage capacity of a pond used for irrigation depends on these interrelated factors: water requirements of the crops to be irrigated, effective rainfall expected during the growing season, application efficiency of the irrigation method used, losses due to evaporation and seepage, and the expected inflow to the pond. Again, your Soil and Water Conservation District can also help you estimate the required capacity of your irrigation pond.

Should you desire to use a pond mainly for fish production, a properly built and managed pond may yield from 100 to 200 pounds of fish annually for each acre of water surface. This is about equal to the beef production realized from average improved grassland.

A dependable water supply is also needed for fighting fires. Although water-storage requirements for fire protection are not large, the withdrawal rate for fire fighting is high. A satisfactory fire stream should be no less than 250 gallons per minute (gpm) with pressure at the nozzle of no less than 50 pounds per square inch (psi). A centrifugal pump operating at 83 psi provides a stream of 265 gpm with a nozzle pressure of 50 psi. Such a stream running for five hours requires a ¼ acre-foot of water. The District can design dry hydrants through cooperation with local fire departments.

In addition to the technical assistance available from your County Soil and Water District, financial assistance to qualifying applicants may be provided through the Agricultural Stabilization and Conservation Service. Working in conjunction with the County Soil and Water Conservation District, Agricultural Stabilization and Conservation Service provides cost-shares on ponds which meet specific conservation needs as determined by the County ASC Committee. In the case of farm ponds, conservation needs is interpreted to mean the exact use intended for the pond. In recent years, ASCS has cost-shared on ponds designed for livestock water, irrigation, or fire protection.

NATURAL COOLER

Natural springs are where underground watercourses break through the ground's surface of their own accord, or are so close to the surface that they may easily be opened by man—intentionally or accidentally—and you are lucky indeed if you have such a spot or discover one near your home (Fig. 4-6). It means that you have an abundance of clean, pure, cold, refreshing water all your own—for free. It is yours: to drink, to supply your home, water your garden, your livestock, and even keep your food cold and wholesome the year round, if you want to build a cooler box for yourself and place it where the spring's overflow can run through the cooler box.

A cooler box is really better than an icebox, for the temperature doesn't fluctuate. Natural springs are a constant temperature the year round.

Most spring temperatures are in the high-40° F. range, some as low as 42° F. Others may be a little warmer, but all are well within the range of good keeping for foods. As with ice, humidity runs high.

Let's look at the spring. Is it just a natural waterhole into which you can dip up a pailful and its outlet is just a tiny trickle of a brooklet or, having been used at some previous time, is it deeper and has it been lined inside with stones, a wooden box, a barrel, possibly concrete, or even a tile section?

In any case, if it's been long out of use, it needs cleaning out. Silts and the natural debris of leaves and sticks will soon fill in any open spring, clogging it to some extent.

Clean-out tools are a shovel and a bucket. Dig and dip out the mud till you come to the clean sand and gravel of the spring's real bottom. As you near the bottom, the water will flow much faster. Be sure to dig out the overflow ditch for 10 feet or so below the spring to help clear the water faster.

When you reach the sand or gravel and the water clears enough so you can see, you'll notice one place, or maybe the whole bottom, where the water rolls and boils up from below.

One place years ago had just such a spring. It had once supplied a house, then long gone, and had been "stoned up" like a water well (Fig. 4-7). Long out of use, it had silted in to the top, and its overflow barely trickled. Dug out and well-ditched, the overflow became a nice little brooklet.

This one bottomed at about 6 feet, and there was clean, almost white, sand that rolled and boiled with the flow of water. Such a place used to be called a well spring, as it was more than 4 feet deep. It had been stoned up and the stones were in good condition, still firmly in place, except for a few around the top. Extra cold, this water temperature was just above 42° F.

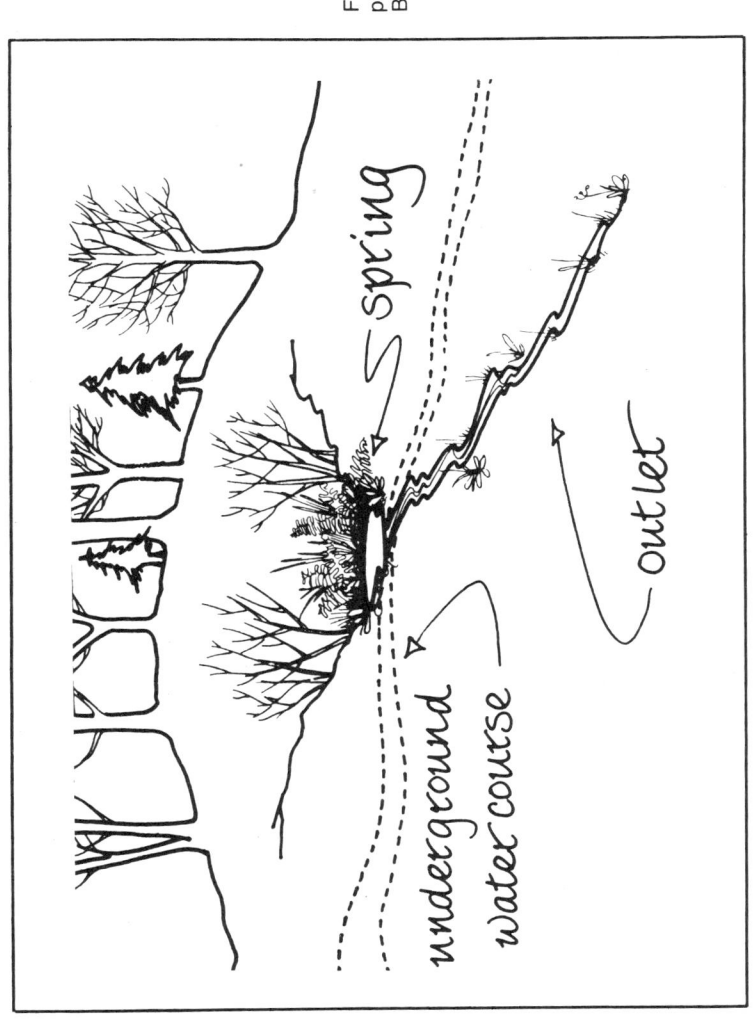

Fig. 4-6. A natural spring provides plenty of pure water (drawing by Liz Buell).

Fig. 4-7. A stoned-up spring (drawing by Liz Buell).

After cleaning out, the stones at the top were replaced. A wooden platform with lift-up door was built to permit dipping a water pail while keeping out debris. The house had no cellar, so a place to keep foods good was needed.

The water outlet ditch was widened, and in it a cooler box was installed, complete with inlet and outlet, so that the brooklet flowed through the box constantly. Both openings were screened to keep out frogs and other would-be visitors.

The box had no bottom, so it was paved with smooth, flat stones (Fig. 4-8). About 6 inches of water was maintained at the inlet end of the box and 8 or 10 inches depth at the outlet end. The shallow end was used for quart-sized glass jars to hold milk and some kinds of foods. In the deep end a 3-gallon earthenware jar was kept into which was put a dish of fresh meat or other food. Using wooden cleats along the cooler box sides, a board shelf was fit on which to set a dish of margarine. Other cleats were put along the sides to keep hold-down sticks for the glass jars, so that they couldn't tip over and spill their contents. All of the containers, set down into the water, had covers, including the earthenware crock (Fig. 4-9). This was heavy enough to stay put without using a hold-down. The top of the cooler box was fitted with a cover and fastener to keep out any animals that might come along (Fig. 4-10).

A little house was built to cover both the spring platform and the cooler box. It has a window and a door that could be locked with a key and padlock.

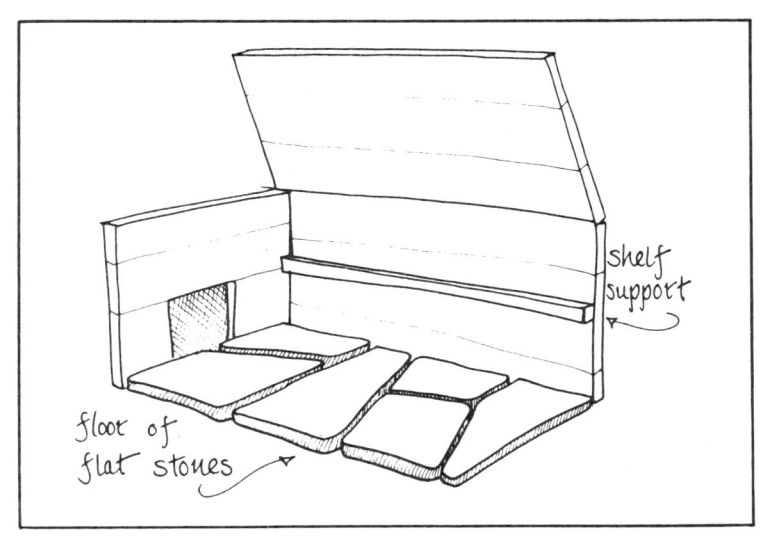

Fig. 4-8. This cooler box has a floor of flat stones (drawing by Liz Buell).

Every area has at least one human thief and may have several thieves about. A house that can be locked is a must, for a thief can easily rip up a cooler box even if it is locked against animals. The house also is a help in winter to keep snow off the platform and box.

A springhouse 6 feet wide by 8 feet or 10 feet long is a good

Fig. 4-9. This cooler box has room for several jars and an earthenware crock (drawing by Liz Buell).

45

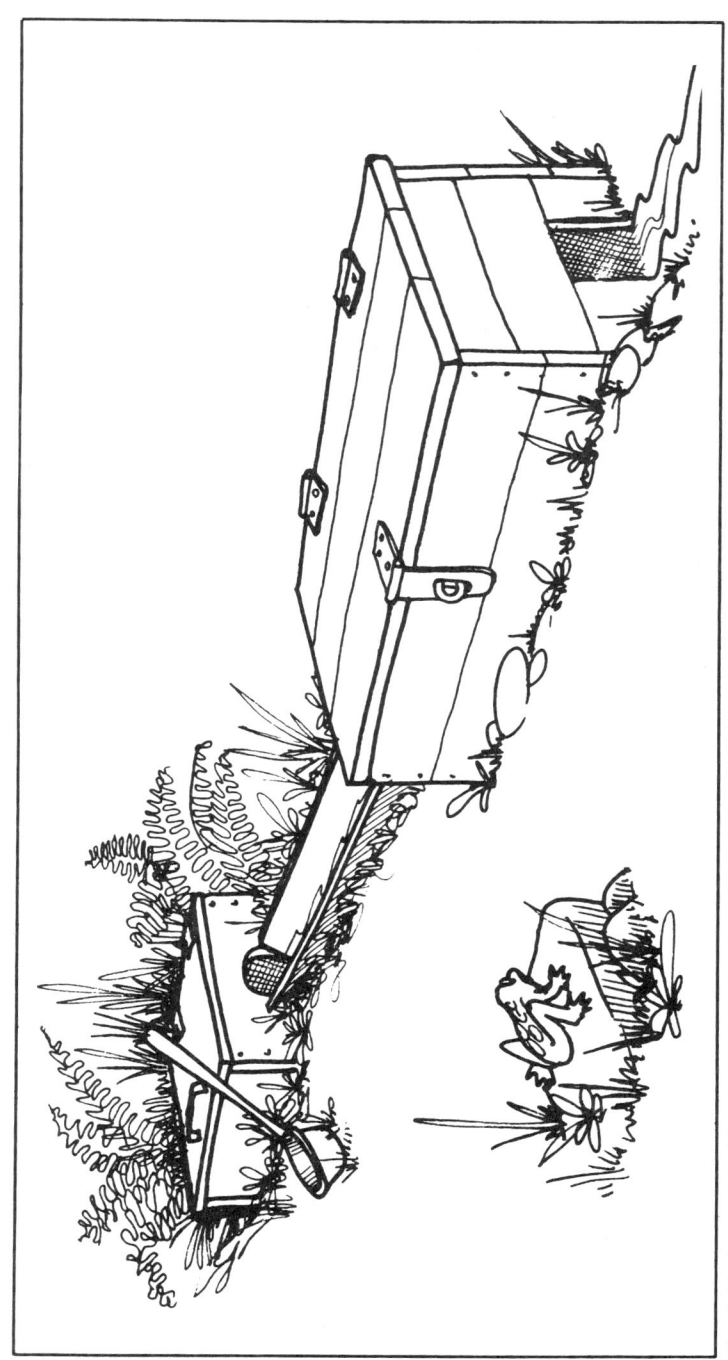

Fig. 4-10. A cover and fastener for a cooler box will keep out animals (drawing by Liz Buell).

size. It needs to be high enough for the user's height both at the door and inside. The springhouse needn't be fancy, but it should be sturdy. Any usable salvage lumber will do; it can be made of pole logs, or sawmill slabs may be used for boarding the sidewalls.

Smooth, flat stones do nicely in the bottom of the cooler box. Pieces of slate are good, if available, or pieces of concrete are also usable.

Nearly all springs have algae of one kind or another. They're natural, belong to the plant kingdom, and make their appearance on stones, boards, or other things in the water. Most of them will not tolerate water that isn't clean, so don't be alarmed when they appear. Just use a stiff-bristled scrubbing brush vigorously, rinse off, and the cleanup is done. Most of these algae are cold-water types.

Clean all glass jars and other containers regularly, even though they still look clean, to keep them fresh. Use lids on all jars, and turn each down tight when you close the container. Should a jar get tipped over, no harm is done.

Spring water that is flowing along doesn't freeze, even in the coldest weather, and that means the low subzero temperatures too. Anything in a submerged jar in the water inside the cooler box won't freeze.

The humidity in the cooler box does, of course, run high. When you lift the lid off the box on a cold winter morning, you may see a cloud of vapor come up, and the inside of the cooler box and the inside of the house may be frosty.

Spills of water on the floor of the springhouse will promptly freeze in winter. It's a good idea to have a pailful of dry sand handy to sprinkle onto the icy floor. Keep the sandpail covered and outside of the springhouse where humidity is lower. Mineral sand doesn't freeze if kept dry. Avoid using salt or salted sand around the springhouse. It would pollute the water supply. If the water level is quite high in the spring, hand-dipping with a pail is fine. If too low for convenience, a handle saved from a discarded broom can be used. Fasten a spring-type snap to the end of the handle to hold the bail of the pail (Fig. 4-11). Bolt-type snaps will freeze and fail to work. Snaps are stocked by all farmers' stores.

To carry the water through the spring's outlet to the cooler box, a section of 4-inch glazed finish terra-cotta tile works fine, or a piece of iron pipe, or you can make a pipe out of four pieces of board of suitable width. Make the inlet opening of your cooler box the size for a neat fit. Put a piece of screen over the opening on the inside of

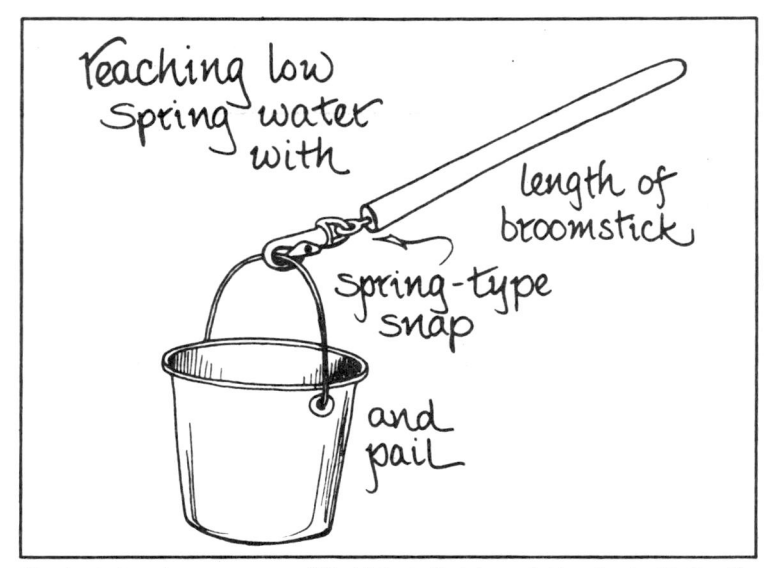

Fig. 4-11. A spring-type snap will hold the bail of the pail (drawing by Liz Buell).

the box. It'll keep out frogs and other small visitors that might come along. Screen the outlet opening for the same reason.

A good spring with a well-made platform and cooler box setup will last for years if well taken care of and sheltered by a good springhouse. A little ditching well done and wisely planned on the uphill side will keep out surface water during heavy storms, spring breakup, snow-melt, or summer deluges. The house will keep snow, rain, and surface debris such as leaves and twigs off the installation. Once a year, if silt accumulates in the spring itself, it's a good idea to clean it out. Late August is usually a good time to do that kind of a cleanup job, because the water level will be close to the lowest for the year. The outlet ditch below the springhouse usually needs checking to be sure it runs clear, just before fall freezeup sets in.

No two spring situations are quite the same, and each cooler box setup will work out a little differently than others. Personal ingenuity on your part can mean a good deal, along with what work you can find time to do, in the interests of convenience.

If the spring is a few feet higher than the cabin, it's sometimes possible to pipe, or even trough the water down to the dooryard, where a cooler box setup can be made to work nicely. No two places are the same, and details have to be worked out by the person who wants a cooler box setup.

Chapter 5

Plumbing

One way of rescuing an ailing septic system is to replace a conventional toilet with a *composting* or *waterless toilet*. The average American family uses 88,000 gallons of water per year, 45 percent of which is used to flush a conventional toilet.

The conventional water-borne system of waste disposal is costly. The Environmental Protection Agency estimates that if present trends continue, 60 billion dollars will be needed to build sewage treatment facilities by 1990. The high cost of sewage systems is the cost of purifying the water, not treating the waste it conveys: sewage is 99 percent water. Freshmen at engineering schools are found of the euphemism that "the only solution to pollution is dilution." Too much of that kind of mentality survives in waste management engineering practices. The tens of billions now programmed in this country for sewage disposal merely take us further down the same road.

Most people tend to avoid the subject of waste disposal, says Helen McKenna, who has written an amusing book on toilets. "It's hard to be an American and say the word 'toilet' without a smirk or snicker. That's because of our hysterical attitudes towards the lower half of our bodies. This is one of the reasons we don't know our toilets, even though we are a nation of toilets."

This was not always so. As a special privilege some European monarchs allowed observers to be present when they were performing these functions. In Rome, performing the basic functions was considered to be a social occasion. In one Roman toilet, 25 highly carved seats were grouped around a room in the center of which was an elaborate fountain. For most of the world, however, bathrooms were largely hidden away or unavailable, "being essentially nomadic" as someone has said.

Queen Elizabeth I, in the late sixteenth century, was the first to have a forerunner of the modern toilet, complete with running water, installed in her castle. Sir John Harrington's invention apparently did not impress anyone else, however, for the idea was not earnestly pursued again until the late 1700s. So elementary were these early toilets that they were often simply connected to an unventilated pipe that lead directly to a cesspool generally located in the basement. In 1872, Thomas Crapper invented the first valveless water toilet. He sold it to his customers with the promise of "a certain flush with an easy pull." The principle behind the "Crapper," which limited the amount of water required, is still used today.

The modern-day flush toilet works quite simply and has changed little in a hundred years. Yet with more people, less water available in many areas, and strict pollution standards, the flush toilet is way overdue for some changes, adaptions, and possibly even substitutions. Alternative household waste disposal systems are urgently needed. Yet products available are in many cases still experimental, the range of choices is endless, and all are billed as providing the ultimate solution.

SHALLOW TRAP TOILET

The impetus for the development of alternatives to the flush toilet occurred in Norway and Sweden as a result of stringent environmental regulations for waste disposal in rural areas. Water shortages and similar environmental constraints have now spurred a burgeoning industry in the United States. In addition to the large number of toilets that use no water at all, there are many that reduce the amount required. All the major toilet manufacturers now produce a water conserving model. Most of these are what is known as a shallow trap toilet, which retains less water in the bowl, uses a smaller diameter trapway, and a significantly smaller tank. At 3 to 3.5 gallons per flush, manufacturers claim an approximately 15 percent savings in water used in the home.

ONE-PIECE TOILET

Developments in the toilet over the past hundred years have focused largely on reducing the noise it produced, eliminating odors, and improving the aesthetics of the units. Many companies now market an eye-appealing, streamlined, low-profile, one-piece toilet. To compensate for the low elevation of the tank, this toilet uses approximately 6 to 8 gallons of water per flush. These toilets are no longer permitted in California as a result of the Keene Bill enacted in 1976. This bill prohibits toilets that use more than 3 to 5 gallons per flush. The early model toilets with tank hung high on the wall provided a much higher water velocity and as a consequence used as little as 2½ gallons of water per flush. The problem with this type of unit is that it tends to be noisy when flushed. Many of these are still in use throughout Europe.

AUTOMATIC SLOP TOILET

Among the many toilets designed in the nineteenth and early twentieth centuries was the automatic slop toilet, which represented the first attempt to recycle water for toilet use. This toilet used waste water from the kitchen sink. Modern waste water recycling toilets aerate, filter, and color kitchen and bath waste water that is then sent on to the toilet. Chemicals may also be added to prevent bacterial buildup. Although environmentally sound, these units are expensive and may not always meet municipal sanitation codes.

The portable self-contained toilet has a long history, having been for many hundreds of years stored under the bed and (in European cities) emptied 5 and 10 stories out the windows to the street. Modern versions require chemical treatment and periodic emptying in predetermined, approved locations. Most of these units were initially designed for use in national parks, recreational vehicles, or pleasure boats. They now offer possibilities for home use, particularly in those situations where only intermittent use is likely.

PRESSURIZED FLUSH TOILET

Another type of low water toilet is the pressurized flush that evacuates wastes by a combination of gravity and air pressure. These toilets use about 2 quarts of water: a 90 percent savings in water over conventional units. Electricity required to operate a small air compressor is a minimal added expense. Also available is a pressurized tank that can be installed on an existing toilet at a cost of approximately $50. This adaption can save 50 to 60 percent of water a toilet normally uses. A potential problem with the low water usage toilets is clogging of municipal sewage lines. For this reason, some municipalities require a minimum of 4 gallons of water per flush.

With the amount of water typically used in the home for other purposes, this should not be a problem.

OIL FLUSH AND VACUUM TOILETS

Instead of water, the oil flush toilet uses a clear, odorless mineral oil as the waste carrier. The oil is screened and sometimes chlorine-treated to remove particulate matter, bacteria, and color and is reused. The oil flush toilet uses no water. It is ,however, significantly more expensive than conventional equipment.

Another waterless toilet alternative is a vaccum toilet, which transports wastes from the toilet bowl to a collection tank for disposal. The vacuum system was used in space by the astronauts. On Earth, an electric pump maintains a vacuum in the sewer line. These units can move waste uphill, using much smaller piping. Although the oil flush and vacuum toilet systems, which are particularly well-adapted for use in ships and mobile units, solve the water usage and pollution problems, disposal of the waste remains a problem. Incineration or removal to a municipal treatment plant are the usual alternatives. Incinerating toilets are available that do solve the waste disposal and waste pollution problems, but at considerable energy costs. The initial cost of incinerating toilets is cost-competitive with conventional equipment. They do provide a convenient method of human waste disposal.

COMPOSTING TOILET

A great deal of attention has been given to the advantages and pitfalls of the composting toilet (Fig. 5-1). The fact remains that despite occasional malfunction and their higher costs, these units are by far the most sensible, environmentally-compatible method of human waste disposal. Problems that have arisen have usually been because persons using these units have been unfamiliar with the composting process.

The composting toilet can have at least three significantly different operating configurations: those units that are relatively compact and require electricity to speed composting activity, those that are large and capable of holding wastes for a long period to assure bacterial reduction, and finally, those units intermediate in size that are in some way solar-heated. The solar-heated units are experimental and often owner-built. No commercial units are yet available. Composting toilets require air, heat, and damp (but not wet) conditions in order for aerobic organisms (bacteria active in

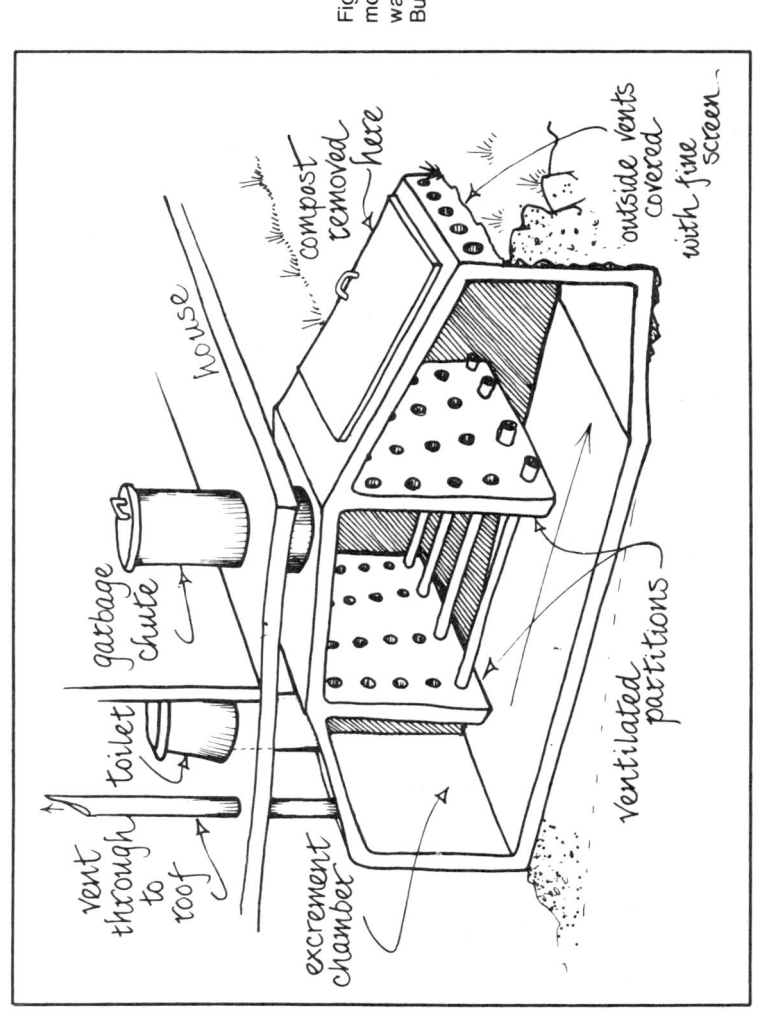

Fig. 5-1. A composting toilet is the most sensible method of human waste disposal (drawing by Liz Buell).

the presence of air) to decompose organic wastes. Too much moisture keeps air away, preventing aerobic decomposition and causing odors. Good venting, a well-insulated tank, raising the pH, and maintaining a loose pile (by adding wood ashes or lime, garden, and kitchen wastes) can eliminate these problems. You may have to learn to live with occasional flies, however. Spiders, beetles, and pyrethrium spray have been used for control.

BIOLOGICAL TOILET

Another alternative that comes close to the practicality of composting toilets is the biological toilet. These units operate somewhat like the composting toilets, except that anaerobic processes are involved. This is similar to what takes place in a septic tank, where bacteria that reduce wastes are those which thrive *without* air. This process produces a small amount of effluent (usually less than 1 pint per person per day) which can be charcoal-filtered and recycled for flushing. The biological toilet requires little or no electricity (depending on whether a fan or heater is needed), but does require that enzymes and starter bacteria be added. The biological toilet may have run aground, however. Only one company is known to be manufacturing the units, and according to the California State Office of Appropriate Technology, there have been operating difficulties reported with the unit.

All of the waterless toilet systems still require some additional means for dealing with gray water-waste water from bathing and washing. The reduced volume of water, excreta, and nutrients in gray water allow for a smaller, usually less expensive filtration and leach field system for handling it. The most prevalent hazard to the environment from gray water is phosphorous from cleaning agents. Considerable research is underway to deal with cheaper, less complicated means of properly treating gray water. One system being tested is a series of interconnected 55-gallon drums filled with sand, pea gravel, and crushed rock to filter and purify gray water

OTHER ALTERNATIVES

Other alternatives for treating human wastes focus on improving the operating efficiency of the conventional septic tank. One device pumps and mixes air, to aid in digesting waste materials—thus, in some cases, greatly lengthening out the cycle for pumping out sludge from the tank. Although these devices do not save water, one manufacturer has developed an aerobic septic tank system that sufficiently purifies effluent to the point where it can safely be recycled to the flush toilet. Before the days of modern pumbing, people had simple means for recycling body wastes back to the land—crude perhaps, but certainly more ecologically sound than today's high-water-usage sewage systems. The waterless toilet, as writer Harold Leich points out, is resulting in a quiet revolution in sewage disposal. The new methods of disposing of waste now being devised promise to solve the sewage problem by disposing of waste on or near the site without the use of large quantities of water. "They offer us the chance", Leich says, "to decentralize human sanitation without going back to the evils of the outhouse."

Many independent self-reliant types don't feel the outhouse is evil at all. In some circles the small, quaint owner-built shed roof structure with a half moon on the door is again gaining in favor. And why not? A well-designed privy can be constructed easily and cheaply. It can be located separate and downwind from living quarters, and it can be designed to facilitate composting and reuse of wastes on the land. Human manure is used extensively in Chinese agriculture. Composting, however, must be undertaken only with great care, for the reason that it can be a carrier of disease. The longest lived of these bacterial are various species of *Salmonella and pseudomonas Aeruginosa*. Compost from human wastes must *never* be used directly on food crops.

Legalization of the common privy still remains a hurdle in many areas despite their possible advantages for some. Proper handling of human manure for composting is definitely not a carefree operation. Wendell Berry, essayist, novelist, poet and farmer, has built a variation of the common outhouse in which he has provided access to the piles of excrement so as to facilitate turning and rotating to aerate and age the wastes. "Some people will no doubt object to this," says Berry, "because they are too fastidious to involve themselves in anything they think may be 'nasty' or 'smelly'—others because of the work involved. In order not to be confronted and offended at home by our bodily wastes," continues Berry, "we continue to swim in them on our vacations."

WASTE WATER TOILET

Harold Fountain has found a way to eliminate the outhouse. No more trips outside in the rain, dark, cold, or snow, and best of all, in these times of needed water conservation, no waste of fresh water just to flush a toilet.

Harold and his wife live in an area where the water table is low, rain is usually scarce through the hot summer months, and it is expensive to have deep wells made, to say nothing of the inconvenience when they go out. So they use cistern water that is provided by the fresh rain and is the best for washing and drinking. There just isn't enough of it to waste on a modern flush toilet, so for years the Fountains used the outhouse.

Harold was born and raised in the city and used to the modern conveniences, but at middle age he began to long for the country and a more simple way of life. Eventually this dream was fulfilled by his buying a small Ozark farm of 20 acres. The Fountains moved onto the bare land and, not having much money, built everything as they could afford it. In about 10 years' time, they had a comfortable five-room house, barn, chicken houses, and garage, with all the land fenced and gardens built up to production. Up to this time, Harold had accepted the outhouse as just a part of this way of life. However, when his first baby was born, he got to thinking of some way to do away with this inconvenience for the sake of his wife, especially during the first few days after the baby came, which happened to be in the worst of the winter.

He had also been doing a lot of thinking about how to use the waste water that was being poured down the drains from dishes and laundry. In the summer when rain was short and the gardens needed water, it seemed a shame to have to lose that water. Finally, the idea of how to do away with the inconvenience of the outhouse and how to use the waste water took shape in a way that put both together for a cheap, convenient, nonwasting, modern-type toilet, right inside the house—just like the modern bathroom (Fig. 5-2). It does not have the noise of a flushing toilet, nor is there a need to pull a handle. There are no parts to wear out and no plumber to call.

Most farmhouses, like city houses, do have a convenient kitchen sink and drain into which all the waste water is poured. They also have a drain for the washing machine and possibly a dishwasher. Usually all these small drains are connected into one larger drain that carries the used soapy water a distance from the house. Because this is relatively clean water, it is usually just allowed to pour out on the ground. To utilize this waste water into the convenience of a modern toilet, all that is necessary is to have the toilet wastes inserted into this draining, soapy water system as it passes beneath the house and to change the drainage dumping area into either a cesspool, septic tank, or whatever seems to be appropriate or required for your particular area (Fig. 5-3). The running drainage water simply picks up the toilet wastes and carries them along way from the house area. So, much like the outside hole,

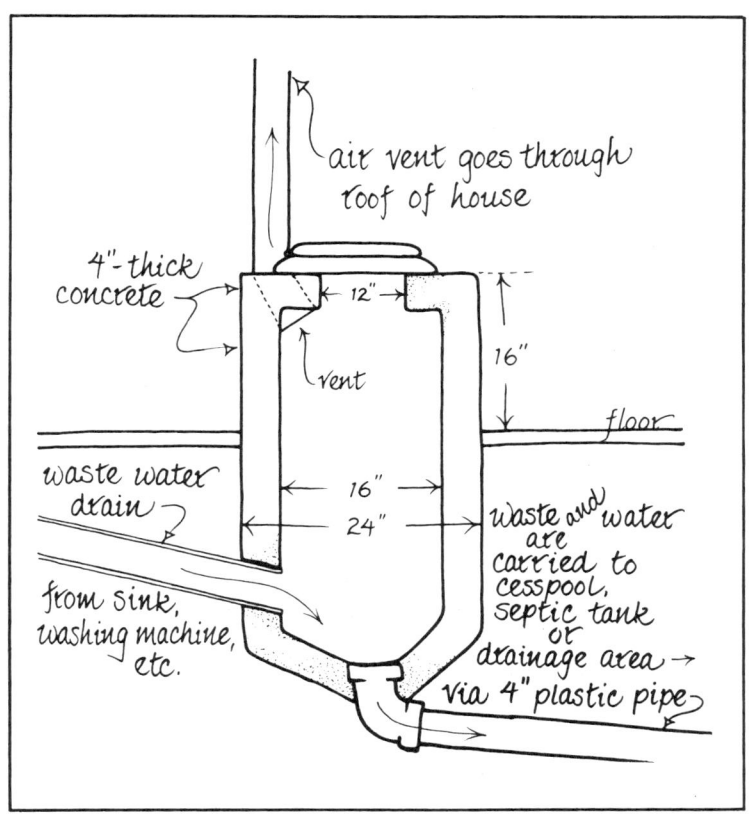

Fig. 5-2. Diagram of Harold Fountain's waste water toilet (drawing by Liz Buell).

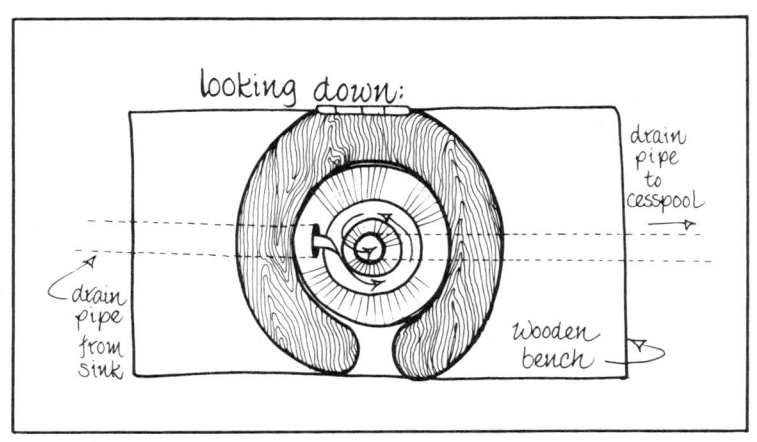

Fig. 5-3. The lower chamber of the toilet is round with sloping "shelves," so the descending waste water swirls and cleanses thoroughly (drawing by Liz Buell).

though which the wastes can be incorporated into the drain. To do this, it is only necessary that the bottom of the toilet hole be low enough so that the house water drains through the bottom of the hole. It is just that simple: nothing to wear out, quiet, inexpensive, nonwasting and convenient.

The Fountains' waste water toilet is absolutely trouble-free, unsmelly, and handy. It is unsmelly because the wastes remain in the bottom of the hole only until the drain water comes through to carry them away, and because all odors are drawn from the toilet by the vent pipe that goes through the roof. Harold believes the savings in time alone from the walk to the outhouse in all kinds of miserable weather would more than compensate for the low cost of its construction. The biggest expense in the system was buying the 4-inch plastic drain pipe needed to carry the wastes about 200 feet to a small cesspool. The entire expense amounted to about $100. Even if you now have a modern toilet in your house, your savings in fresh water would justify your conversion to this system.

Chapter 6

Heating

Space heating requires about 20 percent of our total national energy consumption. Nationally, about half of this space heating uses natural gas and half uses oil, with other energy sources contributing very little. Most space heating is done with imported oil in the Northeast. The experts agree that both natural gas and oil are in short supply and that certainly the price of both will increase rapidly in the future.

The technology to enable us to heat our homes with solar energy is here today. The technology is simple and could be applied by almost anyone designing and building a new home. Solar heating concepts can also be considered when remodeling older homes.

ACTIVE SOLAR HEATING SYSTEM

All solar heating systems are made up of three components: collector, storage, and backup system. A solar heat *collector* is a system of layers of glass or plastic with an absorber in back that intercepts the sun's rays and converts them to heat energy. This energy is then transmitted by a fluid (either air, water, or another liquid) from the collector to the dwellings or a storage unit. The storage unit can be made up of any material that can store this heat energy. This commonly is either rocks (air system) or water (water system). These components and a means of transporting them are shown in Fig. 6-1.

This system is known as an *active* system. It obviously requires

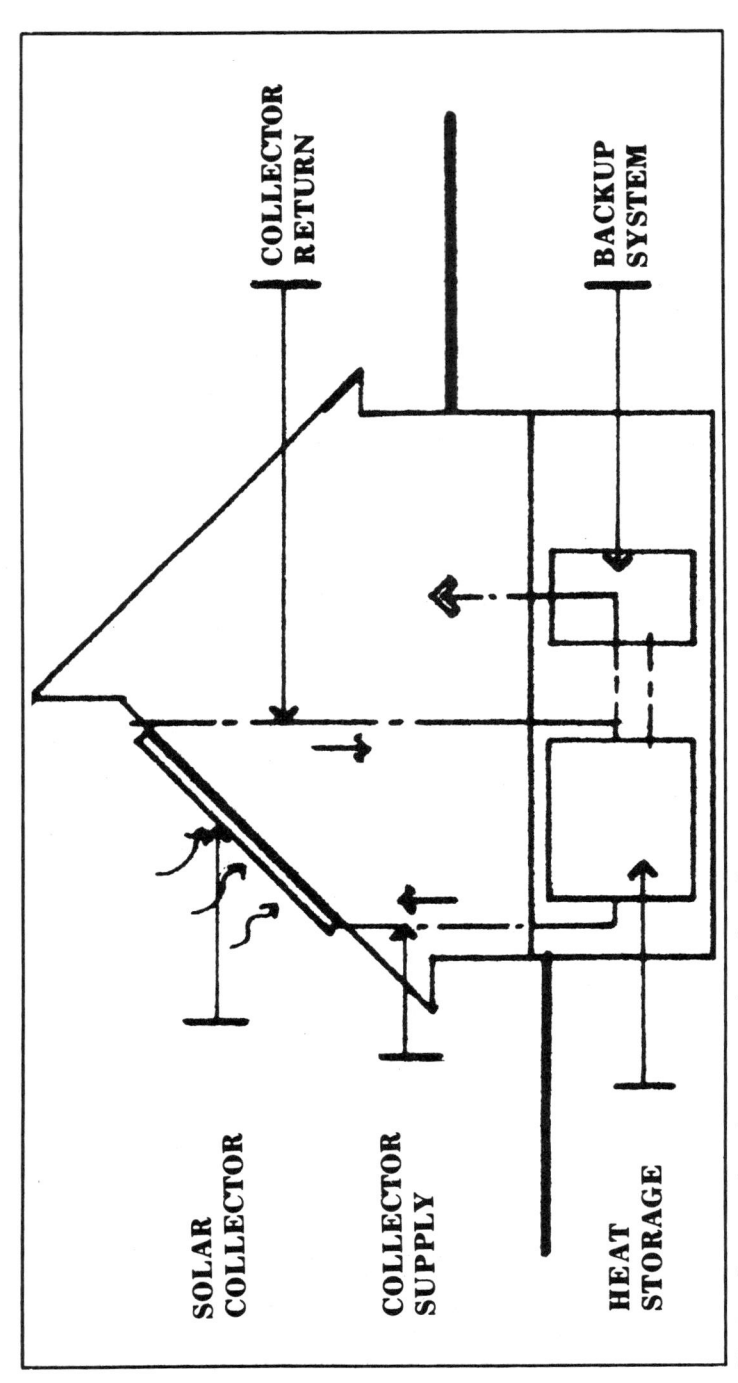

Fig. 6-1. Cross section of a system using active solar energy.

a means of transporting the heat from the collector or storage area to the dwelling.

A pump would be used to transmit the water (or other type liquid) over the collector to the storage in a water system. Another mechanical means then would be used to transport the heat in the storage to the dwelling. The air system would require a fan, ductwork, and control damper system.

The dwelling temperature would dictate mechanically when and from which source (collector, storage, or backup) the heat would come. A relatively sophisticated control system would be required if this operation was done automatically.

This is certainly not to say that active systems should not be utilized. Many homes are currently in design stages or already constructed that have successfully used the above system types. These active systems are not quite competitive with oil at present prices, but they will be very competitive as the price of oil rises.

PASSIVE SOLAR HEATING SYSTEM

A *passive* system contains the same three basic components—collector, storage, and backup. Mechanically moving parts are incorporated to move the heat from the collector to storage and to the dwelling. All components can be constructed by anyone who can do carpentry. Essentially, the collector and storage units are designed to be part of the dwelling. A cross section of a dwelling utilizing passive solar energy is shown in Fig. 6-2. There are no ducts, piping, fans, or pumps to transmit the heat from the collector to the storage. The sun simply heats the collector space, and this heat is absorbed into the storage and, in turn, heats the dwelling.

The orientation of the system is the single most important aspect of the entire solar heating setup. The collector should face south. Direct south would be best, although a deviation of 20

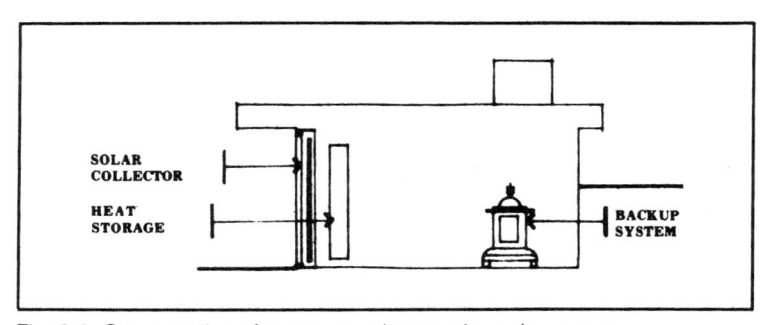

Fig. 6-2. Cross section of a system using passive solar energy.

percent in one direction or another would be acceptable. The area in front of the collectors should be free from trees. Deciduous trees could be planted at some distance in front of the collectors as long as they did not cast large shadows in the winter. Because these trees have leaves in the summer, they actually keep the collector cooler during this period when heat is not required.

The collector operates on the principle of the *greenhouse effect*. The radiation of the sun is in short wavelengths, and these short wavelengths can pass through glass material. Once they come in contact with a good absorption material, they are then converted to long wavelengths. These long wavelengths cannot pass through the glass, so the air around the absorption material is heated.

The layer that the sun passes through must necessarily be able to let the sunlight reach the absorber. This layer need not be glass. There are several materials that have been developed for this purpose. Different materials have different values of solar energy transmittance, which is simply the percentage of solar energy that can pass through. Table 6-1 lists some figures that are a result of studies performed by the American Society of Testing Materials (Test ASTM E-424).

You will notice that the glass and the products by Kalwell are comparable. This is not intended to be a plug for Kalwell, but the material provided by that corporation has been tested and has proven itself. It is a commercial product to consider for solar applications. Other competitive commercial products exist, and as the solar market increases, there will be even more competition. The fiberglass-type products are not clear like glass. This clarity in glass, however, is not evidence of a higher solar energy transmittance value, because the transmittance value is based on energy transmission rather than light transmission.

Once the heat is behind the glass, we want to retain it and not lose it outside again by thermal transmittance. The thermal trans-

Table 6-1. Values of Solar Energy Transmittance for Different Materials.

Material	Solar Energy Transmittance
Polyvinyl fluoride	93%
.025" fiberglass (premium by Kalwell)	87%
1/8" glass (DSB grade)	86%
1/4" glass	81%
Sunwall (by Kalwell)	77%
Double sheet insulating glass	70%
Sunwall II (by Kalwell)	69%

Table 6-2. Thermal Transmittance U-Factors for Various Materials.

Material	Thermal Transmittance U Factor
Sunwall II	.32
Sunwall	.40
Double sheet insulating glass	.65
Glass	1.10

mittance value is called the U-factor, and the lower the U-factor for a material, the lower the energy losses through it.

Table 6-2 indicates that Sunwall has a much lower U-factor than glass and thus transmits much less energy back outside.

Windows should have two layers of glass in the Northeast. The reason for this is to contain the heat inside the building for as long as possible. The same is true for solar collectors, and two layers of transmitting material should be used in this climate.

The absorption layer takes over once the solar radiation has passed through the transmitting materials. Black is the color that will absorb the most radiation and is thus used to cover the absorption surface. Special "selective black" materials are available that have a much lower value of emissivity. The emissivity of a color is the rate at which it reradiates heat. A collector with a selective black absorber can have an efficiency of up to 15 percent higher than the standard flat black paint. The disadvantages of this selective black is the substantially higher cost, and the coating requires a dip or coat manufacturing process. The homeowner making a collector should consider standard flat black paint as the absorption material. Stove black has been used with a high degree of success.

The paint can be applied directly to the storage material. This storage material should be made up of a mass similar to that used in the active system—either water or solid rock material.

If water is chosen as the storage medium, it is held in metal or plastic containers painted with the flat black paint. The containers can be anything from beer cans to old oil drums. Naturally, the larger the container, the longer it takes to heat the water, but also the higher the storage capacity. With these two considerations in mind, a container with a diameter of 12 to 18 inches should be considered. Cylinders are available in metal and plastic in these sizes from various solar manufacturers, and if you use your head many other options may come forward.

The alternative to water is a solid material. This could be an interior reinforced concrete wall, a solid concrete block wall, or a reinforced stone and concrete wall. With either water or the solid wall, the principle is the same. Because solar energy is intermittent, we need to store any excess energy and use it during the sunless periods.

The only addition that might be required for the system is some control over the rate at which the heat is dispersed to the dwelling. If the backup system is intended to be used intermittently, such as a wood stove, then you may not need any control on the solar system. If control is desired, it can be accomplished in various ways. One method is to place an insulated wall between the storage component and the dwelling. This wall could have louvers in the top and bottom when heat is desired, the louvers could be opened and the natural air currents would carry heat into the dwelling space (Fig. 6-3).

An insulated curtain could be installed between the storage unit and the dwelling. When heat is needed, this could be drawn completely away. Then the curtain could be partially or completely closed when the condition is satisfied. Insulation could also be placed between the storage wall and the transmitting material in order to prevent heat from being lost out through the collector at night (Fig. 6-4).

Steve Baer accomplished this by having a lift wall system on the exterior of the house. During periods of no sunlight he pulled the wall up from the inside of the house with a system of pulleys. This insulated wall actually served a double purpose. The back was

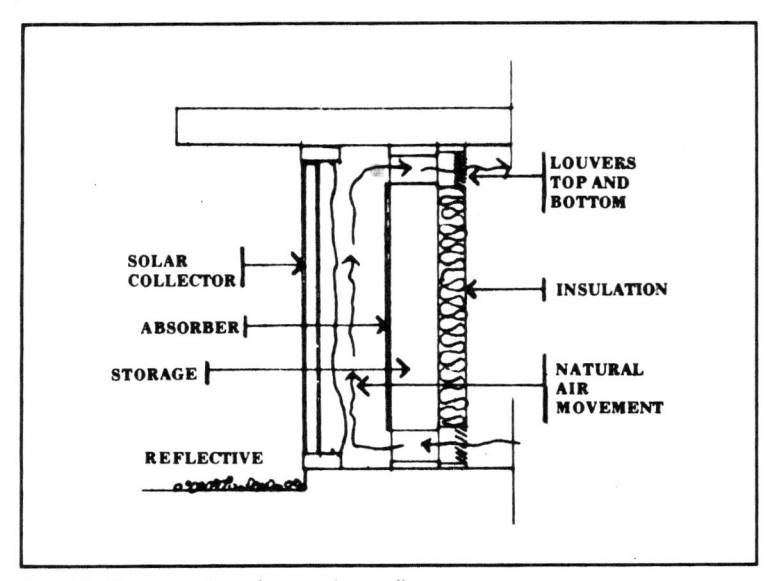

Fig. 6-3. Cross section of a passive wall.

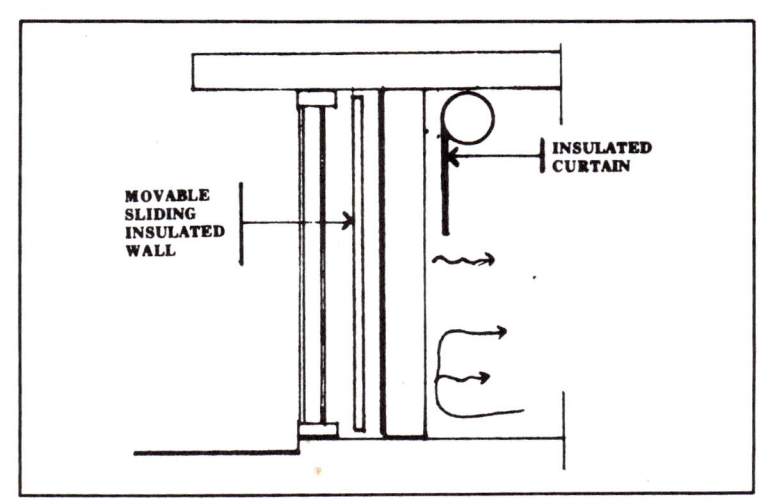

Fig. 6-4. Insulating the curtain/wall.

painted white. When flat on the ground, this white surface reflected more solar radiation onto the panel, thus increasing its efficiency.

Another method of achieving these objectives would be to construct a track so the insulating curtain could actually cross over

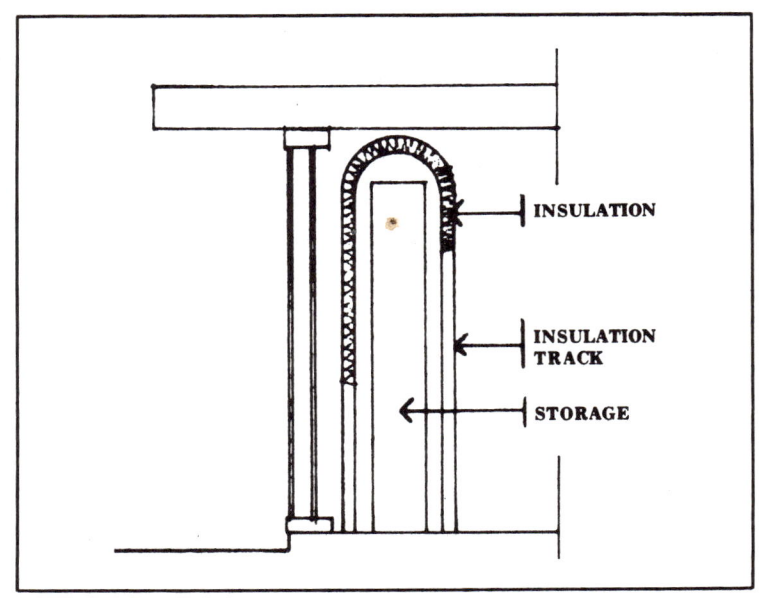

Fig. 6-5. The Kalwell Corporation is producing an insulated curtain and track system.

65

the storage to serve either purpose. A system such as this is already under production by the Kalwell Corporation (Fig. 6-5). During sunlight hours the curtain is placed on the dwelling side of the storage unit to allow the sun to heat the storage. When the sun is not shining, the curtain is placed on the outside of the storage to reduce heat loss to the outside and allow the storage to radiate heat to the dwelling.

I briefly mentioned previously placing an insulated panel on the ground in front of the collector and painting this white to reflect more sunlight. Exterior insulating panels are rather impractical in the north because snow and ice make them difficult to move, but we can still use this effect. When snow is in front of the collector, it reflects more energy into the collector. White rocks could be placed at this location to help during the periods when there was no snow, but heat was still needed. This added reflection can increase efficiency up to 10 percent.

The construction of the house greatly influences how effective any particular solar heating system is. Windows should be avoided when possible on the north side, since virtually no sunlight passes through these windows. Even east and west windows have very little sunlight during the cold winter months. Certainly only the purist would decree no north windows, because a mountain view or other considerations are important. Remember if the house is new that the siting is very important for solar utilization.

Insulation is also an important way that we can control heat loss. We often hear the phrase "insulated for electric heat." This sometimes implies a special type of insulation. What it really says is that the insulation is heavier—usually 6 inches of fiberglass batts in the ceiling and 4 inches in the walls. An even better system is 9 inches in the ceiling and 6 inches in the walls or its equivalent. The amount of heat loss through a given wall is the same no matter what type of system is installed—oil, electric, or solar. In order to do a good job heating a house with a passive solar system, all reasonable efforts should be made to reduce heat loss.

Calculating the efficiency of a system is somewhat complicated and it depends on many variables, such as the size and type of collector, the size and type of storage, the size, shape and expected heat loss of the dwelling, etc. We should mention some examples, however, of what can be expected as guidelines. An active roof-mounted system can be designed that will justify itself financially in approximately 10 years, if the system is designed to supply around 55 percent to 60 percent of the heating requirements. If for the same house a system was designed for 100 percent of the heating requirements, it would be next to impossible to justify the cost over an oil or electric system. The system would be so large in order to handle the month of January that in the spring and fall it would produce more heat than necessary.

A good estimate of the proportion of heat you could supply with a passive system is about 40 percent to 50 percent. Naturally, this would vary with the house, and using good site adaptation, high insulation, berming, good storm windows and doors, and small glazed areas on the north, you could hit 85 percent. At any rate, the need for a backup system is obvious.

In an active system, the backup should be incorporated in with the storage and collector, but a passive system does not lend itself to this. A space heating system would probably be best, either wood stoves or electric baseboard heating.

HEATING WITH WOOD

Not so long ago, a winter's security was measured by the fullness of the woodshed against the cold season. Wood heat is returning as a modern way to self-sufficiency in the face of shortage of nonrenewable fuels, supply breakdowns, and the economic situation.

Heating with wood has many advantages over the usual contemporary heating systems. Power failures often occur when weather is severe, just when you need heat most. Some people keep a wood stove especially for such emergencies, so they can keep warm, heat water, and possibly cook food when electricity is unavailable. Oil and gas fuels may be rationed in the future, and folks may not be able to keep as warm as they'd like. Fuel prices also limit comfort and create a burden for the householder in this northern climate. Supplementing or supplanting such systems can ease the situation greatly.

A wood fire offers more comfort from its direct radiation of steady heat—nice when you've just come in from the cold and want to warm up. A kettle kept on the stove will evaporate water for a more natural indoor atmosphere. One feels a healthy glow from a cheery fire as the sun's energy is released from its storage in the wood. Ancients used to revere the spirit of the hearth that maintained the life within the home by making possible warmth and food cooking. The modern home can enjoy the security of the friendly fire and its peaceful, powerful presence, free from the vibrations of a furnace. Though the fueling of the fire entails many chores, one is the richer for the satisfying exercise and personal experience of interaction with the natural world.

What are the drawbacks to heating with wood? After all, people had switched to other fuels when they became available. It took a lot of (human) energy to provide the wood fuel: to fell, trim, transport, cut to size, split, stack, restack, and stoke. Today, however, most of us understand that there is a great deal more (nonrenewable) energy involved in getting the fossil fuel to the homeowner's storage tank so heat can be obtained "automatically." We pay for that convenience, both financially and environmentally spending from a depleting trust fund. Wood fuel as an alternative is especially reasonable where it is plentiful. Handling it can be simplified somewhat by using a cordwood saw driven from a power take-off instead of chain sawing each individual piece, for example. If you don't have your own woodlot, it's not difficult to work out an arrangement with neighbors, find a local firewood supplier, or waylay a pulpcutter on his way to the mill and offer a better price. You can also reduce the quantity of fuel needed, and the accompanying labor, by using more efficient stoves than were available to our ancestors.

Other disadvantages of wood heat were related to the comfort factor. Given a drafty farmhouse, subzero winds swirling outside, and an old parlor stove, you'd find yourself huddled in the parlor most of the time (when you weren't making a trip to the woodshed). Storm windows and insulation in walls and ceiling will significantly reduce heat loss no matter what fuel you use. Adequate heat production is not so much a question of quantity as it is of quality and management. It is not comfortable to fluctuate between too hot and too cold, with many trips required to regulate the stove. Such uneven heat production consumes an excessive amount of fuel, too. When the area is cooled down during low points in the fuel supply to the fire, it must be heated up to the point where it will feel comfortable again. This recovery of lost room temperature uses more fuel. Later, heat is wasted when all the fuel is aflame, giving off excessive heat.

The burning rate of the wood fire is controlled by the amount of air that reaches it. You ostensibly have control of the air (and heat) by opening and closing the air intake (damper). Stoves that are not airtight also allow air to reach the fire from joints, around the door, cracks, etc. This is the drawback to poorly designed stoves. The fire gets more air than desired, and you get more heat than is needed. Some stoves utilize large quantity and mass of wood so the fire will burn down slowly.

Sheet metal stoves give a quick, high heat but lose it just as quickly when the fire dies down. Cheap sheet metal stoves wear out easily, and safety is a problem if the stove is not properly installed. Sheet metal stoves equipped with automatic dampers give far better control and are more dependable when unattended. Some brands of steel stoves have firebrick or cast-iron liners. The Ashley has a cast-iron top, which increase the life of the stoves and absorb and transfer heat for less severe room temperature changes. Stoves like the Ashley, Riteway, Shenandoah, and Wonderwood control air intake enough to slow down combustion so a long "simmering" process occurs.

Cast iron is more durable and more expensive than steel and is better for equalizing temperature fluctuations. Remember, though, that old stoves can look attractive but may require repair to cracks in the iron, which gets brittle with age. For safety and efficiency, make sure that a stove is in good shape before putting it into use.

The American designs of parlor and box stoves intend that the mass of the fuel will prolong the rate of combustion. European stoves are more efficient, perhaps due to an awareness of Europe's limited fuel resources. In the United States the tendency has been to build bigger stoves to hold quantities of wood to feed a longer lasting fire. The European stoves use materials such as brick, stone, and very heavy cast iron to collect and hold heat for gradual radiation. Baffle systems are used to prevent direct flow of smoke out the flue and consequent loss of heat up the chimney.

Fireplaces let most of the fire's warmth go up the chimney. A shallow design throws more heat forward, into the room. A built-in heat exchanger unit will direct more heat into the room (while the fire is burning); a freestanding model will radiate the greatest amount of warmth. Regulation of the fire for efficiency can be better accomplished with a Franklin-type, or a Jotul combination fireplace style, which closes airtight.

Cookstoves are regaining popularity, since their utility is twofold. The heat is welcome, especially in large, "country" kitchens. A small kitchen may become a miniature inferno, though, with the hapless cook sweating away like a boiler-stoker. It's no disgrace to avail oneself of a compact gas stove or hot plate in the summer. Much more cooking takes place when weather is cooler anyway, and that's when it's very economical to use a cookstove. Long cooking of stews, soups, beans, cereals, and such becomes more convenient as well as less expensive. The oven is always on, so baking is always possible at no extra cost. A few bricks in the oven conserve heat for overnight cereals or all-day baked beans. Each cookstove is unique: some are near impossible, but the majority prove to be excellent kitchen tools. Take time to become familiar with the workings of your cookstove as well as the characteristics of types of wood fuel for various types of cooking. There are new styles of cookstoves designed for cooking the food, not the cook. They are made by Fawcett of Montreal, Canada, and Jotul of Norway.

The ideal is dry hardwood, which gives the most heat and burns most completely and cleanly. For a stove that isn't airtight a mixture with green wood will give more gradual heat, but more creosote may be deposited in the chimney.

When combustion takes place, water in the firewood is evaporated. Chemical changes also occur that produce gases. These gases account for half the fuel value of the wood, but in most stoves they are not burned, lacking oxygen and necessary high temperatures. Few stoves are designed to conduct essential air to the upper part of the firebox, where the gases collect. On their way up the chimney, the molecules in the gases combine with moisture from the wood to form acids. If the chimney draft is slow and the smoke is cool from a smoldering fire, the aforementioned acids dry, leaving a solidified creosote deposit. Wet or green wood will produce more water vapor, aiding formation of acids. Also, heat is used up by the drying-out process of the fuel, so the draft is cooler and favorable to creosote production. The "simmering" method of prolonging the burning rate can cause excessive creosote due to low temperatures in the firebox and flue. Creosote is extremely flammable, and you would want to minimize its occurrence by good stove management. Combustion is more complete and clean at higher temperatures, so a small fire burning at a faster rate would be more efficient than a lot of fuel that is kept smoldering.

Be aware of the condition of the flues. Tap the stovepipe and listen for creosote that may rattle down. This indicates that the pipe should be cleaned of the flammable deposits; the chimney would probably need a check, too. Clean the chimney before each winter and during the midwinter thaw. Another time for attention is during the long, late spring when the stove may be kept damped down for long periods, smoldering and producing lots of creosote. On a cold day, a bigger fire blazing may trigger a chimney fire. Another dangerous situation is when a stove is filled with much wood in hopes of the fire lasting overnight. Sometime in the early morning hours all the wood will be ignited, creating excessive heat in both house and chimney.

When you find a method that works well for cleaning your chimney, it shouldn't take a great deal of effort to keep it safe. A young tree or a hoe on a long pole can be used to scrape the chimney sides; a dangling chain can knock off the deposits. If your chimney has an angle in it, try cropping a rope down it to the cleanout opening and attaching a sack filled with crumbled newspaper or such. Pull it up through the chimney for an effective cleaning job.

Because so much of a stove's efficiency depends on draft, as previously explained, a stove should be operated in conjunction with the chimney. The chimney material (brick, concrete, or steel and asbestos prefab) provides insulation to keep the draft warm and rising. Long lengths of single-wall stovepipe, used from stove to (or instead of) a chimney, may be a possibility of recovering heat that may be lost with the smoke. The uninsulated walls of the pipe will provide a cool surface for condensation to occur, and prodigious amounts of creosote can be expected. The loss through the pipe of the heat of the draft will cause inefficient combustion and its by-products (especially if the pipe passes through a cold area). Such stovepipe cannot long withstand the stress of burning creosote if it should ignite. For safety and efficiency, a chimney is essential. The prefab type is easily installed because it doesn't require a foundation, and it can be moved to another location if desired. A masonry chimney could be less expensive if you provide your own labor, but plan its location carefully because it will be permanent.

Older houses had chimneys and stoves located centrally so heat could circulate through the living areas and rise naturally to upper floors. Even distribution of heat was one more advantage gained when central heating became the style. Heat could be piped to each room, so layout of the floor plan was no longer a critical factor for comfort or efficiency. Some modern house designs will not easily lend themselves to heating with radiant wood stoves, and wood-burning furnaces may be a solution for some situations. Some houses are of older traditional styles that allow heat circulation, especially if insulated. Many owner-designers of new homes who plan for wood heat will be able to enjoy convenience and comfort with their wood stoves. Operation of a stove for maintenance of even temperatures will aid thorough circulation of heat.

Because fire consumes air when it burns, a newly constructed, totally insulated house may be too tight to provide enough oxygen for both the inhabitants and the fire. In old houses there are simply increased drafts pulled in from the many leaky places. A system that is helpful in new houses is a discrete opening in the hearth or floor in front of the stove that connects with a fresh-air flue to the outdoors.

It isn't too difficult to maintain safe conditions for wood heat. The attention required is a good discipline these days when everything else is done in a manner far removed from our personal experience. Operating a stove need not be an intricate process, though you may well appreciate the benefits of economical practices. Your forethought, awareness, and the proper working order of your stove will reward you with economical and self-sufficient warmth to sustain your northern winter's existence.

BUYING A WOOD STOVE

If you want to get the stove you want when you want it, look for it in the summer. Dealers report that fall is hectic. Along with fall's sales increase goes an increase of price. Waiting lists get longer, too. For example, if you order some models in September, you can expect to wait one, two, or even three months for delivery. The waiting lists are almost nonexistent in summer unless there is an unexpected factory backup for a particular model.

Order your stove now. This fall could be worse than ever for stove availability. Many dealers are expected to run out of some models prematurely. The reason is that most dealers do their major purchasing based on the previous year's sales.

In warm weather, when everyone is at the beach soaking up excess solar power, your dealer has more time to help you assess your true needs. During this less pressing time of year, a wood stove dealer is often willing to learn of your unique heating problems and ascertain the best stove for you. Many will even come to your home and help you locate the best stove site. This can also be a good time to trade in your older stove for a newer model, as the dealer feels he has more time to resell your old one. What's more, at this time all the necessary and charming wood stove accessories are more available.

You'll also have more time to see clearly how to get the most out of your stove. This is a good moment to discuss the proper stove size. The more mass a stove has, the longer it will hold heat after the fire burns low, and the more heat output. So consider the weight of the stove you buy. Weight is often one good indicator of how sturdily a stove is built.

Bigger Stove Is not Always Better

Many folks who are purchasing stoves for the first time do not realize that bigger does not always mean better for their individual situation. For example, a stove too large for your needs will not only drive you out of the room, but overly damping the fire means that the wood will never reach the temperature at which volatile gases burn efficiently.

When wood is first heated, the moisture is driven out. As the wood begins to get hotter and burn, it reaches the "charcoaling" stage. Now the combustible gases are released. If your stove is always dampened, you create ugly creosote—a pyroligneous acid that condenses in the pipes and chimney and increases the hazards of a chimney fire as it builds up. You might want to meet requirements to satisfy an insurance company. You certainly want to provide for your own safety.

Speaking of homeowner's insurance, companies generally do not increase premiums for wood heated homes, but are insisting on on-site inspection. They will require a 36-inch clearance from an unprotected wall and 36-inch clearance from any object. If the wall is adequately shielded with asbestos millboard and sheet metal or tile with a 1-inch airspace between it and existing wall, then 18 inches seems to be the general requirement. All stoves should provide a minimum 4-inch clearance from the hearth or stoveboard (½-inch asbestos millboard covered with 28-gauge sheet metal to protect the millboard). The stoveboard should extend 18 inches beyond all sides of the stove where coals or embers can drop, and extend 12-inches on all other sides. Call your insurance company now, rather than at the last minute, to check your policy.

With time at your disposal, your stove can be installed at your convenience and you won't be forced in a last-minute panic, with the dealer telling you when your stove will be delivered and installed. Now you can shop around and get educated, learning to familiarize yourself with a bewildering array of new models. One retailer broke down stove types in this way:

- *Box stove.* This type is basically a horizontal design. They lack grates, so the wood sits on a bed of ashes or 2 inches of sand. They feed from the top or front and can take big logs.
- *Combination stove.* This is a viewing stove with front doors that open so you can observe the fire. They come with screen or tempered glass plate "windows."
- *Freestanding stove* (i.e., a freestanding fireplace). They can be placed anywhere, but preferably in the center of a room.
- *Chamber stove.* This stove takes up less space because of a vertical construction. An arch or heat chamber above firebox increases heat transfer.

- *Cookstove.*
- *Fireplace insert-type.*
- *Circulator stove.* This type allows the heat to pass between an exterior cabinet and the radiant heater and have a thermostatic draft.
- *Wood furnace.*

We counted 150 models of wood stoves and furnaces in one catalog, and each company was not listing all their models. To help you evaluate the stove you want as you shop around this summer, here are a few more pointers.

Stoves Are Constructed of Steel or Iron

Stoves are most commonly made of sheet metal or cast iron. The sheet metal stove is made out of sheets of metal cut to shape with a torch and joined under extreme heat. Steel can be rolled to varying thicknesses. "Sheet steel" refers to metal 1/64 inch-¼ inch thick. "Sheet metal" refers to sheets up to 3/16 inch thick. Sheets 3/16 inch or thicker are termed *plate steel*. What is important is the thickness, or gauge, of the steel.

The thinner bodied sheet steel stoves are the most inexpensive ($100-$200). They may give a first surge of heat, but under the continued stress of heating and cooling, they may bend or warp. Warping most often occurs in stoves constructed with sheet metal of 1/16 inch or less. This warping will let undesirable, uncontrollable air to enter the stove and reduce efficiency. To offset this, some sheet metal stoves are designed so the warping is not visually offensive and have cast-iron doors to help keep the stove airtight.

The highest quality, longest lasting steel stoves are constructed of plate steel or boiler plate, lined with firebrick, and come with a long-term manufacturer's guarantee. Firebrick absorbs the heat, raises the temperature in the firebox, and slows down the heat transfer. This is good if you want a long, steady heat. The lighter the gauge, the more important it is that the stove have a metal or firebrick liner.

Heavy gauge steel stoves are best when the welds are strong and are designed in combination with other materials to make them stronger. They cost from $200 to $650.

The cast-iron stove is made of an alloy, melted and poured into molds. The pieces are then machined and assembled to create a tight fit. The joints are caulked with furnace cement. Even though the seams overlap, they should be caulked each year with furnace cement. Generally speaking, cast-iron stoves last longer than steel stoves, but consequently, they are more expensive, costing from $235-$1400. (The latter price is about what a good cookstove costs that offers a water jacket arrangement to make hot water.)

Cast-iron stoves are quite heavy, and you should carefully consider the size and whether you intend to dismantle it every summer to store in a basement or garage. Furthermore, these stoves require care, because repairs are difficult. They are sensitive to sudden changes in temperature and heavy blows, because cast iron is brittle and can crack, though not under normal conditions. When buying one, you need time to look for a well-bolted, well-cemented stove. Check the cast iron for uniform thickness. Beware an unevenly cast stove that may be porous or badly pitted. Check doors and lid for a tight seal

The Scandinavian stoves are very efficient and offer high quality, and the more expensive models have a deep-baked enamel finish in attractive colors. They cost anywhere from $250 to $610. Most feature interior baffle plates and are designed to burn wood from front to back "cigar fashion." There are many good American-made stoves with this design, also. Baffles retard the passage of air by lengthening the flame path. Thus, more heat is produced because there is greater radiating surface.

Stoves can be loaded from the top, side, or front. Top loading is the easiest because there's no stooping. With side or front loading, the wood is less likely to jam and can be more readily fed into the fire. There is also less trouble with the smoke that may escape while loading with this type. The smaller the door, the more wood splitting you'll have to do. The roomier doors allow for a larger and longer burning chunk.

In giving yourself time to choose the correct stove for you, remember that you're more likely to work out a good surface arrangement with a store whose major specialty is stoves, rather than with a store which only offers a few stoves as a sideline.

During warmer weather, delivery of your stove is less of a problem. Some retailers are willing to absorb the freight cost this time of year. This can save you anywhere from $15 to $50 depending on the weight of the stove. (A 600-pound cookstove would fall into the latter category). Freight cost is surely a good bargaining point, now that there's less pressure. Everything you can save helps. Furthermore, since gasoline shortages are looming, who knows how this will add to your total expense later? Expect the unexpected. A wood stove is not an item to be shipped by United Parcel Service. It is mostly transported by common carrier—big trucks—

and dock or other labor strikes have been realities in the not too distant past.

On the home front, what better time than summer to prepare for the servant-to-come? Does the chimney need cleaning? Any pipes rusted or need to be purchased? For optimum safety, a chimney should be cleaned twice a year. Any masonry work to be done? Perhaps you don't have an existing unused flue; you'll need to send your stovepipe out a window or up through the ceiling and roof. For this project you'll need insulated pipe, perhaps an "insulated tee," wall supports, trim collars, chimney caps, and other accessories. If you're going to do the work yourself, it's much easier to assemble everything during warm weather. You may also want to build a hearth for the stove to safely sit on or construct an attractive wall panel behind the stove. All this takes time.

Another tip we discovered from chatting with people in the wood stove business is that in the summer many retailers display their wares at country fairs. Not only do these exhibits provide excellent places to compare models and values, but usually a special fair discount is offered. The climate of such events is more conducive to bargaining. Some retailers only take orders; others are willing to sell their display models. Many a tremendous deal has been made the last day of a fair, especially if a customer is able to provide the take-away vehicle himself, sparing the dealer the weary task of loading one more weighty piece of equipment back on the truck. Beware that "fair fever" doesn't interfere in your making a rational last-minute decision.

One of the most overlooked reasons for making an early purchase of a wood stove, but an important one, is that you have extra time to gain experience with your new fascination. Even for the wise, getting used to the new model often turns into a time-consuming and nerve-racking romance. Most people are afraid of the novelty of it all, and the beginner will certainly feel intimidated, not realizing his or her new possession needs to be "seasoned"—that is—gradually and gently used. (No roaring fires at first, please.) Every wood stove has its idiosyncrasies.

Therefore, by buying early, on those first few chilly evenings you'll have more time to warm up to your purchase. One person told us that many customers declare that their stove's second year was far superior to the first. The person we were speaking to quickly pointed out that it wasn't the stove that changed; it was the wood-burner who finally mastered his help.

WOOD STOVE SAFETY

Before rushing off to a roaring start with your woodburning venture this fall, stop to consider safety. How protected is your home from the threat of a destructive fire?

The following information will provide you with a good overview of several important areas in your home to examine before you light up your wood stove or fireplace: chimneys, correct wood stove setup and clearances, stovepipes, stove cleaning and safety tips.

Chimney

No matter how proudly the chimney juts past the roof line, if it's not clean and in good repair, it's just a big minus in the area of fire safety.

Chimney fires are no fun. They're caused by the overheating of flammable, crusty creosote deposits that are the result of an accumulation of flue gas condensation. Chimneys with cracks and holes in the mortar can permit sparks or flames to escape and possibly catch on the burnable material in the inner structure of your home.

It's another bothersome step on the treadmill of maintenance, perhaps, but chimneys must be cleaned at least once a year, and twice for optimum safety. They must be repaired if necessary.

Older homes will probably have a masonry chimney. Because flue liners are a relatively new safety precaution, your old farmhouse stack may be unlined. An unlined masonry chimney is a potential fire hazard. The only thing between your house and smoke, flames, and sparks is a thin wall of single brick construction that can transmit heat to nearby combustibles in the event of an overheated fireplace or stove, or a chimney fire.

Unless you are very clever and handy, these chimneys should have professional attention and should be lined by a mason. If you mortar and assemble a flue lining poorly, you'll create bumpy surfaces to collect creosote or hamper the draft. Round flues are best, but they are difficult to install.

There should be a fireclay flue liner, or its safe equivalent, that will resist cracking from hot flue gases. This liner should be ⅝ inch thick and extend above the brickwork.

The newer, prefabricated chimneys are easiest to clean. Most are round on the inside. Many of these can be cleaned from the ground level up.

If you have a masonry chimney that needs cleaning, most likely you'll have to get up on the roof. If you're the type whose knees turn to jelly just looking down out of a second-story window, then maybe you better back gracefully out of the whole project and hire a professional chimney sweep.

What tools will you need if you want to do it yourself? First, you'll need a safe and sturdy ladder. If possible, prop the ladder against the gable of the house rather than against the side of the roof. Place the ladder at a safe slope. This method is good if the stack is near the peak. If the chimney pokes up through the center of the roof on one side, you'll need to situate the ladder against the side of the house and use a second ladder with a ridge hook on the roof.

You'll need a flue brush made of strong, stiff steel wire bristle that fits the flue—round brushes for round flues, square brushes for square flues (Fig. 6-6). The flue size can be determined by looking up into the hearth, past the damper of the fireplace, or into the flue opening, if you have a wood stove. Reach in with a measuring tape. If the flue brush you buy is too large, you can carefully trim the ends with a wire clipper.

Some local fire departments own a set of flue brushes and are willing to loan them. You might want to check this out.

You'll need a rope the length of the chimney to tie to the brush and a weight. The purpose of the weight is to pull the brush down into the chimney. The tighter the brush fits the chimney, the heavier the weight must be.

A broom is another handy item, and you may want to bring one up with you. A flashlight will be useful to illumine the dark and awesome chimney hole (don't fall in) to check the mortar for cracks and holes, or to see how good a job you're doing.

On ground level, you'll want a high-powered industrial or shop vacuum. (Rent one. Your household vacuum is not sufficient, and fine soot may wear out the bearings if it gets into the motor.) Get a drop cloth and strong tape to completely seal off the fireplace, if this is your situation. You'll want a metal bucket and an ash shovel.

Close the damper. Seal the fireplace. You've picked a fair day, of course, with hardly a breeze and not a hurricane in sight. The roof is dry as a bone (no snow or ice). The stove or fireplace is out cold. Your ladder is secure, and you've got on your worst clothes. You've remembered to provide yourself with a dust mask or cloth, but there's one more thing that suddenly occurs to you. The chimney may have a *cap* or *bonnet* that is probably bolted. This will have to be removed, so you must get the proper tools.

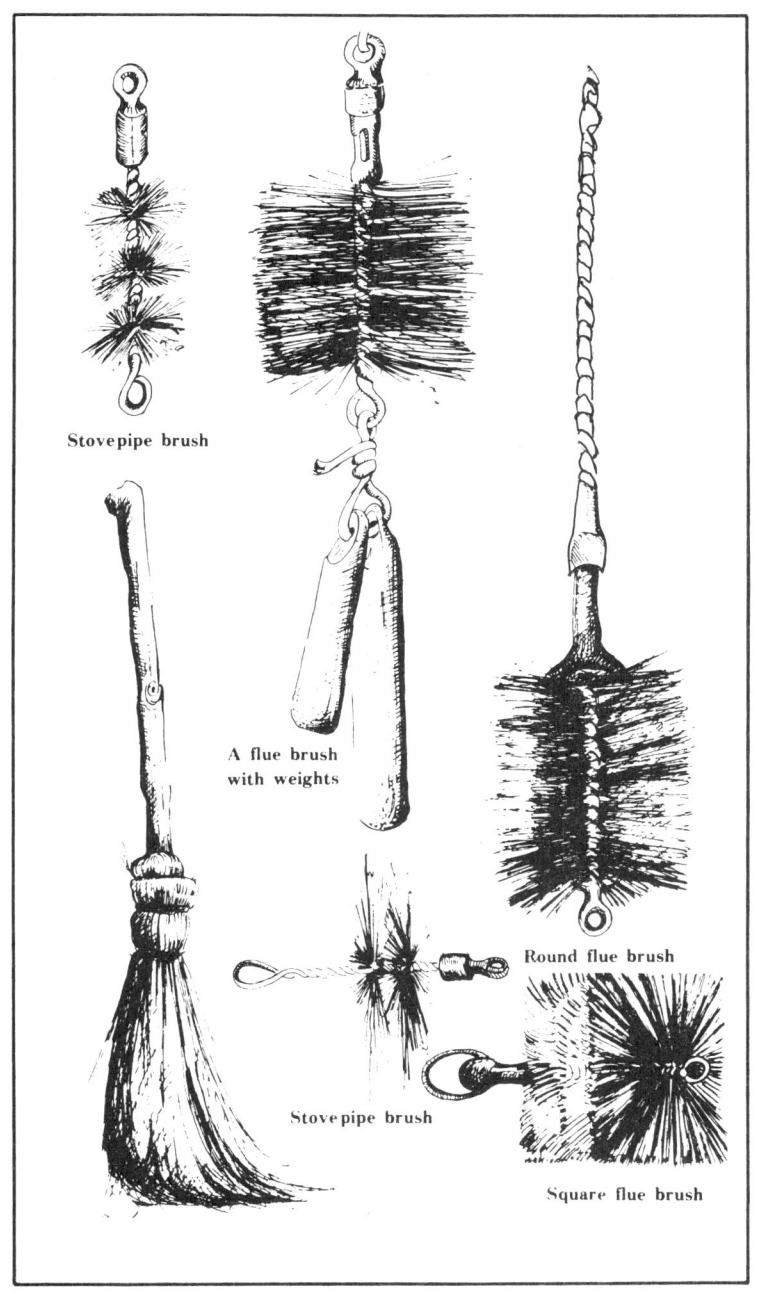

Fig. 6-6. Some flue and stovepipe brushes.

If there was a chimney cap, you've already removed it. You lower the brush, weight first, down the chimney. Don't smash the damper. Gently lower and raise the flue brush the full length of the chimney at least six times.

Here's where you'll respect a good flue brush. It's well worth the small amount you pay for it.

The weight is not necessary if you have a spouse or good friend stationed loyally at the hearthside opening. Attach a rope to both ends of the brush. With one of you on the roof and the other on the hearth end, take turns gently pulling the brush up and down the flue. You'll still want to cover a fireplace opening with a tarp, but an opening should be provided to facilitate working from the hearth.

Climb back down and carefully remove the cloth from the fireplace, or remove the connecting pipes if you have a wood stove. Shut the doors and windows in the house. Then place a sturdy drop cloth on the floor. With a fireplace, open the damper very slowly and gently sweep or vacuum the debris from the hearth and smoke shelf. With a wood stove, you remove soot that's collected in the stove and place it into a metal bucket. Take the pipes outside and brush with a wire brush. There is usually an ash door at the chimney's foundation. Open it and shovel out debris.

You can clean some chimneys without going up on the roof. Find the stack opening on the ground floor level and lay a drop cloth around it. Push the flue brush up into the flue. Keep adding extension handles until the brush has reached the chimney top. A few good strokes, and you'll knock loose the dangerous creosote deposits.

A toilet brush taped onto a plumber's snake will also suffice. Shovel out debris at the bottom of the chimney near the stack opening.

After you've cleaned the chimney, you can further check for cracks and holes in the masonry by what is known as the *smoke test*. Send a trusty friend up on the roof with a wet towel with which to cover the chimney top. Go inside and light a small fire, adding a handful of green leaves or any other material that smokes when it burns. (Avoid rubber or plastic.) Your friend covers the chimney, and you both inspect the entire stack for smoky "leaks." If there are any, mark the spot with chalk and fill the holes with cement, or call a mason.

You may want to place a *spark arrester* (a rounded cone structure of wire mesh) to fit over the chimney top. They don't block the flow of gases, and they'll help prevent sparks from flying out. They'll also discourage squirrels and birds from setting up house in your chimney.

Stove Setup

Most destructive fires that result from burning wood are caused by an unsafe location and installation of the stove.

The stove should sit so the shortest and most direct span of stovepipe is used to connect it to the chimney. This makes for a good draft and for heating the chimney flue. In the long run, these two factors help to reduce creosote accumulation. The lower the stove is in the house, the better for heat distribution. If a stove is located in an insulated basement, it will warm the first floor. If a stove is located near a stairwell, or if the house has floor registers, the heat will rise and heat the second floor.

If you're setting up the stove in or near a fireplace to use its flue, you must block off the fireplace opening with sheet metal or ¼-inch stoveboard in which the size of the stovepipe has been cut. The fireplace cover should be 6 inches wider than the fireplace opening, and 3 inches higher, to allow enough margin on three sides to bolt into the masonry. Run a bead of nonflammable caulking around the edge. You'll want the cover to be airtight.

Another kind of fireplace installation for your wood stove is to run the stovepipe up to, but not into, the chimney flue. You may want to vent the stove into the fireplace chimney above the damper. This doesn't mean you use the wood stove and the fireplace at the same time. You cap the hole for the wood stove connector pipe, so you can use the fireplace for spring and fall. During the winter, connect the stove and block off the flue below the connector pipe entrance. You'll want a skilled mason to install this type since knocking out holes, and otherwise messing around with masonry, can be a complicated business.

Setup Suggestions

Venting a wood stove into an unused existing flue is the easiest. The following are some setup suggestions to be closely heeded:

- ■ Never hook up more than one stove to a flue unless flue openings are at different elevations. Be sure flue is unused. Two or more heat devices may cause the stove to smoke or reduce the draft. A poor draft favors creosote.
- ■ Make sure the flue opening is large enough to accommodate

a good draft. It should be the same size, or larger, as the incoming pipe.
- Never hook up a stove to a flue that also serves a fireplace, unless the fireplace is sealed. Otherwise, flue gas or sparks will enter the room.
- Keep your stove away from passageways.
- Keep your stove away from exits.
- Don't place your stove in a small alcove or closet. There is too little ventilation in such niches.
- Use an interior chimney, if possible. The heat loss from the chimney helps warm the house. Outside chimneys are much cooler and more likely to cause condensation of flue gas, causing more ugly and dangerous creosote.
- Place your stove so you have a good working room to remove ashes.
- Check with a fire prevention official or your local stove dealer about clearances.

NFPA Clearances

Let's take a close look at some National Fire Protection Agency (NFPA) data on how far your wood stove should be placed away from walls, furniture, ceiling, and floor (Fig. 6-7). They may seem fussy but are based on facts. They should be strictly followed.

For example, a cookstove should be 3 feet away (back and firebox) from an unprotected wall. The minimum safe clearance from all unprotected surfaces for a radiant heater (i.e., the typical cast-iron or sheet metal stove) is 36 inches on the front, sides, rear, and above. What's combustible? Doors and window casings, mopboards, plastic walls or gypsum board dry walls if they are attached to wood, and your sofa and other furniture are combustible. The logs you wish to burn inside the stove and all kindling or paper must be kept at a safe distance.

The stove must have legs 4 inches to 6 inches long when it is set on a protective surface called *stoveboard*. Stoveboard is sheet metal not less than No. 24 gauge that cover ¼-inch thick asbestos millboard.

Do not confuse asbestos cement board with millboard. Millboard is a low-density, fire-resistant insulating board. Cement board is high density. It is fire-resistant but easily transmits heat to surfaces beneath or behind it.

Stoveboard should not extend less than 6 inches beyond the

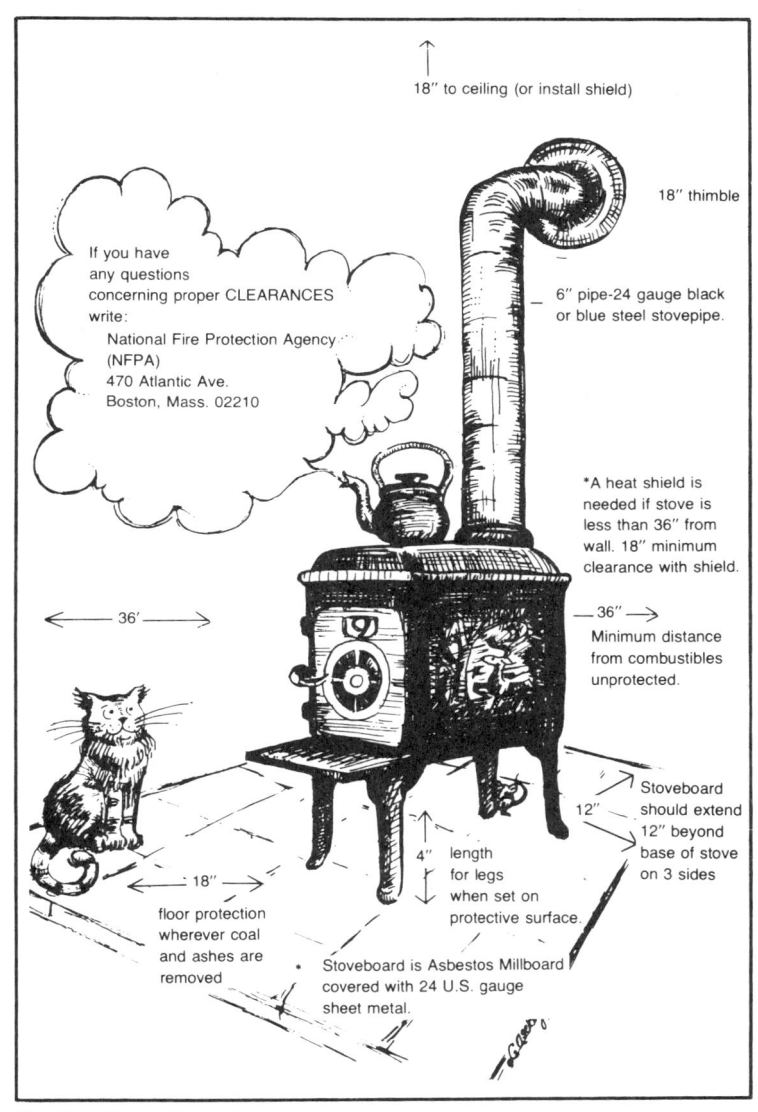

Fig. 6-7. Wood stove clearances.

base of the stove on three sides. It should extend 18 inches on the front.

Decorative and safe floorboards are available today with cheerful patterns in tile or color. You may want to build a masonry floor or wall to add beauty as well as safety to your hearthside.

83

The 36-inch requirement can be reduced to accommodate your wood stove into a tighter area. This is done by installing a heat shield on an exposed combustible wall. Porcelain (hot plastic) electric fence insulators create a convenient spacer for the necessary 1-inch airspace needed between shield and wall.

Stovepipe

The next thing to consider is the best and safest stovepipe. Black pipe or blue steel is intended for interiors. It should be 24 gauge. Galvanized metal can give off harmful gases under extreme heat. Galvanized pipe is designed for oil or gas furnaces and is too thin for woodburning appliances.

Used pipe must be examined for rust corrosion. Beware of thin spots or pinholes. These are extremely dangerous, especially in the event of a chimney fire. Use a stovepipe the same diameter as the stove collar. If the chimney hole is too small, enlarge the opening, rather than reduce the pipe size and consequently reduce the draft. Six-inch stovepipe is a good size for a small stove.

Draft

Check to see if the diameter of the flue is 25 percent greater than the stovepipe. Again, this provides for maximum draft. Avoid using too many *elbows* (bent sections of pipe). The shortest and most direct route of pipe from stove to the chimney is best. Nonadjustable types locked into a 90-degree turn are best. Adjustable elbows for angles 0 degrees to 90 degrees can be bought, but they tend to leak creosote.

If a long span of pipe is unavoidable, create a ¼-inch upward slant to the chimney opening per running foot of pipe. The stovepipe must never be higher than the chimney opening. It should enter the chimney hole horizontally and extend only to the inner surface of the flue, not so far in that it blocks the draft.

How can you tell if your chimney has a good draft? Here's a simple test. Crumple a sheet of newspaper and set it into the chimney opening. Light it. If the paper is drawn up the chimney the draft is good. If not, your chimney may have air leaks.

Damper

Some stoves require a damper, although airtights usually don't. The *damper* is a special section of pipe with a steel pin handle and a disk that fits inside the pipe. It should be installed about 6 inches from the stove collar. Its function is to reduce the amount of draft

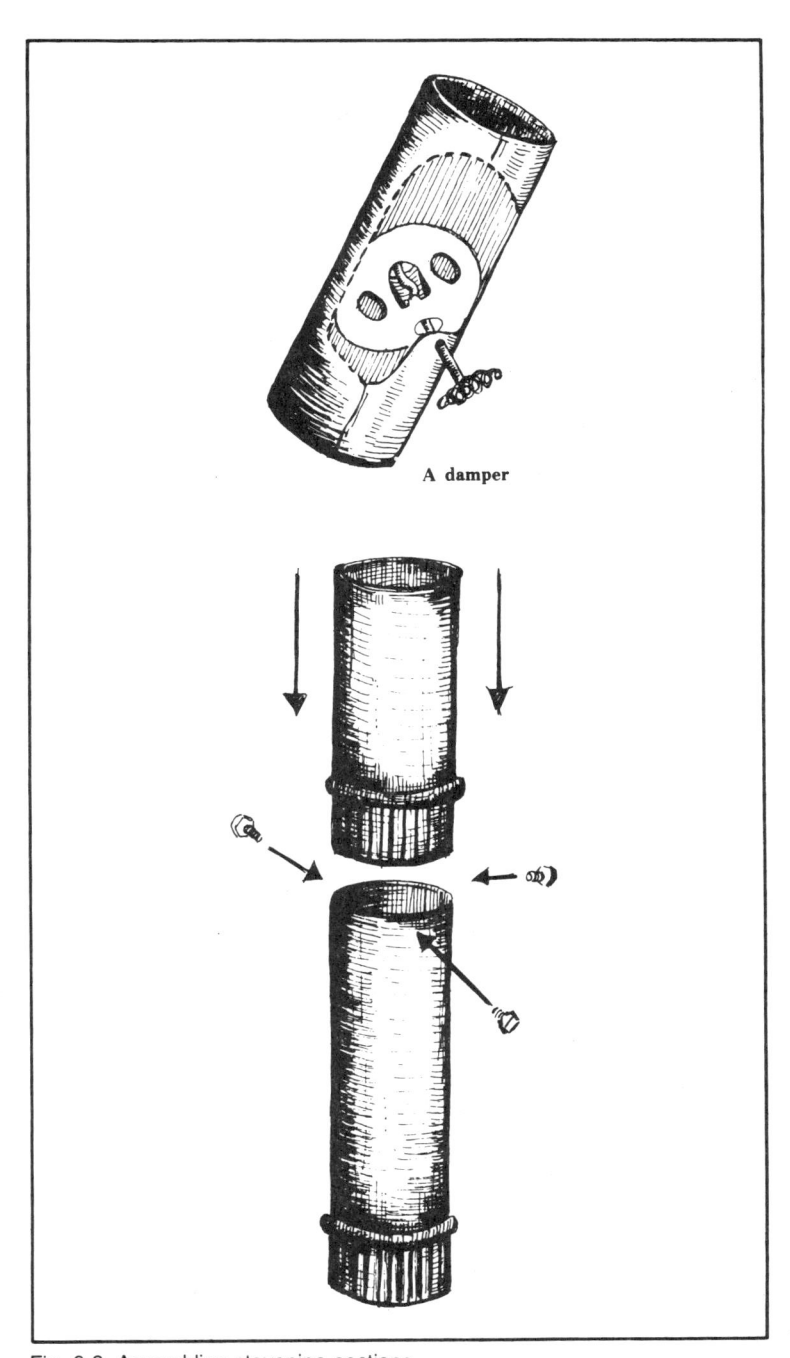

Fig. 6-8. Assembling stovepipe sections.

and thus slow the fire. This section of pipe collects the most creosote and should be cleaned more often than other sections.

Connecting

Great care must be taken in connecting your pipe to the flue. According to the NFPA, a chimney connector should be made of corrosion resistant steel of a 24-gauge steel. It must be as straight and as short as possible, with not more than one, or at the most, two 90-degree elbows. This connector pipe must not be less than 18 inches from the nearest combustible material. This clearance may be reduced if combustible materials are protected with sheet metal or other protective fireproof material.

If the stovepipe enters a wall or other flammable surface, the surface should be cut 18 inches wider than the diameter of the stovepipe and lined with firebrick or asbestos or other noncombustible material.

When your stove is connected to a masonry chimney, a chimney connector is required to extend through the masonry wall to the inner face of the liner, but not beyond. It must be cemented to the masonry. A fireclay *thimble* may be connected with high temperature cement to the masonry wall of the chimney, and the metal connector installed without cement for easier cleaning and replacement. The thimble should be flush with the inner face of the flue liner. If it extends into the flue, it will block the draft.

When the connector pipe is inserted in a thimble, but not cemented, the joint must be tight enough to prevent it from coming loose. Asbestos rope can be wedged into the space with a screwdriver. Thimbles must be surrounded by not less than 8 inches of brickwork or some other equally good fireproofing material.

If you don't use a thimble, all combustible material must be cut out of the wall to provide at least 18 inches of clearance on all sides of the pipe. Use noncombustible and insulating materials to close

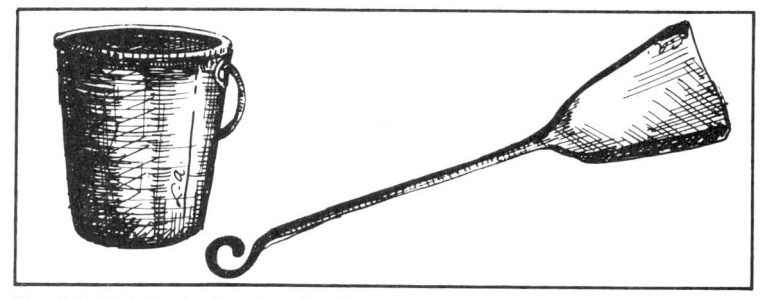

Fig. 6-9. Metal ash shovel and pail.

the opening. The diameter of the hole you made with the 18-inch clearance will be 42 inches.

When installing the connector pipe, be sure the crimped end of it faces the room. Now you can assemble the rest of the pipe. These sections of stovepipe must be fit together so that the crimped ends slide into the smooth ends and face toward the stove. In case of a runny creosote problem, the mess will run into the stove instead of on your floor.

Stovepipe sections are most secure when fastened with short sheet metal screws (Fig. 6-8). Stovepipe wire properly anchored with screw eyes can be used to hold up a long length of pipe.

Cleaning Pipes

Stovepipe is something that must be cleaned regularly. Tap your pipe gently. Does it make a "thud" sound? If it does, you can bet the pipe needs cleaning. A bright little "ping" noise usually indicates clear pipes. Stovepipes that carry cool flue gas from a high efficiency stove may need more cleaning out than stovepipes that carry high velocity, hot flue gas.

In order to clean stovepipes, you have to dismantle the whole affair. (Aren't you glad you hooked up the stove with the shortest possible span?) It's usually easiest to dismantle the pipe in small sections and take it all outdoors. Try numbering the pieces before you take it all apart. It'll be a lot easier to put it back together correctly. Just so you don't leave a trail of soot on the carpet, hold the pipe level or horizontally, as you head through the house and outside.

Use a round flue brush designed to fit the stovepipe or the versatile toilet brush. It isn't necessary to get your pipe shiny clean. Just brush out the creosote and check for corrosion. If the rust is great, replace the pipe.

Cleaning Your Stove

You're ready to clean and inspect the stove itself. By now, it must appear like an iron presence—stonily waiting your attention. Indeed, make sure your stove is stone cold before you begin to clean it. Here are some tools you'll want to have by your side.

- A drop cloth or plastic sheet.
- A trouble light or flashlight.
- An ash shovel (Fig. 6-9).
- A metal bucket.

- Work gloves.
- A small hand wire brush.
- A scraper or putty knife
- A hammer and screwdriver.
- A dust pan and broom.
- A can of furnace cement.

If your stove is the grateless type, there may be several inches of sand at the bottom. This should not be removed as it serves as a liner. If you don't have sand to line this kind of stove, leave at least 2 inches of ashes.

Avoiding Chimney Fires

- Once a day (the morning is a good time), with the damper wide open, burn a hot fire when someone is home. This will clear out the creosote that may have built up the night before.
- A chemical commercial cleaner may be used (calcium chloride/rock salt) if applied according to directions. It should help remove crusty deposits.
- For every three cords of wood burned, clean the chimney. Or clean it twice a year.
- Use only well-seasoned wood.
- Insure the best draft possible for your stove.
- Don't use your stove to burn trash, newspapers, paper logs, or old Christmas trees.
- Don't push your stove or fireplace beyond its capacity.

Outsmarting the Baffling System

Many stoves have a baffle system or a secondary combustion chamber, and it can be quite baffling to clean out this area unless you understand the nature of the beast. Look for a push-out panel on this secondary chamber. It's often sealed with furnace cement, so when you're trying to pry it open, be careful not to give it too direct a blow and make it crack. A wooden block to soften the blow will help. Some baffle systems are fastened with screws, so you may have to do some searching.

With the wire brush, scrape the inside of the chamber. A vacuum cleaner is a wonderful tool at this point. Old, loose furnace cement should be scraped carefully. Now is a good time to troubleshoot with the trouble light and search for cracks and heat warpage. Using your furnace cement and a putty knife or fingers, apply enough to seal the joint, but you'll have to wait 12 to 24 hours for the cement to dry before you fire the stove. If metal plates on either side of the crack are unstable, you'll have to have the parts welded.

Sheet metal stoves should be inspected for thin spots. Test areas with your fingers and palm of your hand for thickness. Discoloration or spots are caused by high heat and may indicate a thin area. A thin spot means your stove is unsafe, and you should not use it.

Cracks in the firebox are dangerous and must be repaired. The doorseal must also be examined and should have a tight fit. If parts of the seal are missing or the stove cannot be tightly shut, order a new seal.

Fourteen Safety Tips

- Do not use a flue being used by a furnace. In many areas this is illegal.
- Don't store flammables near the stove (kerosene, paint, etc.).
- Don't put wood chunks on the top of your stove to dry them out.
- Don't use lighter fuels, such as kerosene, to start a fire or to build one up.
- Put ashes in a metal bucket. Remove the ash container outdoors immediately.
- Prevent small children from playing near the stove. Keep them from opening the door to feed or watch the fire.
- Don't overheat your stove. This puts a tremendous strain on it and increases the danger of combustion of objects near it.
- Keep two dry chemical or CO_2 fire extinguishers handy. Get one that is rated for wood and paper fires. Avoid soda-acid type for cool water can warp or crack a stove. Place the fire extinguisher near the doorway and away from the stove.
- Keep a pound or two of salt or baking soda near a stove. This can be helpful in the event of a chimney fire. (Store salt in a nonmetallic container.)
- Plan ahead. Practice escape from your house in the event of a fire, and agree with the rest of your family upon an outside meeting place. Does everyone know how to use a fire extinguisher or call the fire department?
- Use good quality wood to minimize creosote deposits.

- Maintain a watch for sparks when drafts are open.
- Avoid burning trash in your wood stove. Plastics give off corrosive acids, and such fast fires can burn out of control.
- Watch the damper. It can accidentally close.

Each home presents a unique woodburning situation. When you are in doubt, written information on fire safety, no matter how thorough, cannot replace having your house checked by a fire prevention official or professional. Such authorities should be contacted whenever feasible or possible.

With proper care, a wood stove is an entirely satisfactory and satisfying source of heat for the energy-minded. You must be willing to learn correct operation of your stove and to carry out the necessary inspections and maintenance. With soaring oil prices, a stove can save you money or keep you from freezing in an emergency due to a power failure or a fuel shortage. There can never be too much emphasis on the need for thorough knowledge of wood, wood stoves, and safe practices.

Dealing with a Chimney Fire

A chimney fire sounds like a train roaring through the room. The stovepipe can get red hot and will vibrate violently. Hopefully your pipes are well secured and the chimney is in good repair, preventing fire from advancing through your home.

Don't panic. Most likely, your house will escape danger, although flames shooting up the chimney will be frightening and spectacular.

- Call the fire department immediately (even if you think the fire is under control).
- Close the dampers and vents.
- If the fire continues to burn, dowse fire with salt, sand, baking soda, or a dry chemical or CO_2 fire extinguisher. Do not use water. You could crack the stove.
- Move flammable objects away from the stove.
- Take a second fire extinguisher and check upstairs for possible flames around the chimney.
- The fire may have died out before the fire department arrives, but ask them to check over the stove and the chimney.

BARREL STOVE

The materials necessary to construct this barrel stove, including tools, are a barrel (55-gallon drum), a cast-iron door and collar, a flue, several stove bolts to attach the door and collar to the barrel, a screwdriver and wrench, a saber saw with a metal-cutting blade, and a drill and bit for the stove bolt holes.

It should take less than an hour to set up your furnace. You can use a 6-inch stovepipe. Raise the stove off the cellar floor with fireproof material. Install the damper in the stovepipe leading to the chimney.

There are several noteworthy advantages to this stove. With some sand on the bottom of the barrel, it will probably last two winters before needing replacement. There is greater safety in yearly replacement. When the barrel does weaken or burn through (hopefully you would replace it prior to this occurrence), the collar and door are simply installed on your new barrel. The 55-gallon drums are easy to obtain. Some are free, and some you may pay a very few dollars for, but they certainly are a minor investment.

You can throw in big chunks of knotty wood without all that splitting. The door is quite large, and barrel length allows for nice long pieces. When you are harvesting wood, you can get by with many fewer chain saw cuts since the pieces can be left long. You can use woods for this stove that you might not otherwise wish to use. Woods that produce sparks or dust are not a problem as they might be in a living room. Provided that your cellar is not drafty, the heat produced during the daylight hours in the cellar slowly rises during the night. You should find the house more comfortable when you wake up than it otherwise would be.

If you use this system in your cellar, remember that heat comes to the upper floors through the floor itself by conduction. You may have existing vents for the oil stove through which some heat rises. Leaving the cellar door ajar allows for convection current that increase the efficiency of the heating system.

The system is very safe provided that you start out with small fires until familiar with the stove. It wouldn't hurt to keep a thermometer at the stove area and use a thin sheet of asbestos above the stove. Also, one must be sure that soot is not accumulating along the flue or chimney.

MAKING CHARCOAL

After several minutes of heating you will see a whitish emission from the hole in the lid that is condensed water vapor. This will continue for many minutes before there is a slight change in the color. This change indicates that you now have a flammable gas (mostly hydrogen). Ignite it with a flaming paper or stick to produce a huge blowtorch. Eventually, perhaps after an hour, the flame will begin dwindling. When it finally dies out, metamorphosis has taken place, wood to charcoal (almost pure carbon). The contents of the drum will have been reduced in volume and weight about 65 percent. You have a smokeless, flameless, easily ignited fuel to use at your next cookout.

Don't open the lid, even to just peek, until the kiln has cooled off to the extent that you can handle it with bare hands. (Of course, you can douse the kiln with water.) Don't run the risk of having incandescence cause you to end up with ashes instead of charcoal.

The kids in your neighborhood would be pleased to participate in this project, even in the cleanup aspect. For them it's a spectacular learning experience with plenty of action. That's it. Here's hoping that the local fire warden will give you the green light.

The basic idea: wood is decomposed into charcoal and gas by heating to a high temperature in the absence of oxygen—*destructive* distillation to the chemist.

As a kiln, use a large, heavy metal, unsoldered can, preferably a steel drum with a clampable lid to withstand the high pressure of the gas to be released from the heated wood. Make a hole about 1 inch in diameter in the lid as an exit for the gas.

Fill the kiln with fairly uniform sticks of wood, no thicker than 2 inches (Fig. 6-10). For solid, clean charcoal, use hardwood—maple, oak, or ash. Don't waste your time and energy cutting the wood into chunks the size of charcoal that you buy for, after thorough cooking, the resulting charcoal is very brittle, easily broken into nuggets.

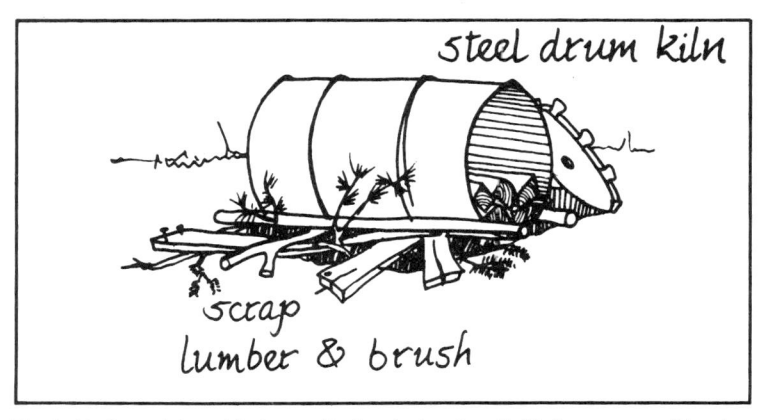

Fig. 6-10. A steel drum kiln is used in the destructive distillation process (drawing by Liz Buell).

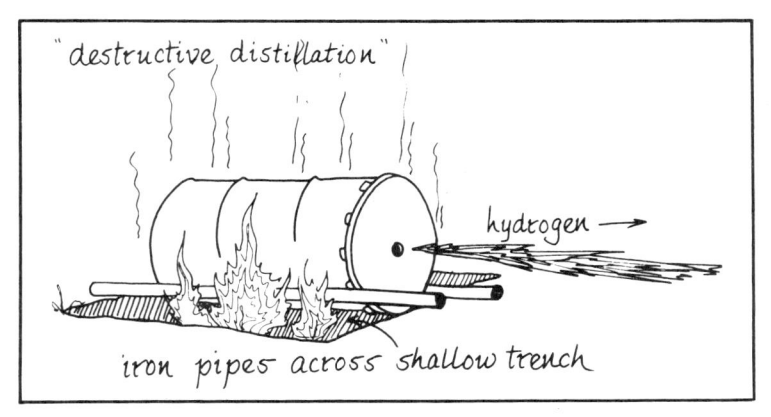

Fig. 6-11. Iron pipes across a shallow trench can be used to support the kiln (drawing by Liz Buell).

Place the kiln on a few rocks, or other support, so that you can have fire under it as well as around it. A shallow trench with two heavy metal bars (or piping) across it may be better (Fig. 6-11). For the fire, use waste wood: rotting lumber, fallen branches, trash, slash, or brush. Have a huge pipe ready to use before lighting the fire. Expect to be busy keeping the fire well stocked, roaring, for a couple hours. The time depends on whether you have green or dry wood in the kiln and on its thickness.

Chapter 7

Energy-Saving Ideas

It would be pleasant if we had some way of conserving summer heat for cold weather. This is obviously wishful thinking. Asking, "Why?" might get, besides a raised eyebrow, a response such as "The wind blows and it gets colder!" This really simplifies the practical understanding that heat flows.

Since heat does flow, fuel gets burned during the winter to replace exactly the amount of heat that flows out of our houses. We do close doors and try to tighten things up a bit. This correctly attempts to reduce the flow of heat from the house. As this flow gets reduced, we can see a reduction in fuel consumption, whether it's oil, electricity, wood, or whatever.

Heat moves at all times from regions of higher temperature to regions of lower temperature, and as a result it leaves our houses by following several paths to escape. We should not rely on any single procedure to do the total job of minimizing fuel consumption. Over-emphasizing one segment of winterizing your house, at the expense of other measures, probably will not be as effective as a more balanced approach.

Let's examine this flow of heat in a little more detail. As a somewhat simplified approach, we may assume that flow of heat from your house consists of two segments: infiltration and conductance.

Infiltration is cold air moving into the house. In springtime, this may be 45° F. air, and in the dead of winter, it might be −20° F. It is probably colder than we would like inside the house, and fuel gets burned to warm it.

The other big factor in heat flow is *conductance*. This term is used here to include heat transfer through any of the solid components of the house, such as walls, ceiling, glass, or doors. Usually conductance also includes heat transfer by convection and radiation when we are calculating heat flow from a building.

HEAT FLOW

To better understand heat flow, let's look at some basic concepts before we attack infiltration and conductance. Heat generally gets measured in terms of Btus, or British thermal units. One Btu is the amount of heat needed to raise 1 pound of water 1 degree Fahrenheit. One single Btu is roughly the amount of heat given off by burning one wooden kitchen match. By way of comparison, a gallon of oil contains a total of 138,000 Btu; a cord of dry hardwood contains about 25 million. We can be a bit more precise about electricity. One kilowatt hour equals 3,413 Btus.

Heat flow from a building depends on several factors. One is the size of the area in question. Heat flow is sometimes given in Btu per square foot to specify area. If we are losing heat through a large area, we would expect greater losses than through a smaller area. A big house uses more fuel than a small one, all else being equal.

Temperature difference affects heat flow. The greater the temperature difference, the more heat flows. For example, in a given area, if the temperature difference between inside and outdoors is 30° F., we will lose only half as much heat as when the temperature difference is 60° F. You are not going to burn as much fuel if it is 35° F. outdoors as you will at zero. Heat flow is directly proportional to temperature difference.

Time is another factor in heat flow. For a given house, the longer time involved, at whatever temperature difference, the greater will be the total heat flow. This seems only reasonable. Heat flow varies directly with time, usually referred to as Btu per hour.

The final factor affecting heat flow is the insulation value across the area separating the two regions of different temperatures. In the case of our house we must consider the R value, or insulation value, of walls, windows, doors, and ceiling that separate our 65° F. indoors from outdoor temperatures. The larger the R value, the better the insulation, and the less heat will flow. Thus, heat flow is inversely proportional to the thermal resistance (R value) of the area we're considering.

All this usually ends up being expressed in Btu per square foot per degree temperature difference per hour, to indicate the relative R value of a material or combinations of materials, such as in a frame wall. R or other insulation measures refer specifically only to single similar sections of the building, such as a square foot of wall or window.

The heat flow we just discussed did not take into account the wind blowing. As far as a wall or window section is concerned, this factor is usually taken into account in the calculation of the R value for them. When considering infiltration, wind velocity certainly is a large factor. Calculation of infiltration losses presents a slightly different picture. If one gets involved with this, the crack width would be determined (usually estimated), and the length of a crack through which air moves, wind velocity, and temperature difference would all enter into the calculations. After much figuring you would come up with a number for the Btus needed to offset the effect of all this air whistling through your house. This all usually gets accounted for by estimating the number of air changes per hour.

Infiltration occurs wherever there is a chance for air to penetrate the house structure—definitely around doors and windows. These are fitted loosely enough to slide or swing, and air penetrates the cracks.

A certain amount of air relentlessly finds its way behind window trim, through laps of clapboards or other siding, or between sheathing and sills. This may end up whistling by an electrical outlet, for example. Another form of infiltration is simply the air exchange when some air rushes out whenever anyone uses the door. Replacement cold air comes in with the person. This exchange makes up part of the infiltration heat loss for the house.

Another effect is warm air rising within the house, especially in a house of two or more stories. With warm air rising, an opportunity occurs for cold air to penetrate, replacing some of this rising warm air. We must assume that some warm air escapes to allow replacement by cold air in the lower part of the house. This may be very gradual, but it is part of the infiltration process. Sometimes this gets referred to as the chimney effect of the entire house. Rising warm air may escape through trap doors into attic space, migrate through plaster or any breaks in the ceiling, flow by light fixtures fitted to outlet boxes in ceilings or go up attic stairwells. It can also escape on the leeward side of the building, moving by loose fitting windows or panes of glass. All these contribute to the chimney effect and allow cold air to penetrate lower regions of the house. Then you burn some fuel to warm it up.

Infiltration causes enough problems that usually the first suggestion for winterizing a house is to provide storm doors and storm windows. Some figures of Btu losses show the effect of adding storm doors and windows. An ordinary outside door occupies 20 square feet (3 feet wide by 6 feet, 8 inches tall). This one exterior door, by conductance and infiltration, will lose about 4,000 Btu per hour when the temperature difference is 75° F. This temperature difference occurs when you maintain 65° F. inside your house and it is −10° F. outside, not too uncommon an occurrence during most winters. Adding a storm door cuts this loss practically in half.

WINDOWS

Let's look at windows (Fig. 7-1). An ordinary double-hung window, single thickness of glass, 3 by 5 feet, has an area of 15 square feet. For our example condition of 75° F. temperature difference, we find 1,580 Btu leaving each hour at each window. This includes the infiltration around the crack that exists because the window can slide. This crack measures 19 feet in a 3 by 5 window. Adding a storm sash to this window provides what is called double glazing. Now the heat loss has been cut in half—760 Btu per hour. These values are for fairly tight fitting windows. Adding a storm sash to a window accomplishes two things at once: it provides an airspace between the double-hung window and the storm window, which reduces conductance; and it sharply reduces the infiltration between the window sash and frame.

It makes little difference whether the storm sash is the old fashioned wooden kind, tightly fitted and attached to the regular window frame, or a combination window, either double or triple track, also tightly fitted and with tight fitting sash. The important part is the second layer of glass providing an airspace and the considerable reduction in infiltration.

Triple glazing cuts heat loss even further (see Table 7-1). You can get triple glazing several ways. One of the simplest is to tape a piece of plastic to the inside window trim. This will provide an inside storm window to go along with your outside storm sash. When you peel the tape off in spring, you will find a redecorating job awaiting.

Another way you can accomplish triple glazing is by placing a

Fig. 7-1. Much heat is lost through windows (photo by Faith Rainbolt).

sheet of plastic on the inside of a wooden storm sash before installing it. This same concept can be used on storm doors. Extra inside glazing is available in clear, rigid plastic panels. These seal windows from inside. The clear panels are held in place by a plastic channel attached to the inside window trim. These channels can be

Table 7-1. Glazing and Heat Loss.

Window Heat Flow[a] (75° F. temperature difference)	
Glazing	Btu loss[b]
Single	1,580
Double	760
Triple	500

a One 3' × 5' window = 15'^{2}.
b Btu loss each hour.

opened to remove the panel during the summer, if you wish. Other extra glazing options include constructing a light wooden framework and attaching plastic film to make a snug fitting inside storm sash.

Anything you do to reduce air infiltration will cut down on fuel bills. The importance of this is emphasized when you consider that a fairly new house, reasonably well insulated, may use one-third to one-half of its fuel consumption to compensate for its infiltration losses.

We have mentioned door openings, window cracks, and this sort of thing as infiltration sources. Other sources of air leakage are kitchen and bathroom exhaust fans that do not have dampers that close tightly when fans are not operating. Ill-fitting dampers on fireplaces let a lot of warm air escalate from the chimney. This air must be replaced by cold air from outdoors.

INFILTRATION

Another source of infiltration is simply the air that must be moved into the house to supply oxygen for combustion of the fuel you are burning. Any open flame, whether oil, gas, coal, or wood, requires oxygen for its operation. This comes from air that has infiltrated your house. This usually may not be too noticeable, but it is nonetheless a very real portion of infiltration into your house. To combat this, you might consider a separate, combustion air duct to supply air directly to whatever fuel burning device is being used.

Banking your house is another practice to reduce infiltration. Today this probably takes the form of plastic or tar paper attached to the bottom of clapboards or sheathing around the house, extended and weighted down to the ground. The effect of banking will be much greater on loose foundations, such as a split granite or rock laid up without mortar. The results of banking on a solid concrete foundation, without windows, will probably not be as significant. The high degree of variability in foundations and the amount of air that can get through make assessment of the effect of banking on your house difficult. If you total all other heat losses, it would not be unreasonable to add a 5 to 10 percent allowance for lack of banking. Any barrier that reduces infiltration makes acceptable banking, and any additional material that provides further insulation around the basement wall offers extra help.

The practice of adding storm doors and windows illustrates the addition of an airspace to slow down the rate of heat loss. The use of common insulating materials sets up a multitude of airspaces. These prevent convection currents inside ceilings and walls and drastically reduce the amount of heat that flows through them.

ADDING INSULATION

Consider a ceiling without any insulation. With a 75° F. temperature difference, this ceiling loses about 23,000 Btu every hour for every 1,000 square feet of ceiling. If your house ceiling is not insulated, you could measure the number of square feet and make a comparison. Table 7-2 provides an idea of the reduction you can expect in the number of Btus flowing through 1,000 square feet of ceiling or wall area, if different amounts of insulation are added.

One myth some people harbor is that insulation can stop heat flow. This is not so. As stated earlier, any time a temperature difference exists, heat will flow, no matter how much insulation is used, but thicker insulation means less heat loss.

Notice from Table 7-2 that adding insulation in the attic does not as much effect per inch of insulation as the thickness of insula-

Table 7-2. Insulation and Heat Loss through Ceiling and Wall.

Ceiling and Wall Heat Flow (75° F. temperature difference)			
1,000 ft^2 of Ceiling Area		1,000 ft^2 Net Wall Area	
Insulation	Btu Loss[a]	Insulation	Btu Loss[a]
0	23,000	0	18,750
2	7,200	3½	4,750
4	4,000	5½	3,250
6	2,750		
8	2,100		
10	1,700		
12	1,450		

a Btu loss each hour.

tion increases. This phenomenon allows a "break-even" point to be calculated. Let's go back 20 years. Anyone constructing a house then could easily have obtained figures that would have shown it was much cheaper to buy oil at 15 cents per gallon (or whatever it was then) than to add more insulation beyond 3 or 4 inches in the attic. In other words, this was the "break-even" point. Placing more than the calculated inches of insulation in the attic would simply cost more than buying oil at the going rate. As far as one's pocketbook was concerned, that was enough insulation.

Applying the same line of reasoning today brings us to the point that we should be figuring about 12 inches of insulation in the attic at current oil prices. If you want to hedge against almost certain price increases, you might want to add a bit more, as you will be in the attic banging your head on rafters and driving splinters into your knees crawling over ceiling joists anyway.

If you are not buying oil but are burning wood, you can console yourself that it will take fewer cords if you put in more insulation. Perhaps you could get to that blissful state where the woodshed holds more than a year's supply, so it has a chance to dry thoroughly before use.

Table 7-2 also shows the amount of heat flow you can expect through an ordinary frame wall with different amounts of insulation. This net wall area does not include doors and windows, which should be figured separately.

Vapor barrier protection should be used on the warm side of any insulation, and the cold side should be vented to outside air. This is very important because water vapor collecting in insulation drastically reduces its insulating quality. Also, water vapor can collect on the inside of outside walls and freeze (Fig. 7-2). In the spring the water vapor will thaw. It will run down the wall and soak into the sills. A few years of this and you might find yourself with rotted sills. Ventilating the cold side of insulation eliminates this problem.

Before insulating your attic, you should lay down a vapor barrier of polyethylene sheet plastic, (Fig. 7-3). Then put in the insulation. At the same time, definite attic ventilation should be provided. Gable louvers should be used at the rate of 1 square foot for each 300 square feet of attic insulation area. This square foot should be at each end of the attic. Use a total of 2 square feet for each 300 if you are using any screening material over the louvers. The screening material is a good idea to keep out bugs next summer. You can further enhance the disposition of water vapor that migrates into

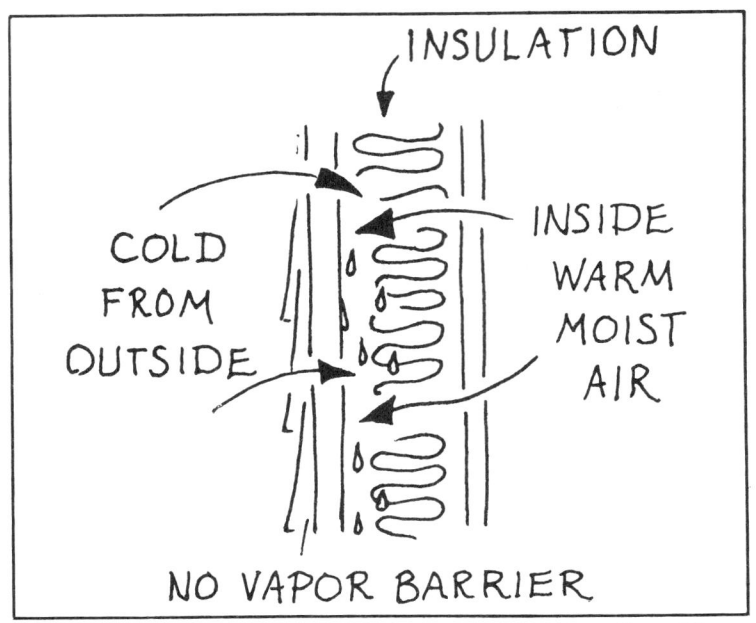

Fig. 7-2. Water vapor can collect on the inside of outside walls and freeze (drawing by Faith Rainbolt).

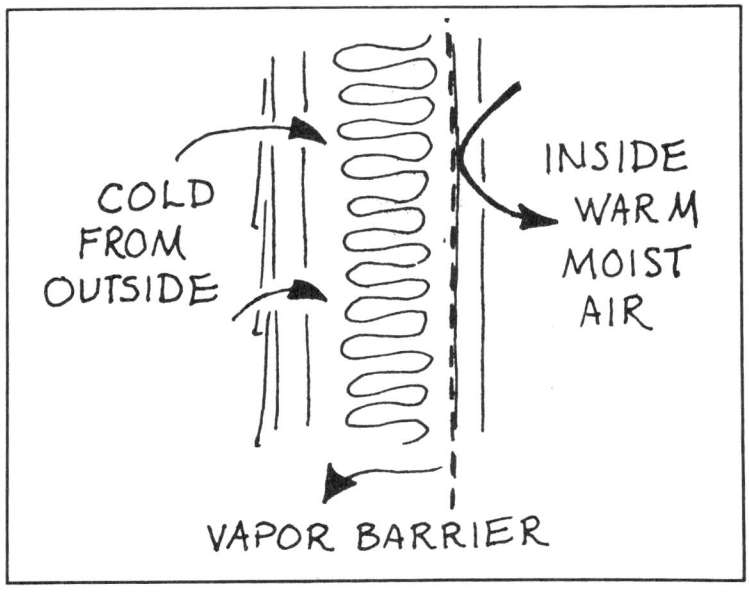

Fig. 7-3. Lay down a vapor barrier of polyethylene sheet plastic before insulating your attic (drawing by Faith Rainbolt).

the attic space by using vents and screened openings along the eaves in the soffit, so air movement can cover the entire attic area (Fig. 7-4).

Installation of vapor barriers in an existing wall is a more difficult process, and a wall presents a more complicated problem. Remember the attic space acts as a large air cushion on the cold side of the insulation. Once a wall is insulated, there is not much of any air cushion to absorb water vapor that migrates into the wall. Possibilities of water condensation become more acute.

Condensation can be alleviated by proper venting of the wall. Providing a small crack between the sill and sheathing admits outside air to absorb water vapor (Fig. 7-5). A path for air to escape at the top of the wall can be had with holes drilled in the plate. Another possibility is to connect wall space with soffit areas vented to the attic (Fig. 7-6). Some improvement in vapor resistance of interior walls can be accomplished with two or three coats of oil-based paints or varnishes or applying vinyl wallpapers. Vapor problems after insulating an existing wall should be handled by a combination of increasing interior vapor resistance and providing venting on the cold side of the insulation.

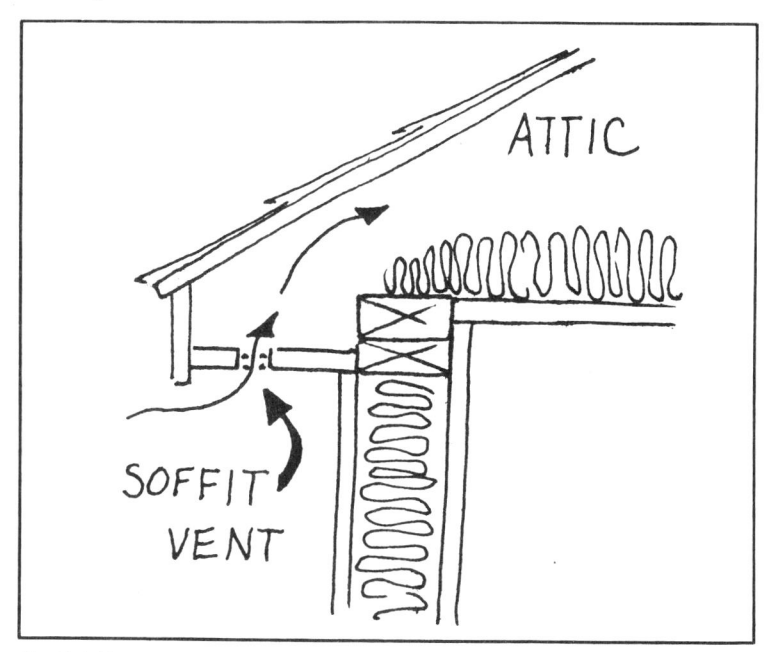

Fig. 7-4. Use vents and screened openings along the eaves in the soffit (drawing by Faith Rainbolt).

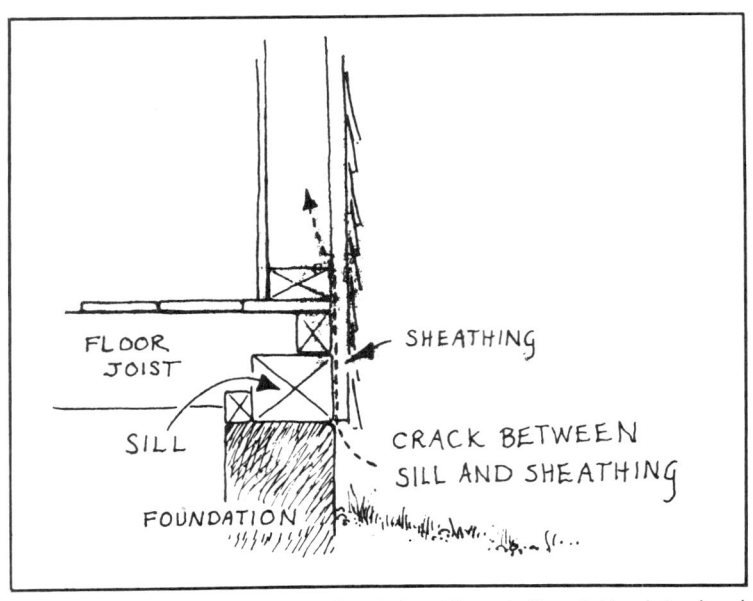

Fig. 7-5. A small crack between sill and sheathing admits outside air to absorb water vapor (drawing by Faith Rainbolt).

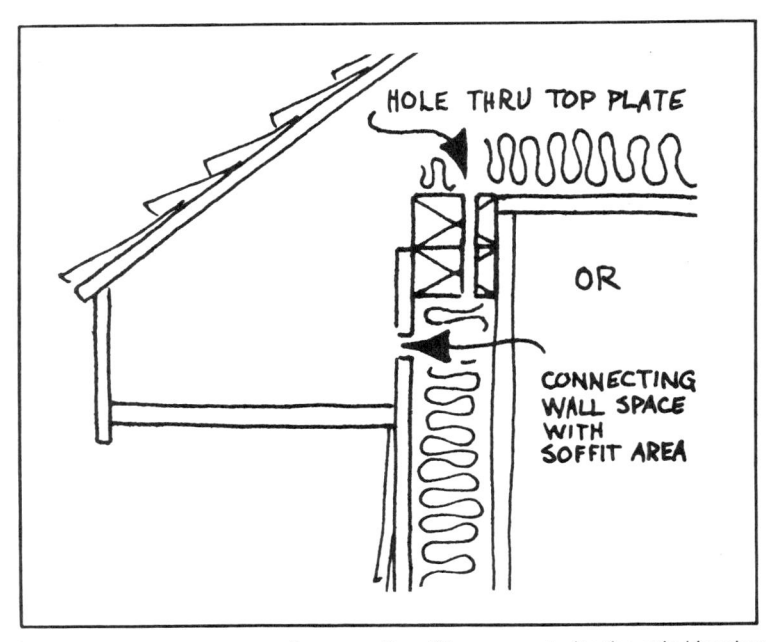

Fig. 7-6. You can connect wall space with soffit areas vented to the attic (drawing by Faith Rainbolt).

Slowing heat transfer relative to all the loss components probably will reduce fuel consumption more effectively than overdoing one item. Consider for a moment the problem you would have heating your house if each window had a pane of glass missing. No matter how well insulated the ceiling and walls were, you would burn a lot of fuel to compensate for all the air that was coming through the broken glass area. Chances are your comfort would also suffer.

Probably the first priority for conserving fuel is to install storm windows and doors to cut down on infiltration and heat loss through areas where flow is greatest. Obviously it would do little good to have a well insulated ceiling and walls if wind was still whistling around windows and doors. The second priority should be proper attic insulation.

FIREPLACES

Using fireplaces to supplement the oil tank may drain the tank faster. Leaping flames in the fireplace require oxygen. The resulting air infiltration takes more oil to warm it. Judicious use of your fireplace may mean not using it at all, but sealing it off. This is particularly true if the only heat to be gained from it is what gets radiated directly from the fireplace and the fire itself. You can't close the damper until the fire dies out, so the draft taking warm air up the chimney may continue even when the fire is radiating little heat to the room.

Taking stock of where your fuel goes this winter will point up improvements you can add to help out next year. There are a lot of things that you can still do inside yet this winter to reduce fuel consumption.

HOMESTEADER'S GUIDE TO INSULATION

Over the last few years, Americans have become relatively sensitive to their energy consumption. This change of attitude has not evolved because Americans have thoroughly examined the energy situation and now believe our society's energy sources are being depleted, and that it is best to conserve what energy remains until other sources are developed. Instead, most Americans have turned down their thermostats or slowed down their cars because of the increased cost of fuels. For instance, the total annual energy consumption for space heating in the typical Boston home built before 1970 with a floor area of 1,500 square feet averages 170 million Btus. In 1970 No. 2 fuel oil cost 25¢ a gallon, so the annual heating costs came to about $425. Assuming that no improvements have been made to increase the thermal efficiency of this pre-1970 house, the fuel bill in 1978 would be nearly double that of eight years ago—$816—since fuel prices have almost doubled over the intervening years. (No. 2 fuel averages 48¢ a gallon.)

This rise in fuel prices has turned a majority of the 70 million U.S. homes into extremely wasteful thermal shelters. The ordinary home was not insulated before 1970 because the insulation investment would not have been offset by fuel savings.

In retrospect, then, housing construction practices of the past were fiscally practical given the assumptions of their times—abundant fuel supplies and low prices. In the 1960s, it was economical to install only 3.5 inches of fiberglass insulation in walls and a maximum of 6 inches in attics. Considering the economics of the period, homes constructed before 1960 were thermally sound shelters with no insulation in the attic. These were the minimum insulation standards set by the Federal Housing Authority (FHA) for the 1950s. In 1977, FHA revised its thermal standards for residential structures. This standard requires 6.5 inches of fiberglass insulation in walls and 12 inches of fiberglass or its equivalent in an attic. Although the government guidelines have been updated, housing design has not yet caught up with economically justifiable conservation techniques.

The construction industry has been primarily concerned with the initial costs of a house, with construction costs and not with the costs of maintenance and heating. The industry has rarely considered operating costs or total life cycle costs. This initial costs approach to housing economics is as much a part of the home buyers' ideology as it is of the home designers' and builders' ethic. Until recently, home buyers were not willing to spend an extra $2,000 on a new house that was designed to conserve energy.

As the nation's vulnerability to energy shortages increases and as the availability of fuels changes, there must be a scrupulous examination of the long-term operating costs of structures and of energy conservation techniques. If energy conservation techniques are not implemented, homeowners will certainly have to change their life-style and suffer a lowered standard of living. Many homeowners are now reeling from fuel bills double those from before the 1973 energy crisis. For example, brownouts are becoming a regular occurrence in the Midwest during the winter months. Natural gas is often unavailable to new customers because of its increasing scarcity. These factors are providing incentives to thermally upgrade or retrofit the vast number of increasingly obsolete structures throughout the country.

An existing structure's energy efficiency can be substantially improved by using insulation. Fuel bills can be slashed by 30 to 60 percent by installing more insulation in the attic, walls, and floor. Life cycle cost analyses done by the National Bureau of Standards indicate that the optimal thickness of insulation is often greater than that recommended by insulation manufacturers.

How much of which kind of insulation is economically feasible to install? Which combination of insulation will save the most dollars over the life of a house? Figure 7-7 shows how this question may be answered. Line A represents the total installed cost of insulation. It does not start at zero because the contractor has a fixed setup cost. This includes such costs as transportation, erecting scaffolding, and drilling holes in the existing wall. From that point, the cost increases in a linear fashion as the thickness of insulation increases.

Line B represents the fuel dollar savings over the life of the house. We start with zero savings and zero insulation. The savings first increase rapidly, since adding 1 inch of insulation usually reduces by 50 percent the heat loss through a wall or attic. As the thickness of insulation increases, the savings get smaller and smaller with each additional inch of insulation. Finally, a horizontal line is reached. The insulation will pay for itself up to the point where line A and B intersect. At that point, the amount spent for insulation is equal to the amount saved. The greatest savings are achieved at

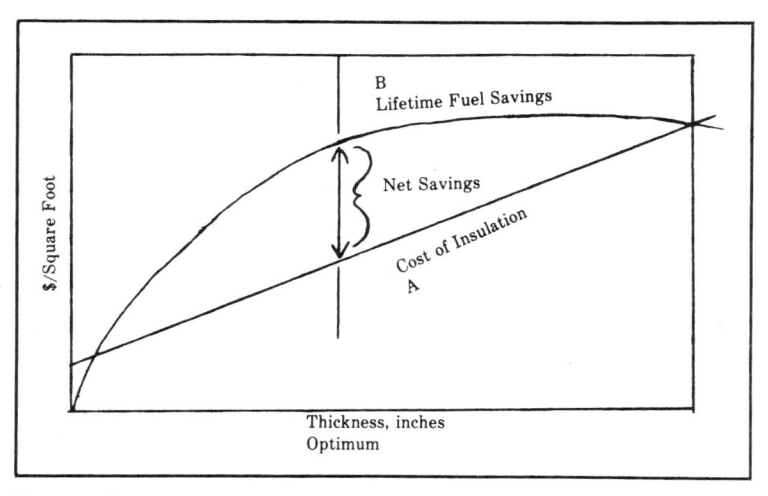

Fig. 7-7. Cost increases in a linear fashion as the thickness of insulation increases.

the point where lines A and B are farthest apart. At the apex of the bulge of line B, there are the greatest savings per invested dollar. This point can be determined exactly by using an economic technique called the *marginal savings analysis*. This determines the maximum dollar savings generated by the last inch of insulation.

Optimal insulation thickness for six applications and nine commonly used insulations are presented in Table 7-3. The optimal thicknesses were computed using 10,000 degree days and a delivered fuel cost of $1 per 100,000 Btus. (The number of degree days for a given day is computed by subtracting the average temperature for that day from 65° F. These daily degree day figures are added together for the entire heating period to obtain totals for different localities. In New England, this varies from about 10,000 in northern Maine to about 5,500 in coastal Massachusetts.)

You can compute the optimum thickness ("Topt") for your locality for any of the insulations in Table 7-3 by using Table 7-3 and Fig. 7-8. Look at the bottom horizontal scale in Fig. 7-8 for your fuel cost per delivered therm (one therm equals 100,000 Btu). Examples of types of fuels are given. Then find the total number of degree days for your locale on the curves going up and to the right. Run a line straight up from the estimated fuel cost to your specific degree day curve and then straight over (left) to find a K value, which is called the insulation thickness adjustment factor. Then multiply this K value by the insulation thickness given in Table 7-3 for the type of insulation and installation you desire. This will yield the optimum insulation thickness for your specific location.

Here's an example on how to compute a Topt:

Location: Portland, Maine
If: degree days = 8,000 fuel cost per delivered therm = 50¢
Look these values up in Fig. 7-8. Then: K = .64 (vertical scale on Fig. 7-8)
Select insulation type from top of Table 7-3 and the application from the left side of Table 7-3
Condition: conventional stud wall desired type of insulation: cellulose, contractor installed.
K × Topt = .64 × 8″ = 5.12 inches.
This is then the optimum thickness of this type of insulation you can install.

Before purchasing insulation yourself or phoning a local insulation contractor to install it for you, there are a few things you should know.

Table 7-3. Optimal Insulation Thickness for Six Applications and Nine Commonly Used Insulations.

Optimum Insulation Thickness Assuming 10,000 DD And F=1.0. To Find Optimum Thickness For Other DD And F Values, Multiply By k from Figure 7-8.	Labor By:	Blown Fiberglass R=2.2 Reff=2.2	Fiberglass Batt R=3.2 Reff=2.7	Cellulose In Attic R=3.7 Reff=3.7	Cellulose In Wall R=3.3 Reff=2.8	Urea Foam 0% Shrinkage R=3.3 Reff=2.8	Urea Foam 3% Shrinkage R=2.6 Reff=Estimated	Beadboard R=3.9 Reff=3.2	Styrofoam R=5.25 Reff=3.9	Urethane R=6.25, Reff=4.3
Open Attic	Owner Contractor	36" 36"	27" 19"	20" 20"						
Cathedral Ceiling	Owner Contractor		21" 15"	18" 15"				14" 11"	9" 8"	7" 6"
Conventional Stud Wall (Stud space not free)	Owner Contractor		12" 8"		11" 8"	8" 6"	9" 7"	9" 6"	7" 5½"	
Wall Insulated Outside Framing	Owner Contractor		18" 13"					12" 9"	8" 7"	6" 5½"
Floor, No Perimeter Wall	Owner Contractor		20" 14"	16" 13"				13" 10"	8" 7"	6" 6"
Floor Over Unhtd Basement or Crawl Space	Owner Contractor		11" 8"					8" 6"	3" 2½"	

109

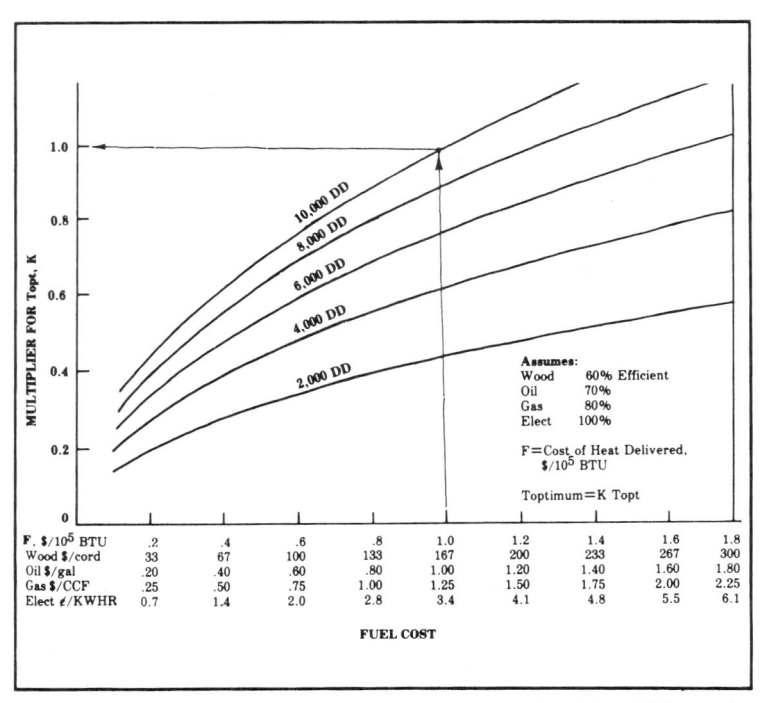

Fig. 7-8. Use this information to help find the optimum insulation thickness for your locality.

Contractors

In the last few years, the number of insulation contractors in the country has increased drastically, like fruit flies at the dump on a hot summer day. Unfortunately, a few are in the business to make a quick buck at the customer's expense. These contractors feed the public's increasingly skeptical attitude toward insulation contractors. Here are some guidelines to remember when dealing with contractors:

—When hiring a contractor of blown-in insulation, be sure he is licensed by the manufacturer of the particular brand and has a reputable standing in the community.

—Two or three estimates should be obtained for a job, because prices vary considerably among contractors.

—Check the density of insulation to be installed. With the blown-in urea formaldehyde, the preparation and rate of application determine density of the installed insulation. All manufacturers publish recommended densities of their products; the government publishes recommended densities for some products. Be sure the contractor you hire follows the established guidelines. This can be accomplished by obtaining a copy of the guidelines from a manufacturer.

Fiberglass Insulation

For the right material to be chosen for the right task, it is essential to know the characteristics and qualities of available insulation.

The purpose of insulation is to retard the rate of heat flowing from inside a heated building to the cold external environment during the winter; the reverse is true during the summer. Depending on the space and location to be insulated, some insulators are better than others because of their ease of installation and their cost. For instance, it would be a long, laborious effort to put fiberglass batts or blankets into an existing wall unless the wall was

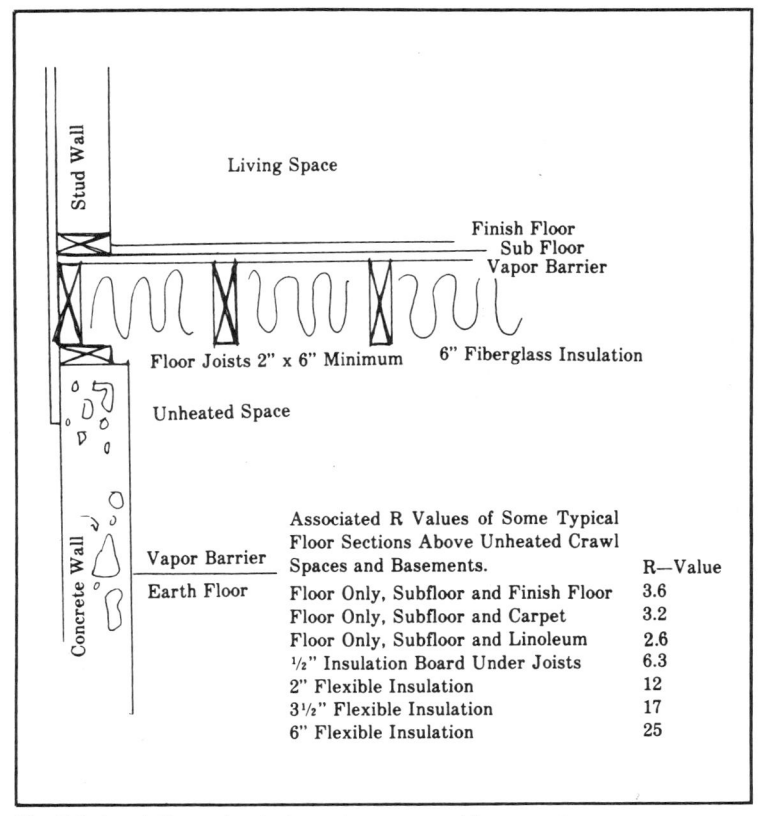

Associated R Values of Some Typical Floor Sections Above Unheated Crawl Spaces and Basements.	R—Value
Floor Only, Subfloor and Finish Floor	3.6
Floor Only, Subfloor and Carpet	3.2
Floor Only, Subfloor and Linoleum	2.6
½" Insulation Board Under Joists	6.3
2" Flexible Insulation	12
3½" Flexible Insulation	17
6" Flexible Insulation	25

Fig. 7-9. Insulating unheated crawl spaces and basements.

to be ripped out anyway. Fiberglass batts are semirigid and come in strips that are 4 feet long and either 16 inches or 24 inches wide.

In new construction, the most widely used insulation is fibrous glass—commonly called fiberglass. It is the least expensive insulation per R (R being a measure of the resistance of a material to heat flow) and usually the easiest to install in a wooden frame house. It is available in thicknesses of 2 inches, 3½ inches, 6 inches, 7 inches, and 9 inches and in either a batt or roll. The roll is recommended whenever possible, because its fewer seams make it less likely to be improperly installed. In the retrofit of existing buildings, fiberglass can be easily applied in any exposed area such as attics or floors and exposed underneath to a basement or crawl space (Figs. 7-9 and 7-10). This material is available in only two widths—16 inches and 24 inches—so before purchasing, measure the space between the wall studs or joists to be insulated.

Fiberglass is available with a one-sided facing (or covering) of foil or paper or with no facing. Recent reports from the National Bureau of Standards and Owens Corning, the world's largest manufacturer of insulation, contend that the foil or paper facings do not provide adequate moisture barriers for a building. It is necessary to install a continuous vapor barrier on the living space side (the warm side) of the insulation material to prevent rotting and other forms of moisture degradation within the structure's wall and roof cavities. Polyethylene film is most generally used as a vapor barrier. R values and cost per square foot may be found in Table 7-4.

Styrofoam

Extruded polystyrene foam—*Styrofoam*—has recently earned a wide reputation as an excellent insulation material for new and old construction. The exceptional performance of Styrofoam is caused by its unique cellular structure—tiny, rigid bubbles closed off from each other and free of airspaces.

Styrofoam is moisture-resistant and durable. Its closed cells prevent water absorption caused by capillary action and provide good compressive strength for a lightweight material. Its excellent resistance to both water and water vapor helps Styrofoam maintain its insulating value despite long exposure to adverse climatic conditions. This is often used below ground to insulate concrete foundation walls to prevent excessive heat loss.

Styrofoam is often used in new housing construction to sheath exterior frame walls and basement walls (Fig. 7-11). The insulating sheathing covers the whole walls and basement walls, with the

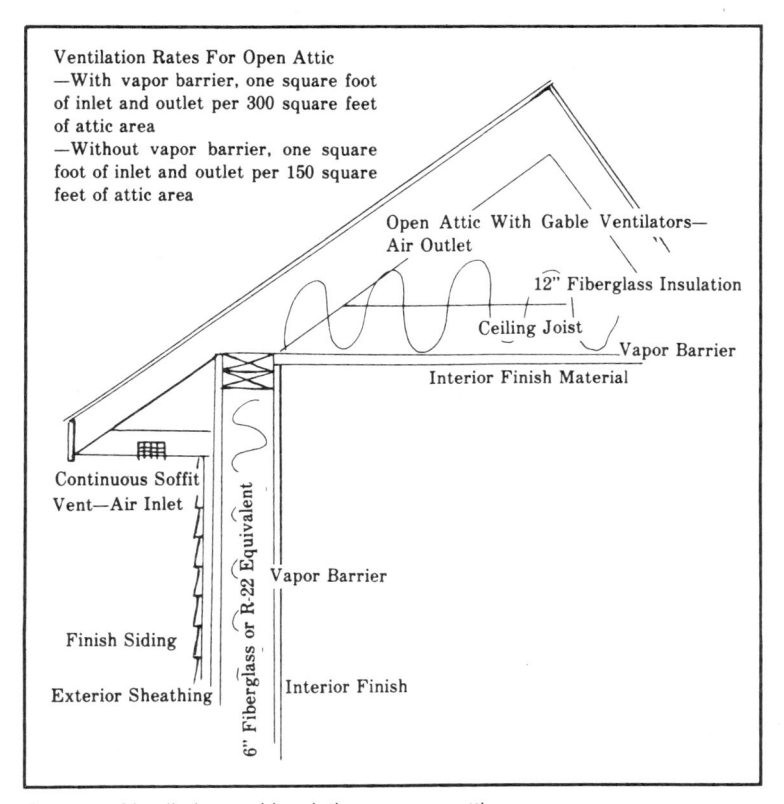

Fig. 7-10. Ventilating and insulating an open attic.

exception of window and door openings. It completely insulates studs, plates, headers, and masonry foundation from the roofline to the frost line and eliminates the thermal weak spots that commonly exist with other insulation systems. By completely enclosing an entire building, this insulation system also reduces drafts and excessive infiltration.

Through comprehensive testing done in 1974 and 1975, Ohio State University found that extending 1 inch of Styrofoam insulation from the roofline to the frost line slices the heating bill of a conventionally-framed three-bedroom house by about 24 percent.

In slab-on-grade construction (concrete floor poured directly on ground), good thermal efficiency can be achieved by making the best use of the tendencies of the concrete slab and walls to absorb and emit heat (Fig. 7-12).

When placing Styrofoam as sheathing on the exterior of any building, it must be protected from sunlight. When exposed to

Table 7-4. R Values and Cost per Square Foot of Insulation.

	Insulation value (R per inch)	Cost ($ per square foot)	Cost per R (per square foot)
Blown fiberglass	2.2	.0275	1.3
Fiberglass blanket and batt	3.15	.033	1.0
Blown cellulose (attic)	3.7	.055	1.5
Blown cellulose (wall)	3.3	.07	2.1
Polystyrene "beadboard"	3.9	.10	2.6
Extruded styrene "Styrofoam"	5.25	.24	4.6
Blown urea formaldehyde (walls)	4.2	.18	4.3
Urethane	6.25	.35	5.6
Vermiculite	2.2	?	?
Blown rockwool	3.3	?	?

Styrofoam used to sheath exterior frame walls completely insulates studs, plates, headers and masonry foundation—reducing infiltration and conductive heat loss through the building frame.

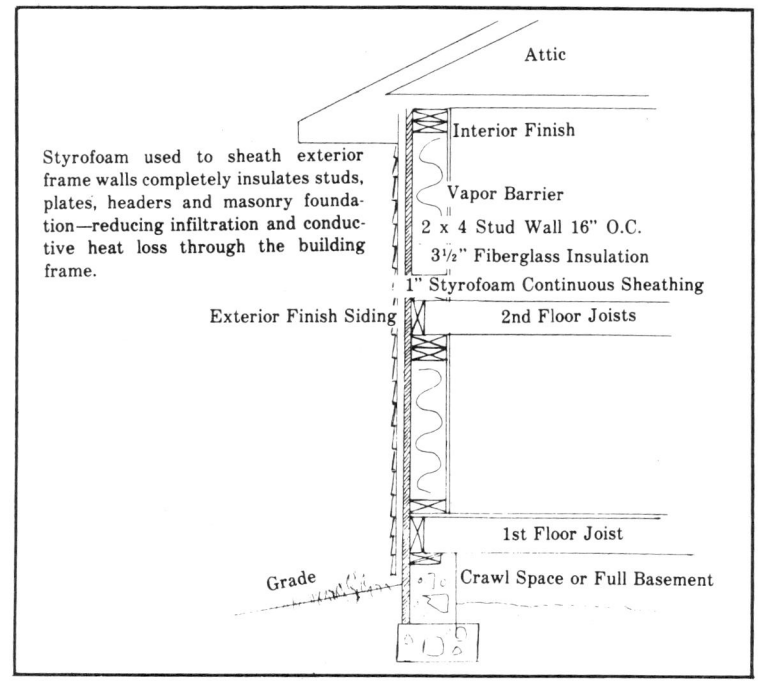

Attic
Interior Finish
Vapor Barrier
2 x 4 Stud Wall 16" O.C.
3½" Fiberglass Insulation
1" Styrofoam Continuous Sheathing
Exterior Finish Siding
2nd Floor Joists
1st Floor Joist
Grade
Crawl Space or Full Basement

Fig. 7-11. Styrofoam is used to sheath exterior frame walls.

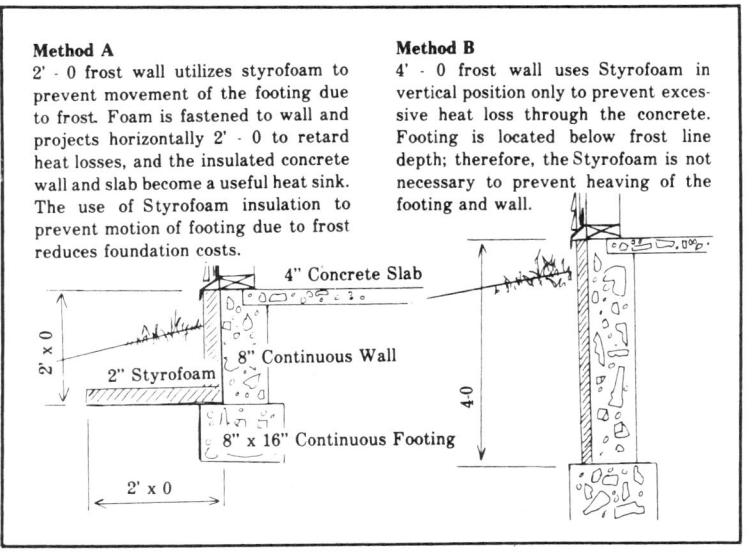

Method A
2'-0 frost wall utilizes styrofoam to prevent movement of the footing due to frost. Foam is fastened to wall and projects horizontally 2'-0 to retard heat losses, and the insulated concrete wall and slab become a useful heat sink. The use of Styrofoam insulation to prevent motion of footing due to frost reduces foundation costs.

Method B
4'-0 frost wall uses Styrofoam in vertical position only to prevent excessive heat loss through the concrete. Footing is located below frost line depth; therefore, the Styrofoam is not necessary to prevent heaving of the footing and wall.

Fig. 7-12. Methods of insulating concrete slabs that enable the slab and foundation wall to act as a heat sink, which helps to temper extreme temperatures in the living space.

sunlight for an extended period of time, Styrofoam goes through *photodegradation* or begins to decompose. This is apparent when its normally blue color turns to a tan or a yellowish brown. The foam can be protected by covering it with a vinyl-acrylic latex coat or stucco with chicken wire reinforcement. Contact the Styrofoam manufacturer for a list of recommended protective coverings and associated distributors.

It is often assumed that Styrofoam sheathing is an adequate vapor barrier. According to the Dow Chemical Company, this is not so. Dow has concluded that buildings—regardless of their insulation system—have great potential for moisture condensation problems. This is due to higher relative interior humidities and tighter, better insulated homes. These conditions call for a continuous vapor barrier properly installed on the warm side of the building membrane, regardless of the insulation materials used.

Styrofoam is available in 2-by-8 pieces of varying thicknesses—½-inch, 1-inch, 1½-inch, and 2-inch. Methods of application are mastics (glue) especially designed for foam application, or nails or staples. See Table 7-4 for cost and thermal resistance data.

Beadboard

Polystyrene, often called *beadboard*, is a rigid, sheet-type insulator. Foam coffee cups are made of this material. It is lightweight and durable, but must not be exposed to harsh conditions such as extreme low temperatures, or subjected to physical abuse such as being kicked, battered, and knocked.

Polystyrene can be used in wall and floor cavities, although its insulation value per inch—or R factor—is considerably less than the Styrofoam. This material comes in many thicknesses, from 1-inch to 4-inch and overall dimensions of 2 feet by 8 feet, and 4 feet by 8 feet. Its availability in many sizes and shapes makes it appealing for special applications. Polystyrene is less than half as expensive as Styrofoam. Like other insulators, beadboard is not an adequate vapor barrier (since water vapor easily permeates it), so a vapor barrier must be installed on the living space side of the structure on which it is used.

Polyurethane Foam

Although urethane foam was once hailed as the solution to the insulation problem, it has since become the black sheep of the insulation family. It does rank among the most efficient insulators per inch, but it has been outlawed by the building codes of many states because it is highly volatile. When ignited, it emits an extremely toxic cyanide gas. It is usually recommended for insulating roofs where there is the least danger of human inhalation of the noxious gas. Urethane foam should be covered with a fire-rated material wherever it is used.

The price of urethane foam is significantly greater than any of the other commonly used insulators. When coupled with its other inherent qualities, this diminishes its appeal.

Polyurethane foam is most commonly used in industrial buildings to insulate refrigeration systems where space is limited and the maximum R is required. Unless you intend to use it for this specific purpose, it is best if you use another insulation material.

Urea Formaldehyde Foam

Urethane foam insulation should not be confused with urea formaldehyde foamed-in-place thermal and acoustical insulation. This material is commonly known by its trade names: Rapco Foam, Insulspray, and Tripolymer Foam System. When burned, urea formaldehyde is no more toxic than wood and will not ignite at temperatures below 1208° F. These qualities, as well as its ability to flow into such odd-shaped spaces as around wires and pipes, make it a valuable insulator for retrofitting. This material has a higher R value than blown wool, fiberglass, cellulose, vermiculite, perlite, and insulated aluminum siding. It is easily installed by trained applicators, who usually blow it in from the outside of a home through 1-inch diameter holes.

Although urea formaldehyde is mold-resistant, a vapor barrier must be used to prevent vapor transmission into wall and roof cavities. This could create a dry rot problem.

Urea formaldehyde cannot be used when exposed to sunlight: like Styrofoam, it then decomposes. The National Bureau of Standards found in 1977 that when this material is subjected to temperatures over 100° F. and to a relative humidity of over 92 percent, decomposition occurs within a few weeks. The result is a fine dust. Therefore, using this material in ceilings and roofs is strongly discouraged. Lengthwise shrinkage of the urea formaldehyde in wall cavities after application is a controversial subject among insulation specialists. Reports of shrinkage vary from 3 percent (as reported by the National Bureau of Standards) to 8 percent (as reported by the National Bureau of Standards) to 10 to 12 percent (as reported by independent researchers). This shrinkage leaves gaps between the wall and the insulation—gaps through which much heat can escape.

Until this controversy is resolved, it is hard to predict the effective R value of urea-foam. It can be said that any amount of shrinkage has the tendency to reduce the efficiency of the insulation. As the material recedes from the studs and from the sheathing, cold air enters, increasing the infiltration rate and reducing the effective R value of the material. Since shrinkage can be controlled to some extent by properly applying the insulation, finding a manufacturer-licensed applicator is critical.

Cellulose Fiber

Cellulose fiber, another blown-in insulation, is actually recycled newspaper treated with boric acid, a fire-retardant chemical. This material is rated class I, II, and III. Class II is the best buy for residential work. If installed at less than proper density, cellulose settles and leaves uninsulated areas. Manufacturers suggest a maximum area that each bag can cover, so be sure to check the manufacturer's recommendation to ensure that you have sufficient coverage. The density can be calculated by dividing the total area filled by the number of bags used.

Small amounts of moisture always pass through the wall membrane with little effect on the performance of the insulating material.

Of all the insulating materials discussed, cellulose is more adversely affected by the extraordinary amounts of water encountered with ice, wind-driven rain, flooding, or extreme household moisture problems such as wet basements. Cellulose, like newspaper, severely settles when wet and—unlike other insulation material—it does not rebound to its original state when dried. When installing cellulose, be sure to install an adequate vapor barrier and provide for adequate ventilation of the exterior wall surface.

Cellulose insulation's flammability is currently under attack by *Consumer Reports Magazine*, the Tennessee Valley Authority, and the federal government's General Services Administration. While there are federal standards governing the flammability of cellulose insulation, these are not mandatory. Congress is now drafting mandatory safety standards for cellulose insulation.

Until adequate safety measures are enforced, cellulose should be your last choice, if other materials are available. If cellulose must be used, find a reputable contractor for installing it.

When the installer arrives, check the bags. Don't use any unless the label specifies that the cellulose meets one of three existing standards: that adopted by the manufacturer's trade group (N-101-73), a separate voluntary specification (ASTM-C-739-77), or the stronger of two GSA specifications (HH-515D).

When installed, be sure the material is 3 inches from recessed electrical fixtures and ventilators.

Older Insulations

Blown fiberglass, vermiculite, and rock wool are somewhat obsolete. These materials are found in many older buildings and reduce the heat flowing from warmer to cooler zones. When adding insulation to increase thermal performance, it is recommended that fiberglass, Styrofoam, or urea formaldehyde be used. The reason is threefold. One, compared to blown fiberglass, vermiculite, and rock wool, these insulators have a higher R value per inch. Usually, their slight additional cost is justified by the simple payback calculation. Second, these older outdated insulators generally experience extraordinary settling and leave uninsulated gaps in the wall or ceiling cavity. Third, they often absorb moisture. This causes rotting in older buildings.

Whenever insulation is installed in a wall cavity between the studs, the effective R value is often less than that stated by the manufacturer. This is true because heat is lost through the framing material usually at a faster rate than through the space filled by the

Table 7-5. Nominal Versus Effective R Values in Framing.

Values based upon theoretical calculations using an air cavity R of .92 and 6 percent area shrinkage. The National Bureau of Standards reports Reff/in=2.6 with 3 percent linear shrinkage and S4S 2×4 at 16" O.C. framing in a single test.

Rnom=Nominal Thermal Resistance to Heat Flow
S4S=Lumber planed on four sides.
O.C.=On-Center Spacing—the distance from the center of one stud to the other.
RGH=Rough Sawn Lumber.

Cavity Insulation	S4S 2×4 at 16" O.C. Rnom	S4S 2×4 at 16" O.C. Reff.	S4S 2×4 at 16" O.C. Reff/in	RGH 2×4 at 24" O.C. Rnom	RGH 2×4 at 24" O.C. Reff	RGH 2×4 at 24" O.C. Reff/in	S4S 2×6 at 24" O.C. Rnom	S4S 2×6 at 24" O.C. Reff	S4S 2×6 at 24" O.C. Reff/in	RGH 2×6 at 24" O.C. Rnom	RGH 2×6 at 24" O.C. Reff	RGH 2×6 at 24" O.C. Reff/in
Fiberglass Batt, R=3.2/in.	11.2	9.2	2.6	12.8	10.5	2.6	17.6	15.0	2.7	19.2	15.8	2.6
Cellulose, No Settling, R=3.3/in.	11.6	9.4	2.7	13.2	10.7	2.7	18.2	15.4	2.8	19.8	16.1	2.7
Cellulose, 6% Settling, R=3.3/in.	11.6	6.3	1.8	13.2	6.9	1.7	18.2	8.4	1.5	19.8	8.6	1.4
Urea Formaldehyde, No Shrink, R=4.8/in.	15.8	12.0	3.4	19.2	13.7	3.4	26.4	20.1	3.7	28.8	20.6	3.4
Urea Formaldehyde, 3% Shrinklin., R=4.8/in.	15.8	7.3	2.1*	19.2	8.0	2.0	26.4	9.5	1.7	28.8	9.7	1.6
Beadboard, R=3.9/in.	13.7	10.5	3.0	15.6	12.0	3.0	21.5	17.6	3.2	23.4	18.0	3.0
Styrofoam, R=5.25/in.	18.4	12.6	3.6	21.0	14.4	3.6	28.9	21.5	3.9	31.5	21.6	3.6
Urethane, R=6.25/in.	21.9	14.0	4.0	25.0	16.0	4.0	34.4	23.7	4.3	37.5	24.0	4.0
Solid Softwood, R=1.25/in.	4.4	4.4	1.25	5.0	5.0	1.25	6.9	6.9	1.25	7.5	7.5	1.75

insulation. The average of the R value for an entire wall or structure includes the insulation value of the wood framing and the nominal R value of the insulation (the insulation manufacturer's R rating of his product). In other words, what you see on the package is not what you get. Table 7-5 presents the nominal R values versus effective R values in framed walls using currently available insulation and conventional framing techniques.

Insulation alone does not solve the energy dilemma in the home. This is one of many tools that can be used to convert energy waste havens into energy-efficient shelters. Weatherproofing techniques such as storm doors, weather stripping, caulking, sealing unused entries for the winter, closing unnecessary rooms, nighttime thermostats, and automatic flue dampers are only a few of the hundreds of energy-saving measures that can be done without the slightest reduction of the present living standard. If anything, you'll end up with a few more dollars at the end of each month.

Chapter 8

Wood

Wood has been a long-used energy resource in rural areas throughout the country. As technology advanced during the past century, wood steadily gave way to gas, coal, and oil. This trend away from the use of wood—a renewable resource—continued until we recently realized that fossil fuels are nonrenewable and thus will become increasingly scarce, more difficult to obtain and more expensive.

We are now rediscovering wood. Many homes and farms are returning to the use of wood as both a primary and secondary energy source.

FOREST MANAGEMENT

Wood is one of the best alternatives to oil heat in the Northeast. An added advantage is that firewood harvest can actually be used to improve forest stands and greatly increase the value of forests to the landowner. Poorer quality trees can be thinned from the stand for firewood, leaving the better quality trees to grow for valuable wood products (Fig. 8-1).

In the broken farmland of the Northeast, most every farm has its woodlot. By not practicing sound forest management, farmsteaders are missing an important potential source of farm income.

Firewood cutting can improve forests stands by thinning, releasing, and properly spacing the best quality trees for other valu-

Fig. 8-1. Poorer quality trees can be thinned from a forest stand for firewood (drawing by Liz Buell).

able uses. This is possible because any species of any size and form can be used for firewood.

Furthermore, no small benefit will be realized in savings and satisfaction by using firewood you have cut and "fitted" from the woodlot. Not only real benefits are resultant, but that special something that defies identification will embrace the firewood user. There is something about the heat from a wood stove that penetrates chilled bones and envelopes the user in a warm, stimulating blanket that could never be duplicated by any central heating system.

Before going further, let's define and explain several terms used in forest management and firewood use in order to avoid any confusion.

Cord. A stack of wood 4 feet by 8 feet by 4 feet. In some areas cord wood is usually cut into 4-foot lengths, and a pile 4 feet high by 8 feet wide equals a cord. In other areas, cord wood is cut in 8-foot lengths, and the pile needs to be only 4 feet high and 4 feet wide. A smaller cord measure used in some areas is a face cord, which is a pile 4 feet high by 8 feet wide. A face cord is always smaller than a regular cord.

Stand. A forest stand is simply any definable area that is relatively uniform and composed of the same mixture of species throughout.

Forest Type. A forest type is a larger area with similar species and soil conditions throughout. You may have several stands on your property of the same forest type.

Site Quality. A term used to delineate the value of a specific area for growing trees. On a good or high site, trees grow more rapidly and are taller at any given age. On a poor or low site, trees grow more slowly and do not get as tall. Usually if an area has tall straight trees that do not taper rapidly from the trunk on up the stem, it is of good site quality. If the trees are relatively short and taper rapidly, it is a poor site. Diameter growth is usually related more to tree spacing and the history of the particular stand than it is to site quality.

Form. The form of a tree relates to its shape. A tree with good form is one that is tall and straight and does not taper rapidly from the bottom to the top. The better the form, the more valuable the tree is for use as saw timber.

Pulpwood. Wood sold to make pulp and paper.

Saw Timber and Saw Logs. Wood sold to make dimension lumber.

Bolt Wood. Wood sold to make dowels, spools, wooden handles, etc.

Veneer Logs. Usually hardwood logs used for making paneling.

Softwood. A term used for all evergreen or coniferous tree species, such as pines, spruces, and firs.

Hardwood. Deciduous species that lose their leaves each year.

FOREST TYPES

Forest types are sometimes confusing, and there are several systems of classification. Basically, however, forest types may be broken down to softwood, mixed wood, and hardwood (Fig. 8-2). In reality, this is too general a classification to be of great help in choosing fuel wood harvest areas. It is important to separate these three basic types into upland areas and wetland areas, because the species composition and management practices vary so much.

Let's talk about upland hardwoods, wetland hardwoods, upland mixed wood, and wetland mixed wood for a start, because these are the areas that may be most suitable for firewood management. The forest types we will describe are representative of northern New England, the northern Great Lakes area, and eastern Canada. All of these types do not occur outside this area, but it should be possible for you to interpolate to your own situation.

Fig. 8-2. Examples of hardwoods and softwoods (drawing by Liz Buell).

Upland hardwoods may consist of the following species: sugar maple, red maple, American beech; white, gray, and yellow birch, all commonly associated with hemlock; and elm, basswood, white pine and some white spruce. The beech, birch, and maples are the most abundant.

Wetland hardwoods will consist in the majority of red maple, black ash, small amounts of white ash, American beech, basswood, and American elm, along with scattered balsam fir and Eastern larch.

Upland mixed wood will include white and red pine, associated with Northern red oak, white spruce, balsam fir, American beech, Eastern hemlock, sugar maple (few) together with a small component of white ash, bigtooth and trembling aspen, white birch, and gray birch.

Wetland mixed wood consists predominantly of red maple, Eastern larch, balsam fir and hornbeam (few), along with a minority of gray birch and an occasional white pine. Generally, these woods are in grassy, wet areas varying in size from small pockets to large swamps.

The softwood types, both upland and wetland, are often not suited for management for firewood. They usually contain only a small component of hardwood species, but where there are hardwoods, these types can be improved by cutting firewood.

The first step in managing your forest for firewood is to identify these types and determine approximately how much of each type you have. Then you should determine the best stands in which to concentrate your firewood harvesting efforts.

There are a number of criteria you should consider when selecting your best stands. Access, site quality, equipment available for use, species present, age, size, and density of trees are among these criteria.

How much land will you need to produce your firewood? That's also an important early question in your forest management planning.

GROWTH RATE AND ACCESS

The growth rate is the most important factor in determining how much land you'll need for a perpetual harvest. In northern New England the accepted growth rate is about ½ cord per acre per year. This is for unmanaged stands, however, and with management, the growth rate can be increased substantially. Using the conservative figure, however, 10 acres would produce 5 cords of wood per year. If you are considering using thinnings, cull trees, and inferior species for firewood, while leaving the better quality trees of better species to grow for other wood products, it might take 20 acres to produce the 5 cords/year over the long run. At this moment in time, however, most forest lands in the Northeast in small private ownership are dense and in need of improvement cuttings. You could certainly consider taking ½ cord per acre per year for some time, while still leaving the better trees to grow for future crops.

Access is another important consideration. Many farmsteads will have old skid or logging roads that were used in the past. These roads can be difficult to locate, as they may be grown over with new forest cover. Look for old wheel ruts, and start with openings that may appear more readily at field edges. These roads usually will require very little work to make them passable other than cutting small trees and down timber and will also serve the areas of best timber growth. If no old roads can be located, you must choose a location to establish new roads.

Establishment of a road system will result in more than the benefit of access of fuel wood. These roads may be used for fire control, insect and disease control, and will most certainly result in access for other benefits such as hunting and scenic trails for the owner. Establishment of a new road system is time-consuming and will require much work. In most cases, wood removed during road building will be utilized for firewood or pulpwood. In choosing a road site, be aware of slopes, final distance from point of firewood use, and impassable areas such as streams and bogs. Stay away from steep slopes, try and follow the contour of the land, and walk the entire proposed road before cutting any trees.

Your decision to build or utilize a wood road will also depend on the type of equipment you have available for use. Most farmsteads have some type of farm tractor or wheeled vehicle for use around the farm. These vehicles will serve during winter to skid the harvested wood to where it may be utilized. Some owners skid small trees with a snowsled, so if one should be available, make use of it.

Upland hardwoods will yield an abundance of firewood. An average cord of dried hardwood will produce the equivalent heat of 193 gallons of home heating oil. All species of wood produce almost an equal amount of heat per pound of wood, but the density of wood varies greatly. The species that produce the most heat per cord are hardwoods (Table 8-1).

CRITERIA FOR SELECTING TREES TO CUT

The species to be found in northern New England in upland hardwoods that will serve as good firewood are: sugar maple, red

Table 8-1. Heating Values of Different Woods.

Species	Heating Value (Millions of Btus Per Cord, Air Dried)
Hickory	25.4
White oak	23.9
Beech	21.8
Sugar maple	21.8
Red oak	21.7
Yellow birch	21.3
White ash	20.0
Red maple	19.1
Tamarack	19.1
Black cherry	18.5
White birch	18.2
Red pine	17.8
Elm	17.7
Gray birch	17.5
Hemlock	15.0
Spruce	15.0
Aspen	14.1
Balsam fir	13.5
White pine	13.3
Basswood	12.6

Fig. 8-3. The tree at the left has good form in terms of timber value. The tree at the right has bad form in terms of timber value (drawing by Liz Buell).

maple, American beech, the birches, and a few elms. Criteria for selection to cut must be established because many of these species have higher value if utilized for other products. Initially, every tree considered for cutting should be examined on the following basis: form, size, health, and vigor.

Many species that may be utilized for higher value products, such as boltwood, sawlogs, and veneer logs, may be separated on the basis of form (Fig. 8-3). If a tree has small-diameter branches, a good straight bole or stem, and a small number of branches on the lower bole area, probably this tree should be left as a high value tree and not removed for firewood. If, on the other hand, a crooked stem, many large branches, and generally poor form are apparent, the tree may be put to better use as firewood.

The size of the tree, or diameter of the bole at about 4 feet above ground, should also be considered. Timber stand improvement, which basically means an improvement in light, moisture, nutrients, room to grow, etc., as applied to the trees you will not cut, should be a consideration. The younger stems will respond to improvement work much better than the older veterans.

The best size of tree to leave in an improvement program would be demonstrated by leaving a good species of tree of about 3 to 8 or 9 inches in diameter at breast height. The larger veterans, from about 10 inches and up, may be removed to ensure more light, moisture, and room to grow for some of the smaller crop trees you plan to leave. Some smaller trees of good species may be taken due to poor form, or disease, as ascertained by your first selection.

The first selection should also include an inspection for health and vigor. Many times what appears to be a good tree to leave will have some defect that will affect your selection. For example, trees with dead branches extending upward and that are located in the main lower bole will have a certain amount of decay inside. Also, some decay fungi will leave an apparent blemish on the stem. Damage from nature or by man's activities, which is located on the main stem, will also reduce the value of the tree. These trees should be selected for firewood if they suit your criteria for size in felling, bucking, and splitting. Vigor, or apparent aggressive competition with adjacent trees, is also an important consideration. A tree of good form, with a large crown or leaf area in relation to its size, with good uniform green color, and which shows dominance over its neighbor to some extent, is growing valuable wood for you and, if of the proper species, should be left to compound its value over future years. Each of the foregoing criteria should be considered for each different area and for each different tree you plan to examine for firewood.

Site quality is measured by the height of the dominant trees in relation to their age. Site quality can be estimated by visual examination of the existing dominant trees. If the dominant trees in a stand have exceptional height growth in relation to other trees of the same species you have noticed in other areas, the site quality is probably pretty good. A little practice in observation will aid the farmsteader in site determination. Site quality is an important criteria in choosing an area to harvest for firewood because if you desire the added benefit of timber and stand improvement, it is best to begin on the better sites.

It would be impossible to tell you exactly which trees to save during timber stand improvement, because it would depend on your specific stand, local conditions, and local markets. A few examples, however, might illustrate how to select the valuable trees that should not be cut for firewood.

Local markets are important. The farmsteader interested in obtaining maximum value from his woods must investigate local markets and determine which forest products are most valuable. Select grade hardwoods; straight and with very few knots are often very valuable. If there is a veneer mill close, good quality sugar maple, yellow birch, large white birch, and elm can be worth $200 or more per thousand board feet in the woods. Ash and oak are also valuable wood if the trees are straight, tall, and with few lower limbs. White birch bolt wood is much more valuable than firewood if there is a mill near that makes dowels and spools. Clear white pine sawlogs are becoming more valuable all the time, and good spruce logs are used mainly for construction timbers. Hardwood species that should be selected as firewood because they have little other value are red maple, beech, and gray birch. Other hardwoods should be selected on the basis of form.

Wetland hardwoods will serve for fuel wood harvest during winter months when the ground is frozen. Red maple, ash, beech, elm, and basswood can be selected for firewood in this type. All the above-mentioned criteria for selection should be applied to each of the areas in which you intend to work. Upland mixed wood produces oak, beech, maple, birch, and some ash. These are the species to prefer for firewood. Wetland mixed wood areas may be harvested for red maple, birch, and black ash. The majority of the hardwood species mentioned for each area will serve adequately for firewood because of the heat output and, if selected by the correct criteria, will result in improved woodland areas for future harvest of higher value products much earlier than if left alone.

There are often some hardwoods in the softwood forest types, and softwood types can be improved by firewood cutting, but the amount of good firewood per acre is limited. It would be time-consuming to harvest it. The softwoods species can also be used for firewood, but conifer thinnings are probably more valuable as pulpwood if there is a good pulpwood market in the area. Tamarack has the same heating value as red maple and is the only softwood species that makes good firewood. At any rate, softwood types would have to be considered low priority areas for improvement with firewood cutting. If that's all you have to choose from, however, by all means use it.

DRYING WOOD

With the preceding information in mind, the worst thing you can do is grab your saw and head out to cut some trees. Before any cutting, examine the areas on the ground and select the trees to remove beforehand and mark them. Nothing is more confusing than to try and select trees to cut during the process of harvest. Once the trees are marked and cut, and after they are transported to the area that you will "fit" and use them, the trees should be split to suit your stove and stacked for drying where the wind and sun can do their work.

Wood dries almost 100 percent from the cut ends rather than the side or bark area. Pile your wood so that the ends will be open to the wind and sun. Fuel wood should be dried for at least one year before burning. The amount of heat you receive from wood is greatly increased if the wood is dry. Also, much less creosote is produced by dry wood.

Time can be saved in drying wood by a process called *wilting*. This is done by cutting the trees in June or early July after leaf growth has matured. The tree is left intact, and the leaves draw moisture from the stem. The trees are then cut up, split in the fall, and stored for use. Not as much moisture will be removed as in cutting, splitting, and drying, but a sufficient amount will be removed to ensure good burning. This practice should be a second choice to proper drying methods. One problem with wilting is that you must determine how many cords you have cut while the wood is still in tree length. A rule of thumb would be that for 8-inch diameter trees, about 12 trees will be required to make a cord. See Table 8-2.

FELLING A TREE

Woodcutting is a dangerous activity and probably the most dangerous part is the actual felling of a tree (Fig. 8-4). With the increase in use of wood as fuel, there has been an increase in the number of inexperienced people cutting wood. It is often said that experience is the best teacher, but in the case of dangerous activities like woodcutting, a certain level of knowledge of safe practices should be attained before you attempt to get experience. Safe woodcutting is a must in order to fully enjoy the benefits of self-cut wood heat.

Before you begin to fell a tree, in fact before you even start to work, make sure your saw is fully gassed and oiled, the breather and oiler unobstructed, and the chain sharp and properly tightened. Proper tension may vary with the type of saw. With some saws the

Table 8-2. Available Heat from a Pound of Wood.

Percent Moisture	Available Heat Btus
0 overdried	7100
10	6300
20 air-dried	5400
30	4500
40	3600
50	2900
60	2100

Fig. 8-4. Exercise caution when felling a tree (photo by Faith Rainbolt).

tension is adjusted so that at rest, the chain does not hang. If pulled, it will yield about ¼ inch. Always carry your "duty tool" in your back pocket when cutting, as a chain will loosen after use and need readjustment. Running out of gas halfway through a tree necessitates a long walk back to the gas can or tools while leaving the tree hanging. A dull saw, madly overrevving and spitting sawdust rather than chips, is dangerous. A chain not getting oil will tighten and stall the engine eventually, but it may damage itself and the bar in the meantime.

The next step is to choose a tree and determine which way it will fall. By and large, without heavy equipment, a tree will fall according to its own inclination. Though the trunk may lean one way, the greater weight is given to the upper limbs and leaves, especially in the spring and summer. This weight is in a position of advantageous leverage. The wind can play havoc with you, tossing the treetop to and fro, and always changing the tree's inclination.

The wind's direction and velocity are the most variable factors in woodcutting. It is the fickle wind that causes most of the accidents among experienced loggers. Do not cut if the winds are high and gusty. A tree may lean obviously to the right but rock back to the left as a gust passes, inviting disaster. Also present on windy days, lurking unseen above, are the *widow-makers* dead limbs and treetops waiting only to be dislodged and come crashing down.

Once you've determined which way the tree wants to fall, cut away vines, brush, and lower branches to give yourself plenty of room to move while cutting. Pay special attention to the route you may want to bail out on should you have to get away fast. Now you are ready to make the face-cut (Fig. 8-5). The face-cut will influence the direction of the tree's fall, taking advantage of whatever factors may be present. Should you wish to swing the tree slightly to either side of its line of inclination, cut the face a little further (Fig. 8-6) around the tree in the direction you wish it to fall. There is danger in trying to borrow too much, because you may lose the center of gravity and wind up with your saw jammed as the tree rocks back away from the face. The reason for the face is to remove a surface for the tree to jam on or pry against as it begins to fall. The danger of eliminating or undercutting the face, even on trees which may be growing almost horizontally, is the prospect of splitting.

Some trees are notorious splitters. A tree may split because it is hollow inside or from grains, internal twists, and stresses that may not be apparent unless the wind shifts or the face is cut improperly. Stand to the side as you cut the face—usually on the side to which you expect the tree to come as it falls. This protects you from splits. Cut as low as possible on the trunk as this will give you more wood and is standard good logging practice. The lower the stump, the less danger it presents as obstruction. Also, by bending to make the cut, you give yourself a split second to straighten up and avoid a murderous split. It takes longer to fall backwards than to straighten up. On high risk splitters, you may make a *small* notch first, on the back side of the tree, slightly above the expected back-cut level (Fig. 8-7), to give the trunk a chance to snap off rather than split.

Always be sure you've cut yourself room to move all around the tree, so you can move in any direction in a hurry. Make the horizontal cut first on the face, anywhere from one-third to even two-thirds through, depending on the acuity of the tree's inclination. The

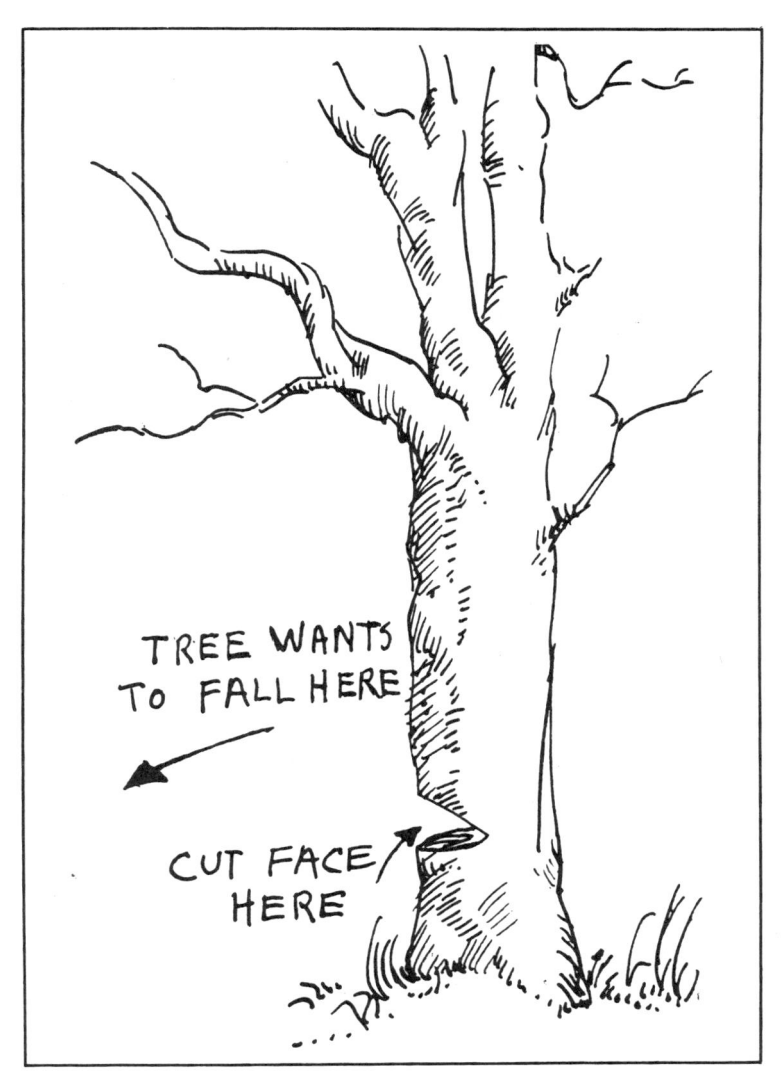

Fig. 8-5. Making the face-cut (drawing by Faith Rainbolt).

greater the inclination, the less need for a deep face. The danger of undercutting is splitting on the back-cut; the danger of overcutting is the tree falling, in any direction, before you can even make the back-cut. With the horizontal cut made, take out the notch, generally from the top down, endeavoring to make the cuts meet neatly (Fig. 8-7). In some situations, upcutting the notch may be in order, but it's easier to work with gravity whenever you can.

The back-cut comes next, and in making it you may influence the tree's line of fall by *hinging*. This hinge is the last piece of wood still holding the tree as it begins to fall. It will continue to pull the tree towards the hinge until the last bond breaks.

Generally, you would position yourself on the side of the hinge to protect you from splits. Begin the back-cut on the far side and pull

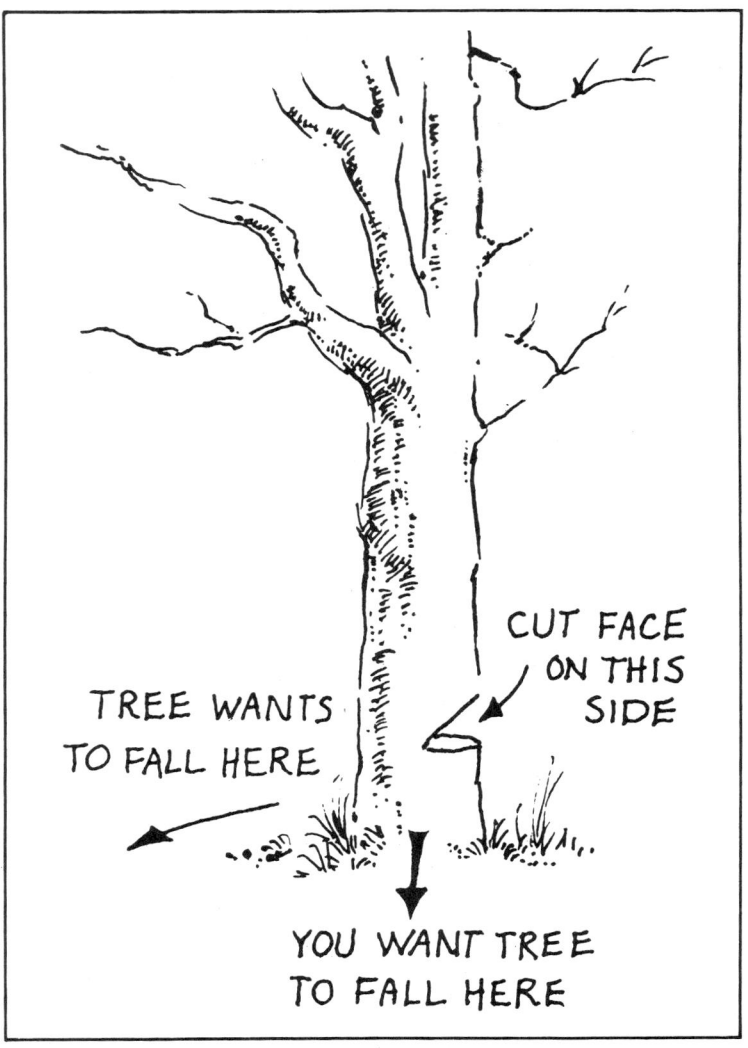

Fig. 8-6. You can cut the face a little further around the tree in the direction you want the tree to fall if you want to swing the tree slightly to either side of its line of inclination (drawing by Faith Rainbolt).

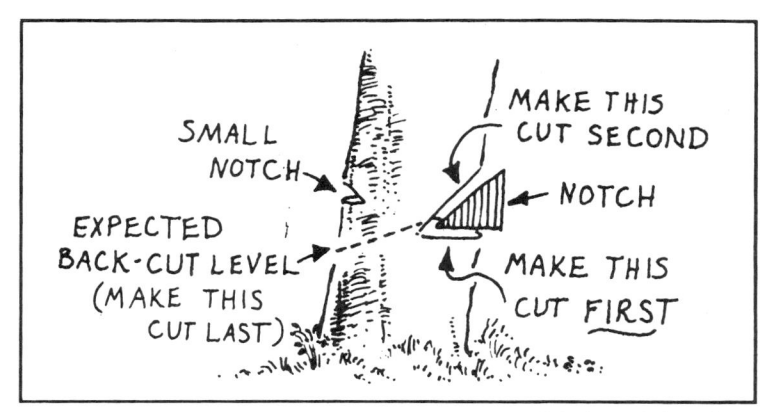

Fig. 8-7. You can make a small notch on the back side of the tree slightly above the expected back-cut level (drawing by Faith Rainbolt).

the saw across the back towards you (Fig. 8-8) until the tree begins to fall, and the hinge twists the tree on the stump and pulls it in your direction. Step around the rear of the tree so that it falls away from you, but don't commit yourself until you know for sure the direction it is going. Should a tree ever begin to fall towards you, never succumb to the irrational urge to outrun it. Panic seems to make this a natural human reaction, but with foreknowledge, you need only step around the tree behind the line of fall.

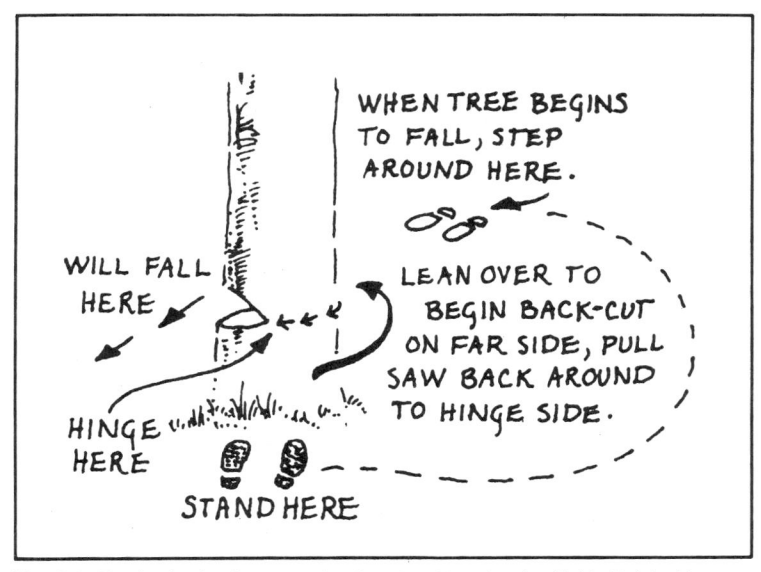

Fig. 8-8. Begin the back-cut on the far side (drawing by Faith Rainbolt).

Sometimes, just as it seems the tree must topple, the wind or a miscalculation may rock the tree back on the stump, pinning your saw and/or jamming tight against the narrow back-cut. If you cannot snatch the saw out of the bind, don't linger. Shut the saw off, step back and with one eye on the treetop to determine where it might go, and the other out for stumbling blocks and brush, carefully choose the safest line and back off. Once safely away, you may analyze the situation and choose one of several courses.

The safest course is to let the wind blow the tree over. The problem here is the wind's unpredictability. You cannot go off and leave a potentially murderous situation poised indefinitely. The tree can come down in seconds or months later. You are responsible for the tree; it must fall before your responsibility ends.

The best choice of tools in this situation is a wedge. For all its simplicity, pound-for-pound it's the most powerful tool you may own. If your saw is not pinched in the back-cut, the wedge is inserted and driven in with a small sledge or mall. Many trees are likely to pinch back and spit the wedge out by rocking back in reaction to the first one or two blows. Once the wedge has been tapped in place, hit it a good lick. As the tree rocks forward, quickly set the wedge by hitting it again, before the tree rocks back. Whenever driving wedges, be aware that sharp metal chips may fly into your or an observer's eye and cause severe injury. Wedges should be kept trimmed of burrs and splintered edges, and safety goggles are the best insurance against eye injury when using any tools. It is best to carry two wedges, as most jobs will require more than one.

If the fully-driven wedges do not influence the tree enough to tip it back along its intended line, or if your saw is still stuck in the way, and if you have another saw, make a new cut below the first attempt, reversing the face and back-cut (see Fig. 8-9). Be sure you have room to move because this tree could go anywhere at this point.

If the wedges haven't worked, or the tree is looking down on your barn or the neighbor's fence, and you can't drop it back where it wants to go, a long, stout rope or cable and block are in order. Try to anticipate problems such as nearby buildings, etc., beforehand and attach your block and line before beginning to cut. Hooking onto a delicately balanced, wind-sensitive toppler is an adventure of rushing peril. The block should be chained to a solid base; the line is run through it and set around the trunk or a limb as high as possible to gain maximum leverage. How to set the line is up to you, but it is

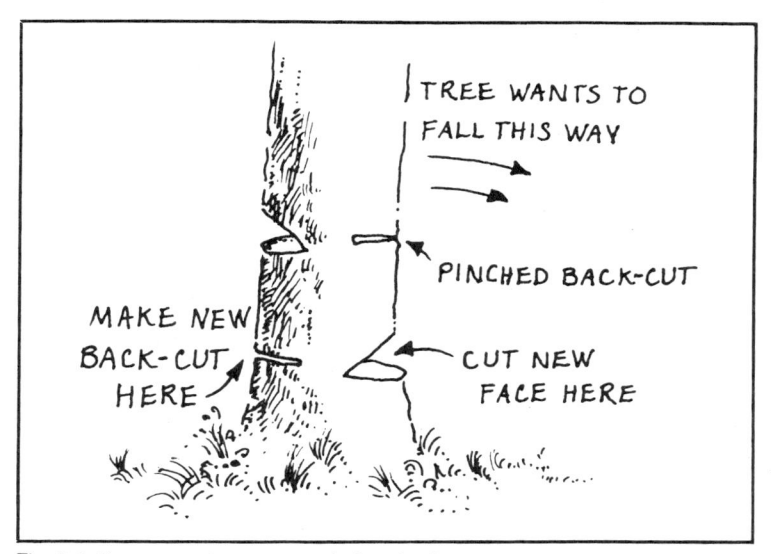

Fig. 8-9. You can make a new cut below the first attempt, reversing the face and back-cut (drawing by Faith Rainbolt).

foolhardy to climb the tree. If there is absolutely no other way, add your weight to the situation on the side of greatest balance. Before you even consider climbing, tie a light rope to the heavier rope or cable, weight it with a rock, toss the rock over a limb, and haul the cable up and around the tree. Listen for cracking and groaning and watch the treetop. Have partners well clear and watching for you. Once the line is set, if sufficient pull-power can be applied by truck, tractor, partners, or neighbors, the tree will fall towards the block. If you do not have a block, the line can be run around a nearby tree or stump and pulled to, but this is less efficient than a block. In the absence of a suitable tree or stump, you may pull directly towards the power source. Be sure your line is long enough to take you beyond the falling tree.

A tree may begin to fall only to get caught in adjacent trees. This may happen often until you learn to fall the trees in a stand with a mind always to open a path for the next tree to fall. Don't jump into the biggest tree or the one nearest the truck. Walk around a bit before beginning to cut. Usually one tree will be so inclined as to fall into an opening. This may open a whole logical order and hangers may be avoided. It usually pays to treat the whole operation as a series of smaller operations.

Sometimes a tree is going to hang up. When that happens, you have a dangerous situation. First, watch out for the tree's butt. It may still be in contact with the stump, and at any time it may slip off and jump back, battering ram style. Don't be behind the stump. As the tree begins to fall and the problem is developing, back off and keep eyes up for dislodged widow-makers. If possible, pull the tree free with cable and truck. Be alert. It may take many minutes for stress to wear down a supporting limb, but with a loud snap the tree may roll free and fall to either side. Usually you can perceive the direction of the stress and with cautious circling, approach the hanger from behind and hook a cable to its butt.

If you cannot pull the tree free, you may be able to free the bind by upcutting with your saw. Your upcut will be made from the stressed side, but do not stand on the side your saw will cut from (Fig. 8-10). It may take several cuts to finally loosen the entangled top and each cut is perilous. Again, always make yourself plenty of room to move. Be prepared to simply release the saw if it should be wrenched. Any time a tree wants to take your saw, let the saw go. Do not resist the irrestible force, and it is likely the tough bar and chain will be undamaged. Even if the saw is totaled, it can be replaced. Do not wrestle with a tree; step back and keep yourself intact.

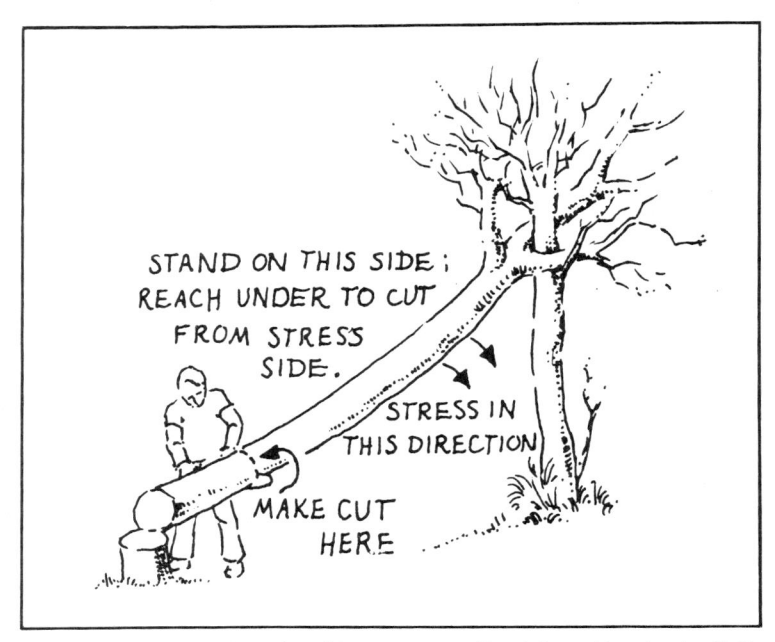

Fig. 8-10. Don't stand on the side your saw will cut from (drawing by Faith Rainbolt).

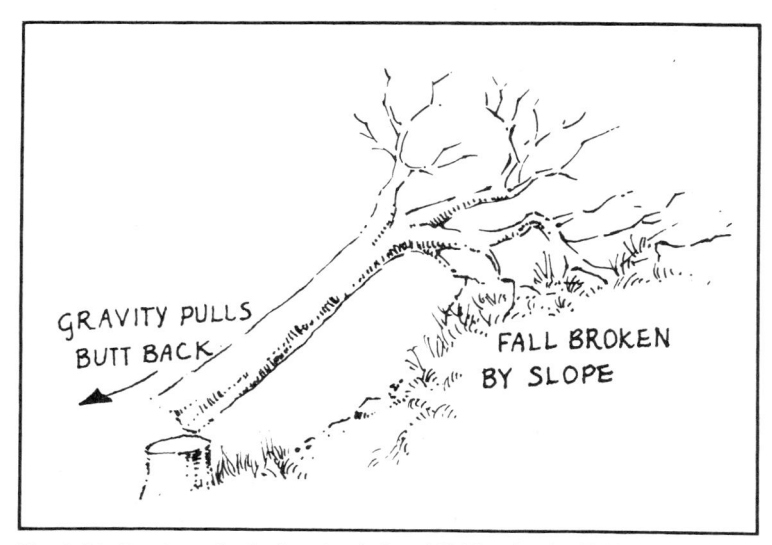

Fig. 8-11. Gravity pulls the butt back downhill (drawing by Faith Rainbolt).

It is safer to have company in the woods, but whenever cutting with others, only one saw should be running in the same area. Everyone should focus his attention on the same tree. The cutter should never begin until he *knows* everyone is well out of the way.

Resist the temptation to "jackpot" by falling the tree in which the first in hung. You'll wind up with two leaners, domino fashion, and this can go on indefinitely.

If you've got the tree on the way down, here are a few more things to consider. A tree falling uphill may kickback off the stump just as if it had caught in nearby trees. The limbs break the fall and gravity pulls the butt back downhill (Fig. 8-11). A tree falling downhill will jump out and down the hill, sometimes for many feet. The larger the tree and the greater the slope, the broader the jump. Consider the effect in determining cutting order, positioning self and equipment, and avoiding obstructions. Speaking of obstructions, a tree may fall across something—a fallen tree, stump, or land configuration—and the resultant lever action will flip the butt about (Fig. 8-12).

Even when the tree is down, you may not be through. The tree may have fallen over tough, pliant brush or smaller trees. Sometimes these will be unbroken and pinned, and when cut as you clear brush, will spring up like some jungle trap. Stand aside; be alert. As you limb, be aware the trunk may shift and roll as supporting limbs are cut out. Also, cut limbs from the stress sides, as when upcutting,

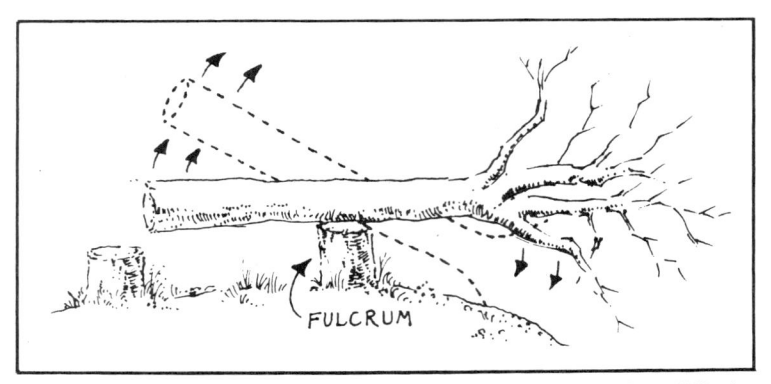

Fig. 8-12. A tree may fall across a stump, and the resultant lever action will flip the butt about (drawing by Faith Rainbolt).

to avoid binds and the jungle trap effect. If you follow these precautions, you should come out with a good pile of firewood, cozy winter fires, and all of your own limbs to enjoy the heat.

SPLITTING WOOD

If you cut your own wood, cut close to large knots so they will be in the short chunks only for easier splitting. Choose wood that can be split. Straight-grained, well-seasoned softwoods split most easily but burn rapidly. Among hardwoods, ash is one of the easiest to split. Oak splits fairly well if the grain is straight; so does maple. Fruitwoods, such as apple, make excellent firewood, but they are generally crooked-grained. Since they are usually small in diameter, little splitting is necessary. Birch and ironwood, though tough to split, are often too small to need it. The larger pieces can be saved to keep the fire through the night. Elm is a fooler. The straight, knotfree trunk appears to be a lot of clear wood for the fire. The grain is usually so crooked that many folks despair of ever splitting the stuff. Use only elm that is small enough to burn unsplit, or plan on using wedges and a sledge hammer—a tedious chore.

Get yourself a chopping block. Soft earth under the chunk to be split absorbs the shock of the ax blow and makes the work hard indeed. Concrete floors destroy axes. A large tree trunk cut so that the combined height of the block and the wood chunk to be split is about level with the lowest swing of your hands as you swing your ax to split is best.

Use a good, single-bitted ax (Fig. 8-13). A double-bitted ax has a straight handle and cannot be controlled properly for effective splitting. A few nicks in the blade won't matter, as long as the ax is reasonably sharp. An ax worn so that only a stub of the head is left will only sink dully into the wood and reduce even an experienced splitter to an amateur.

The diameter of the chunk of wood is unimportant. If it has been sawn to stovewood length (16-20 inches), and there are only a few small knots, an ax will split it easily if properly used. At this point comes the temptation to tackle the really large ones with wedges and a sledge hammer. Don't. Reserve the wedges for rails and furnace-length wood or for extracting a stuck ax while you're perfecting your technique.

If the chunk of wood is large enough to need to be split in more than two pieces, start at the outer edge and work toward the center, turning the chunk after each piece is split off (Fig. 8-14). This way you'll only be splitting an ax-size bite at a time.

Swing the ax until it's nearly to the wood chunk, then relax your swing (but not your grip on the ax handle), and let the momentum

Fig. 8-13. Use a single-bitted ax.

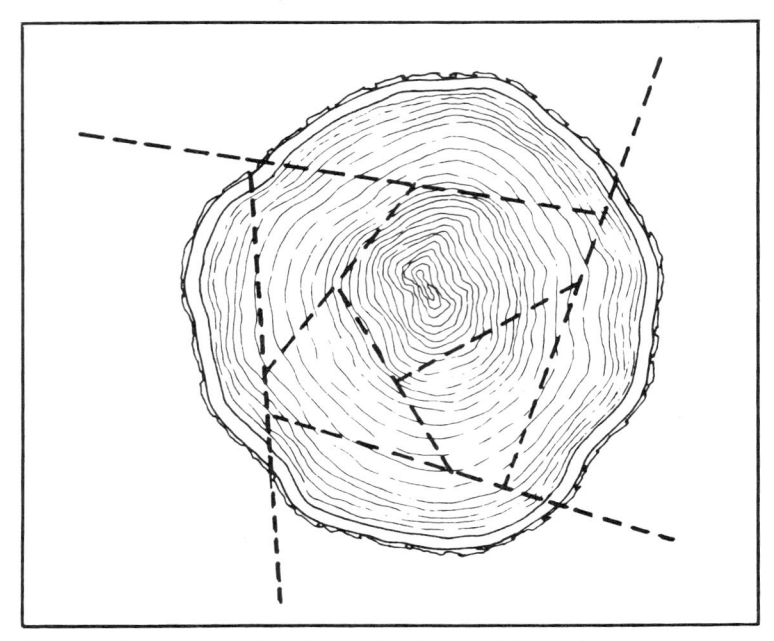

Fig. 8-14. Start at the outer edge and work toward the center.

carry the ax head for the last several inches. At the point your blade strikes the wood, both hands should be together at the end of the handle and cross-handled from your usual chopping position. As the ax enters the wood, twist the head sharply over—done properly, the wood will split, and the piece split off the larger chunk will topple over or flip away in a spiral (Fig. 8-15). Twist too soon, and the ax head lands sideways with a "clop," perhaps breaking the handle. If late, you've probably stuck the ax into the chunk.

Work on your splitting technique as diligently as you would a golf stroke. A few weeks of practice will pay off in many years of pleasurable, frustration-free wood splitting. Then you can boast that you get heat from your wood before it burns.

RECYCLING LUMBER

Everything today costs more than it used to, and the price of building materials is no exception. Fortunately the homesteader is not locked in to high prices. He needn't insist on new materials—only good ones. He is often surrounded by very good or even superior building materials at a fraction of their cost when new.

Thousands of buildings are standing idle or falling down (Fig. 8-16). Many of them are available for little or no cash. In some cases

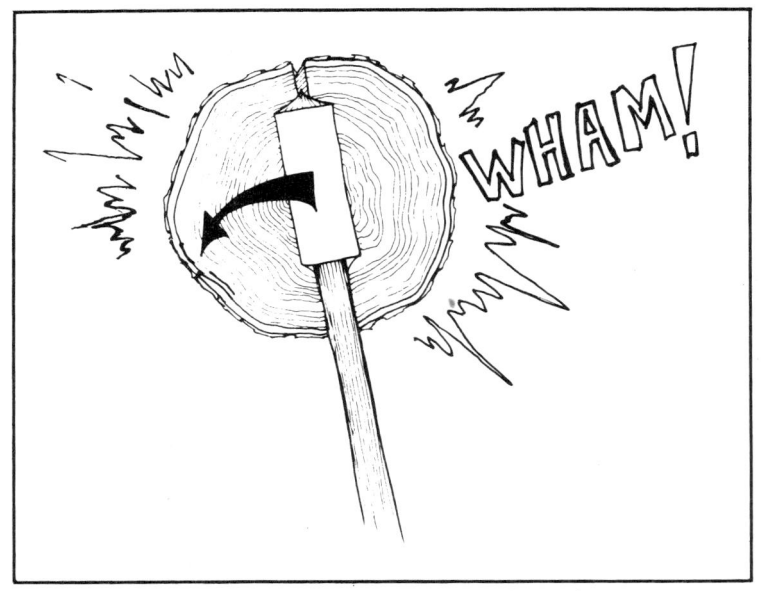

Fig. 8-15. As the ax enters the wood, twist the head sharply over.

they can even turn a cash profit for the enterprising farmsteader. Tapping this wealth of good lumber is a three-part affair: finding, wrecking, and reclamation.

Finding this supply is your first problem. Start looking and asking. Some people won't sell you a leaky doghouse that hasn't been used or maintained in 50 years. They prefer to let it go to pieces on its own. Others will let you take apart $3,000 worth of dry, sound lumber just to get rid of an eyesore. Your biggest problem will be to select just the right building for your needs.

While houses contain some of the most obviously reusable material in the form of studs, joists, sheathing, flooring, and often plumbing and electrical fixtures, these things are not accessible without digging. Plaster, you see is the problem. It is dry, dusty, lung-clogging, heavy and, when mixed with the lath that held it to the studs, often nearly impossible to shovel out. It requires a lot of handling unless you have a dump truck. It may cover every wall and every ceiling in a house from ½ to 1-inch thick. It cannot be reused or recycled.

Small barns, poultry houses, garages, and sheds will usually provide the most good lumber with the least mess and effort. These buildings don't have plaster. They aren't likely to be strung together with too many electrical wires, and what they do contain (2×4s,

Fig. 8-16. Old buildings are a source of good lumber.

2×6s, 1×8s, 1×10s, 1×12s, and wider) will be most useful to you. They will be most easily converted into your own sizes and for your own best use.

Many poultry buildings were built within the last 20 to 50 years, folllowing specifications which the poultry industry and the state agricultural offices considered to be most suitable for their intended use—housing laying hens on the floor in deep litter with natural daylight supplemented by electric lights. They are now obsolete, many of them are rotting, and because they are not likely to be used again, should be available for salvage in some quantity. They are also big. Don't tackle one unless you have time, a fairly large work crew, and a good amount of knowledge and experience. They should net you a large amount of 6-inch-by-6-inch timbers, dimension lumber of all widths, and thousands of board feet of sheathing, as well as odds and ends of window sash, screen, welded wire mesh, and insulation, depending upon how long the building has been empty, how well it has been protected from the elements, and how well it was cleaned out. The building may present a few problems, such as matched lumber on the interior walls—difficult to remove, and time-consuming; a much-repaired roof of tar, nails, and asphalt roofing paper—if it has a metal roof in good condition you're lucky indeed; a feed bin, bolted, nailed, screwed, and tongue-and-grooved together—hard to take apart, and likely to be rotten.

If you're looking for something smaller, try outbuildings or attached sheds. These are often newer than a main barn and are frequently of less use to the owner. If they are built on mud sills or timbers laid directly on the ground, be prepared to lose a few inches or feet of each stud to rot. Sheds are low, small, and relatively safe for the more inexperienced.

Unless you really know what you are doing, stay away from big old barns of two, three, or more stories. Their timbers are heavy, the roof is high and slippery, and the wrong move could kill you.

There are too many shapes, sizes, and styles of buildings to list here. In deciding what to look for, take into consideration your needs in terms of dimensions, types, and quality of lumber, your own ambition and skills, and what is available within a reasonable distance. If you can get someone to pay you to tear down a building, do so. In that case, you can obviously afford to take on a job that requires more cleanup or offers less salvage. If, on the other hand, it is you who must pay for hauling away the junk, make sure before you start that you can really use what you're getting.

If the wood is rotten, burn or bury it. If it's green slimy, but still seems strong, it might dry out well enough to be used for interior paneling, as in a barn or chicken house, but should not be used in any load-bearing capacity, such as roofing or exterior siding. If it's to be used as a sill, joist, stud, rafter, or foundation post, it should be dry, sound, and straight. If you've chosen your lumber well and salvaged it carefully, you can affort not to use the questionable pieces and still save money. If the board or timber in question has been kept dry over the years, has not been subjected to abnormal loads, and was of good quality to start with, it is almost certainly able to do any reasonable job that can be expected of its size and kind. We would rather use an older piece of wood in many instances than one bought in the lumberyard. The former, even though it was only used as barn sheathing, was likely to be wide, straight, a full inch thick, and of No. 3 or even No. 2 grade. The latter, by contrast, may be crooked, knotty, full of pitch pockets, and still dripping sap. Wood today is not cut from the same stock as it was a century ago. It is often rushed to market while still relatively green, and while you can buy D-select lumber for framing and sheathing, you are more likely to buy No. 4.

Wrecking is dangerous business—far more so than construction, for obvious reasons. Poor carpenters can often build a perfectly adequate building which, if not entirely square or plumb or attractive, can at least bear its own weight for several years. The reason for this is that in construction every nail driven and every piece of wood attached will begin to pick up a part of the load. With each passing minute and each stroke of the hammer, the floor or wall or roof or whatever you are working on becomes stronger and less likely to dump you to the ground. With demolition, exactly the opposite is true. Each nail removed and each timber cut or dislocated weakens the overall remaining structure, and at some point (perhaps with the removal of the very nail you're working on at the moment) the accumulated load will be too much for some rusty nail or punky board to hold. You are therefore advised not to be standing on, under, or even particularly near anything which might collapse. You're even better off if you know enough to either control the rate and nature of that collapse (much as in felling a tree), or to prevent it altogether, and to pick out your boards one at a time.

You should wear work shoes, preferably high-top, (steel toes are nice too), long pants (and long johns in winter), a close fitting shirt with tails tucked in, gloves, hard hat, and a hammer holster. Tools required include chain(s), several wrecking bars from 16 inches to 3 inches, crowbar, 16-foot ladder, stepladder, 16 or 20 ounce hammer, 2-foot level, 3-pound hammer, wood chisels, lots of good rope, hatchet, nail claw and a handsaw.

Start from the top and work down. Take off wood and asphalt shingles with your short wrecking bars. Pull the nails in metal roofing and remove it a piece at a time; it can be salvaged, but wood and asphalt can't. Junk the latter and use good, dry wood shingles for wedges or kindling. Remove roof boards, then rafter ties, collar beams, and rafters. Work the walls of each floor down to floor level before dropping to another floor (unless it is balloon construction, in which case the studs may run from the foundation to the second floor top plate uninterrupted). If a window was installed properly, it will come out as a unit by removing the interior trim and those nails in the exterior trim that hold it to the building. Sheathing can be removed fastest by beating on it from the inside with the sledge, working along the length of each board, banging next to the studs. Or you can pull the nails from the outside and the board should drop off. Make sure you are in no way connected to any source of power. Chop old wiring loose with your hatchet.

When removing matched boards, start at the side of the floor or wall that has the tongue exposed, and remove that board. Remove each succeeding board by pulling the nails in its tongue and lifting it out, or you can drive the nails on through with a punch.

Face the fact that you can't save everything. If a board is pinned in, don't spend an hour working it loose. Cut it and keep the job going. Reclaiming lumber only pays in inverse proportion to the amount of time it takes you to secure it. It is wise it inspect each board or timber before you move it. Check to see what it will take to free it, how that will affect the remaining structure, where that board will drop (and who is in the way), and if removing it will make it easier or more difficult to proceed with the rest of the operation. When cutting a board or timber, stop frequently to see if the cut wants to open or close, thus giving you an idea of whether the piece is under tension or compression. If a wall is too shaky to work on, it may be advisable to loosen the bottom plate and pull it over with a rope. Watch out that it doesn't land on someone or get hung up halfway so you don't dare go near it.

Now that it's all on the ground, in an unsightly heap, how do you reclaim it? First, decide what its most likely use will be. If you want timbers for a barn, save nothing but the best. If you only want some 6×6s to make raised beds in your garden, you can use some half rotten things. If you think hard enough, you might be able to use almost all of it or at least burn it for kindling. If you are short on storage space, keep only what you know you can use so you won't be stumbling over an 18-inch piece of odd molding for the next five years.

Most lumber can be reused in some way. Bricks and cement blocks can be if you chip away the old mortar. Metal roofing is usually good for another go-round, even if only for a wood pile cover. Metal pipe is probably too full of scale and rust to be reused in its former capacity, but it can be used to tether animals or mark property lines. Windows can often be reused directly if you can frame the right sized hole. Even large pieces of broken glass can be recut into smaller usable pieces. Hardware, such as hinges, window locks, and door pulls, can be salvaged if they aren't rusted shut or twisted out of alignment. Large bolts can be cleaned up, but wood screws will probably have their slots bunged up during removal.

The following most likely can *not* be of any use to you or would require so much time to reuse that it would be cheaper to buy them new: shingles, asphalt siding and roofing, Sheetrock, electrical wiring, sheet metal flashing, and nails.

Some of your best pieces will be suitable only for a particular job: a nice varnished stair bannister, a 12×12 timber as good as new, some stanchions from an old barn, a heap of chain, long forgotten in a cellar, or a colored glass window.

Cleaning up your booty should be a systematic job. Strip the nails from a few 2×4s each day and pretty soon you'll have a nice pile of good studs. Set up a pair of sawhorses somewhere where you can just let the nails drop to the ground or floor, then sweep or shovel them up. This saves much time over carefully putting each individual nail into a pocket or can. Pile lumber in a heap on one side of the work area. Build a neat pile of boards on the other, segregated as to kind and length.

Do not cut lumber to a standard length or even square off the ends in order to make it look neater in storage. As surely as you do, you will someday wish your board was just an inch or two longer.

When reusing boards, it makes good sense to hide the ugly ones and use the best where they'll show. You can use stained and dirty dimension lumber for framing and cover it with new paneling or wallboard. This stretches your new lumber dollars by letting you use them only on what shows.

Your own ingenuity should allow you to use old boards in a variety of ways. Just don't sacrifice quality to save money. Don't try anything you haven't done or seen done successfully before if there is any danger involved. By using old lumber you will be brightening the landscape, saving trees, increasing your own self-sufficiency and carpentry skills (taking it apart gives you a better idea of how it was put together—and vice versa), and saving money. That's not bad for several afternoons of hard, dirty work.

Chapter 9

Tools

Many factors contribute to the success of any farmsteading endeavor today, but one of the most important is the need for a well-equipped toolshop. Without a good selection of quality tools, the homesteader today is simply increasing the odds against ever making it on the land. Tools are needed to build your cabin or renovate an existing building, to erect livestock shelters, install stoves, and carry out normal maintenance.

What you select or require in the way of equipment will, for the most part, be dictated by your special plans and requirements. If you intend to live in an area where electrical power is available and to make use of that facility, your choice of tools and equipment will be different than for someone living without power. If you intend to use gasoline-powered machinery, you will need a larger selection and some specialized equipment to keep that machinery in operating condition.

Perhaps the only concession to big business you'll make is to use a battered old half-ton for running back and forth to town or a part-time job. Even so, you'll require some basic tools to perform at least minimal maintenance and repair jobs, such as a ratchet and socket set with spark plug socket, oil filter wrench, battery terminal cleaner, jack and tire iron, plus tape and clamps for emergency repairs.

Major automotive or tractor maintenance and repair will require a timing light and a dwell-tach unit and voltage indicator. If your major powered equipment is a tiller, do you have the tools necessary to perform your own tuneups and repairs? Most small engines require special instruments for removing flywheels and other parts. Do you have spares of the most likely to be replaced parts, such as sparkplug, points, or belts?

Horse-drawn farming equipment doesn't negate the need for the proper tools to perform maintenance and repair functions. Hammers, wrenches, welding torches, files, and screwdrivers are just as important here as they are to work on motor-driven implements.

Horses also require their own special tools on the well-equipped farmstead. A farrier's hammer, hoof nips, and hoof knife, as well as a hoof pick and rasps, are just some of the gear you'll need in your shop. Consider part of your purchase requirements to include awls and other gear for emergency repairs, and harness and trace lines.

Buy the very best tools you can afford. You may pay more initially, but you will save a lot of time, frustration, and expense because you won't have to shell out dollars at a later date. Stay with nationally well-known brands such as Stanley, Fuller, Craftsman, Nicholson, or Disston. For power tools, select at least the medium or top-line categories.

Once you have your tools, learn how to use them properly, maintain them, and store them where they won't get lost or damaged. You'll have big dollars invested in equipment that can literally mean the difference between life and death and the difference between success and failure. Treat your tools as "friends," and they should last you a lifetime. A tool should be checked for wear or possible breakage, then cleared and stored where it won't get damaged or lost.

The ideal situation is a separate workshop with benches and lots of storage space where tools can be hung on racks in plain sight (Fig. 9-1). If this isn't possible at first, at least keep your tools in special boxes or drawers where they can be stored without damaging each other or getting misplaced.

Don't lend them to anyone. Most tools that are lent out to friends or neighbors don't come back in good condition. Tools or implements returned in broken or misused condition upon which you depend for your living are absolutely of no further use to you in that state without time (and sometimes money) being spent to get them back in working order.

There are three solutions to this problem of tool borrowing.

Fig. 9-1. Have plenty of storage space for tools (drawing by Liz Buell).

First, you can absolutely refuse to lend any equipment, perhaps resulting in broken friendships and poor feelings. Second, you can keep old, broken-down tools on hand especially for this purpose, which could result in the loss of friends or neighbors. The third solution is to offer the use of the tool and yourself when required. Using this solution means you keep an eye on your tools, offer your expertise (hopefully in its proper use) and, in addition, you may gain some valuable knowledge or even an offer of labor or goods in trade at a later date.

To anyone contemplating a move from the city to a farm or homestead situation, delay your move, if necessary, until you have enough cash to finish off your major tool acquisitions. The delay may only mean another week or two at your present job, but it's better to face that problem now than when you become involved in the busy aspects of building your dream in the country when cash may be even more difficult to obtain. At the very least, be prepared to budget some of your nest egg for future tool and equipment purchases. Proper planning at this stage can mean a lot towards your eventual failure or success.

HAND TOOLS

The following are hand tools essential for the workshop of any homestead. We have not listed a large variety of specialized tools relating to engine repair, metalworking, etc.

- *Wood ax*—single bit, 4 pounds. It's a good idea to have two on hand. Also, purchase a spare handle (Fig. 9-2).
- *Bow saw*—36-inch with spare blades. For trimming branches and pruning trees, consider buying a 24-inch model (Fig. 9-3).
- *Handsaw*—22 to 26-inch, eight-point crosscut.
- *Handsaw*—22 to 26-inch, five to seven-point rip.
- *Adjustable frame hacksaw* with 24 spare blades.
- *Back or miter saw*—14-inch with 10 points per inch.
- *Keyhole or compass saw*—14-inch, eight point.
- *Miter box*—for making accurate angle cuts. Stanley makes a nice bench mount device for around $24. You can buy a cheaper wood model.

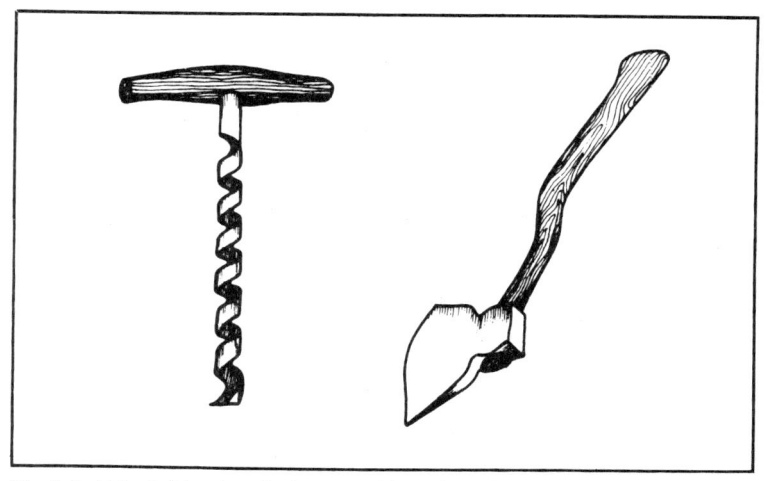

Fig. 9-2. At the left is a barefoot auger without the spiral tip. At the right is a broad ax with an offset handle to prevent scraped knuckles (drawing by Liz Buell).

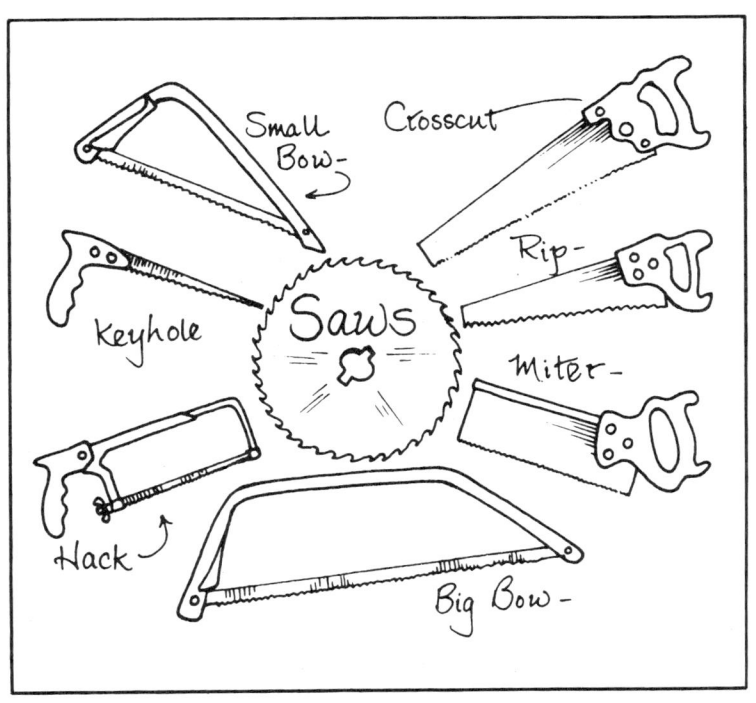

Fig. 9-3. Saws are essential tools for the homesteader (drawing by Liz Buell).

- *Sledge hammer*—6 or 8-pound model.
- *Utility club hammer* with 2½-pound head.
- *Woodchopper's maul*—6-pound head should be sufficient.
- *Steel splitting wedge*—at least 5-pound. Get two.
- *Broad ax*—needed if you are into squaring your own timbers. Lightest you should get is with 3-ound head.
- *Peeling spud*—for peeling logs, rails, and posts.
- *Claw hammer*—16-ounce is best. Get two. If you prefer wood handles, pick up two spares.
- *Ball peen hammer*—16-ounce size for main use.
- *Screwdrivers*—a large selection is essential. Range from shorties for tight spots to those with 8 or 10-inch shanks. You'll need some for Phillips, Robertson, and slot screws. Buy one inexpensive slot type expressly for prying open paint cans, etc.
- *Wood chisels*—at least four. Range in width from ¼ inch to 1¼ inches.
- *Handyman or carpenter's ratchet brace.*
- *Auger bits* with tapered square shanks for above brace. At

least ¼, ½, ¾ and 1-inch sizes. For boring above 1 inch, get an expansive bit ⅞-inch to 3-inch capacity.
- *Hand drill*—get a heavy-duty model. If possible, buy one with breast plate for heavy work.
- *Twist drills* for above in-set from 1/16 inch to ¼ inch by thirty-seconds.
- *Pliers*—like screwdrivers, you never seem to have enough on hand. Your toolbox should have at least an 8-inch lineman's plier, a 9-inch slip-joint multigroove plier, a 7-inch diagonal cutter, and 8-inch long-nose with side cutter. Pick up at least two locking pliers in 7 or 10-inch size.
- *Tin snips*—one pair straight cut and one pair circular cut.
- *Combination square.*
- *Rafter square.*
- *Steel tape*—minimum 10-foot.
- *Level*—24 size is best for all-round use. For extensive masonry work, also buy a cast aluminum mason's level.
- *Line level*—lightweight. Hooks to line.
- *Jack plane*—14-inch is best for all-round use.
- *Drawknife*—straight or curved blade. For shaping wood, especially ax or hammer handles, etc.
- *Spokeshave.*
- *Chisel and punch set*—cold chisels, drift and pin punches. Add two nail sets in 1/16-inch and ⅛-inch sizes.
- *Wrecking bar*—30 inches.
- *Combination fence tool*—has two wire cutters, staple puller, and hammerhead all in one tool.
- *All-purpose socket set with ratchet handle*—best to buy ⅜-inch drive for all-round use. Get ½-inch drive set if likely to be working on heavy machinery.
- *Files and wood rasps*—include those needed for sharpening axes and chain saws. Include a file card for cleaning.
- *Oilstone.*
- *Woodworking vise*—at least 4-inch jaw capacity.
- *Mechanic's vise*—at least 4-inch jaw capacity.
- *Staple gun*—great for tacking up chicken wire, plastic on windows, hothouses, insulation, or window screening. Buy a healthy selection of staples while you're at it.
- *Box and open-wrench set.*
- *Adjustable wrenches*—8 and 12-inch lengths with jaw capacity from ½ inch to 1½ inches should do for most jobs.

Large Stillson-style wrench for really heavy jobs is nice to add to your selection.
- *Oxygen-propane welding torch*—one of these rigs won't tackle the really big jobs, but it should be sufficient for most occasional work encountered around the farm. It will cut ½-inch bolts and braze 3/16-inch steel.
- *Clamps*—a good assortment of C-clamps and bar clamps make any number of projects possible.
- *Grease gun*—not only for truck or tractor maintenance but for tillerss, mowers, wagons, etc.
- *Hydraulic jacks*—get two. One with 1½-ton capacity and one with 3-ton range.
- *Wire*—in all forms and sizes from snare wire to the heaviest you can find. It's great for repairing ax handles, bucket handles, bracing stovepipes, etc.
- *Gear-type clamps*—relatively expensive but great for repairs to radiator hoses, water lines, etc. Keep a good selection on hand. While you're at it, lay in a supply of electrician's tape for the same purposes.
- *Adhesives*—a couple of tubes of five-minute epoxy as well as other adhesives are invaluable in making repairs to a variety of materials from water buckets to rubber work boots.

POWER TOOLS

The use of electricity can make life a lot easier around the farmstead. Even a limited selection of power tools can make your workload more productive. When purchasing power tools, always select professional or industrial rated equipment if you can afford them. If not, aim at the better or best categories of home-use tools from such lines as Black and Decker or Craftsman.

- *Portable power saw*—7¼ inches. This saw will handle 90 percent of your cutting chores. Never get one with less than a 9-amp motor. Unless involved in quality, precision woodwork, put your money into one of these over a bench saw.
- *Drill*—better to buy ⅜-inch chuck capacity rather than ¼-inch. Three-amp motor minimum. With attachments, the drill can be used for sanding, grinding, mixing paint, etc.
- *Half-inch drill*—to handle those larger jobs, especially in metal. A 4.2-amp motor is best here.
- *Saber saw*—selected blades make this item suitable for

straight and curved line cutting in wood, plastic, and light metal. Get nothing less than a 3-amp motor.
- *Drill press*—a top-quality model can be used for precision drilling and for buffing, grinding, and routing with the proper attachments.

The first four items on this list should cost around $200. With care, they should last a lifetime with no other expenses than replacing brushes and blades or bits.

HAMMERS

How many hammers should a homesteader or a householder have? Most homeowners start out with two basic types, the nail or claw hammer and the ball peen hammer, but both of these can be purchased in different weights and sizes. Certainly every homestead needs to plan on having one hammer in the house so it's not necessary to chase out to the barn or workshop.

Heft incorporates many meanings—weight, balance, feeling, a sense of rightness in size and movement. A hammer with the right heft is the hammer that feels right to the person using it—right for the particular purpose for which it is being used.

A hammer with a long handle can be a great impediment if you are doing close work hour after hour in cramped quarters. On the other hand, if a good amount of heavy hammering is done, a tool with a short handle would soon tire your muscles. Analyzing your needs correctly should lead to better choices in purchasing hammers.

Hammers are one of the most important hand-wielded tools —an extension of man himself—and, therefore, made in many forms to serve many uses. Quality tools are a good investment. Inexpensive tools are often harder to use and will have to be replaced. In the long run, buying quality hammers will save you money, time, and the frustrations of working with poor equipment.

When you find a particular hammer that feels especially comfortable to use and has a handle and head relationship that fits you, make a pattern of the handle and of its angle and balance with the head. If you ever break the handle, such a pattern could be used to shape and fit a new one.

The basic nail or claw hammer can be purchased with a straight or curved claw. The straight claw is used for ripping and does a fine job in quickly removing old lathing during remodeling. Generally used for rougher framing work, the straight claw hammer is frequently called the lifesaver because the claw, quickly driven in, can act as a handhold and keep a workman from falling from a roof or a scaffolding (Fig. 9-4).

The curved claw, used in working in more confined areas, prevents striking others with sharp points opposite the face of the hammer and will not get wedged into something behind the hammerer. The claw, in either case, is used for pulling out and for straightening nails.

Fig. 9-4. The straight claw hammer can be a lifesaver (drawing by Liz Buell).

Nail hammers can be purchased with heads of various weights ranging from 5 to 28 ounces. The 12-ounce and 16-ounce sizes are the most common. The lighter hammers are used for driving small nails. The heavier ones are used for driving large nails into softwood or ordinary nails into hardwood. When a hammer is too light for the job, it will cause the nail to bend. Generally speaking, a hammerhead weight is right if you can drive in a large nail with five blows.

In addition to wooden handles, most hardware stores today display hammers with steel and fiberglass handles. The average handle length on the 12-ounce and 16-ounce hammers is 12 inches. Only by holding, hefting, or trying to balance a hammer can you decide on the weight, handle length, and shape best for you. Preferences are usually the result of the type of tools a person learned with originally or from the arm length and physical proportions of the user.

It's nice to note that today, as more people become interested in learning crafts and trying new skills, there are fewer broken hammers tossed in dumps. Shaping and fitting new handles to old hammerheads often means another 70 years of use. White ash, white oak, and hickory were the woods used in the past for farm-crafted handles. Sometimes they were treated with linseed oil, but a well-used hammer has its handle preserved by the sweat of the hand of the wielder.

The terminology or vocabulary associated with hammers is helpful for those who are just beginning to use these tools. An adze-eye hammer has a head with metal (a continuing united part of the head) extending down the handle for reinforcement. The plain-eye hammer does not (Fig. 9-5).

The term *peen* means to enlarge, to straighten, or to smooth. A ball peen hammer has a flat face for striking and, opposite this face, either a spherical or a wedge-shaped end. This peen end is used to "head over" metal so it will not protrude or stick up.

A *swage* (and there are many kinds) is a tool for bending cold metal to a required shape. To swage is to reduce or taper an object, or to stretch to shape, and sometimes to pound a flat surface of metal so as to spread it. Thus, for instance, is done on a rivet.

A *quoin* is a wedge-shaped piece of wood or metal driven in between two *shims* that are longer, narrow strips. In rock cutting, a line of holes was made with a drill hammer and then, when the shims and quoins were put into the holes, the quoins were hammered (Fig. 9-6). The force of the hammering upon the quoins split the great

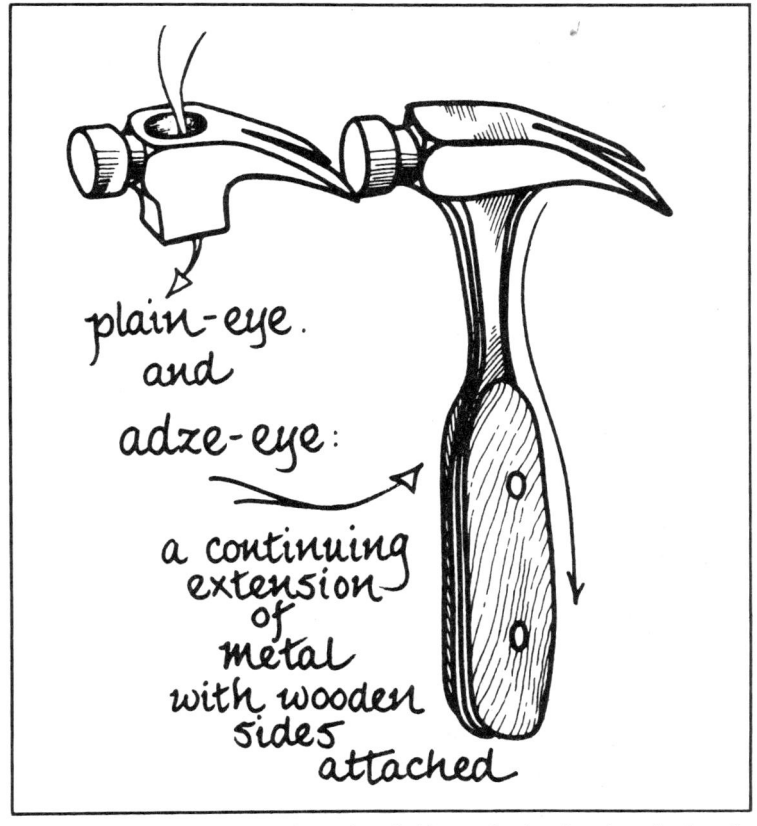

Fig. 9-5. An adze-eye hammer has a head with metal extending down the handle for reinforcement (drawing by Liz Buell).

chunks of granite. Many old homes in the Northeast have foundations of granite with these quoin marks still showing.

The term *to broom* refers to the splintering or fraying of hammers by careless use or by using the wrong tool for the job. Sometimes this is expressed as *to mushroom* or to change shape quickly—to spread out as a result of being hit too hard with the wrong choice of hammer.

A *hammer blossom* is the indentation made in wood by hitting a nail too hard or by not hitting at its center. Sometimes such dents are called the *footprints* of a careless, sloppy, or inexperienced worker.

Mallet usually refers to a wooden type of hammer used with one hand—thus, it has a short handle. The long-handled *"maul"*—

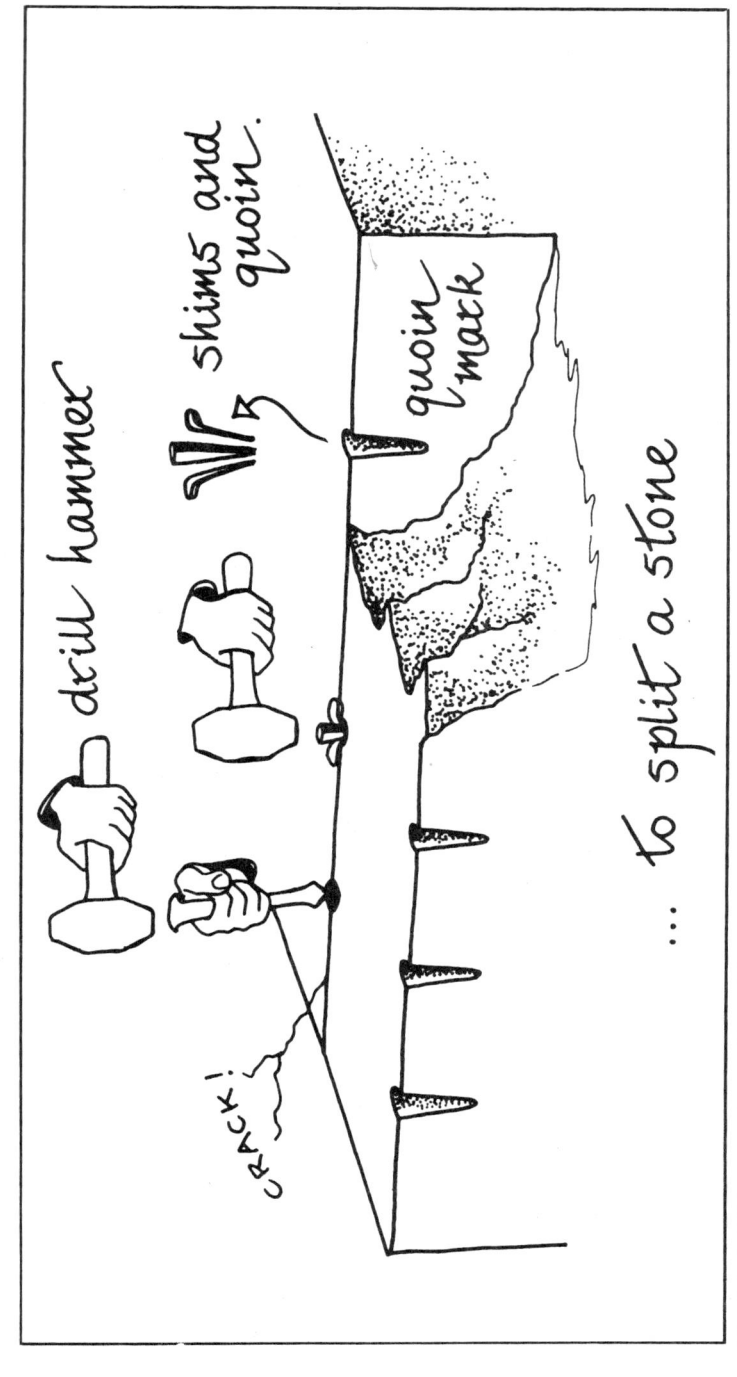

Fig. 9-6. A drill hammer is used in splitting stones (drawing by Liz Buell).

also made of wood—is used with two hands. These terms, however, are often interchanged in different parts of the country. The *beetle* was a crude, rough type of maul often made from the burls in maple trees. These hammer-type tools were generally used to strike other tools to provide the cutting force.

The 12-pound *sledgehammer* is the one most useful for general work. The spiking sledgehammer was used in driving railroad spikes, and the head was longer so that the workman could strike down over the rail in driving the spikes. These were also used in shipyards and in putting together the huge timbers in barns.

Among the smaller hammers are those used by cobblers, farriers, and upholsterers. From either a collector's point of view or that of homesteaders learning to do for themselves, these small, adaptable tools are a delight to view and handle. Often the upholsterer's hammers have one short head and one long one in order to reach deep inside the work.

Tack hammers usually have one end magnetized to hold and set the tack. The opposite end is used to whack it firmly into place. With practice, the skill of "tap and whang" increases.

Other combinations of these work terms involving quick use of both ends of the hammerhead are "flip and hit," "start and drive," and "set and pound." The word "tunk" means a gentler type of hit usually to move something into place.

For everyday care of hammers, wipe the handles and heads with a lightly oiled cloth. Regular care will prevent accumulations of rust. Care should also be taken in storage. Dampness will cause the wood of the handles to swell and fray. Heat will dry the wood and the handles will loosen. A metal hammerhead flying through the air can be a lethal projectile.

Hammers were made and are made in many shapes and sizes (Figs. 9-7 and 9-8). The old Yankee snow-knocker, used to whang out balls of snow that formed on horses' hooves and caused them to skitter and go down, may be needed again as farm horse populations increase. As new materials are used in modern construction, new hammers may need to be invented.

You'll save yourself time, money, energy, and frustration if you can find the right hammer—the right tool for the task. Take the time to try each one to be sure that your hammers have the right heft for your hand.

CHAIN SAWS

Loud, dirty, and dangerous they may be, but nothing has done

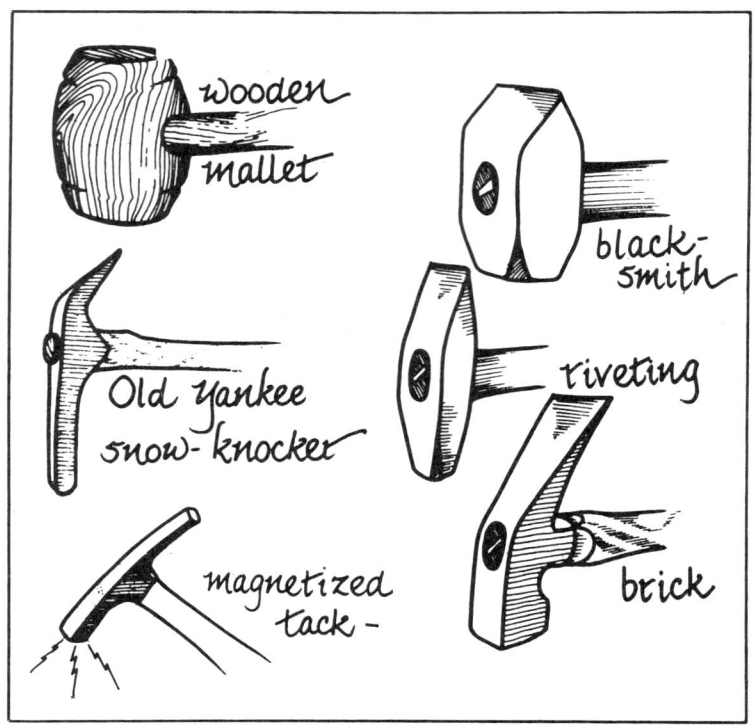

Fig. 9-7. Hammers come in many shapes (drawing by Liz Buell).

more to bring the age-old art of woodcutting to latter twentieth century practicality than modern chain saws (Fig 9-9). Light years ahead of the earliest generations of chain saws that ripped and roared through the nation's timberlands, today's models are more subdued of voice, easier to handle, and powerfully efficient.

Buyer's Guide

Chain saw manufacturers offer a wide range of models and sizes (Fig. 9-10). Before selecting one, it's important to know what saws are available, the jobs they are designed to do, and what features will be useful for the type of cutting you plan to do. Table 9-1 is a representative sampling of the choices available in the chain saw market. After considering the chart, visit local dealers, try out the demonstration models on hand, and take your time selecting the chain saw that's right for you.

Chain saws are usually powered by gasoline engines ranging from a tiny 1.6 cubic inches to a monstrous 6 cubic inches in displacement. The cutting chains are mounted on bars that may be as short as 10 inches in length for occasional, light-duty cutting, or as long as 36 inches. Most people find a 16-inch blade sufficient for cordwood cutting without being too awkward or unwieldy; the longer bars—needed for cutting only very large trees—can be dangerous in inexperienced hands.

Modern chain saws also come equipped with a wide range of options, ranging from handy automatic oilers with manual oiling overrides and safety chain brakes, to luxuries such as heated handles, electric starters, and automatic chain sharpening systems (Fig. 9-11). While many of these extras may seem inviting, they can also complicate operation and maintenance of the basic machine. Experienced woodcutters have learned that exotic frills can be more trouble than their convenience is worth, so careful, personal consideration of the options under inspection and actual cutting conditions at your dealer's woodpile is a good idea.

If you're in a position to invest in extras, one good buy to consider is a chain saw that has a slightly larger engine than is required for the bar length you choose. Not only will the extra

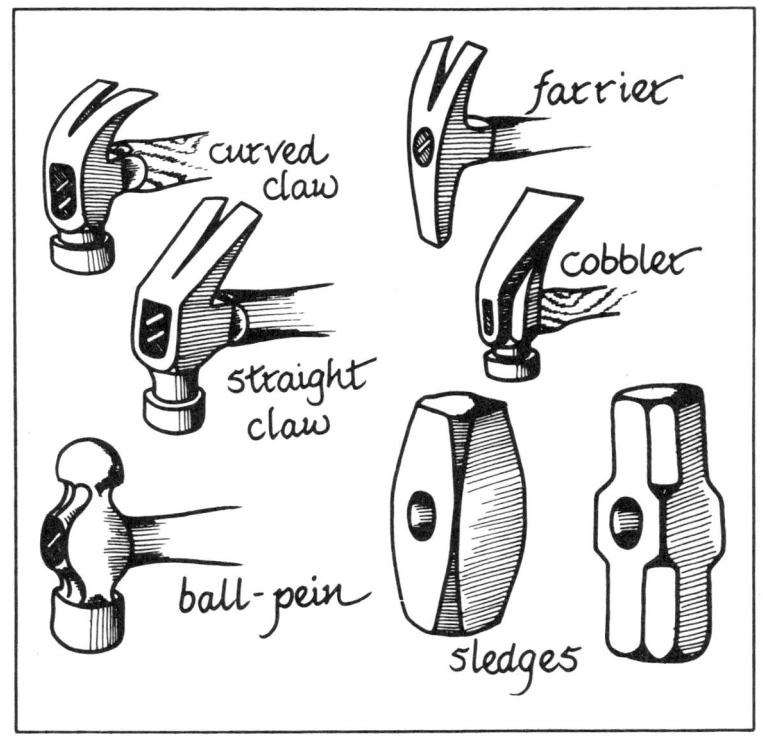

Fig. 9-8. Hammers also come in many sizes (drawing by Liz Buell).

Table 9-1. Chain Saw Manufacturers and Distributor Addresses.
Names and Location of Local Dealers May Be Obtained by Contacting the Distributor or by Checking the Yellow Pages.

Chain Saw	Distributor	Chain Saw	Distributor
Homelite	Homelite Homelite Distribution 60 Chapin Road Pinebrook, NJ 07058	Montgomery Ward	only by catalog
Husqvarna	Jesse F. White Route 16 Mendon, MA 01756	Olympic	Tilton Equipment Route 1 Rye, NH 03870
Jonsereds	Tilton Equipment Route 1 Rye, NH 03870	Partner	R.D. Faulkner 146 Parkway South Brewer, ME 04412
John Deere	John Deere Company P.O. Box 4949 Syracuse, NY 13221	Pioneer	Crandall Hicks Company Route 9 Southboro, MA 01772
Lombard	R.D. Faulkner 146 Parkway South Brewer, ME 04412	Poulan	R.E. Jarvis Route 9 Fayville, MA 01745
McCulloch	McCulloch of New England Reading, MA 01867	Sears Craftsman	only by catalog
		Stihl	Hampton Equipment Lancaster, NH 03584

Fig. 9-9. A chain saw makes cutting wood easy.

power provide added protection against long-term wear and occasional strain on the saw, it will allow you to step up to a longer bar and chain, if needed, or add accessories to make your saw more versatile without buying a new chain saw later.

While testing a chain saw, don't forget to examine it for quiet running, low vibration, and good balance of the saw's weight in your hands. When working in the woods, there's nothing that does more to bring on early fatigue than a whining, unmanageable machine.

If you are buying a saw for nothing more than some backyard tree pruning, or perhaps to cut up a few slender logs for the fireplace, a minisaw will suit your purposes well. These saws are usually manufactured with engines of about 2 cubic inches displacement. They are equipped with guide bars ranging from 10 to 12 or even 14 inches in length. Minisaws are light, easy to handle, and

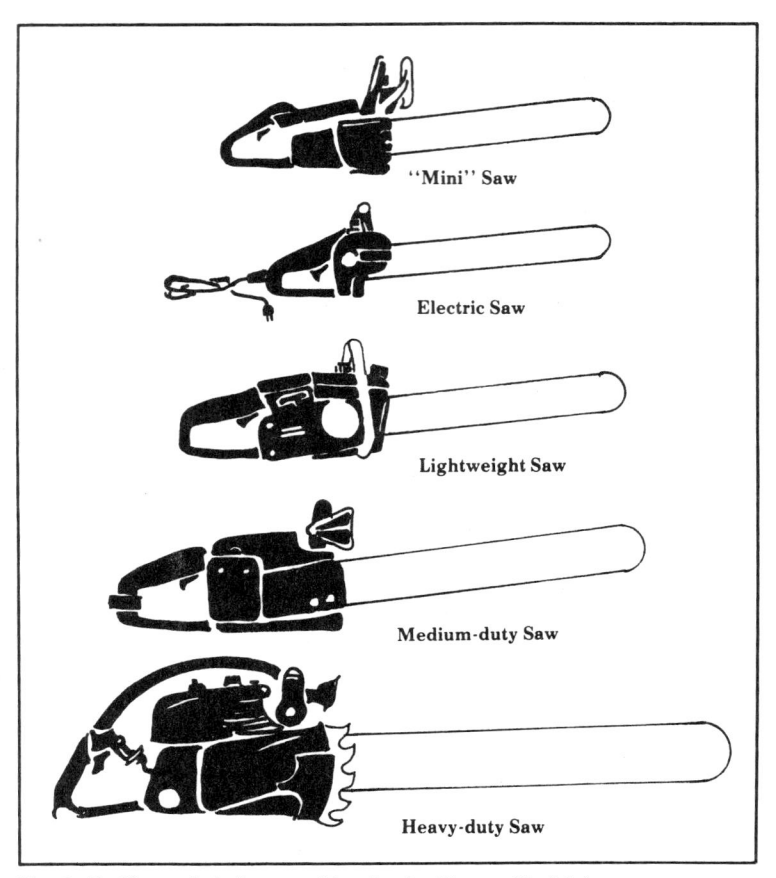

Fig. 9-10. Sizes of chain saws (drawing by Dianne Shelble).

inexpensive. Despite their diminutive size, many brands are also rugged and reliable. Before the newfound, mass popularity of backyard chain sawing, these machines were manufactured for tree surgeons and orchardists who used them for treetop cutting. It is easier for them to climb to lofty heights with a small-sized saw simply by hanging it from a belt. They then lop off branches by holding the lighter-weight equipment in one hand.

Many makers also offer electric minisaws, and because they are less costly to manufacture, electric chain saws may sell for only about half the cost of equivalent gas-powered models. Electric saws must be plugged into a service outlet, so their use is limited by the length of your heavy-duty extension cord. If you are in the market for a handy, inexpensive tool for the sole purpose of whittling down the backyard woodpile, an electric saw might be a good investment.

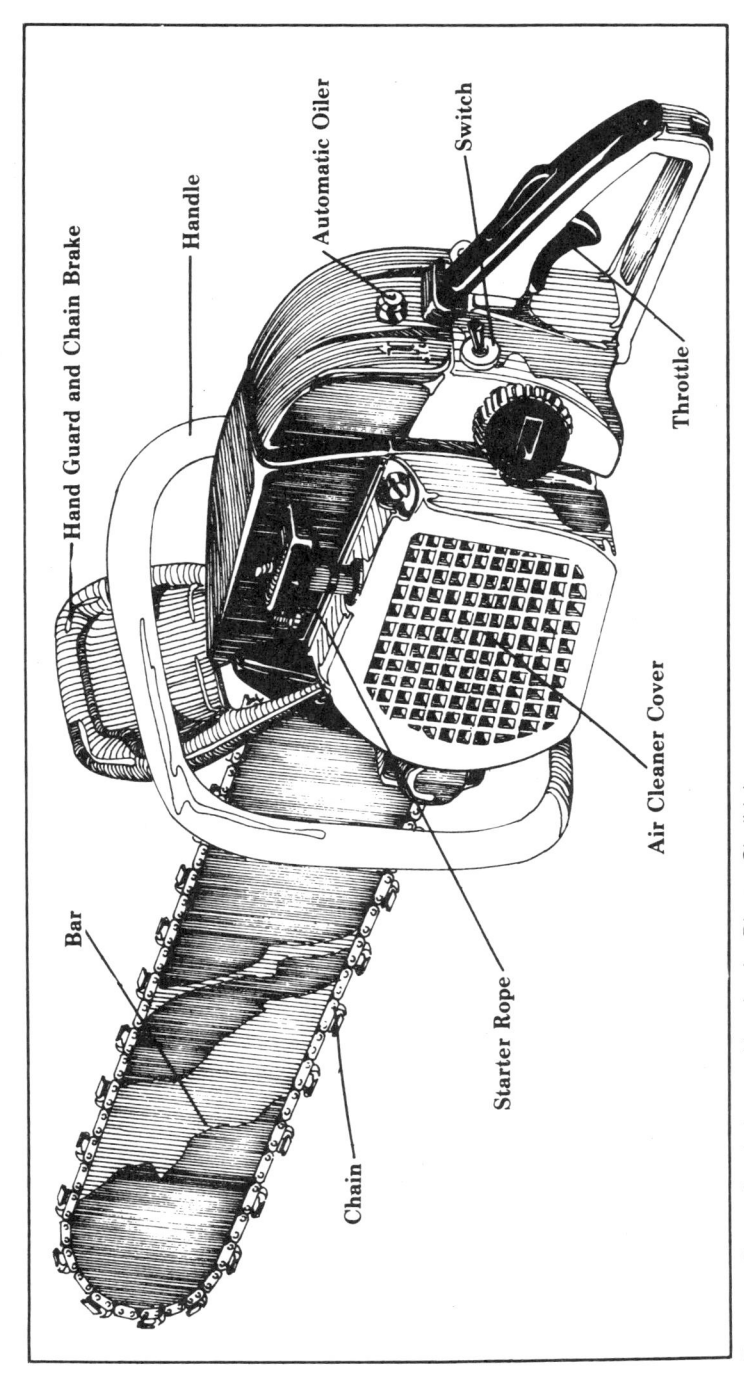

Fig. 9-11. Parts of a chain saw (drawing by Dianne Shelble).

Not only are electric saws lighter, easier to start, cheaper, and quieter than their gas-fueled counterparts, but they produce no exhaust fumes. Therefore, they can be used for woodcutting and construction projects in the woodshed or basement.

If you don't need to climb trees with your saw (a dangerous practice in the best of circumstances), and you'll be doing more than occasional cutting, a lightweight production chain saw might be the one for you. These saws are usually powered by engines in the 2.5 to 3 cubic inch displacement range and are commonly outfitted with bars 14 to 16 inches long. They hold more fuel than a minisaw and therefore run longer without refueling. They are also quicker to start and easier to maneuver than the heavier production models.

Chain saws with displacements ranging from 3 to 3.9 cubic inches are called medium-duty saws. These machines are best suited for regular logging and pulpwood cutting, and they will usually accept a wide range of brush cutting, hedge trimming, stonecutting, and drilling attachments. Saws from this category are best suited to the year-round cutting done by professional wood suppliers, because they provide more power than is often required for cutting a single home's wood supply. These chain saws will certainly do the job around the homestead, but their size, weight, and power may take a little getting used to.

Heavy-duty chain saws, the smallest of which have displacements of about 5 cubic inches and bars ranging from 16 to 36 inches in length, are not for everyone. They are bigger, heavier, stronger, and louder than other production saws. Unless you plan to do contract logging in the White Mountain National Forest, convert your saw to an Alaskan sawmill for the production of lots of rough lumber, or cut giant trees every day, these formidable machines with their giant attachments may be more than you would care to handle.

If you're ready to buy a chain saw this year, first examine the following list of models, specifications, and features to determine which machines might be right for you. Then, by all means, try before you buy. Ask questions. Talk with other woodcutters you know besides the salesperson at your local chain saw dealer's showroom. When all else is carefully considered, make your final choice the saw that feels the best as you work with it. After all, you'll be cutting with that saw for a long time.

Care and Use

All major saw brands have similar maintenance requirements.

Two criteria should be used when buying a saw for the first time: availability of parts (distance to saw shop), and what you will use it for. Choose one that is light enough to handle comfortably. Old clunkers are fine if that's what you have.

Proper care of gas and bar oil is the first step to good maintenance. Use relatively new gas. Saw manufacturers recommend regular gas. Nonleaded high test Amoco gas burns cleaner and smokes less. Mix whichever gas you choose with two-cycle engine oil according to the directions on the can. Don't necessarily follow the saw manufacturer's recommendations, as many times the proportions given for mixing only apply when using their special high-ratio mixing oil. We buy Jonsereds two-cycle oil and mix 1 quart with 4 gallons of gas. Be sure to shake the mixture well each time you use it, as two-cycle oil tends to sink to the bottom of the can. Use clean, airtight containers to store the fuel. Avoid storing a small amount of gas in a large container, as this will make a greater surface area available for condensation. Never use the last few tablespoons from the container; it may contain water.

Bar oil should also be kept in clean cans. Dirt can clog the oil filter screens and prevent the oil pump from working efficiently. Use special grade bar oil rather than engine oil. We use 10-40W bar and chain oil, available in most saw shops for about $1.60/gallon.

Your saw must be cleaned regularly to work right. Soak the air filter in gas or kerosene a few minutes to remove the sawdust and oil that covers it. If you attempt to scrape it off, you will damage the filter. To clean the carburetor compartment, remove its outside cover and pour gas or kerosene over it. An old toothbrush will help remove the caked-on grit. Next, find an old hacksaw blade and run it between the engine's cooling fins to remove grit that may cause overheating. Every so often, the pullcord starter mechanism should be removed from the body of the saw and cleaned. Be sure to clean and oil the two fingers held to the flywheel's center by springs, while you have the mechanism off. Failure to do this will cause the fingers to disengage from the pullcord mechanism in cold weather, and you won't be able to start the saw.

Tuning your saw seems difficult at first, but it really is very simple. The high-low adjusting screws located on the side of the carburetor control the gas-air mixture. Turn the high screw in enough to get maximum power out of a full throttle. The engine should accelerate smoothly to a level which sounds clear and powerful. If the saw seems to scream or rattle, or the engine has a tendency to cut out as the throttle is increased, then the high screw is in too far. Having the screw out too far will cause the engine to smoke excessively. The low screw will maintain a continuous idle when your finger is off the throttle. If screwed too far out, the engine will stop. If screwed too far in, the chain will spin around the bar. At an idle the chain should not move. The idle adjustment screw (located next to the carburetor) should be turned inward a slight amount if an idle cannot be attained by using the low adjustment screw.

If you've become totally confused by this description, try turning both the high and low screws all the way in, then turn them out 1¼ turns. This will give you a good point from which to start again.

You will spend more money on bars and chains than on any other parts for your saw. Treat them well. There are three types of bars to choose from: sprocket nose, roller nose, and hard nose. The sprocket nose and roller nose are the fastest and smoothest cutting bars. They are, however, the most expensive. Many times they will not last as long. The hard nose bar is best for most cutting jobs. Correct chain tension is essential to long bar life. The chain on a hardnose bar should have ¼ inch of slack if you were to gently pull the chain away from the bar. If it's too tight, the chain will hiss and smoke. If too loose, the chain, bar, and sprocket will undergo excessive wear. Also, your chain will be more likely to fly off the bar. Sprocket and roller nose bars should be kept a bit tighter. With any bar the chain groove will enlarge with wear to the point where the teeth of the chain will not feed properly into the wood. Take the bar to a saw shop and have them grind it down. This process can be repeated a number of times before the groove becomes too shallow to use. It's also a good idea to file off any lips that might develop on the bar's edge before they interfere with your cutting. Be sure to flip the bar over every time you replace a chain. Hardnose bars with worn out or chipped tips can be retipped at some saw shops.

Watch for wear on the sprocket (either rim or star) located on the engine's drive shaft. Excessive wear on this part can cause premature wear on the chain drive links. If you have a choice between a rim sprocket and a star sprocket, buy the rim, as it is less costly to replace and also keeps the chain lined up better with the bar groove.

Always make sure the chain gets plenty of bar oil. If your oiler stops, stop the saw immediately. Running it without oil will cause the chain to kink—a condition that renders the chain worthless.

Chain sharpening is a difficult subject to discuss. New chains from the factory are *not* sharp. To make them ready to use, remove the metal lip left from machine sharpening at the factory.

Next file down the rakers using a raker gauge and a flat file. The best gauge is made by the Carlton Chain Company and is called a file-o-plate. It is flat and can be carried in your wallet. Saw manufacturers recommend that the saw teeth should have a cutting angle of between 30 degrees and 35 degrees. It really depends on what kind of wood you're cutting. For hardwoods, use a smaller angle—maybe 25 degrees. On softwood, an angle of 35 degrees seems to work fine. How you cut the side plate angle (the angle you see on the chain teeth looking from one side of the bar) is up to you. Chain manufacturers recommend 85 degrees.

Troubleshooting saw problems is something that takes time and experience to learn. If the saw won't start, unscrew the spark plug, reconnect its wire cap, and place it against the engine block. Pull the starter cord a few times slowly. If there is no spark, it's either bad points, condenser, or spark plug.

If you've been pulling the cord a while trying to get it started, it may be flooded. This means that there will be a lot of gas in the ignition cylinder, which means that if your plug fires, your saw will be on fire. Don't panic, smother it with your glove or something. If you know the saw is flooded beforehand, wait awhile before trying to start it again. If the spark plug has fire, yet the saw won't start, either there is water in the gas or the carburetor isn't working right. Take the cover off the top diaphragm of the carburetor (bottom diaphragm if a Partner saw) and clean out the various compartments you see. If there is a lot of grit in the filter screen, maybe the fuel filter (located in the gas tank) has come off. If your saw starts but does not run smoothly, it's probably either water in the carburetor or diaphragm or a bad spark plug. If the saw revs up and won't slow down, there must be an air leak between the carb and the engine or in one of the engine seals.

Saws are not the only thing you must keep in good running order. Keep your body in one piece by using the following safety devices. A chain break will stop the chain's movement in about .13 seconds if the saw should slip from your right hand and buck up at you. The extra $30 it costs is well worth it. Shock absorber handles reduce the saw's vibration you receive and therefore give you better cutting control. Continuous use of a saw without these special handles causes permanent capillary damage in your fingers. Earplugs are necessary when you are using older saws with straight pipe mufflers. Newer saws also can cause ear damage when run for long periods of time. When working in the woods, wear a hardhat and steel toe boots.

Anticipate how the saw will react and don't take foolish chances with it. Saws buck up at you, jerk you here and there, and can fly out of your hand in the blink of an eye. Paying attention to what you are doing is about the best advice we can give you.

SHOVELS

If you're not really too unfamiliar with shovels, perhaps a rundown of different types and uses is in order. For all practical purposes, there are three basic types of shovel heads and two types of handles. There are one or two special purpose tools that may not fit exactly into these categories. See Figs. 9-12 and 9-13.

Let us first take handles. They are either long and straight or short with a "D" grip. Some shovels come with either, and some with only one type. At an auction you may find one that some country cobbler has custom designed for a special job.

By far the most common shovel is the *round mouth* with a long handle. Primarily it is used for digging and moving or loading sand, soil, gravel, and crushed stone by hand. It is a great tool for leveling uneven ground, or spreading sand or gravel. With some practice you can throw a shovelful a distance of 10 feet, and either leave it in a small pile or spread it to fill a small hole.

Sharpening the edges of a round mouth shovel greatly increases its usefulness. Not only will it penetrate hard earth easier, but it will also cut small roots. This lets you remove sod, cut weeds below ground level, and trim the sides of a round posthole.

With a few refinements, foresters have developed a *fire shovel*, which is very useful in the hands of an expert when fighting forest fires. This is just one of many specialized uses.

A round mouth shovel with a "D" grip on a short handle can do many of the things a long-handled one can do. Its basic use is for digging, especially in close quarters such as a well, a trench, or a hole for a corner fence post. This short-handled, round mouth shovel is also handy for carrying in cars or trucks when you travel muddy country roads.

The *square mouth shovels* are usually used around buildings where they can be used on level floors. Because of their construction, they are more apt to be used for scraping or carrying than digging. A square shovel is handy for moving hard packed snow.

One square shovel that is used for digging is the *garden spade*.

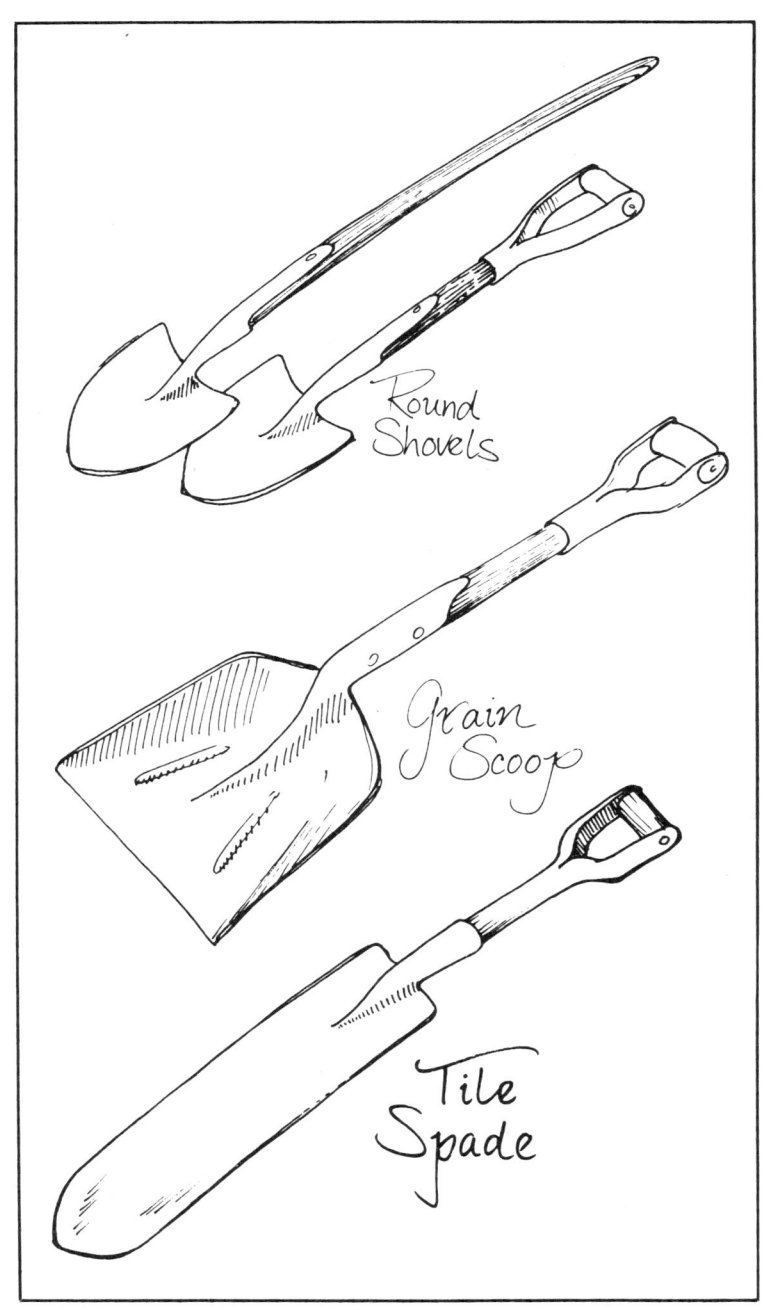

Fig. 9-12. Round shovels are the most common. A grain scoop has a short handle. A tile spade can save work (drawing by Liz Buell).

Fig. 9-13. A square shovel is used for carrying and digging. A garden spade is used for digging (drawing by Liz Buell).

It is a very efficient, short-handled digging tool. Not only can it be used for digging up the garden, but when sharpened, it is wonderful for edging the flower bed.

Scoop shovels usually come in two sizes and two materials. All have short handles. A large steel scoop is used mainly for grain, while a small aluminum one is handy for carrying in the trunk of your car in winter. Both can be used for shoveling or carrying material that is not too heavy and does not require much digging to load the shovel.

In these days of mechanization, you may never have seen a *tile spade*. If you have only a short run of tile to lay, such a spade can save you a lot of work or a lot of money. It was made to save digging a trench wide enough to work in all the way down to the full depth the tile was laid. The wide trench was only dug down perhaps 2 feet, and the tile spade is used for the last foot and a half or so.

The blade of the tile spade is about 5 inches wide by 18 inches long. It is rounded at the end. Handles are short and sturdy with a "D" grip. This gives a tool that not only can chop hard earth but is also strong enough to lever a small rock. Tiles are lowered into this narrow trench with a tile hook, a tool quite often homemade simply by putting a bent rod in a hoe or shovel handle.

Chapter 10

Construction Projects

This chapter has plenty of building suggestions for homesteaders to tackle. Projects vary from a woodshed to carving spoons.

WOODSHED

This woodshed, built by Frank Booker, is 16 by 24 feet—big enough for a year's supply of wood and gardening tools. It has three sides and an open wall facing south.

Site selection is important because a building takes on an air of permanence and tends to alter the pattern of the world around it—such things as orientation to the sun (remember the south-facing wall), accessibility (you want to be able to back the truck up to it), and nearness to the house so you don't have to lug the wood too far. Because this woodshed has an earth floor, the site had to be well-drained to avoid having to dig the last few weeks' supply of wood out of a frozen swamp.

Booker had just such a site out back of his house—fairly level and clear to the south. The nippers and a chain saw made short work of clearing the brush that was in the way, except for a few of the larger alder roots, which were wrapped with chain and hauled out with a pickup.

For a foundation, Booker decided to use cement blocks set on the ground. Forms about 18 inches square and a foot deep were nailed up and set into shallow holes dug by removing the sod. A ½ yard of gravel and rocks from an abandoned pit and a half bag of

175

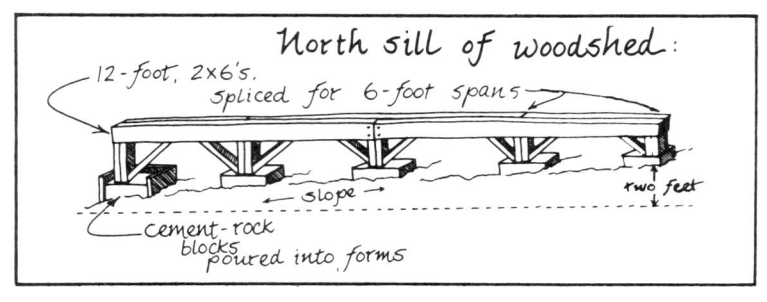

Fig. 10-1. The shims are braced.

cement were soon mixed into mortar and filled the forms. Most of the volume was taken up by larger rocks, with mortar being used to hold them together, making for level tops. Large flat rocks would have served just as well.

Because the ground slopes about 2 feet over the length of the building, no attempt was made to bring these blocks to the same height. Instead, a sill was installed around the perimeter and brought to the level of the highest block with shims or short posts as needed. The short posts were braced (Fig. 10-1). The sill is 4 inches by 6 inches made up of 12-foot long 2×6s and spliced as shown, with a support post being placed under each joining of the wood. This gave Booker a maximum span across the back of 6 feet—adequate to support the light framing and the rafters. The same thing was done on 8-foot centers along the sides, where the weight carried by the sills is less (Fig. 10-2). The sills were joined at the corners.

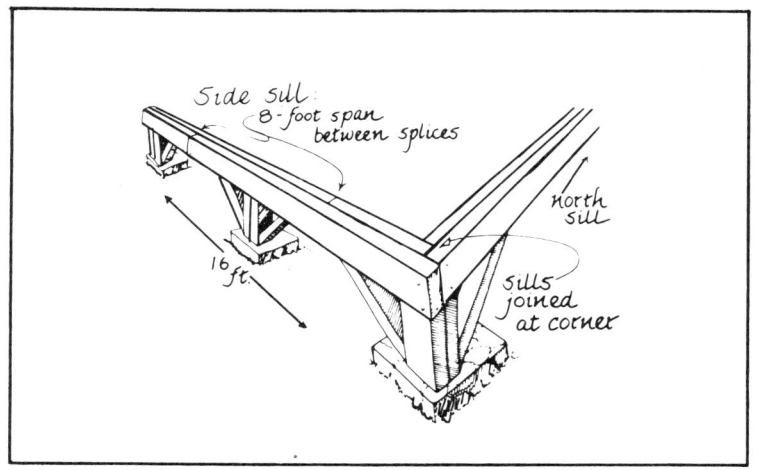

Fig. 10-2 Sills are joined at the corners.

This gave Booker a foundation of 24 feet along the back, 16 feet along each side, and open at the front. Four more blocks were poured at 8-foot intervals across the front and across the center for support posts (Fig. 10-3).

The wall framing, gable ends, and end rafters were cut and assembled (Fig. 10-3). Booker used a stud length of 4 feet and two 2×4s for a top plate. This gave him an opening across the front of almost 9 feet in height at the highest and 7 feet at the lowest end.

The long rafters are supported by a 4 by 6 carrying timber made up of two 2×6s running down the center of the building. Another such carrying timber was set at the same height across the front to support the front rafters. These beams were supported by posts at 8-foot intervals that were set on the concrete blocks poured earlier for the purpose. These posts were braced off against the carrying timbers with short lengths of 2×4s.

The wall bracing was nailed on. For this bracing, Booker used a few long boards nailed diagonally across the studs on the inside. These diagonal boards give the wall framing triangulation and make the building rigid. Make sure that the building is plumb before this goes on, as it tends to "set" the building into its final position and shape. Additionally, these boards give all kinds of nooks into which tools can be stashed. Rakes, hoes, and shovels stay conveniently against the wall.

The remaining rafters were cut and nailed in next. Each pair of rafters was tied together with a 4-inch wide board nailed to the rafters and running horizontally between the carrying timbers. These are called collar ties, and they give the rafters the rigidity of triangulation and prevent their spreading (Fig. 10-3).

The roofing boards were nailed on, and tar paper was put on for temporary roofing. This tar paper was run up and down the roof. Each course was lapped about 4 inches and stuck with some roof sealer. The seams were then secured by nailing on battens to keep the wind from lifting the roofing. This roof supports a couple of feet of heavy snow with nary a sag nor sway.

Sidewall boards were next nailed on vertically. This kind of boarding works quite well to keep out all but the most driving rains and snows without siding.

A few of the cedar shingles can be used for a roof and siding.

CHIMNEYS

Few of us are happy in the thought that the product of man's skill in manipulating such commonplace materials as clay, lime, and

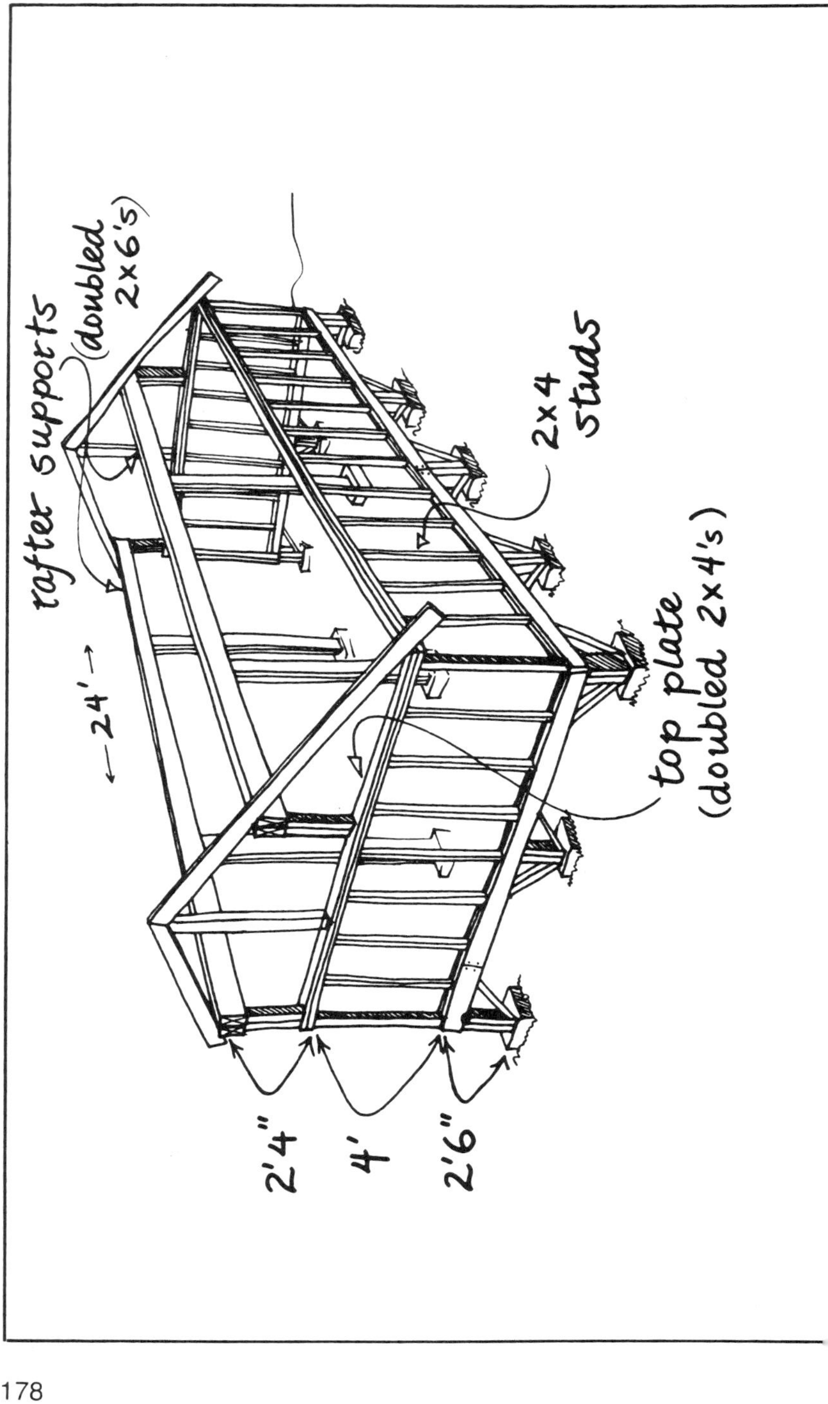
rafter supports
(doubled 2x6's)
2x4 studs
top plate
(doubled 2x4's)
24'
2'4"
4'
2'6"

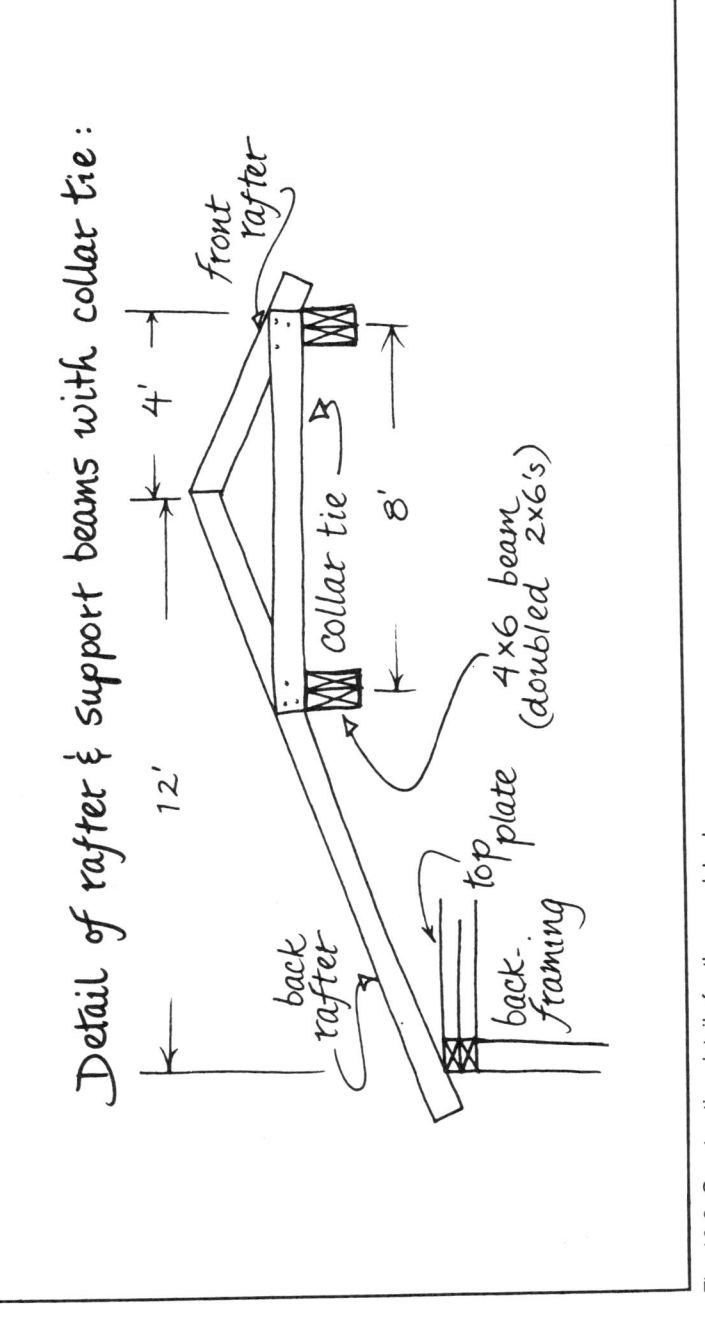

Fig. 10-3. Construction details for the woodshed.

sand can even occasionally be possessed of such innate contrariness as a bad acting chimney. It seems strange that a change in the direction of the wind can make the difference between smiles and contentment, and tears and discomfort to those whom the chimney was created to serve. Perhaps even more exasperating is the ordinarily well-behaved chimney which decides to give a demonstration of its temperamental vagaries on a day or occasion when the need of the best possible service is peculiarly urgent.

The lack of an ample supply of air at the fire end of the chimney is the cause of many failures commonly blamed on the chimney itself. The top of a chimney may be so much lower than a nearby ridge, part of a building, or a group of tall trees that eddies of wind blow down the chimney and force puffs of smoke back into the room. Chimneys built from architects' plans and specifications or in a city in which building laws are strictly enforced are well protected, but perhaps more than half of our population live beyond the range of these benefits. Those contemplating the building of modest homes or summer refuges in small towns, in villages, or in the rural districts without assurance that expert service is available, should know enough chimney philosophy to keep tabs on the progress of the work. Chimney permanence largely depends upon the thoroughness with which the craftsman fills the joints with mortar.

Unless rocks of suitable shape and size were available, our pioneer ancestors used the most convenient substitute and built their first chimneys with sticks thickly plastered inside and out with clay, sometimes laying stones as high as the fireplace if no more were available. Chimneys and log houses similar to Fig. 10-4 that have sheltered several generations may still be found in remote districts, their contemporaries having either decayed or burned because chimney inspections and repairs were neglected. As frontiers were pushed further on, the frame house supplemented the cabin for it marked a step in both economic and social progress. In such houses thousands of chimneys were built upon plank platforms supported as shown (Fig. 10-5) and well braced to the frame of the house. Often the chimney was built upon a frame (Fig. 10-6) supported from the sill of the house, which rested upon a stone or post foundation.

Perhaps this is not safe according to building laws and insurance inspectors' opinions, but the significance of the word "safe" depends on whether simple safety or super safety is considered safe. Thousands of such chimneys, built three or more generations ago, are still in active service. More are being built in modest

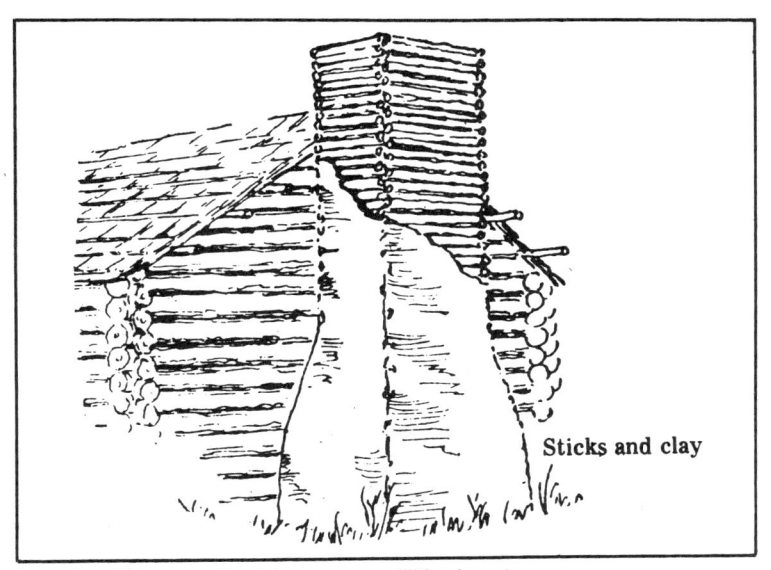

Fig. 10-4. Chimneys like this one may still be found.

dwellings beyond the pale of building ordinances. It would seem that the safety of these chimneys would stand comparison with the same quality in others, for it is not an unheard of thing for a recently built modern house to vanish in smoke because of a defective flue. If we can forget the ideal of super safety, we can easily convince our-

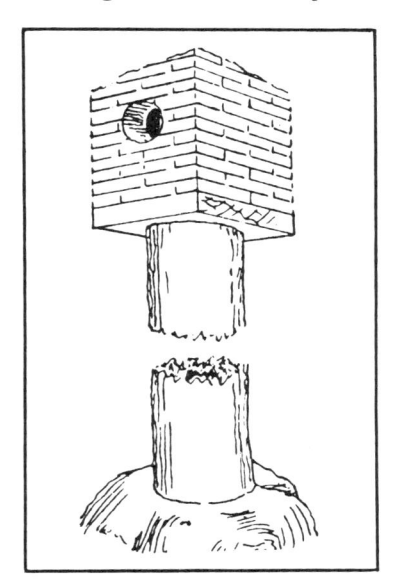

Fig. 10-5. This chimney is supported on a post in the ground.

181

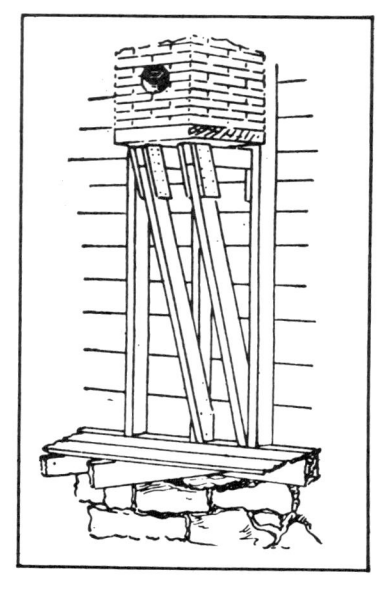

Fig. 10-6. This chimney is supported on a frame from the sill of the house.

selves that if the support is strong enough, if protected by sheet iron under the lower course of brick, and the chimney itself is well built, this chimney is safe enough for a light building, especially if bricks are as expensive and as hard to get as in some localities.

Ceilings and partitions are sometimes built closely against the sides of a chimney, and walls, ceilings, and chimneys are plastered at the same time. After a year or so the plastered corners will crack and break away (Fig. 10-7) because the difference in the rate and direction of expansion and contraction of both the brick chimney and the frame of the house will inevitably break plaster joints. Another method is to nail strapping on the chimney and lath and plaster thereon (Fig. 10-8). This is little if any better, for the plastered

Fig. 10-7. The plastered corners will crack and break away.

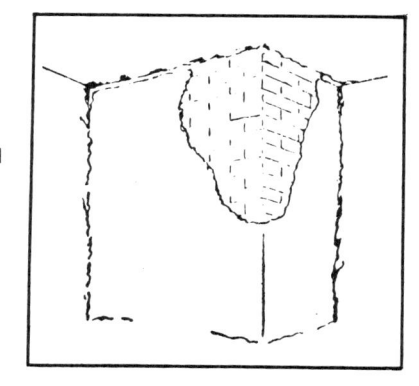

Fig. 10-8. Strapping is nailed on the chimney.

angles will break about as badly for the same reason. The correct method is to build the frame by placing 2-inch-by-4-inch studding flatwise 2 inches from the chimney and lathing and plastering as shown (Fig. 10-9).

Another method of unwise economy is the building of a chimney by placing bricks edgewise (Fig. 10-10). The element of safety is practically nonexistent, yet houses with such chimneys have stood for years, the result of propitious fate rather than of any constructive merit in the chimney. Many other such chimneys have been responsibile for fires that burned the houses down. Figure 10-10 shows such a chimney built around a terra-cotta or fireclay lining that makes it less unsafe. If a chimney must be built in a

Fig. 10-9. Build the frame by placing 1-inch by-4-inch studding flatwise 2 inches from the chimney.

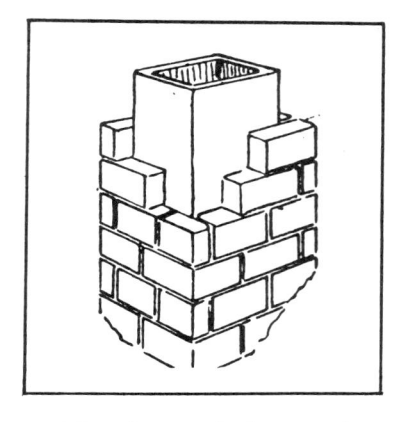

Fig. 10-10. Terra-cotta tile lined chimney brick laid on edge.

restricted space during repairs, we may place the lined chimney in the safe category. All joints must be well filled with cement. The form of the top or cap influences the safety and efficiency of the chimney; a cement top (Fig. 10-11) of the form shown built above the tile lining will prevent water from entering between the bricks and the lining that would soon wreck the chimney. Such a top tends to divert the wind as suggested, which will help the draft appreciably.

The ancient custom of pargeting (Fig. 10-12) is still followed to some extent in the belief that the smooth surface helps the draft. The owner of the house should insist that all plumb joints be entirely filled with cement and pargeting omitted, for often when that drops or scales off some of the mortar in the joints will come with it. This may leave a crevice that will reduce the draft and offer a passage for sparks; eventually you have a defective flue. A pargeted chimney is not acceptable in any place where building laws are in force.

Fig. 10-11. A cement cap is built above the tile lining.

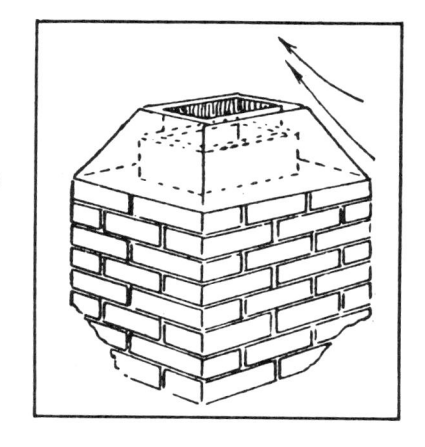

Fig. 10-12. Pargeted chimney flue.

Two examples of bad construction (Fig 10-13) illustrate a method of framing still followed in some places where building laws do not interfere. The construction at A protects the ends of the timbers from sparks for a while, but the capacity of the flue is reduced 25 percent. No chimney has greater capacity than its smallest area. Both methods are affected by the expansion and contraction of the building and chimney which may open dangerous cracks between the bricks. The method shown at B is as bad as it can be, but it has been used. No part of the frame of the house should rest on the chimney. The construction of the floor should be similar

Fig. 10-13. Two examples of bad construction.

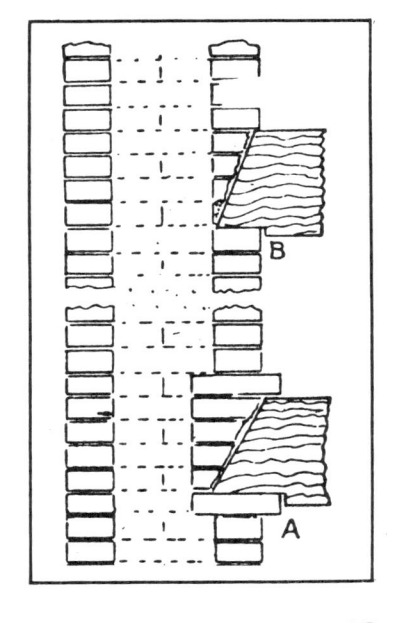

185

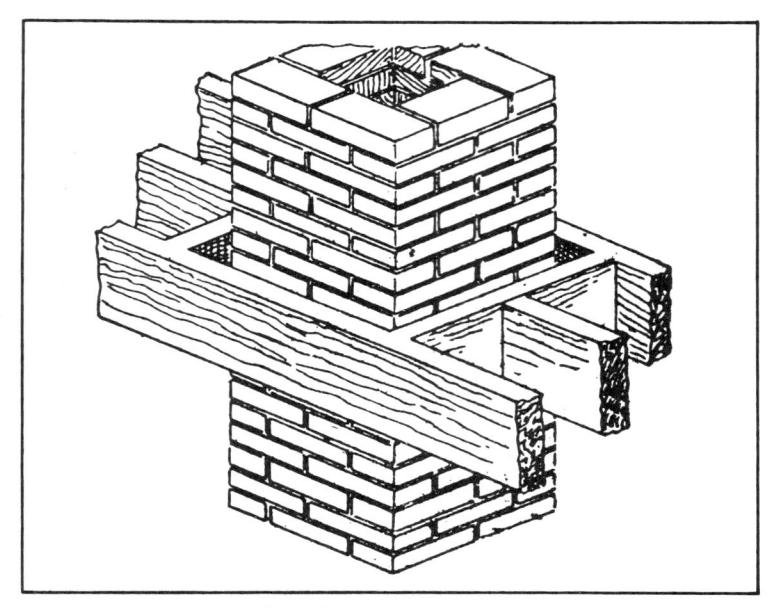

Fig. 10-14. An example of good construction.

to that shown (Fig. 10-14) in which there is no connection between the chimney and the frame of the house.

The chimney of the stove-heated house (Fig. 10-15) has for more than 40 years escaped some of the penalties of ignoring chimney philosophy; with eight stove connections the chimney certainly strains the idea that each connection should have its private flue. The house is built on a side hill which permits a basement tenement. Ordinarily the chimney gives satisfactory service for seldom are more than two or three openings in use at once. When a high wind blows over the hilltop, an occasional down draft blows smoke back into the various rooms, but not worse than in neighboring houses in which the chimneys were built with due regard for chimney efficiency. This is simply an instance of chimney temperament.

The offending of the rule regarding placing flues opposite each other (Fig. 10-16) brought dire results. The builder took a chance for it seemed that all things considered, there was no better way to serve the one-story ell kitchens of a double house. One kitchen range behaved itself with perfect courtesy no matter how the wind and weather conducted themselves, but the range in the other kitchen seldom allowed anyone to stay in the room until long after

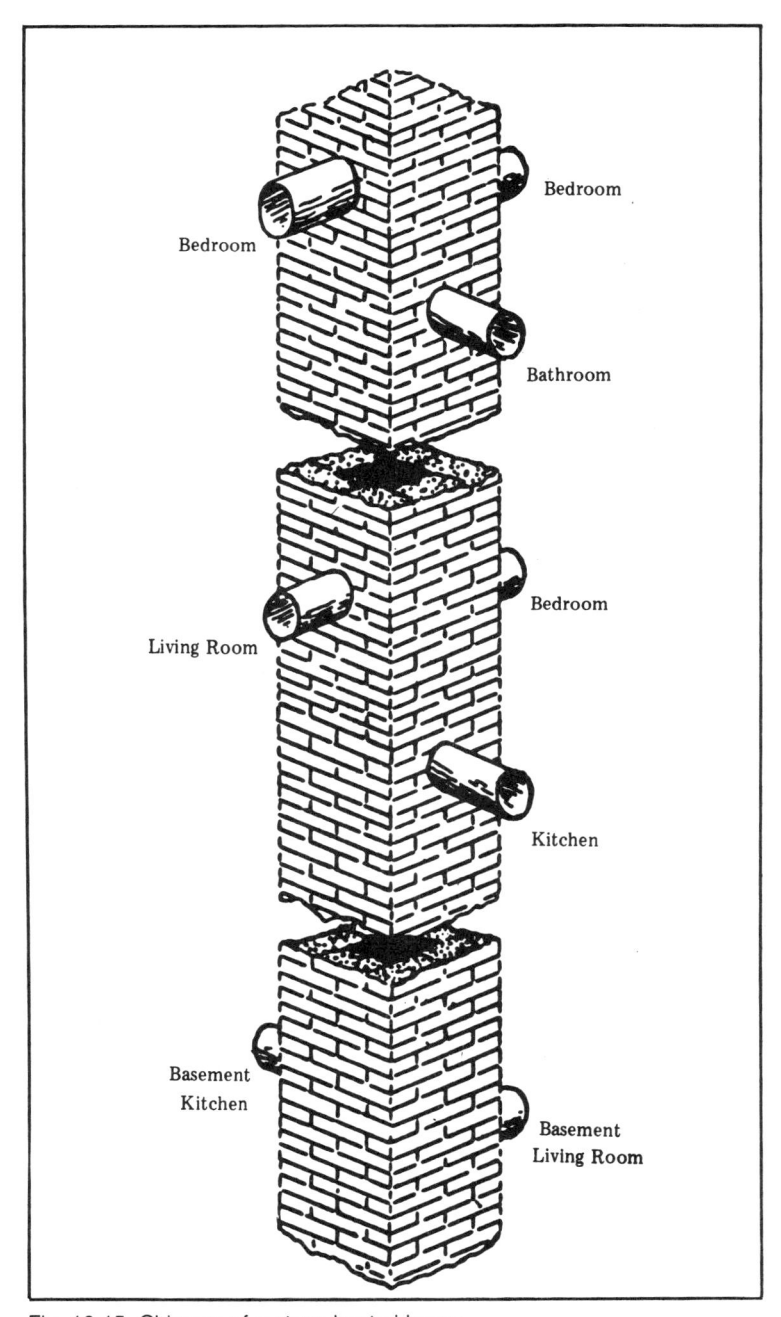

Fig. 10-15. Chimney of a stove-heated house.

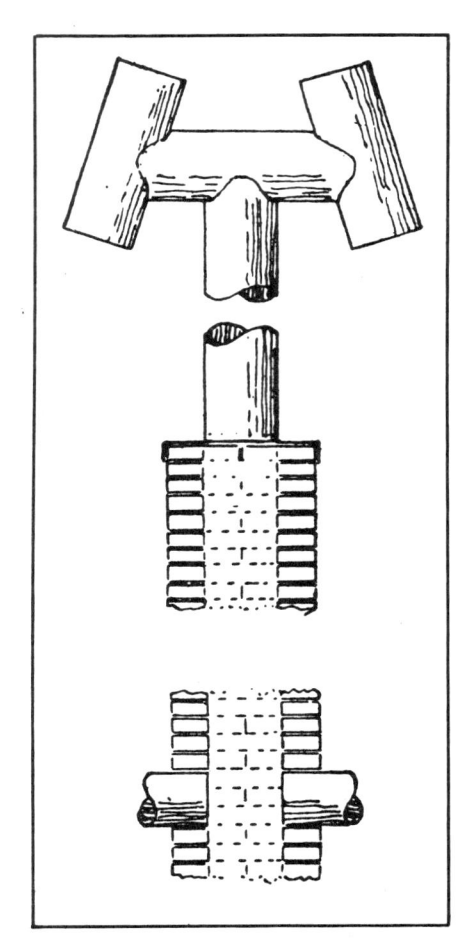

Fig. 10-16. A bad smoker and how it was cured.

the fire was lighted. Whether the first range was busy or not made no appreciable difference. The owner in desperation, but with little faith, followed a suggestion and had a galvanized iron chimney top made. It was brought to the house just as the lady of the house had built a fire in her range and retreated to the back porch until the smoke had assumed a texture that would allow her to return. The instant the chimney top dropped into place, the smoke in the kitchen seemed to tumble over itself as it was drawn through the open draft of the range, until in a few minutes there was no trace of smoke in the kitchen. The chimney has not since behaved itself in any manner the most meticulous could criticize.

Many flue connections (Fig. 10-17) have been made by placing a stovepipe thimble from the flue to the face of the plastered wall. In time pinholes made by the action of smoke chemicals will appear, but these can be seen only by drawing the pipe out of the chimney and inspecting it, which is seldom done, for its safety is taken for granted until a fire starts from the dust that settles upon the iron thimble. This is likely to happen on a cold day when the stoves are being pushed to their utmost. Instead of the iron pipe, a thimble of vitrified drain tile should be used. This will not be affected by smoke acids, nor will it become so hot as to endanger the house. Often in setting up a stove, a length of pipe will be pushed into the flue as at C, which shuts off the draft. The chimney is wrongly blamed for the smoke that backs into the room.

In building any chimney it is wise to leave its outside exposed wherever possible in the basement, in closets, and in the attic, for at best a chimney is more or less of a gamble. Once built, thorough inspection and repair are out of the question in most homes. A newly finished chimney may be given the smoke test by covering the top tightly, stopping all flue connections so no odor can pass out, and building a smudge fire of oily rags in the bottom of the flue. Smoke leakage may then be tested by the odor, but repairs may be made from the outside only unless so near the top that the chimney can be taken down to the leak and rebuilt if a bad leak cannot be reached otherwise. Sometimes the oil of peppermint or other pungent liquid or gas is used instead of the smudge. The flue itself may be inspected for stoppage or for the accumulation of soot (Fig. 10-18) by using a small hand mirror as suggested.

Every chimney should be fitted with a cleanout (Fig. 10-19) near the bottom for the accumulation of soot, scale, and perhaps

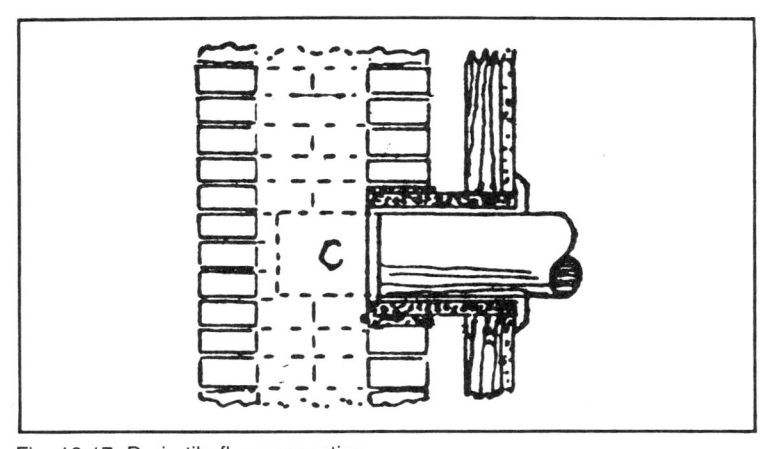

Fig. 10-17. Drain tile flue connection.

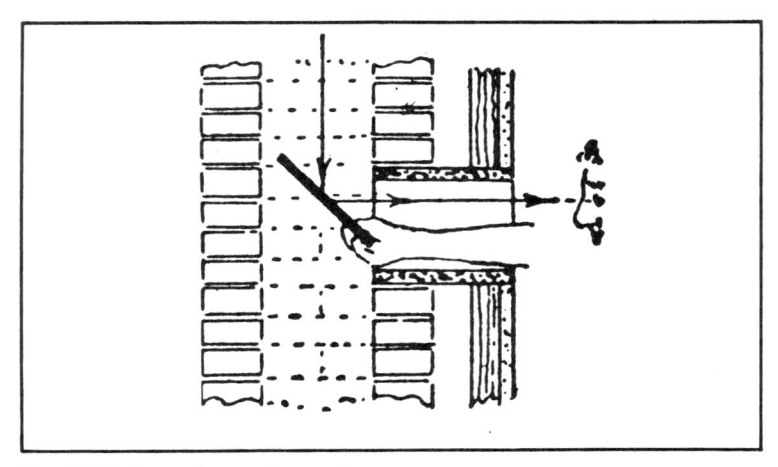

Fig. 10-18. Inspecting a chimney flue.

birds nests. This debris should be removed occasionally, or the flue may become filled to the lower connection when trouble is near at hand.

FENCE

There are two basic ways to construct fences. One is to simply hang the fence on posts set in the ground, and the second is to stretch the fence. A stretched fence is stronger, looks better, and will last longer.

Cedar is the best wood to use for the posts as it resists rot naturally better than any other type of common wood. If you can cut

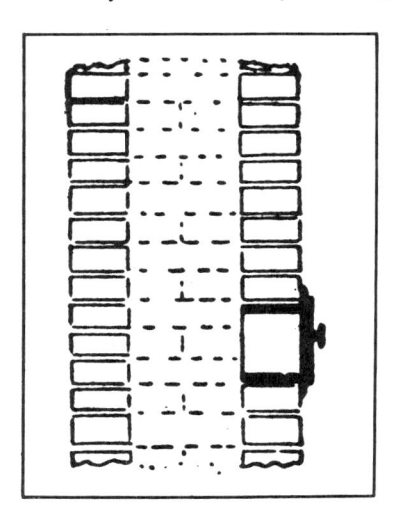

Fig. 10-19. Every chimney should have a cleanout.

and peel your own cedar, then your only expense for the posts is labor. If you do not have a source of posts, you can buy cedar posts or pressure-treated posts (pine or cedar), or you can use metal posts. Cut and peel the posts between May and mid-July, since that is the time when it is easiest to peel the logs. It is best to cut the logs a year in advance of the planned time of use. Not only are the logs easier to handle, but they absorb creosote better and resist rot better than green wood.

The length of the posts depends on the type of fencing that you are using. We use a woven 4-foot fence with an added strand of barbed wire above the fence, so we use a 7- to 8-foot post. We don't use any posts less than 3 inches in diameter at the smaller end. Corner and brace posts should be larger than the line posts, usually about 6 to 8 inches in diameter.

Before we put the posts in the ground, we treat the ends with a preservative—1 part used motor oil to 3 parts creosote. If you do use green wood, give the ends as many coats as you possibly can so the creosote has a chance to soak in somewhat. It is best if there is the space and time to soak the ends in the solution for about a month.

The postholes should be dug 30 inches to 36 inches deep, and at least twice the diameter of the post to allow room to tamp down the soil around it. The distance between each line post should be about 15 feet, and between the corner post and the brace post about 6 to 8 feet. Get the postholes dug as early in the spring as you can work the soil. It is much easier to work the soil when it is still wet. Don't, however, try to set a post in a hole with standing water as it is impossible to tamp down mud effectively, and you will not get a good solid post. Also, make sure to dig your postholes in straight lines, and line the posts up when you set them. You can't stretch a good fence on an uneven fence line. Besides, it looks a lot better. If you put in the corner posts first and sight visually or run a line between them, it is not hard to get them reasonably straight.

If you have the misfortune to have ledge close to the surface, it is still possible to put a post in as long as you don't have to put in too many in a row. If there is any soil above the ledge, dig as deep as you can, put the post in and with another smaller post, lay the second post on the ground, mark where they cross, notch them both, nail or bolt, then run a brace diagonally to a point 3 feet from the base (Fig. 10-20). Be sure to put the diagonal brace on the opposite side from the side that the fence will run on. You can also use this method even if there is no soil, starting at the base of the post. For corner posts, it is best to use the dead man method (Fig. 10-21). Bury a log about 10

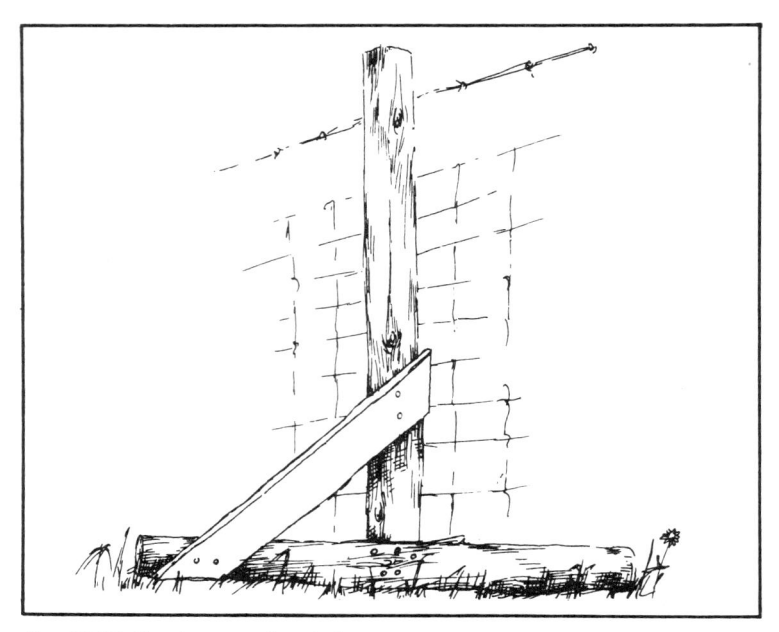

Fig. 10-20. Bracing a post on ledge.

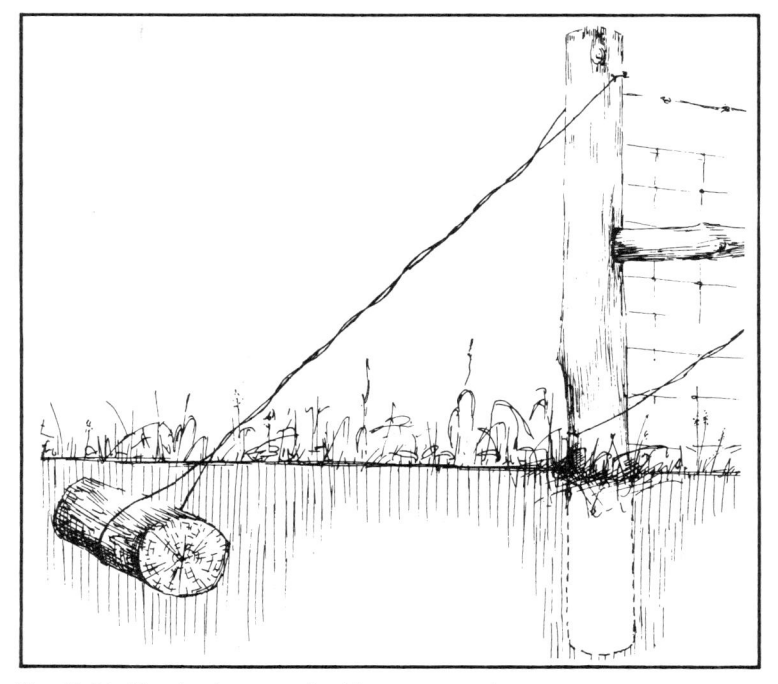

Fig. 10-21. The dead man method for corner posts.

feet away on the outside of the fence and wire the fence post from the top to the buried log.

The corner posts and the brace posts (next post up on either side) have to be braced against the strain of the stretched fence. We set brace posts about 6 to 8 feet from the corner posts; then we take a third post and run it horizontally about midway up, notching it in, and nailing (Fig. 10-22). The thing is then wired diagonally from the bottom of the corner post to the top of the brace post, and vice versa. To wire them we use a 12-gauge wire and cut the wire twice the distance of the diagonal plus 1 foot. Staple the one end to the top of the post and run the wire to the bottom of the other post and staple, then run the other end back up to the other side of the top of the first post and staple again. Take a large screwdriver and twist the wires together until they are good and tight, but not too tight or they will pull the bottom of the post out. Repeat the process for a diagonal running the other way.

After you have dug your postholes in a straight line, and you have painted the large end with preservative, stick it in the ground. The reason for putting the larger end in the ground is that it makes it harder to pull out, which is the whole object, unless you have to move the fence at some later date. Make sure that the post is perpendicular to the world rather than to the ground. It is best to use a level on uneven ground. Throw a couple of shovelfuls of dirt in

Fig. 10-22. The corner post has to be braced.

around the base of the post and tamp it down. We use a piece of wood about 5 feet in length and about 1 inch in diameter. If you don't get the post in solidly, no amount of stretching is going to give you a solid fence. You also get much better results from a small diameter tamping stick than from a larger one as you put more pressure per square inch on the soil. Do not put in any rocks bigger than a small stone, since they are very hard to tamp in properly and tend to move around in the freezing and thawing. Strangely, there is never enough dirt to fill the hole back in, so just dig some from a couple of feet away to finish. Be sure to fill the hole, tamping every couple of shovelfuls until it is filled all the way.

Now that the posts are in and the corner posts are braced, it is time to stretch the fence (Fig. 10-23). The equipment that we use is a tractor, truck, car, or block and tackle, in that order of preference, two 5-foot 2×4s with four bolt holes drilled through them, and four 4½-inch bolts with square heads and plenty of washers. Use square-headed bolts instead of carriage bolts as the wood will lose its grip after a couple of boltings. You also need hammers, heavy-duty wire staples (not a staple gun), and lots of friends. A good strong chain is needed unless you are using a block and tackle. If you do use a block and tackle, you need a six strand one.

Attach the fence to the corner post at one end by wrapping the horizontal wires around the post, then wrap them around themselves. Roll the fence along the posts up to the next corner post. Stretch only one side at a time.

Attach the 2×4s to the far end of the fence just behind a vertical strand for that little added gripping power. Wrap the chain around the middle of the 2×4s and attach it to your tractor, truck, car, or block and tackle. As you position your pulling vehicle, be sure to get the fence next to the posts so you don't have to stretch it sideways as well as lengthwise to staple it to the posts. Have someone stand near the starting corner post—not too close—and have him yell if the corner post starts out of the ground. Stretch the fence to a point of maximum tension, but just short of pulling the corner post out. Then staple like mad. Put the staples in on a diagonal so they do not hit the same grain of the wood. When you get up to the corner post, use two staples per wire to hold it from slipping when you release the tension from the tractor. Continue around the fence, one side at a time.

When stretching barbed wire, we attach the chain directly to the wire. Stretch all wire fences slowly and stand clear of the fence (especially barbed wire) when it is being stretched, in case either the staples holding it come out, or the wire breaks.

Fig. 10-23. Stretching the fence.

To stretch a very short length of fence, it is impractical to use a tractor, etc. Attach at one end as before. Roll the fence out and pull as tight as possible. Then bolt the 2×4s right next to the end to be pulled and use either a post or a crowbar as a lever and stretch it around the endpost. This is good only for short distances.

MODULAR COLD FRAME

A cold frame is a useful and sometimes necessary tool for gardening enthusiasts. It can be used to grow salad vegetables in early spring, to harden off plants on their way to the garden, and to grow salad vegetables in late fall and early winter.

Positioning a cold frame over an open basement window or using a soil heating coil can provide a heat source and thus extend the use of cold frames into winter and early spring.

A cold frame can be used, initially, to grow spring and fall salad vegetables and to harden off garden bound plants in spring. The design of cold frames can be improved in several ways. Windows on top of a cold frame should be positioned at an angle to receive the sun's rays as close to perpendicular as possible for any time of the year that the cold frame is to be used. Construct the cold frame in bolt-together, modular sections in order to change locations easily. An insulated cover that can be put over the top of the cold frame at night will reduce heat loss when temperatures are low.

Calculating the Angle of the Cold Frame Top

The correct angle for the top of a cold frame depends on the position of the sun during the period the cold frame is used. The angle of the sun from the horizon (a_n) for any day of the year is calculated by using the following formula: *$a_n = 90$ degrees $+ D - L$.* D = declination, or the sun's angular distance north or south of the equator at solar noon. For the Northern Hemisphere, D is positive for north declinations and negative for south declinations. Declinations for each day of the year are listed in the *Farmer's Almanac*. L = latitude of the location where the cold frame is to be changing constantly from day to day, and it is necessary to calculate an average angle for the period the cold frame is to be used. In this way the angle of cold frame top (a_r) will receive the sun's rays as close to perpendicular as possible for the period of the cold frame's use (Fig. 10-24). The angle of the cold frame top from horizontal (a_t) is calculated as follows: *$a_t = 90$ degrees $- a_n$.* For a location in, say, southeastern Massachusetts (approximately 42°N latitude), the spring use period is approximately from April 1 through May 15.

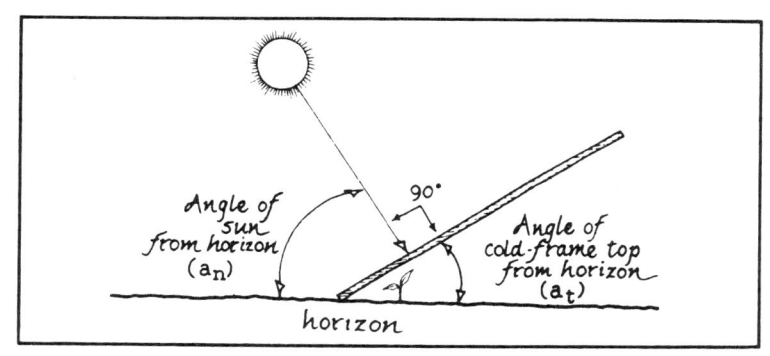

Fig. 10-24. The angle of the cold frame top will receive the sun's rays as nearly perpendicular as possible for the period of the cold frame's use (drawing by Liz Buell).

The fall use period is approximately September 15 through early November. The early, midpoint, and late day angles for each period are calculated as in Table 10-1.

It is good practice to cater to the cold or short day side of the period of cold frame use in choosing the angle of the top (a_t). Choose angles that correspond more to the midpoint of the short day half of the use period. This corresponds to approximately April 8 or $a_t = 35$ degrees for the spring period and October 28 or $a_t = 55$ degrees for the fall period.

Modular Design

Constructing a cold frame in modular, bolt-together sections permits the gardener to change cold frame locations very easily. In this way the cold frame can be moved to cover fresh soil from season to season or stored easily when not in use.

Figure 10-25 shows a side view of the cold frame used for spring and fall applications. The modular insert is added or removed

Table 10-1. Early, Midpoint, and Late Day Angles for Spring and Fall.

Spring Use Dates	a_n	a_t
April 1	43.5°	46.5°
April 22	60°	30°
May 15	67°	23°
Fall Use Dates		
September 15	51°	39°
October 15	39.5°	50.5°
November 15	29.5°	60.5°

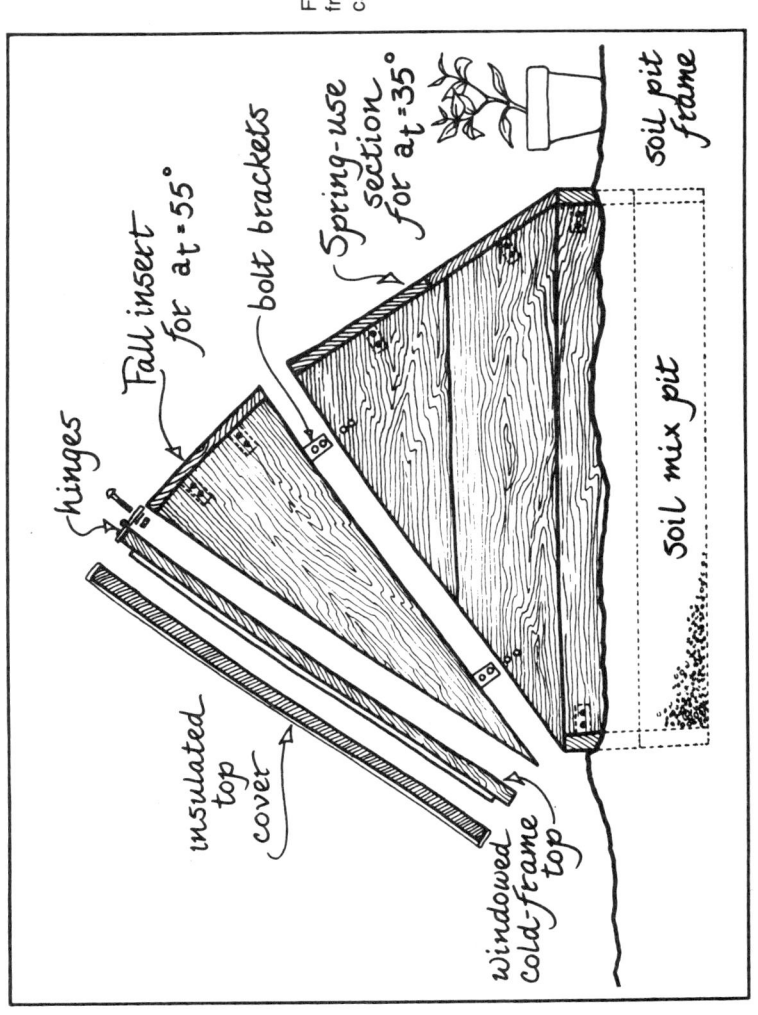

Fig. 10-25. Side view of the cold frame used for spring and fall applications (drawing by Liz Buell).

to change the angle of the cold frame top according to the season. An insulated top cover can be used to prevent heat loss on really cold nights. Also, the back of the cold frame is sloped 90 degrees from the top in order to maximize the surface area of the soil protected by the cold frame.

Construction

Basically, the cold frame can be constructed from any suitable materials available. Its size depends on the size of area you need, but two large storm windows often make a convenient top. You may make the frame from salvaged planks and level the bottom plank of the rear section in order for the cold frame top to close flush. Each section is fastened together using stove bolts and angle brackets. To minimize heat loss, the adjoining edges of each section are insulated with weather stripping. The top cover is hinged to the rear section for easy access into the cold frame.

The fall insert section is also constructed with planks and requires additional beveling in order for the top to close flush. The insert is also weather-stripped and bolted to the rest of the cold frame with straight brackets and stove bolts. The insulated top cover is simply a sheet of ⅝-inch plywood with a 1-inch-by-2-inch frame large enough to fit over the windows of the cold frame top. The inside of the cover is lined with Styrofoam (from throw-away packaging) for insulation. Leave room for an airspace between the cover and the cold frame windows.

This cold frame can be used in spring and fall. The insulated cover allows you to start plants earlier and protect them during cold nights. The fall insert provides greater heating efficiency during the fall period, and the modular design allows you to move the cold frame to the most convenient location.

HOTBED

You should get a jump on the growing season with sturdy plants of your own. Your tomatoes and peppers should be the best you ever raised, and your cole plants ought to crawl with vitamins. You can do this by raising your seedlings in a hotbed.

There are no hard and fast rules (for making a hotbed, which is an enclosed bed of soil used to force or raise seedlings with the heat emitted by its fermenting manure.

A hotbed is nothing more than a wooden box with a transparent cover. If you can't get secondhand windows, simple frames covered with 4-mil plastic are suitable.

Use materials at hand. Just make a reasonably tight box with a transparent sloping top. Partly fill it with horse manure covered with loam. Assure yourself of a quantity of horse manure that is fairly fresh, without too much bedding mixed in. Pile it in a spot where you can fork it over at three- or four-day intervals before you expect to use it. If left undisturbed for a few weeks, it will heat. You will find a batch of gray ashes-like stuff of no value. Don't get it more than a couples weeks ahead.

The size of the hotbed will be determined by two things:

- How big your operation will be. Dozens and dozens of plants, naturally, will take more space than a few.
- How many windows or frames and materials you have on hand.

When you have collected the materials, take your saw, hammer, square, and nails, plus your ingenuity, and get busy. Because a hotbed is really just a slanted box with a transparent top, its size and construction depend on your preferences and the material you have at hand (Figs. 10-26 and 10-27).

Assemble the hotbed so it will face south. It preferably should have a windbreak formed by a building or solid fence behind it.

Pile the manure you have so carefully nurtured into a depth of a foot or more. Horse manure seems just made for the job. That from cows doesn't heat well, and what hens make gets too hot and doesn't last long enough. Pack it down firmly, but don't beat it into a cake. Sprinkle it with up to 10 gallons of water and cover with about 4 inches of loam. Put on the windows and let the mass cook for a few days until the heat really begins to generate.

The time in the spring when you do all this will be determined by how far north you live. It's best to wait for the snow to leave, but experience will teach you. It goes without saying that sometime in late winter you have started, in a sunny window, the plants you want to raise.

As soon as the hotbed is working, you can transplant seedlings into it. Leave space for growth because you won't move them until they go into the garden.

Keep an eye on the temperature. A thermometer hung in the shade of that top board is a good thing. The heat can reach 100° F. without half trying. That is one reason for having easily moved window sashes. You can regulate the temperature and ventilate by raising them as needed. Early on, a small block of wood is sufficient under them.

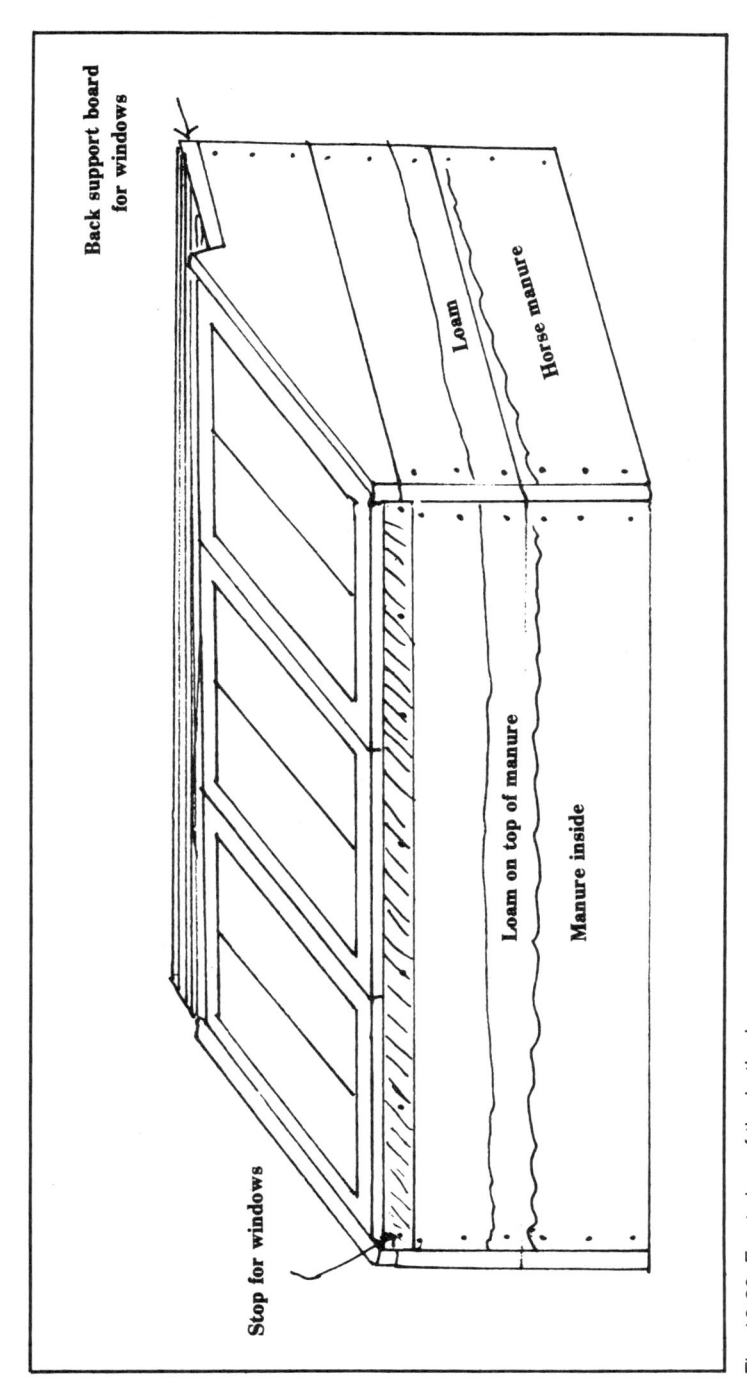

Fig. 10-26. Front view of the hotbed.

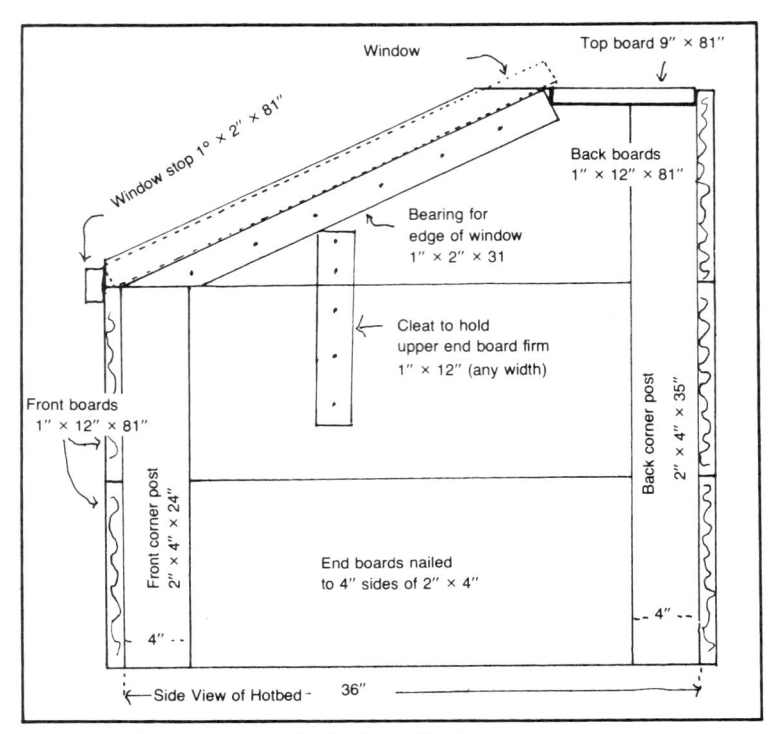

Fig. 10-27. Construction details for the hotbed.

On the other side of the coin, be prepared for cold nights. Horseblankets, old quilts, old rugs, or covers of like nature will help maintain an even temperature.

As the weather gets warmer, you'll want to ventilate more and more until a few days before transplanting. Then completely remove the windows to harden the plants, but keep an eye on the weather reports. Don't let a stray frost catch you with your windows off.

HONEY EXTRACTOR

It's called the Apel-Fisher honey remover. The chief designer and builder is Fred Apel. Even Apel admits that there is little new about the remover.

"I've seen the design before. I just built it better, simpler, cheaper," he says (Fig. 10-28).

The extractor will hold eight frames—four frames full depth and four smaller (shallow or medium) frames (Fig. 10-29). You can

Fig. 10-28. Designer Apel (left) and cobuilder Jeffrey Fisher (right) go over details of the honey remover (photo by Susan North Fisher).

Fig. 10-29. View of the honey remover showing the barrel, drill, pulleys, belt, shaft, and top support. Note the eight-frame capacity (photo by Susan North Fisher).

make the remover accommodate six medium and two full-depth frames if you like (Fig. 10-30). The remover has the following important features (Fig. 10-31).

- It's motor-driven.
- It has an "automatic" clutch.
- It features centrifugal removal of honey.
- It's all metal and durable.
- It costs less than 10 percent of commercial models.
- It's made mostly from used or scrounged parts.
- There's no reversing necessary.
- It requires low maintenance and is easily sanitized.
- It works.

The remover's outer container was made from an old 55-gallon steel drum. With the upper one-third removed with a friend's torch, the drum stands 24 inches high. It costs $6. The cutting job took five minutes. To be fancy, you can use a metal file around the new rim to smooth off any edges.

Handles were placed on the outside of the drum. We scavenged two aluminum ones from an abandoned boat, but anything strong will serve. Because of the size of the barrel, handles are necessary for convenient lifting and moving.

The "dynamic" centerpiece is an old washing machine spin cylinder. There is about ¼-inch clearance between the outer drum

Fig. 10-30. Top view of the loaded extractor. Note the two full-depth and six medium-depth frames (photo by Susan North Fisher).

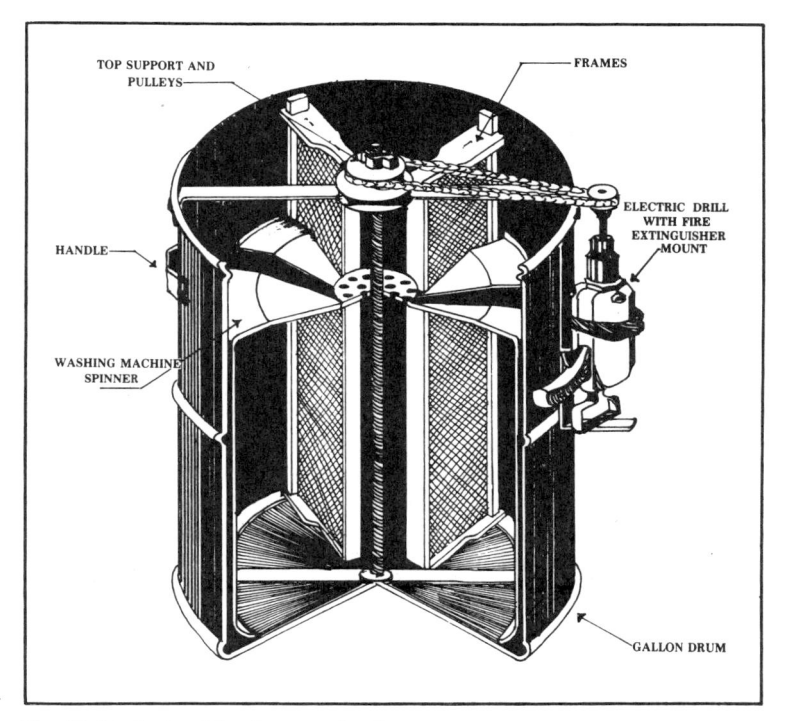

Fig. 10-31. Parts of the honey extractor.

and inner spinner. Because the spinners are enameled, they have a beautiful finish and don't need additional coatings. The drum can be primed with an epoxy-polyester clear finish. A pint can cost less than $3. A galvanized drum is also acceptable.

Turning the spin cylinder upside down, you cut slits to accommodate the number and sizes of frames you desire. We used a Carborundum blade on a circular power saw (Fig. 10-32). It may be necessary to cut out small tabs on the bottom edge to accept one corner of the frames (Fig. 10-33). Remember that you must equalize the distance between frame slits to maintain weight balance. Note, also, that you reverse the spinner. Its bottom in the washing machine becomes the top in the remover.

Mounting the spinner in the drum is probably the most challenging job. We fitted and glued a strong piece of plastic from the bottom of an old bucket and placed it into the bottom of our spinner. The plastic can be sterilized. A few extra holes can be drilled into it to permit honey escape. The washing machine spinner already has holes, so no extra drilling is needed.

Fig. 10-32. Top view of the spinner showing cuts made with the Carborundum blade on a circular saw (photo by Susan North Fisher).

A ⅝-inch, galvanized, 26-inch-long, all-threaded shaft rod is mounted down the center of the spinner (Fig. 10-34). Two nuts are fastened—one from the top and one from the bottom to secure the

Fig. 10-33. Bottom view of the spinner showing plastic insert and shaft nut. Note the small tabs cut out to accommodate the corner of the frames (photo by Susan North Fisher).

Fig. 10-34. Apel removes the spinner with frames in place by holding the threaded, galvanized shaft (photo by Susan North Fisher).

spinner on the shaft. Have about ¾ inch extending below the bottom nut. All bolts and nuts can be stainless steel.

The mounting device is simply top and bottom support bars (Fig. 10-35). Two ¾-inch ball bearings were "cannibalized" from an old wheel barrel. They are simply fitted into the holes drilled in the support bars. The bars were scrap flat iron. The bars are fastened to the drum with the stainless steel bolts. The spinner rests on the bottom support while the top one locks it in place. Measurement is crucial in hole drilling. Your spinner will wobble if you're not exact here.

You can fashion a hand crank and extract honey manually. In an earlier model we used a washing machine motor (2,000 RPM) with a 10:1 gear reducer and some pulleys and belts. We achieved 200 RPM (ideal for honey extraction), but we felt the system was cumbersome and complex.

A far easier and simpler system is to employ your electric shop drill with a belt/pulley arrangement. An excellent drill mount is to

Fig. 10-35. The top support bar is removed after the pulleys (photo by Susan North Fisher).

fasten an old fire extinguisher mount to the outside of the drum. This permits the drill to be snapped on and off easily. Be sure to place it at the proper height.

Ours is a ½-inch drill with 575 RPM. By placing a 3-inch pulley on the shaft and a 1-inch one on an old and broken drill bit, we achieved an approximate 3:1 reduction. We estimate that our spinner turns 175-190 RPM.

Our belt is a hollow braid polypropylene rope. It is slightly loose, so at slow speeds it slips. This slipping prevents honeycomb damage from abrupt jumps when starting and stopping (our automatic clutch). No reversing is necessary. Honey is removed from both sides of the comb.

A final feature permits honey removal from the drum. We drilled a 1-inch hole in the bottom of the barrel. A simple wine cork makes a seal. We strain the honey through the hole, using cheesecloth and 60 mesh nylon cloth. The best cleaner for the remover is the honeybee. Simply place the sticky machine in the sun near a bee yard. By the next day it will be spotless (Fig. 10-36).

ELECTRIC SEEDLING MACHINE

Walter Thompson starts vegetable and flower seedlings in a growing area he built in the basement (Fig. 10-37). He used a door for the base of his unit, raising it up to a comfortable working height. On each corner he nailed a 30-inch piece of 2×4 in an upright position. Across the top he nailed a 1-inch-by-4-inch piece of board for a rail. He covered the top of the frame with clear plastic, stapling it to the board rails. Next he drilled two holes ½ inch in diameter in each of the end rails about 8 inches from the 2-inch-by-4-inch corner posts.

Plastic side and end panels completely enclose the growing area. These panels are stapled only at the top, so Thompson can roll them up to tend the plants. He installed a 70-degree heating cable on the door, being careful not to let the wires touch each other, and held the cable in place with masking tape.

A 4-foot ceiling fluorescent light fixture with growlux bulbs are hung inside. The hanging chains are threaded through the holes in the end rails and fastened with a nail through the chain and across the hole. This arrangement allows Thompson to vary the height of the light as the plants grow larger. One end of the light can be raised higher than the other to accommodate plants of different growing rates.

Thompson plants seeds in a sterile growing mixture in flats.

Fig. 10-36. Giant hive that necessitated designing and building the honey remover (photo by Susan North Fisher).

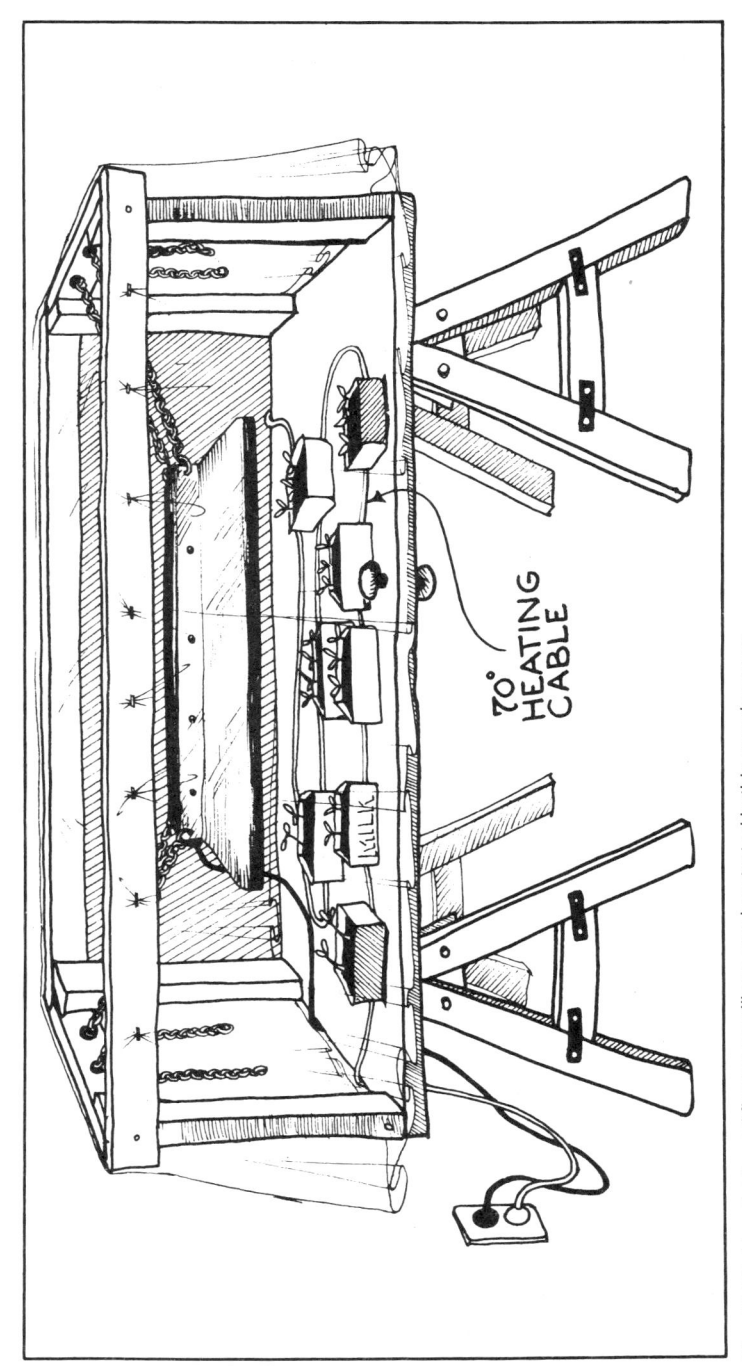

Fig. 10-37. Vegetable and flower seedlings can be started in this growing area.

After planting the seeds, he encloses the flat in a plastic bag to maintain a high humidity and puts them in his growing box on top of the 70-degree heat cable. After a few days he turns on the growlux light, so when the seedlings first appear they will get plenty of light to develop into sturdy healthy plants. At this time the light is only about 4 inches above the flat. A timer on the light keeps it burning 16 hours each day.

The side and ends of the plastic curtains are kept closed except to water the plants. The 70-degree cable and the enclosed area keep the temperature and humidity near the ideal level. The 16-hour light is also near optimum for these seedlings.

Thompson has added another 4-foot lighting fixture, and he now has a growing area 3 feet wide by 6 feet long. The two lights cover this area well, and he can grow a lot of plants in this area.

SNOWSHOES

One of the necessities of winter life is the snowshoe. From the first deep snowfall of late autumn until the spring thaw, the snowshoe is used for hunting, trapping, ice fishing, and hiking. At home, snowshoes can be the only means of reaching the mailbox, the wood pile, or the barn. Before the advent of the snowmobile, the snowshoe was the most important mode of winter transportation. On snowshoes a man could go where no sleigh could, and even now, there are hills too steep and woods too thick for the snowmobile. With a little ingenuity and a bit of patience, a good pair of serviceable snowshoes can be made.

Materials and Tools

4	white spruce	¾" × ½" × 60"
4	white spruce	¾" × ½" × 10"
4	white spruce	¾" × ½" × 7"
4	bolts	10 × 32 × 1½"
2	bolts	10 × 32 × 2"
6	nuts	10 × 32
12	washers	
16	rawhide	⅜" × 60"
16	rawhide	¼" × 60"
1	varnish	pint
1	white pine	2" × 4" × 60"
8	wood screws	
24	nails	6 or 8 penny

1 handsaw
1 hand drill
1 7/32-inch drill bit
1 sandpaper—fine grit
1 water tub
1 source of hot water
1 sharp knife
8 bricks
4 wooden sawhorses

Frames

Snowshoe frames are usually made of white spruce, although there's some disagreement over which wood is the best. Professional snowshoe makers claim that white ash is the best wood available. Amateur snowshoe makers who make snowshoes for their personal use have used the following wood with success: quaking aspen, Oregon ash, paper birch, slippery elm, hickory, maple, white oak, white spruce, and black willow. White spruce bends easily without cracking and is readily available.

To prepare the frames for bending, take the four 60-inch-long pieces of white spruce, check them for warping, and then sand them. Drill one hole 2 inches from one end (the toe) and two holes at 2-inch intervals from the other end (the heel) in each piece of wood. Drill a hole 20 inches from the toe and another hole 36-inches from the toe. Run a 10×32×2-inch bolt and washer through the toe hole and fit a washer and nut onto the bolt. Do not tighten. Run a 10×32×1½-inch bolt and washer through each of the holes at the heel and fit a washer and nut onto each. Tighten (Fig. 10-38).

Fill your water tub with boiling water. The ideal water tub is the bathtub, but get permission first from the rest of the household. If you do use your bathtub, get the water as hot as possible. Put the frames into the tub, then drape heavy cloth or towels over them. Get boiling water and pour it over the towels. Keep the shower curtain

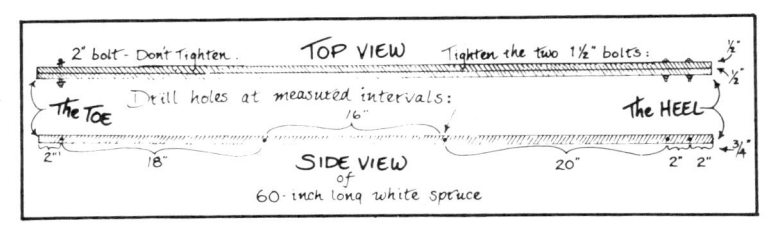

Fig. 10-38. Drill holes in the pieces of white spruce as indicated (drawing by Liz Buell).

closed and the bathroom door shut. Let the frames stay in the homemade turkish bath for two hours.

While the frames are steaming, make your bending jigs. To do this, place two sawhorses 16 inches apart. To form the stretchers, nail a 10-inch piece of white spruce on one sawhorse. Nail a 7-inch piece of white spruce on the other. Form an open-ended 12-inch-by-12-inch square of white pine and secure it to the sawhorse with the 10-inch piece of white spruce (Fig. 10-39).

Remove the frames from their bath, and one at a time place the toe into the square you made on the sawhorse. Slowly bend the frame down towards the sawhorses. At the same time pull the two pieces of white spruce apart until they fit around the stretchers. Weight the frames down with bricks and allow them to dry for one week (Fig. 10-40).

When the week is up, remove the frames from the sawhorses. Quickly insert the ½-inch-by-¾-inch-by-10-inch crossbars and ½-inch-by-¾-inch-by-7-inch white spruce. Secure them with wood screws. Lay the frames in a warm, dry place for two weeks.

Lacing with Babiche

The rawhide that fills a snowshoe is called *babiche*. Rawhide is simply the hide of an animal without the hair. Cowhide makes excellent babiche, deer hide is almost worse than none. When rawhide is dry, it's tough and inflexible. Only when it's wet is it

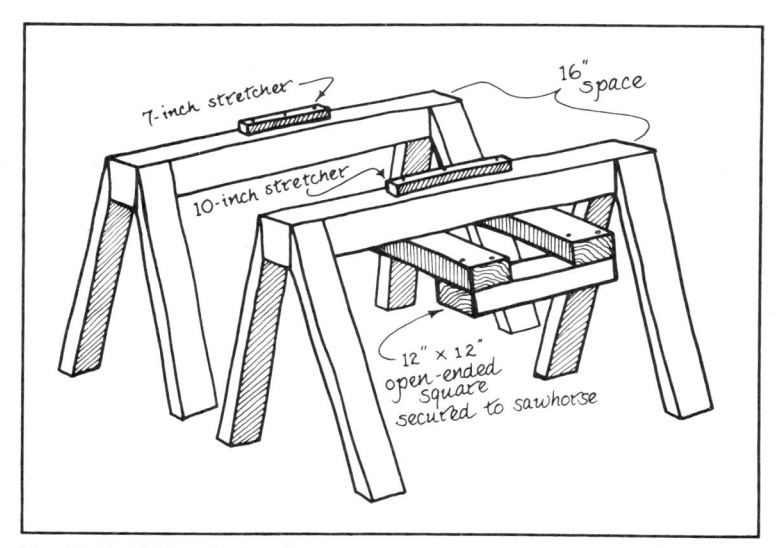

Fig. 10-39. Making the bending jigs (drawing by Liz Buell).

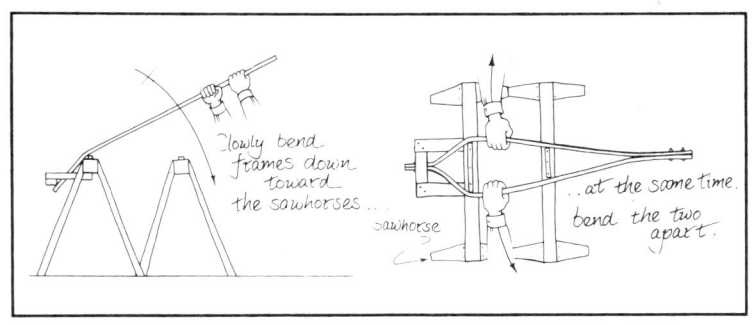

Fig. 10-40. Procedure for bending the frames (drawing by Liz Buell).

pliable enough to be worked. After obtaining your rawhide, check it for uniform thickness. To make the rawhide pliable, soak it in warm water just before lacing the frames.

Lacing the frames isn't as complicated as it seems, but it does take practice and patience. It is also very important to be sure to keep the tension on the rawhide at all times. You will find that you will have to splice the rawhide strips together. Splicing should always be done at the frame for added strength (Fig. 10-41).

Lace the center section first using the ⅜-inch rawhide. Work slowly and be sure to understand the pattern before starting. After the center sections of both frames have been laced, lay the frame flat to dry over night (Fig. 10-42A through 10-42F).

The next day, lace the toe and heel sections of the frames using ¼-inch rawhide. Lace each frame one at a time. If you look at Fig. 10-43, you will notice that lacing this pattern is like playing dot-to-dot. The pattern used by the Abanaki Indians is unusual. Instead of the hexagonal effect seen in the commercial snowshoe, the Abanaki

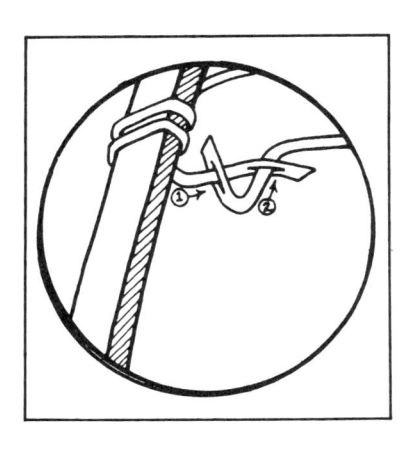

Fig. 10-41. Splice close to the frame (drawing by Liz Buell).

215

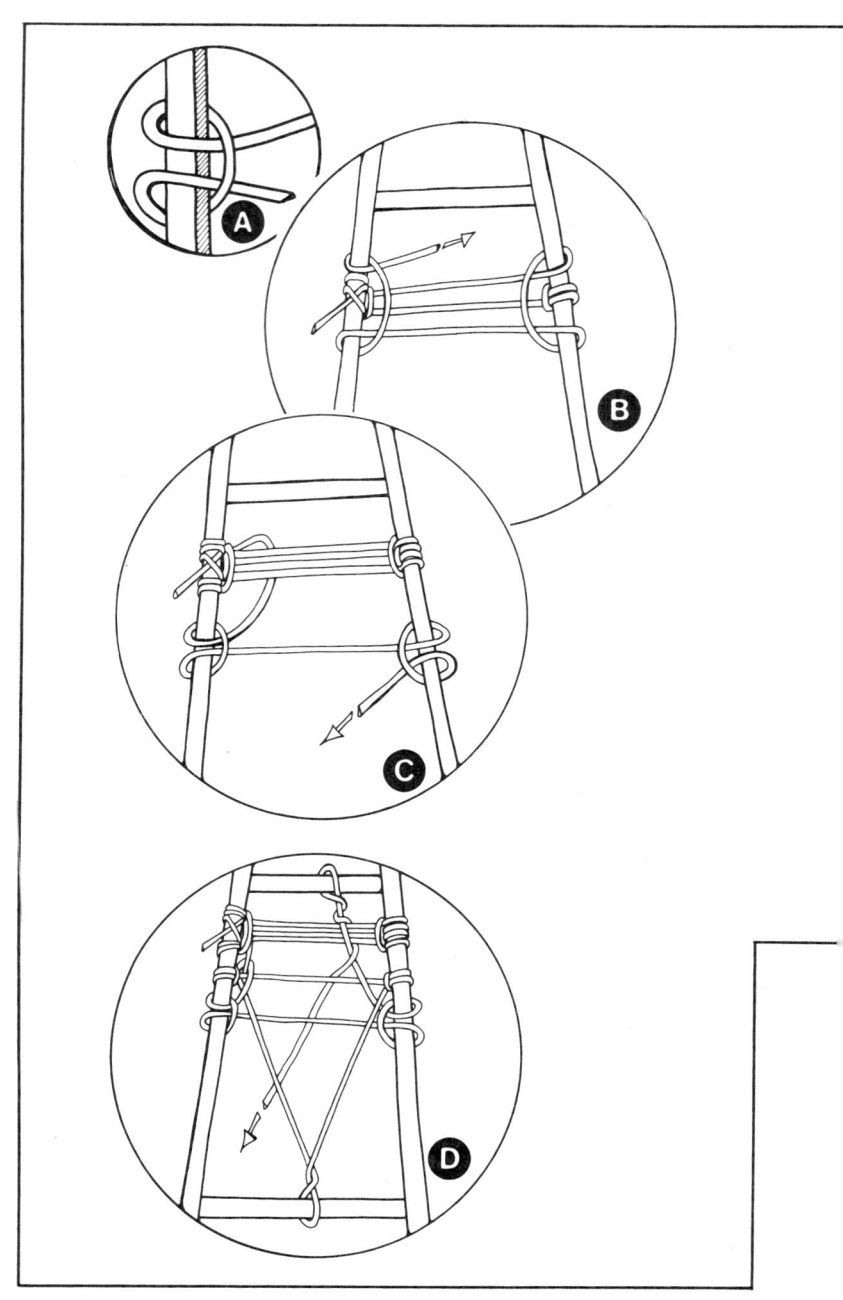

Fig. 10-42. Sequence for lacing the center sections of the frames (drawing by Liz Buell).

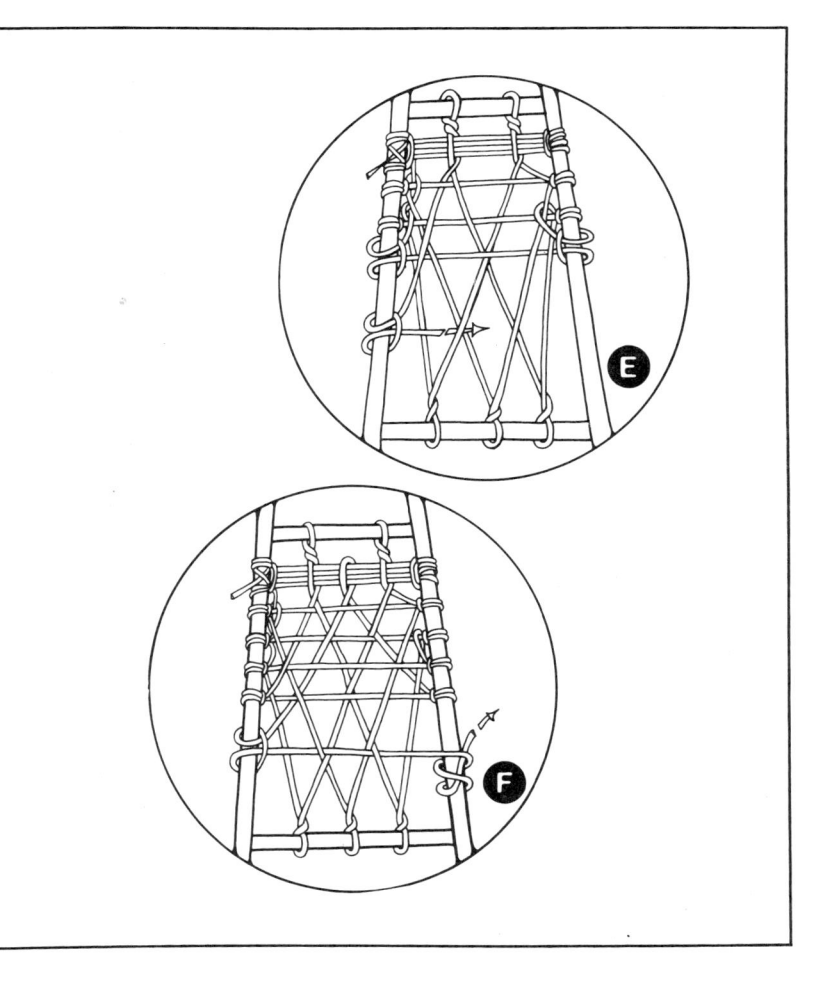

used the squared pattern. There seems to be no functional difference between the patterns—only an aesthetic one.

After lacing the toe and heel sections of both frames, lay them flat and let them dry thoroughly for at least one week. When dry, apply a heavy coat of varnish. A colored varnish can be used if a dark finish is desired.

The bindings for a pair of snowshoes can be made by using leftover rawhide. Two pieces 1 foot long and two pieces 3 feet long will be needed (Fig. 10-44).

Now all you have to do is wait for snow. When it comes, it won't take long for you to learn the knack of walking in your new snowshoes.

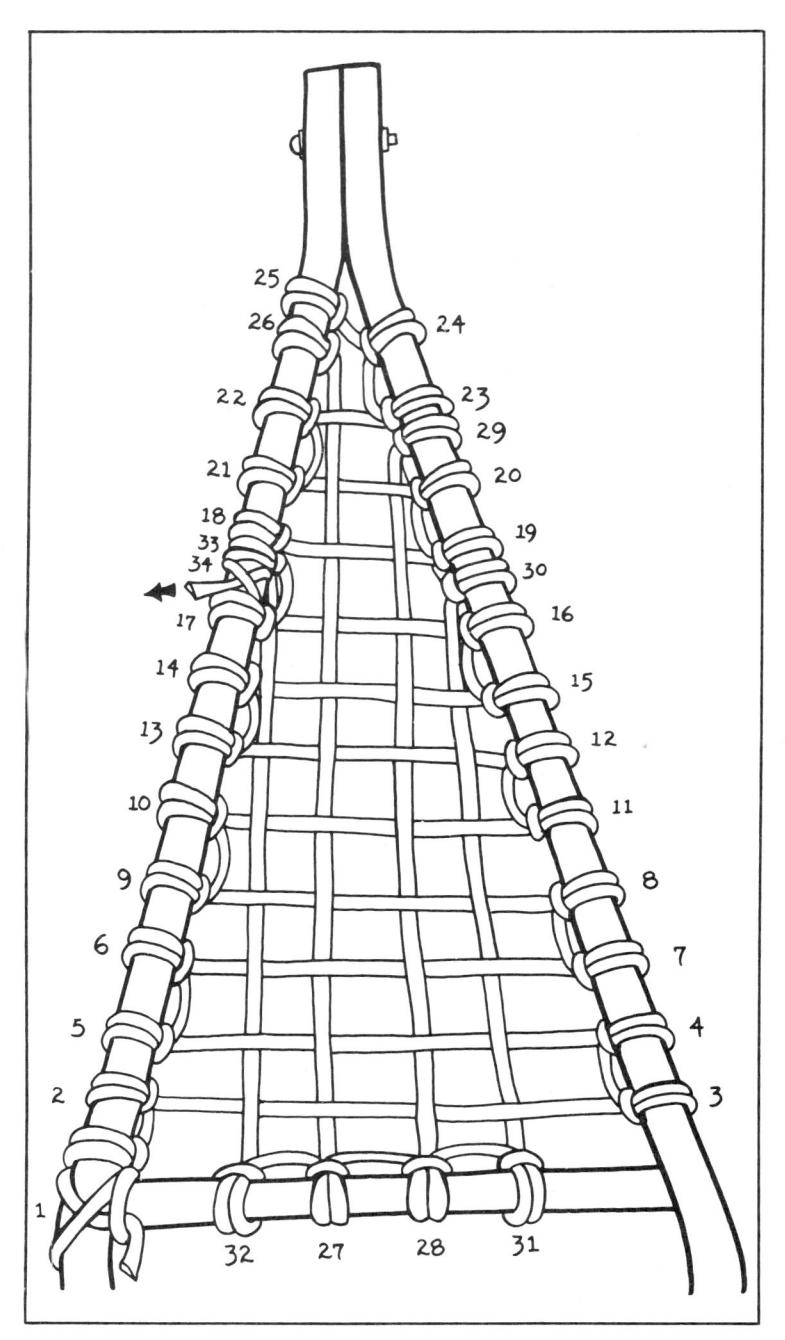

Fig. 10-43. Lacing this pattern is like playing dot-to-dot (drawing by Liz Buell).

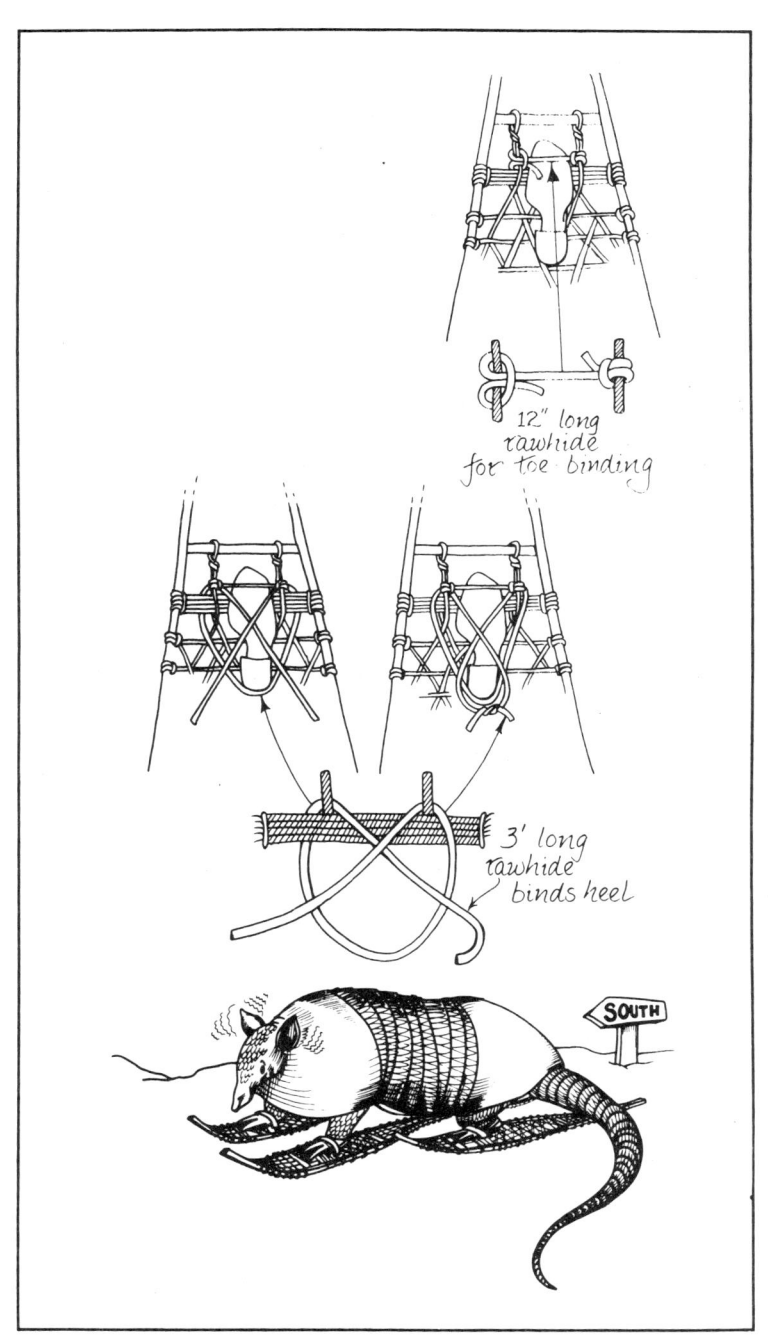

Fig. 10-44. Using leftover rawhide to make bindings (drawing by Liz Buell).

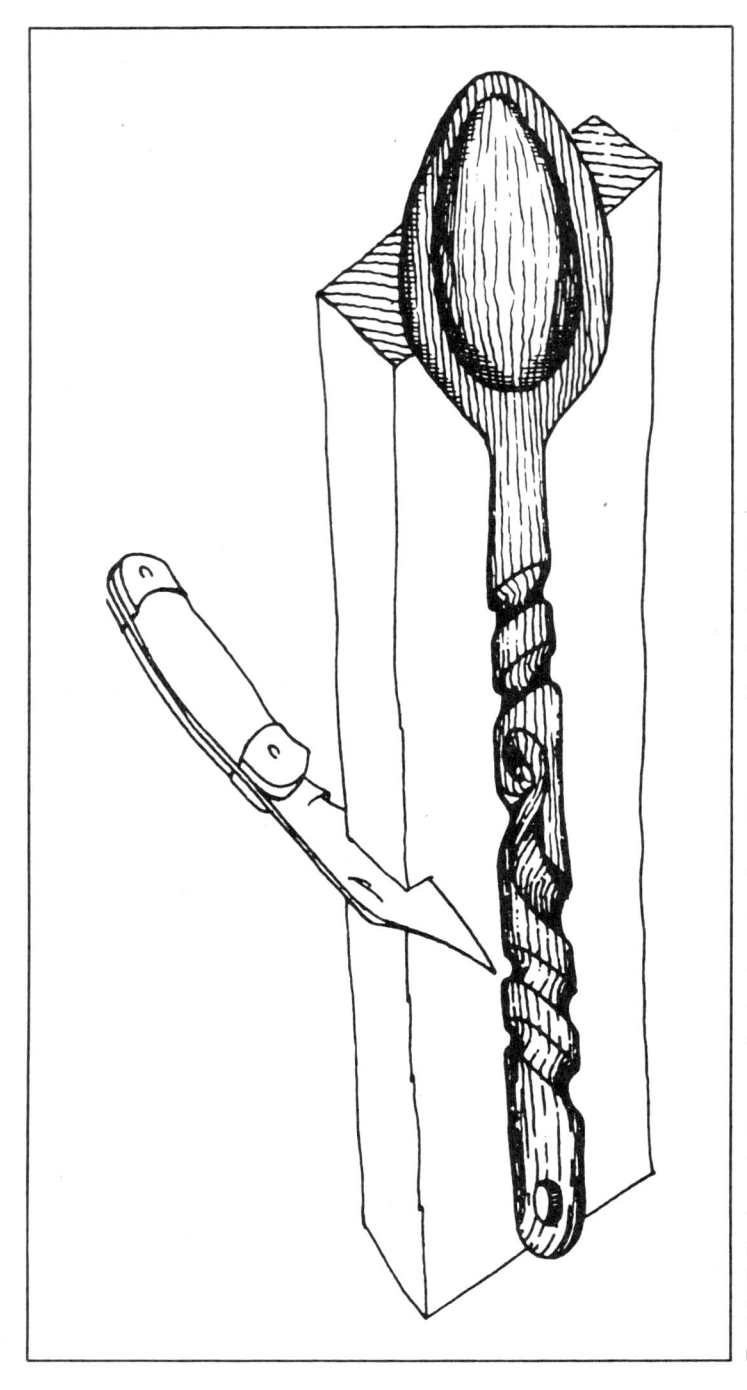

Fig. 10-45. Maple, red oak, or another hardwood works well for spoons (drawing by Liz Buell).

CARVING SPOONS

Hardwood is best for spoons (Fig. 10-45). Maple and red oak scraps from school shops, college woodworking studios, and small furniture factories are good. These small pieces, 10 to 15 inches long and 2 to 3 inches wide, are plentiful and are usually thrown out or burned.

Essential tools are a pencil, rasp, pocketknife, some form of gouge, and sandpaper. It is possible to start with wood so neatly sized that a saw is not necessary.

After wood and tools are assembled, draw a pattern or two (Fig. 10-46). Choose the most appealing one.

From the sides of the drawn handle, saw away excess wood. Cut angles to take off the square corners where the bowl will be and where the bowl will join the handle.

Begin to rasp, rounding the handle and bowl. Be prepared for a long process. Stop often to see how the spoon is progressing. Is the handle uneven? Is the bowl too square? Use a rasp more than anything else. The pocketknife is not as forgiving; it can take off a lot of wood quickly, but slips can cause changes in the shape of the spoon or leave marks that can't be removed.

The bowl and handle should progress evenly. The spot where bowl and handle join is always ticklish.

The bowl should be roughly rounded outside by now. Begin to dig it out. Start in with the gouge. Watch for slips. Leave enough wood so that there is no risk of gouging through the bowl.

After the spoon is rasped and gouged, it's time for sanding. Coarse sandpaper smooths out the gouge marks; fine sandpaper takes off the coarse sanding grooves. About here, after a lot of sanding the spoon will start to look good. Sanding is another long process best done outside.

Run the spoon through the dishwasher or wash it thoroughly. After it dries, oil it with mineral oil and let it dry again. Mix, beat, scoop, and spoon.

Wooden spoons will serve you well mixing bread or stirring soup or chili. Oiled regularly and kept away from hot stove lids or burners, they will last for years. Hung on the wall, they'll add class to the kitchen.

pattern...

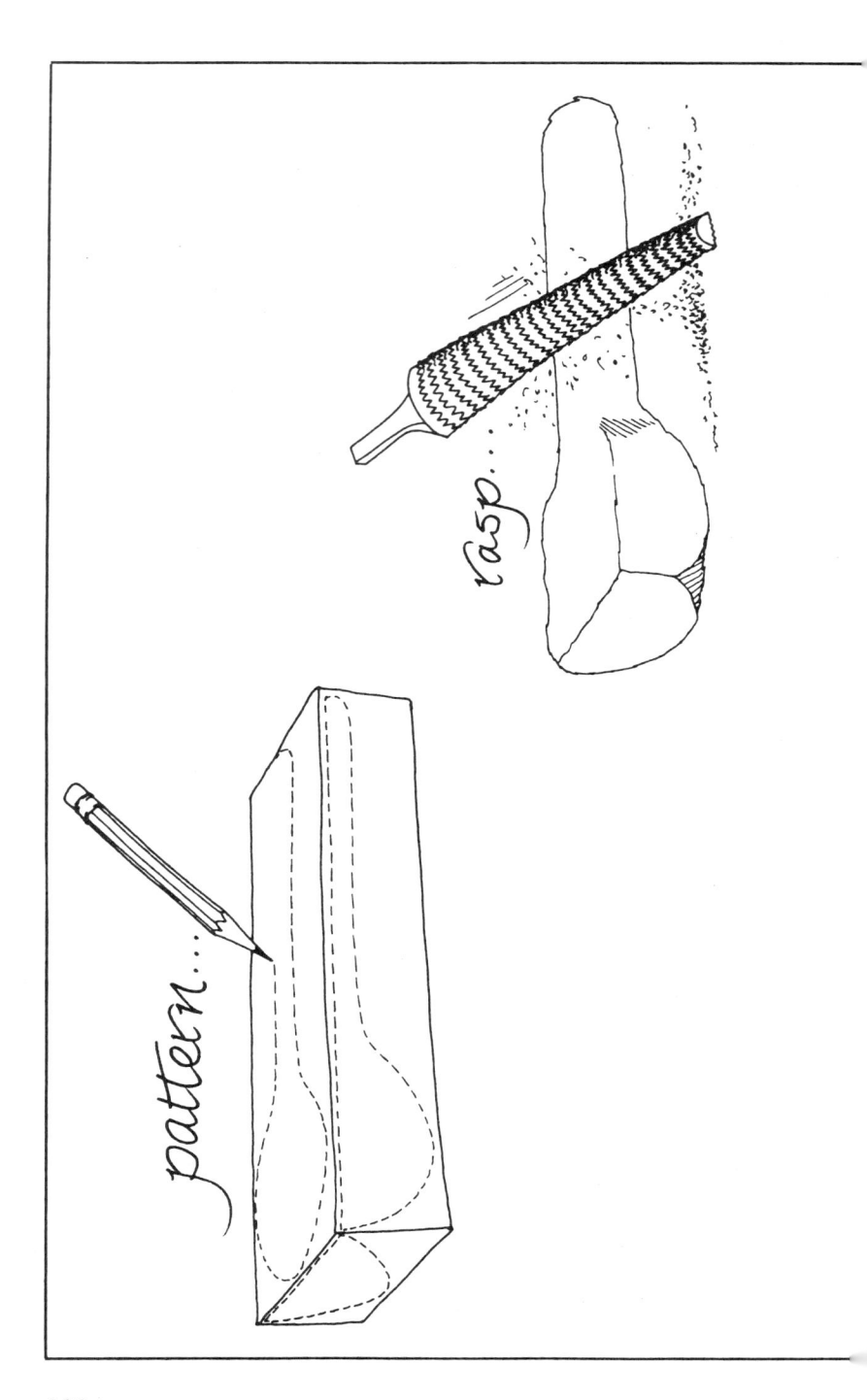

rasp...

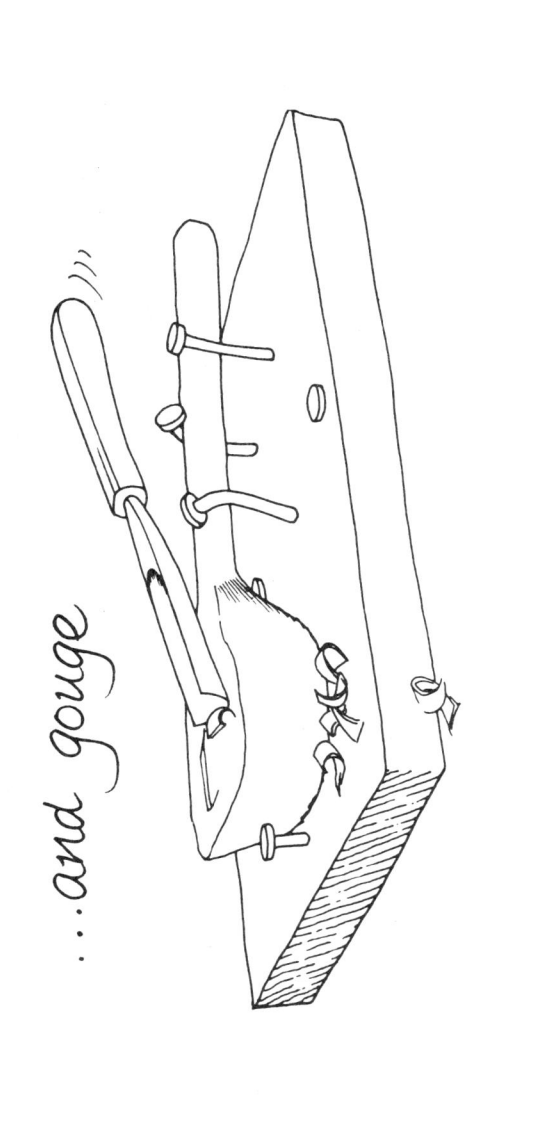

Fig. 10-46. Procedure for making a spoon (drawing by Liz Buell).

Chapter 11

Crafts

Sewing, quilting, spinning, and weaving are popular with homesteaders. This chapter examines these activities. Plus, there are instructions for making mittens, socks, and rugs.

SEWING

With a sewing machine, you can remodel used clothing and confidently sew new material. Thrift shops are good sources of material for your sewing fun. Those run by charitable organizations usually have the best prices. Garage sales may be your treasure house of secondhand garments.

Consider these points in judging used clothing. The more "yes" answers, the better.

- Is it washable?
- Does it have notions (zippers, lace, buttons, snaps) that can be used now or later?
- If it is to be ripped apart, does it have several large areas of useful material? Is it suitable for a new project?
- Will the scraps be handy for such homestead projects as quilting, doll clothes, or rug braiding?
- Will it fit someone with just a minor alteration?
- If it is a coat or jacket, are both the lining and other material in reasonable shape?
- Is the price, if any, right?

Ripping apart used clothing is not as traumatic as you might suppose. Do the first few stitches with a seam ripper or scissors. Grip the material on both sides of the seam and pull the pieces in opposite directions. (By this method you can usually rip apart a whole coat in five minutes.) Pressing the material is next. When you put on the pattern pieces, try to avoid worn places or spots.

When looking at a used item, try to visualize it in a different form. A worn terrycloth robe may become washrags. (Cut in squares. Zigzag around each edge twice.) A furry coat lining may be turned into a teddy bear. An old quilted bedspread may replace a worn coat lining. Worn overalls have a few good places. These can be combined with red bandanna handkerchiefs to make a boy's quilt.

The following jobs are easy: making pant legs shorter, changing buttons or trim, changing most hemlines, making a dart larger or smaller, changing long sleeves to short, and sewing from a simple pattern, regardless of the source of material.

Used clothing is wonderful, but you should spend about half of your sewing time with new material. Learn when fabric sales are held in your area. Buy flannel and fake fur in late winter sales. Obtain cotton and thin material in the early fall.

Some remnants are fantastic bargains. Others are merely short pieces of material at the regular price. Flawed material is often sold at reduced prices. A spot, a faded section, or a tear may be to your advantage. Experience helps you decide if you can put pattern pieces around the flaw. "Flat fold" material may be cheaper than that neatly rolled on a bolt. A big investment? Yes, but that was two years ago, and I haven't bought any thread since.

Keep a reasonable amount of thread, elastic, buttons, snaps, and zippers. It's simply more fun to have the things you need.

Sewing is not an old-fashioned little old lady type of occupation anymore. It's true that we still make dresses and aprons, but we make so much more. The pattern catalogs have pages of men's wear (including Western and formal), Christmas ornaments, and sleeping bags. Backpacks, stuffed toys, and tablecloths all have available patterns.

Sewing is not always a long process. *Simplicity* brand patterns have their "Jiffy Super Patterns." *Butterick* has their "Sew and Go" patterns. *Vogue* has a similar line called "Very Easy." *McCall's* has a new visual sewing system in selected patterns. This includes a guidebook. Basic patterns are good investments and can be used for years. Styles will change, but modifications can frequently be made without buying new patterns.

A sewing book is a good sewing friend. All the pattern manufacturers have paperback sewing books. Your public library may have many general books like *McCall's Sewing Book, Vogue Sewing Book*, and *Better Homes and Gardens Sewing Book*. There are specialty books about making gloves, doing alterations, and sewing for children. If your library does not have a desired book, you can usually obtain it through the interlibrary loan system.

There are fewer items needed for sewing than for many money-saving ventures. Nevertheless, you do need something besides a bone needle. These items are basic necessities:

- Sewing machine—electric or treadle.
- A good pair of scissors—poor quality scissors will tire your hands (Fig. 11-1).
- Tape measure, pins, and needles (Fig. 11-2).
- Sufficient material, thread, and patterns (Fig. 11-3).

These items are nice to have:

- Pinking shears (good ones).
- Pin cushion.
- Basic sewing book.
- Seam ripper.

Sewing can be fun, creative, and thrifty. It can supply some of our most primitive needs.

TREADLE SEWING MACHINES

Quality clothing at low cost is important to us all. By sewing your own on a treadle sewing machine, you will not only be a step closer to self-sufficiency without using electricity, but you will also have exactly what you want (Fig. 11-4). You will enjoy the task as well. Graceful in design, sturdy, and dependable, the treadle has no rival.

Sewing machines became common for the homemaker in the late 1800s. The earliest ones were hand-cranked; later the treadles

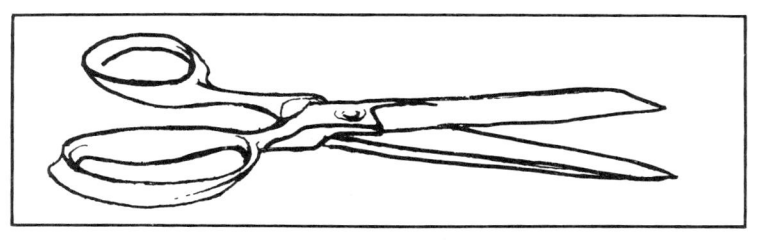

Fig. 11-1. A good pair of scissors is essential.

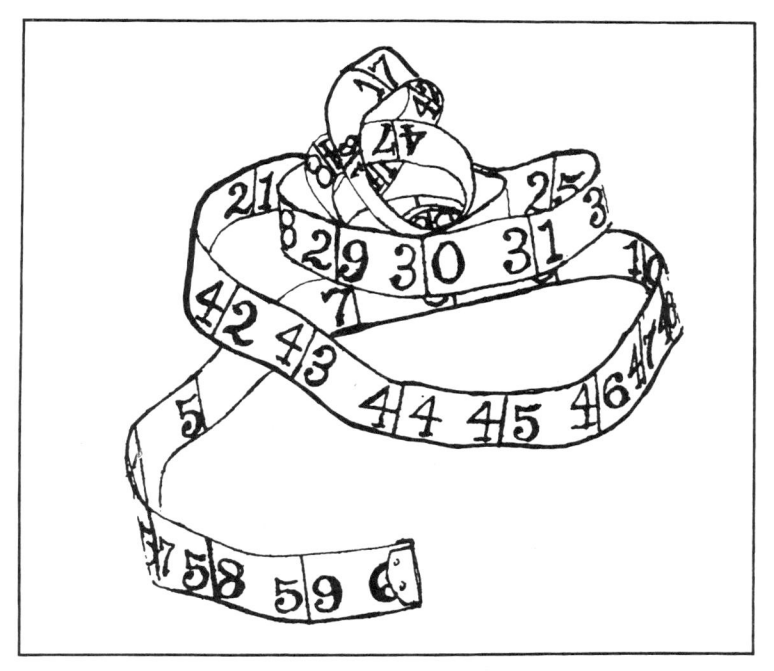

Fig. 11-2. A tape measure is a sewing necessity.

became popular. There were many makes; among them were Howe, Davis, New Home, White, Wheeler, and Wilson, Singer and Standard. Isolated homesteaders in the midwest bought thousands of treadles from Montgomery Ward and Sears, Roebuck and Company.

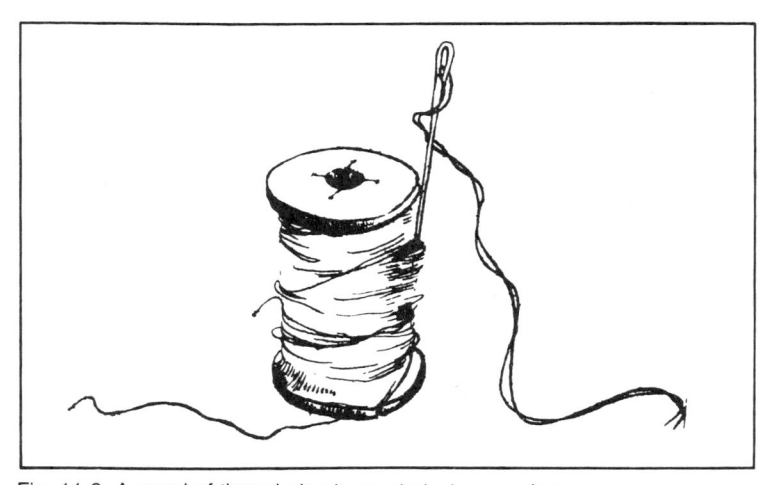

Fig. 11-3. A spool of thread also is needed when sewing.

Fig. 11-4. A treadle sewing machine is sturdy and dependable.

Both of them started their mail order businesses in the 1870s and marketed their machines under many different model names. Sears sold the "New Home Queen Sewing Machine" for $11.25 with a 90-day guarantee. It was shipped to the nearest railroad station where the buyer could inspect it before paying. By the turn of the century, treadle sewing machines were an integral part of almost every home.

How can the treadle sewing machine compare in quality with the new machines of our present technological age? Aren't the new models better? It all depends on what you want in a machine. If you feel the need to zigzag and do machine embroidery, and don't mind the hum of the electric motor, the treadle would have little appeal. The basic stitch, however, hasn't changed over the years and is just as strong (if not stronger) as those on present models. Its simple design means less moving parts with very little that can malfunc-

Fig. 11-5. Left—vibrator shuttle and bobbin (in older models). Right—rotary shuttle and bobbin.

tion. Treadle machines are so sturdy that most can even sew leather.

Since treadle sewing machines were so well made, many are still available today. Watch the classified ads in newspapers, go to auctions, and inquire at sewing machine dealers who resell trade-ins. Surprisingly enough, you may find a beauty for under $40. Some treadles can be found at antique stores, but go there only as a last resort. Their prices will be inflated, and their customers are often unappreciative.

Learning to use a treadle is easy. After threading the machine and bobbin and after putting the presser foot down on the material, turn the balance wheel slightly toward you to get the flywheel started (Figs. 11-5 and 11-6). This is then kept in motion by the

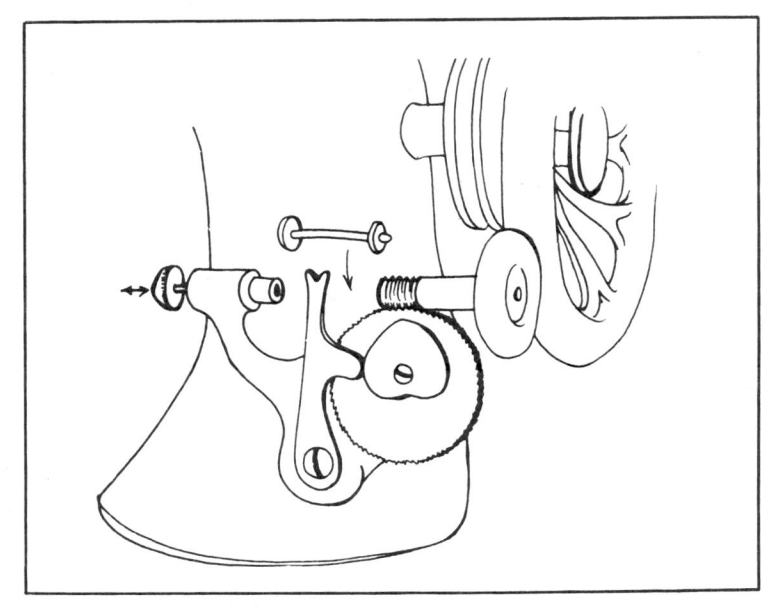

Fig. 11-6. A bobbin winder.

steady backward and forward rhythm of your feet (Fig. 11-7). Once started, you can continue at whatever pace you choose. You will be able to go as fast as you can handle the material. Although the movement is different, you won't exert yourself any more than when pressing the accelerator in a car.

Take care of your treadle and it will last forever (Fig. 11-8). As with any machine, it's important to keep it cleaned and oiled to run smoothly. If you don't use your machine often and fold it up when not in use, your tune-ups won't be frequent. Keep your machine dusted. Clean and oil it at least once a month. Sewing machine oil, available at any sewing machine dealer, dropped on each moving part is all you need to do. Plates attached by thumbscrews on the machine head should be removed. Put a drop of oil in each of the oil holes and joints inside. Oil holes on top of the head are provided for bearings that can't be directly reached (Fig. 11-9). Underneath the machine there are more oil holes and bearings. Oil them all. Oil should also be dropped underneath the bobbin case, which is usually removable. Be sure to also clean off the lint and dust that readily accumulates there. When oiling your machine, it's also a good time to check that

Fig. 11-7. Start the motion by hand and keep the rhythm while treading.

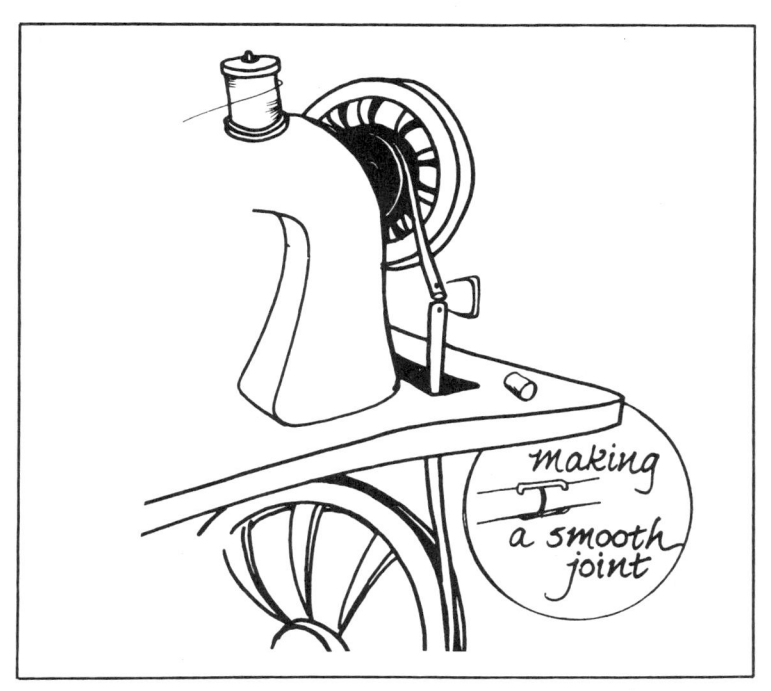

Fig. 11-8. If the leather belt loosens, snip off a piece and restaple.

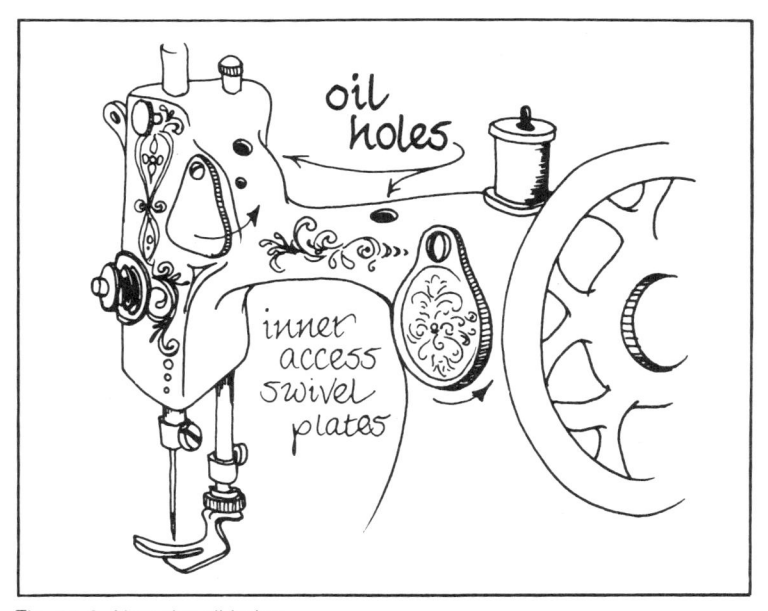

Fig. 11-9. Note the oil holes.

231

all of the bolts on the pedal are tight. The occasional overhaul will make your treadle purr.

In the drawers of your sewing machine you may find any number of fancy-looking attachments. There are hemmers, binders, edge stitchers, gatherers, and the most elaborate of them all, the ruffler. If you are fortunate enough to get an owner's manual with your machine, look up the procedures for their various uses. Although they're not so practical for our purposes today (i.e., we can buy binding rather than make it), they do work and are fun to try. If you ever need to make a ruffle, put piping on it and sew it onto your dress all at the same time.

Changing the tension on the machine is likely to be the only adjustment you will need to make. This is done by turning the tension thumb nut on the face of the machine head. The bobbin thread tension in the bobbin case shouldn't need to be changed once it's been properly adjusted. In the perfect stitch, the needle and bobbin threads are locked in the center of the material. If the needle thread is too tight (bobbin thread too loose), the needle thread will lie straight on the upper surface of the material. If the needle thread is too loose (bobbin thread too tight), the bobbin thread will lie straight along the underside of the material. Always keep the presser foot down when regulating the needle thread tension.

The only drawback to the straight basic stitch made by the treadle sewing machine is that there is no reverse. Backstitching at the ends of seams is important to keep them tight. To compensate, turn the material around to backstitch. If you're sewing a noticeable area, topstitching for instance, pull both threads out of the underside of the material and tie a knot.

If the cabinet of your treadle is in need of refinishing, treat it like the fine piece of furniture that it is. Sandpaper and linseed oil may be all that you will need. Enjoy your sewing tasks. Let your creations flow with the treadle's steady rhythm. You, too, will appreciate its quiet beauty.

THE ART OF QUILTING

Quilting is an ancient art—more than 4000 years old. It was born of necessity as a means to produce warm clothing and bedding. One of the early uses of quilted clothing was as an undergarment to prevent chafing under heavy armor.

The very cold winters in Western Europe in the fourteenth century made quilting very important to create warm clothing and bedding. During these years, quilted bedcovers were a necessity.

Quilting increased the flexibility of fabrics for use in both clothing and bedding. Many things were used to fill quilts, including lamb's wool, moss, feathers, and even grass.

After centuries of using quilting for practical reasons, the art of quilting was developed. Stitching became more elaborate, with scrolls, ornamental motifs, and applique as common decorations. Quilting frames were invented, and special tools were devised for joining layers of fabric.

The British and Dutch called quilts bed furniture, and most Pilgrim families came to America with complete sets of bed furniture. The early settlers were isolated from European conveniences, and everything was used and reused. Quilts were repaired with scraps of old clothing and thus gradually acquired the appearance of a patchwork top. Those early tops were not as colorful as we know patchwork tops today. They were usually made of dark red, blue, and brown. Some were knotted or tied together. "Crazy patch" was the name given to one of the earliest patterns, because unequal sizes of patches were used. Later, quilts were patched or made with native, handwoven material usually of wool, which was dyed with natural dyes.

Shipping lines began to bring European material to the New World, making it possible to use finer material and many more colors. Patchwork quilts became more decorative, and more interesting arrangements of colors and patterns were used.

Some of our most beautiful quilts in museums are quilts made of silks and then embroidered. Some quilts were made of pieces of cherished garments, thus preserving some of the history of the family.

Making quilts became community social events, a friendly way to pass a cold winter day with friends. Young girls shared in these events and started to make quilts for their home when they were very young. Often when girls became engaged, their friends and relatives would make blocks for a quilt with the engaged couple's names and the date of their wedding on them. This led to the betrothal party to put the quilt together.

Eventually American production reached a point where fabric could be produced in many colors and more cheaply than the material carried from Europe. As a result, applique work grew in popularity. *Applique*, the practice of laying one fabric over another for design purposes, was frowned upon by the early settlers because they considered it a waste of material. *Patchworks*, which are pieces of material sewn together to make a design, also became more elaborate and decorative. The stitching often followed the pieced patterns, making the pieced pattern stand out. If the pattern included a large plain block or border, very interesting patterns of stitching could be developed. Some of the early patterns, inspired by the settlers' natural environment, were: log cabin, pine tree, wedding ring, flower garden, sunbonnet, nine patch, and blazing star (Fig. 11-10).

Quilts are usually made of three layers: backing, filling or batts, and either a pieced or plain top. Fillings can be made of almost any material from feathers or down to a single layer of muslin material, depending on the weight of quilt desired. The batting most commonly used today is a commercially produced synthetic fiber, usually dacron, and is readily available at most fabric or department stores. It is a ½-inch layer of loosely fused fibers and is quite easy to handle. If synthetic fibers don't meet your fancy, you can use whatever is at hand. It was not an uncommon practice to take an old warm quilt and use it as a batting, putting a new top and backing over it.

Fabric for the tops and backing should be smooth, soft, nonraveling, colorfast, and with a firm weave. If they are not preshrunk fabrics, they should be washed before using so that there is no

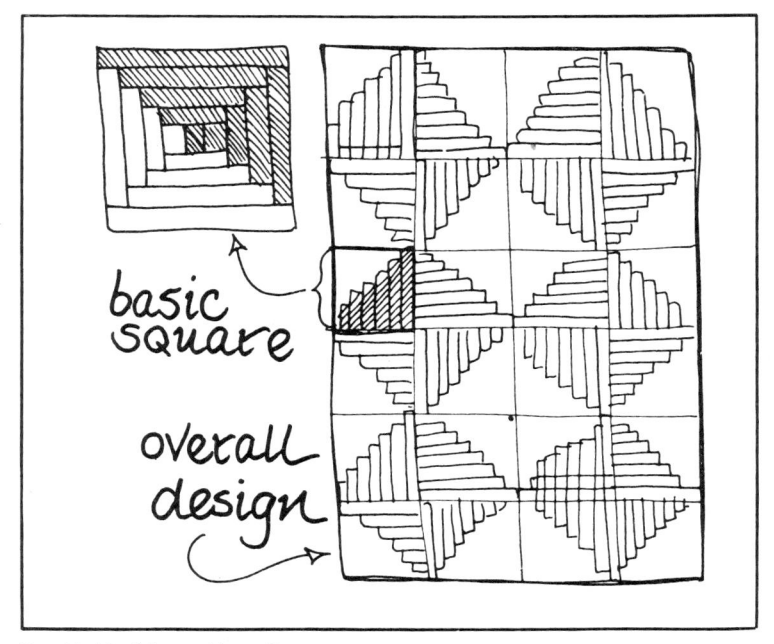

Fig. 11-10. A log cabin pattern.

chance of shrinking after they are stitched. The fabrics good for piecing or quilting are: broadcloth, calico, cotton, cotton satin, flannel, gingham, muslin, satin, silk, velvet, velveteen, wool, and the newer knit fabrics.

Inexpensive muslin sheeting or flannel makes a sturdy backing, as do any of the materials mentioned for use in piecing or quilting, especially if you want the quilt to be reversible. Fabrics which are hard to penetrate with a needle, such as permapress, percales, expensive heavy satins, and stiff material, should be avoided. Loosely woven cloth and transparent fabrics are also not good choices for backing or tops. It pays to use good quality material, because quilts require a lot of work and should be durable. Different types and weights of material should probably not be used together as they might produce problems in cleaning.

Needles for quilting should be short and strong. Number 7 to 10 needles are best to make short, even stitches. Quilting thread should be strong and almost stiff. It comes in several colors. Thread can be waxed with beeswax to make it stronger.

Glass-headed pins are better than ordinary pins because they are easier to see to remove. Pinking shears are not generally used. Sharp, straight shears with a good point are best. Yardsticks, rulers, and tape measures are also useful.

If the stitching pattern does not follow a design in the patchwork or material, the pattern must be marked on the fabric. A semihard pencil is best for marking the pattern. Be sure the point is sharp. If the pencil marks are made light enough, the quilting stitch will remove most of them.

Use sandpaper as a pattern guide. For example, if you want a heart in the pattern, cut the proper sized heart out of sandpaper, place it on the top of the quilt, and draw around it with a sharp pencil. By placing the rough side down, this creates a convenient, stiff pattern guide that does not slide around on the quilt.

Thimbles are a must. Make sure the thimble fits your index finger properly.

Frames are important to make a smooth quilt. You will need two pieces of 1-inch-by-2-inch knot-free fir or pine as long as the width of your quilt and twice the lengths of the quilt. Some quilting frames are large enough to accommodate full-sized quilts, but you can make smaller quilts by using C-clamps.

Ticking is strips of denim or other material that must be attached to the quilting frames (Fig. 11-11). It must be tacked or stapled to the entire length of the frames, leaving at least 2 inches of

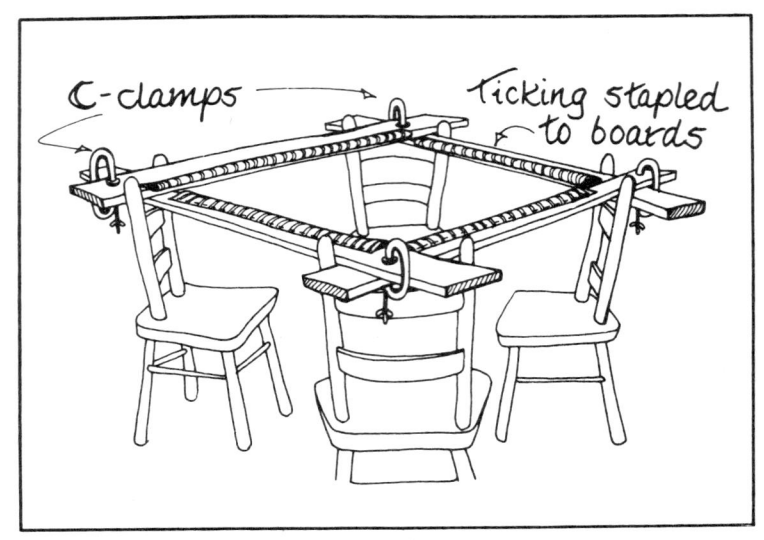

Fig. 11-11. Ticking must be attached to the quilting frames.

material sticking out along the edge of the frame. The purpose of the ticking is to provide a means to pin the quilt to the frame (Fig. 11-12). After clamping the four pieces of frame together, it works best to set the frames on four straight-backed chairs.

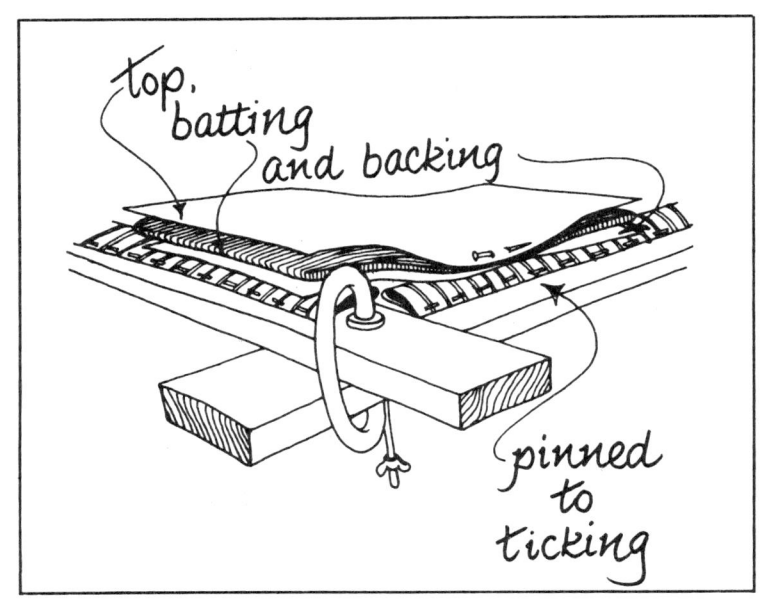

Fig. 11-12. The ticking allows you to pin the quilt to the frame.

After setting the frames on the chairs, pin the backing onto the frames. First, pin one side of the backing fabric to one side of the frame, placing the pins about 2 inches apart and parallel to the frame. Then pin the opposite side of the backing to the opposite side of the frame, making sure the backing is stretched firmly. Pin on the other two sides, making sure there is equal tension on all four sides of the frame. Next lay the batting out on the backing fabric. Smooth it out, but do not pin it. Then lay on the top fabric, either plain, pierced, or applique, and pin it in the same manner as the backing was pinned. Last, check to make sure the frame is square and clamp the corners firmly.

Start stitching the quilt around the outer edge. You can stitch about a 1-foot border around the quilt before you roll the frames. To roll the frames, loosen the C-clamps and turn the frame piece under (Fig. 11-13). It is important to keep the frame even at this point, or your quilt might not lay evenly when it is finished.

One hand is kept under the quilt at all times while doing the quilting stitch. After practice, it is possible to do two or three stitches at one time through all three layers of the quilt (Fig. 11-14). In the beginning, you should do one stitch at a time. The needle should penetrate the fabrics at close to a right angle. Stitches should be made as small as possible, six to eight stitches per inch. When you graduate to more than one stitch at a time, as soon as the needle goes through the bottom, it should be pushed up by your underneath hand. This makes the stitches somewhat embedded and tends to

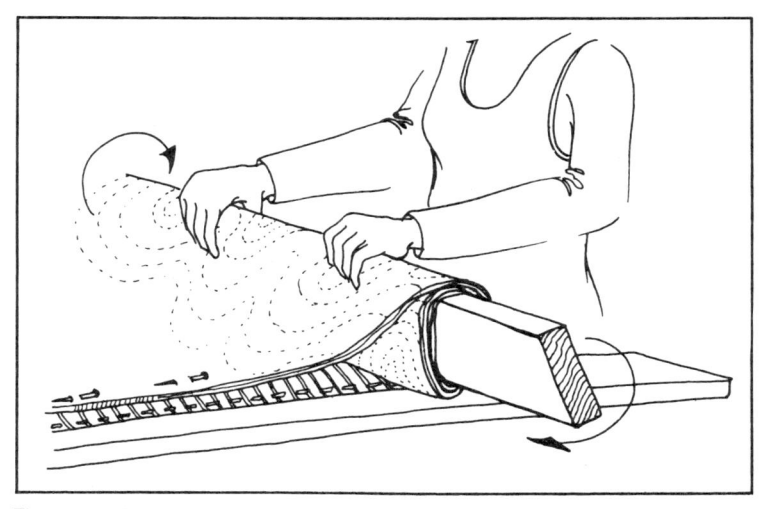

Fig. 11-13. The finished portion is rolled under as quilting progresses.

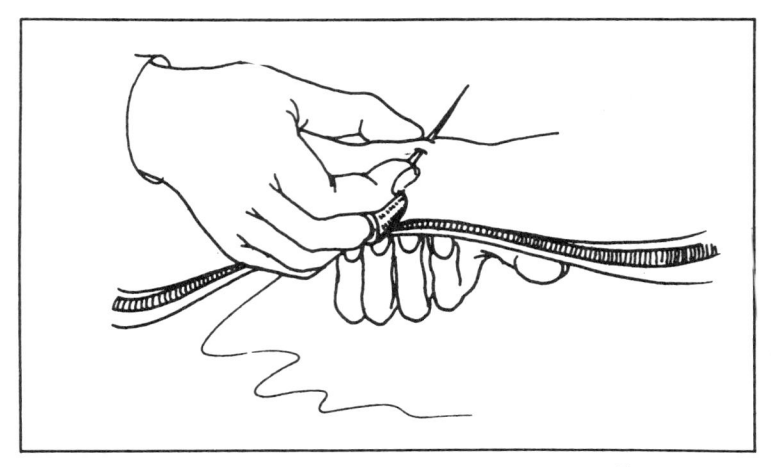

Fig. 11-14. Stitch through all three layers. Work toward yourself.

puff up the pattern. If the stitch is just a running stitch, the thread lays on the top of the quilt and does not show off the pattern.

Patterns and designs of quilts are as varied as the people who create them. The patchwork and applique tops are usually sewn together by machine, but interesting applique designs can be hand-stitched. Many beautiful quilts are also made with elaborate stitching designs on plain fabric.

After stitching the entire quilt, you are ready to remove the quilt from the frames and bind the edges. You can use a bias binding for your quilts. Cut bias strips about 2 inches wide of the same material you used for the quilt. Stitch the strips together to form strips at least as long as one edge of the quilt. Fold the strips lengthwise as straight as possible. Pin and sew one side of the strip to the top of the quilt, using a blind stitch. Then fold the strip around the edge of the quilt, pin it, and stitch it to the backing (Fig. 11-15). Bind each side in this way and then sew the corners together (Figs. 11-16 and 11-17).

QUILTING PROJECTS

When late night embers crumble to ashes, do you ever long for a warm, fluffy quilt to cover your cold toes? Perhaps the prospect of endlessly hunching over hundreds of tiny patchwork pieces makes Grandmother your only hope.

Well, don't despair? Here are two quick, inexpensive quilting methods which any homesteader can handle.

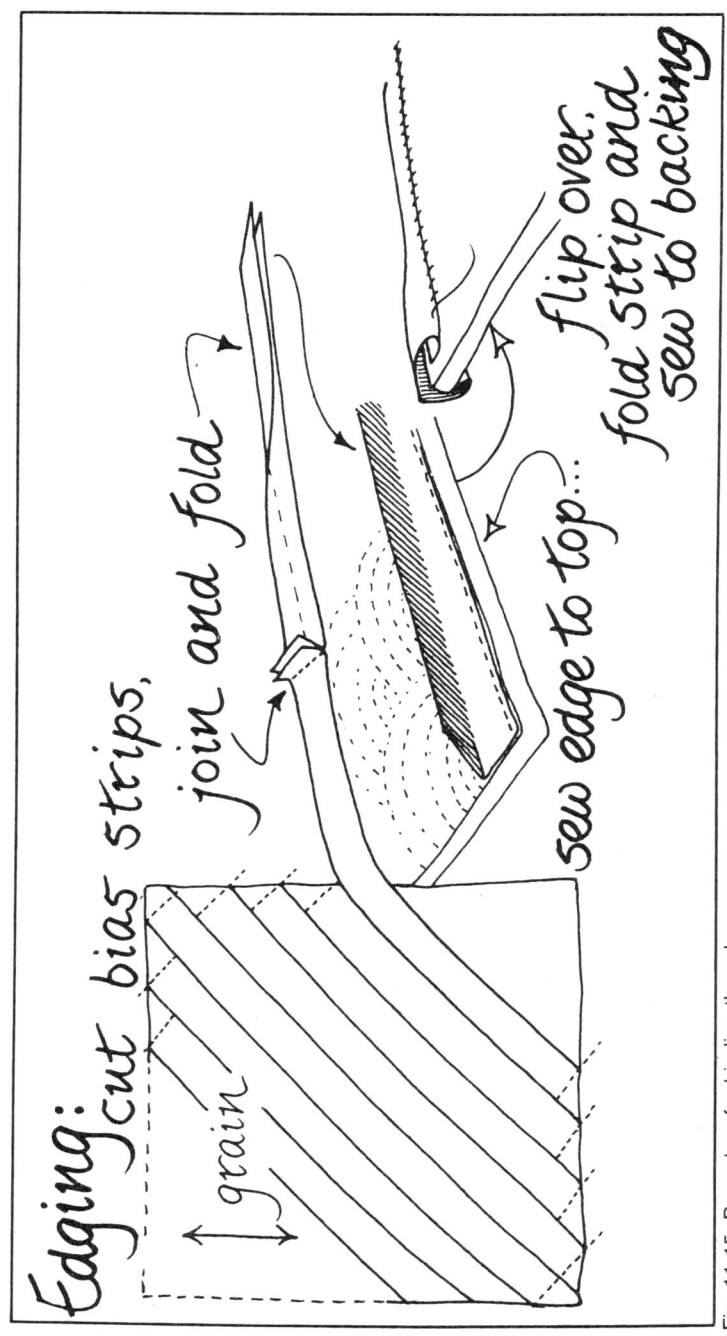

Fig. 11-15. Procedure for binding the edges.

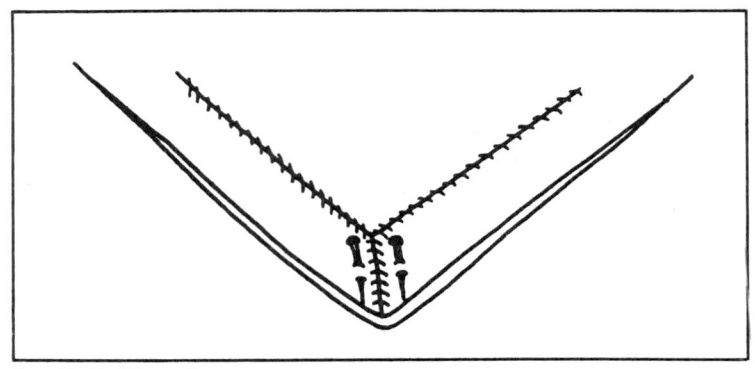

Fig. 11-16. Mitered corner sewn at a 45-degree angle.

Comforter

Materials:

- 224 6-½-inch cloth squares to top; this allows for ¼-inch seams.

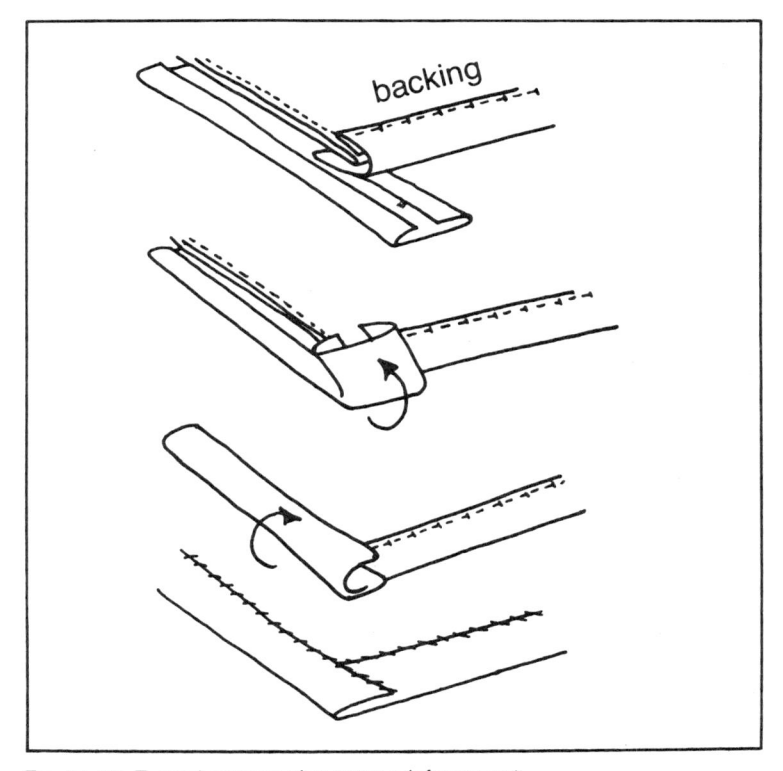

Fig. 11-17. Turned corners give extra reinforcement.

240

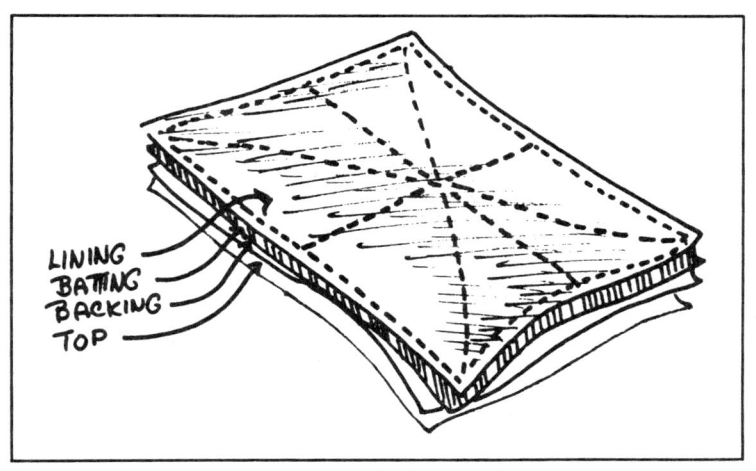

Fig. 11-18. Placement of the backing, batting, and lining.

- 7-by-8-foot liner.
- 7-by 8-foot backing.
- Batting.

Cut out squares following a cardboard pattern of the same dimensions. Sew squares together into 16 7-foot-long strips. Sew the 16 strips together into one 8-by-7-foot piece. On a flat surface, place the quilt right side up. On top, place the quilt backing right side down, then the batting and liner (Fig. 11-18). To make sure that pieces do not slip, tape ends together and down on a flat surface with masking tape. Baste around entire edge of all layers and diagonally, vertically, and horizontally across the quilt (Fig. 11-18).

Machine stitch around the outer edge, leaving ½-inch seam allowance. A large opening (about 2 feet) should remain on one side

Fig. 11-19. Tuft the quilt at 1-foot intervals.

so that you can pull the quilt right side out after stitching. Trim seams around the corners and pull out the right side of the top through the side opening. Slip stitch the opening and retape corners of the quilt to the flat surface. Using a large eyed needle and knitting worsted, tuft the quilt at intervals of 1 foot as shown (Fig. 11-19). To tuft, push the needle down from the top of the quilt, leaving 2 inches of yarn exposed at the top. Push the needle back up from the bottom of quilt, tie yarn, and clip off ends.

Tube Quilt (Single Bed)

Materials:

- 18 4-foot-by-4-inch cloth strips (bright solids or checks work very well).
- 6-by-4-foot liner.
- 6-by-4-foot backing.
- Batting.
- 7 feet of 1-inch wide bias tape.

Sew strips into one 6-by-4-foot quilt top. Baste layers as for the comforter except in regular order (bottom, batting, liner, top right side up). Machine stitch along the edges of the strips (Fig. 11-20). Baste ½-inch strips of batting to the wrong side of the bias tape. Along top edge of quilt, sew bias tape, wrong side up, to the quilt (Fig. 11-21). Slip stitch the other side of the tape to the bottom of the quilt (Fig. 11-22).

CRAZY QUILT

Our pioneer ancestors knew how to take what they had and make it go as far as it could, then recycle it to make it go a second mile. The patchwork quilt is a beautiful example of their frugal art. Quilt historians speculate that the earliest patchwork quilts in this

Fig. 11-20. Machine stitch along the edges of the strips.

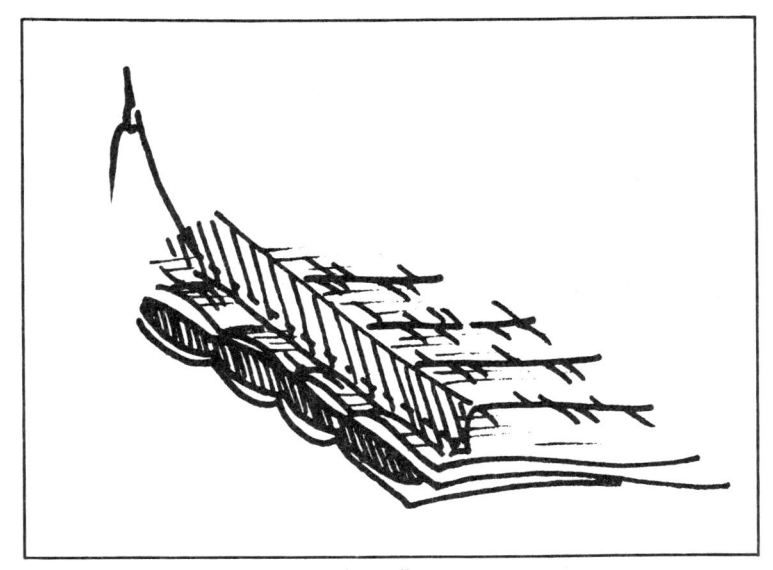

Fig. 11-21. Sew the bias tape to the quilt.

country may have been crazy quilts—patch upon patch fabric collages using homespun fabrics cut from worn-out dresses, pants, and shirts. Old blankets were often used as filler, and backings were also pieced.

Later, in the Victorian era, the crazy quilt was a popular way to recycle the elegant clothing of the day. There was velvet from ball gowns and silk from blouses and ties. The crazy quilt's charm lay in the exquisite embroidery covering not only the seams, but many patches as well. Many of these Victorian crazy quilts survive today because they were made to be admired, not used. With the ruffled edge, they reclined on the little-used parlor divan. People in this

Fig. 11-22. Slip stitch the other side of the tape to the bottom of the quilt.

century still make crazy quilts of both traditions—the earthy and the elegant.

We have seen one crazy quilt made entirely of knits—all sewing scraps. These were machine stitched to a worn tablecloth and backed with more knits sewn in strips to make a single "striped" fabric. The crazy pieces on the top were outlined with the simple feather stitch. A few tacks held the layers together. Our favorite crazy quilt had denims mixed with plaid flannels.

Mary Ann Woodman of Lowell, Massachusetts, has completed a crazy quilt equally as elegant as its Victorian forebears. The quilt top is made entirely of used fabrics: velvets, silks, and cottons all attached to 12-inch squares of old sheeting (Fig. 11-23). The squares, joined together, produced a quilt so heavy it needed no filler. A colored sheet was used to back it and was folded around the edges to the front, forming a self-binding. More than 200 embroidered designs plus dozens of embroidered outline stitches make the quilt a masterpiece. No motif is repeated. Some designs are copies; most are originals.

Fig. 11-23. Used fabrics are attached to 12-inch squares of old sheeting (drawing by Liz Buell).

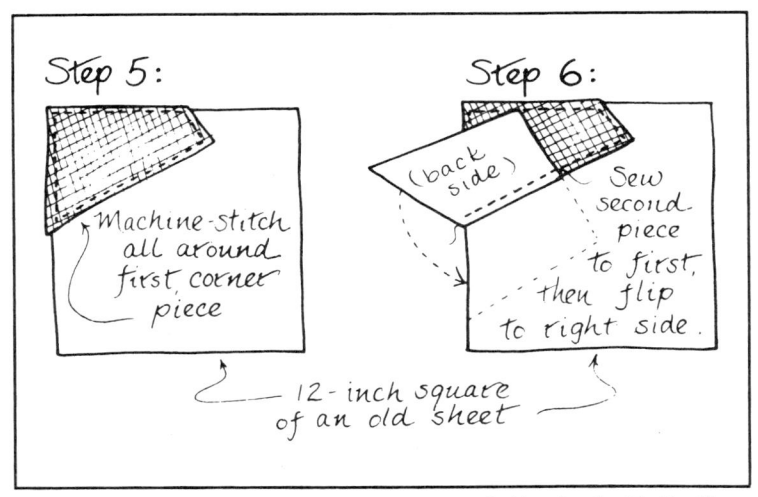

Fig. 11-24. Steps 5 and 6 in making the crazy quilt (drawing by Liz Buell).

Like any craft, making a crazy quilt is not cut and dried. Everyone seems to do it a bit differently from the next person. Here's one method:

1. First, wash all clothing you might use in the quilt.
2. Cut open seams, trim off buttons, etc. Discard overly worn areas.
3. Cut an old sheet into 12-inch (or larger) squares. Measure your bed and decide how large you want the quilt to be. Cut blocks accordingly. (It is much easier working with 12-inch blocks and sewing them together later than to crazy patch the whole sheet.)
4. Play with the colors, shapes, and textures of your fabrics until you find a pleasing arrangement on top of your 12-inch block. Be sure pieces overlap by at least ½ inch all around.
5. Take a second 12-inch block and sew the pieces to it, one by one, starting at one corner. Do not turn under the edges of the first piece to be placed at the corner. Machine baste all around this piece (Fig. 11-24).
6. Lay the second piece over the first, right sides together. Machine sew where the first and second piece overlap. Flip to the right side. Attach all the remaining pieces in this manner (Fig. 11-24). Some edges will be impossible to do by machine and will have to be turned under by hand and blind stitched.
7. Select some embroidery floss. Outline the edges of the patches with the simple feather stitch or other embroidery stitches (Fig. 11-25).

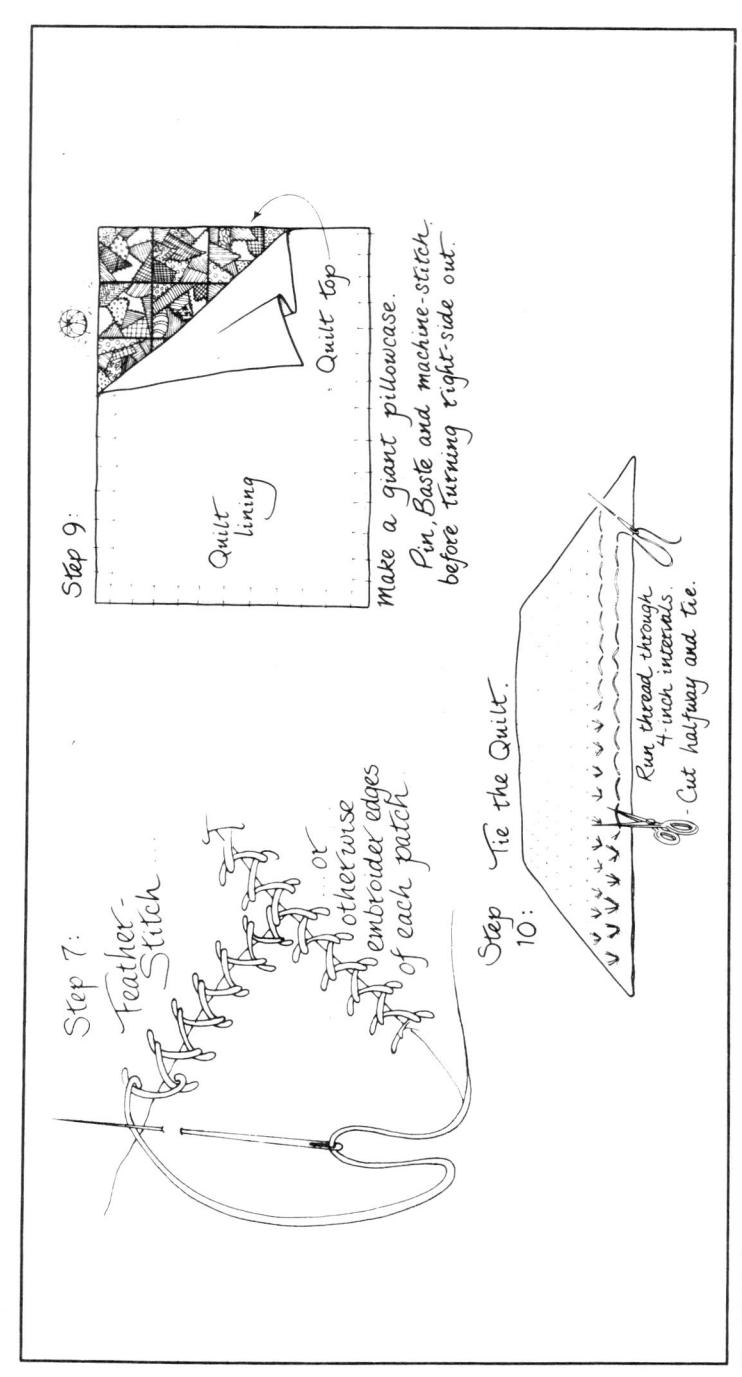

Fig. 11-25. Steps, 7, 9, and 10 in making the crazy quilt (drawing by Liz Buell).

8. Repeat this procedure with all blocks. Then stitch the squares together in long rows the length of the bed. Stitch several rows together to make the quilt top. Using feather stitch again, outline the seams joining the squares.

9. Line the quilt with a single fabric (old draperies seamed together, for example). Lay the quilt out flat on the floor right side up. Lay lining fabric on top, right sides together. Pin and baste around three edges. Machine stitch this giant "pillowcase." Turn to right side and turn in raw edges of fourth side. Blind stitch in place (Fig. 11-25).

10. The final step is to tie the quilt. Lay it out on the floor and using yardstick and chalk, dot it at 4-inch intervals. Using a long double strand of crochet cotton and needle, insert the needle at the edge of the first chalk dot. Come up through the fabric about ¼ inch away from where the needle was inserted. Go on to the next dot and the next until you run out of thread. Cut the threads halfway between dots. Tie a knot at each dot. Leave ½-inch long ends. Trim all ends evenly. Continue this process until the whole quilt is tied.

Your crazy quilt is now completed. Enjoy its warmth and the memories of the former lives of its fabrics.

SPINNING AND WEAVING FLAX AND WOOL

Every well-furnished farmstead should have a spinning wheel and a loom. Spinning and weaving have always been a necessity when a family or community has had to be self-sufficient, and spinning and weaving are surely among the pleasanter tasks that contribute to supplying the necessities of the household (Fig. 11-26). While the current interest in handweaving is focused principally upon its decorative and ornamental uses, the weaving of articles for wear and household use, governed by considerations of utility and suitability to their function, as well as aesthetics, can be a highly challenging undertaking.

The earliest settlers had to bring cloth for their needs with them when they arrived on these shores. Among their first and most pressing tasks were the raising of sheep and the sowing of flax in order to be able to replace the stores they had brought with them and used up or worn out. Although eventually possible to buy, cotton, wool, linen, and tow were dear, money was scarce, and so these goods continued to be produced at home. One or more of the processes—from the growing of fiber through the carding, spinning, and weaving to the sewing—were familiar occupations of the women until the mid-1800s and later. Carding and spinning, the

Fig. 11-26. Spinning and weaving help supply the necessities of the household (drawing by Mary A. Chase).

processes which required the greatest relative expenditure of time and labor, were the first to be taken over by the burgeoning mills with the coming of the industrial revolution. Weaving and sewing continued to be home industries for a longer time.

The preparation of flax fiber—from which both linen and tow are obtained—is a time-consuming and arduous task, more so than preparing fleeces for spinning. Because of this, as soon as cotton became available at low cost with the invention of the cotton gin and the rapid development of power carding and spinning in the early 1800s, flax raising was virtually abandoned. Wool continued to be raised and woven at home even into the twentieth century.

The site selected for the flax patch should be open, as flax wants sun and wind, and it does not tolerate drought. The ground should be finely worked and free of weed seed. The seed is sown broadcast and quite thickly so the plants will be crowded and grow tall and slender, not branching until quite high. This diminishes the bloom and consequently the yield of seed from the next crop, but produces superior fiber.

Flax must be hand harvested by pulling it up by the roots, then tied in bundles and dried, keeping the stalks neatly aligned all through the processing. To separate the fibers from the woody parts of the stalks the plants are retted, either by spreading them on the grass and leaving them in the rain and dew for a period, or by standing them in slowly moving water—a pond or stream. Another drying-off is following by breaking the stems in a *flax brake*, by *scutching*, swingling which is flailing with a wooden knife against a wooden block, and *hackling, hatcheling, hetcheling*, drawing the bundles of fibers through successively finer sets of very sharp steel teeth set in a heavy block, to comb out the shorter fibers and remaining bits of stalk and align the long fibers in parallel. At this stage the flax is at its most beautiful—long, lustrous fibers of a shining white-gold color. It is now ready for spinning. Tow is spun from the shorter fibers separated out in the scutching and hackling processes. Tow is a coarser, rougher material, still very strong, which was much used for coarse toweling, sheeting, heavy sacking, and even clothing. Linen is a very strong fiber, very absorbent, and even gains strength when wet.

For those of us who enjoy doing it ourselves, the raising of sheep, the growing of flax and the preparation of these fibers for spinning and making them into yarns can be interesting and enjoyable on an experimental scale. The spur of necessity is absent so far, and our production will scarcely suffice to fill our needs. Weaving, like sewing, can, when done on a domestic scale, go much farther toward filling some of those needs and wants. We may have to buy some of the yarn we use, but we can incorporate any we have been able to spin and grow.

Weaving is an interest that can be enjoyed on many levels. It can be extremely simple—on the little frames on which children weave pot holders—or quite complex—as in drafting and weaving a coverlet, perhaps in an 8-or-12-harness double-weave. The process can be very free—even-woven-off-the-loom as some fiber sculptures are—or it can be very controlled, as in a 10-harness linen damask tablecloth. There is a special satisfaction in being able to furnish some of one's own household necessities in this very time-honored fashion.

MITTENS

If you have some worn or outmoded winter coats or jackets,

don't throw them out. Recycle them into rugged, warm mittens for next winter. These mittens are very easy to make, and comfortable to wear. Use the knit tops of old socks for wristlets.

Cut out a back and a front, then reverse the pattern for the other hand and cut out another back and front (Fig. 11-27). They may be made larger or smaller by cutting the pattern wider all around or narrower. Pick a part of your material that is the least worn.

To sew the mittens, pin the two pieces, right sides together. Start sewing at the base of the thumb on the wrong side of the material. Sew up around the thumb while the mitten is open; then you sew around the mitten. Take the knit top of an old sock and bind one end of it to the wrong side of the mitten. Turn the mitten right side out, fold the knit top in two, and bind onto the right side to form a cuff for the mitten.

SOCKS

Here's an easy and fast way to make socks (Fig. 11-28). Note the following abbreviations: K—knit, P—purl, Sts—stitches, Rnd—round, Tog—together, Sl—slip one stitch, Ch—chain stitch, and Psso—pass stitch over last stitch just worked.

Materials

- Size six double-pointed needles.
- One skein, 4 ply, 4-ounce yarn.
- Cast on 36 sts (12 on each of three needles).
- Work K2, P2, ribbing for 3 inches.
- Change to stockinette stitch (K every rnd till desired length to heel, about 10 inches from beginning).

Divide for Heel

K across the first nine sts on first needle.

Slipping sts place nine sts on each of next two needles.

Place last nine sts on needle with the first nine sts that were knitted (this is heel needle).

Working on heel sts only:

Row 1: P across.
Row 2: Sl-1 st, K across, sl last st.

Repeat these two rows until desired heel length (about 2 inches) ending with second row.

Turn Heel

Row 1: Wrong side, P10, P2 tog, P1, turn.
Row 2: Sl-1, K4, Sl-1, K1, Psso, K1, turn.
Row 3: Sl-1, P5, P2 tog, P1, turn.
Row 4: Sl-1, K6, Sl-1, K1, Psso, K1, turn.
Row 5: Sl-1, P7, P2 tog, P1, turn.
Row 6: Sl-1, K8, Sl-1, K1, Psso, K1, turn.
Row 7: P across 12 sts.
Row 8: K across 12 sts.
With spare needle, pick up seven sts along instep.
K these with heel needle.
K across the next two needles with spare needle; there will be 18 sts on this needle.
With spare needle pick up seven sts along other side of instep.
K these plus six sts off heel needle.
Row 1: K around.
Row 2: 1st needle—K across to last three sts, K2 tog, K1.

    Second needle—K across.
    Third needle—K1, Sl-1, K1, Psso, K across.

Repeat these two rounds until 36 sts remain. Now work even until 2 inches shorter than the desired length of foot.

Toe Decrease

Row 1: first needle—K to within three sts from end of needle, K2 tog, K1.

    Second needle—K1, Sl-1, K1, Psso, K to within three st from end of needle, K2 tog, K1.
    Third needle—K1, Sl-1, K1, Psso, K to end of round.

Row 2: K around.
Repeat these two rounds, ending with first round. There will be 12 sts remaining. Leaving about a 12-inch length of yarn, break off the yarn, pull tight, and weave the remaining strand of yarn into the sock.

RUGMAKING

Rugmaking in America has become an art over the years, but the first floor coverings were scarce and devised solely for utilitarian purposes. When wintry drafts blew under the door or up through the cabin floor, colonial homemakers began creating the first American rugs to make their crude homes more comfortable and add a bit of color in the process.

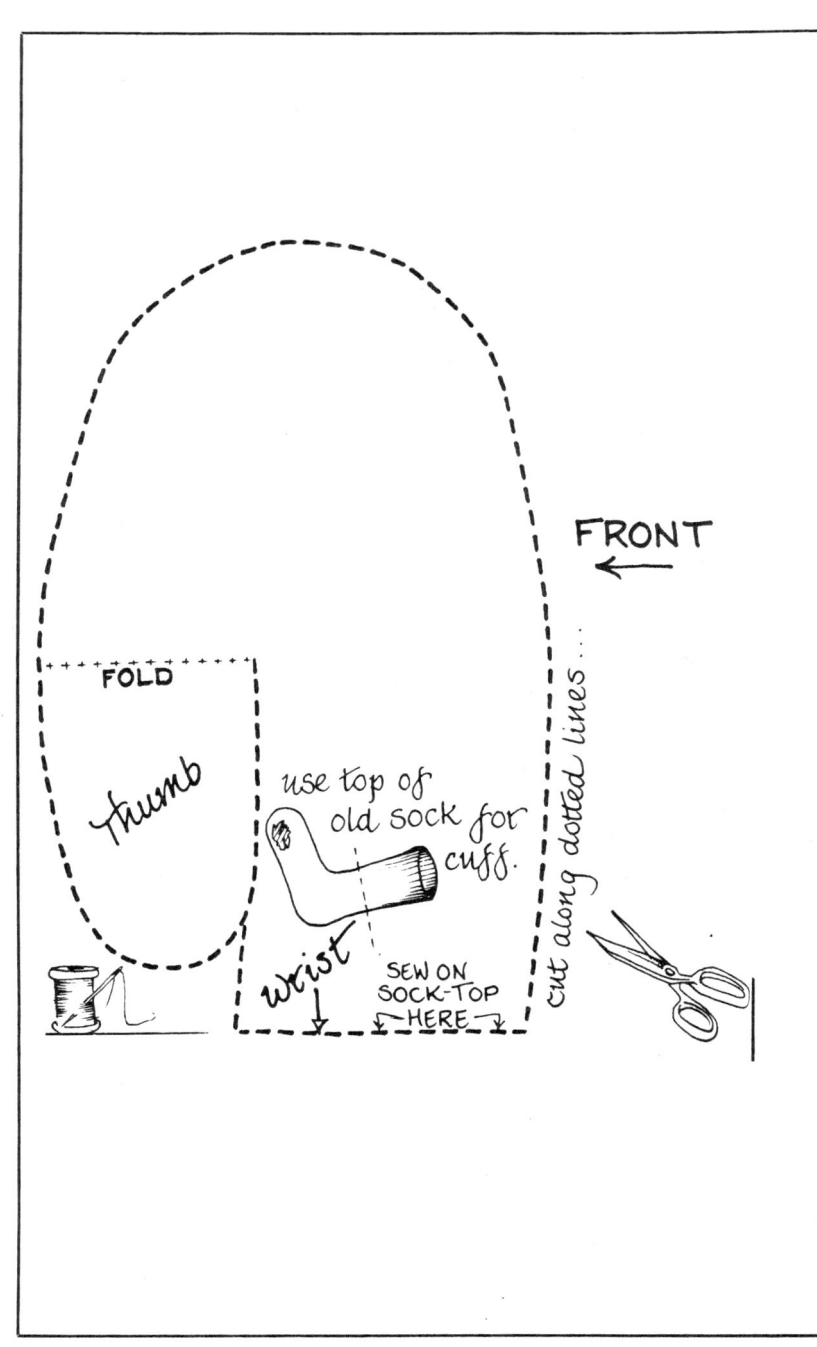

Fig. 11-27. Procedure for making mittens.

INSTRUCTIONS:

Cut out one FRONT and one BACK pattern piece. Reverse patterns and cut out one more FRONT and BACK for the other hand.

To assemble:

Place right side of material of BACK piece against right side of material of FRONT piece so wrong side of material will be on the outside.

Fold over thumb on BACK piece.

BACK →

FOLD

Fold up thumb on FRONT piece.

BACK

FRONT

Slide FRONT piece over BACK piece and match thumb parts. Baste or pin together.

Machine stitch around mitten (starting at Ⓑ).

Turn right side out after sewing cuff to wrist →

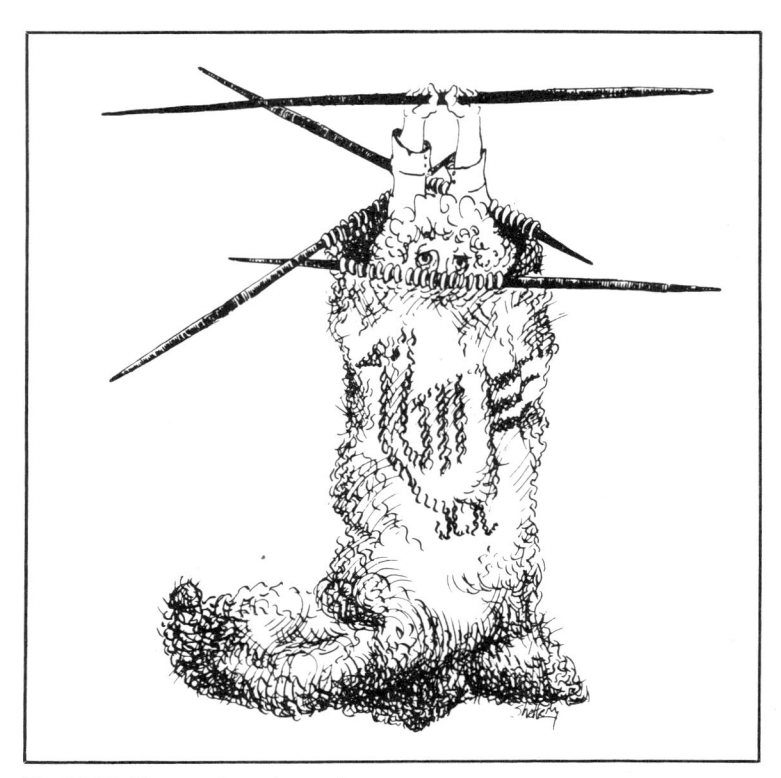

Fig. 11-28. It's easy to make socks.

The main materials on hand for making those first rugs were rags and worn-out clothing when they could be spared. With those rough materials, the pioneer homemakers let their creativeness come forth and even the simplest rugs might be objects of beauty. The faded old fabrics were dyed with dyes made from bark and berries to give new brightness to the rugs thus created.

Rugmaking in America is still going on as women create these works of art for their homes. Our American spirit of individualism still survives as people take time from their busy days to make these unique items of beauty to brighten their homes with something a bit different than those found in any other home.

There have been a variety of methods used for making rugs in America, and no one is quite sure which is the oldest. Among these are braiding, weaving, knitting, crocheting, and hooking.

Braided Rugs

Braiding is thought to be one of the older of the rugmaking arts in this country and is still being done by industrious people to create floor coverings. In addition to using rags for braiding, pioneer rugmakers used corn shucks when the rags were scarce. Although our ancestors didn't always have the time to make extremely precise braided rugs, their creations served their purpose by adding warmth and color to the home.

Braided rugs were round and oval. They were made by braiding into long plaits the cloth strips cut from rags and old clothing. These then were coiled up and sewn together to hold them securely.

To make truly braided masterpieces, much care and patience is involved. The colors must be blended harmoniously, the raw edges must be folded in so they do not show, the strips must not wrinkle in braiding, and care must be taken in sewing the braids together.

Cut your rags into about 2-inch strips. Woven materials usually are cut on the bias. Stitch the ends of the strips together. These long strips can be rolled into balls until you're ready to use them (Fig. 11-29).

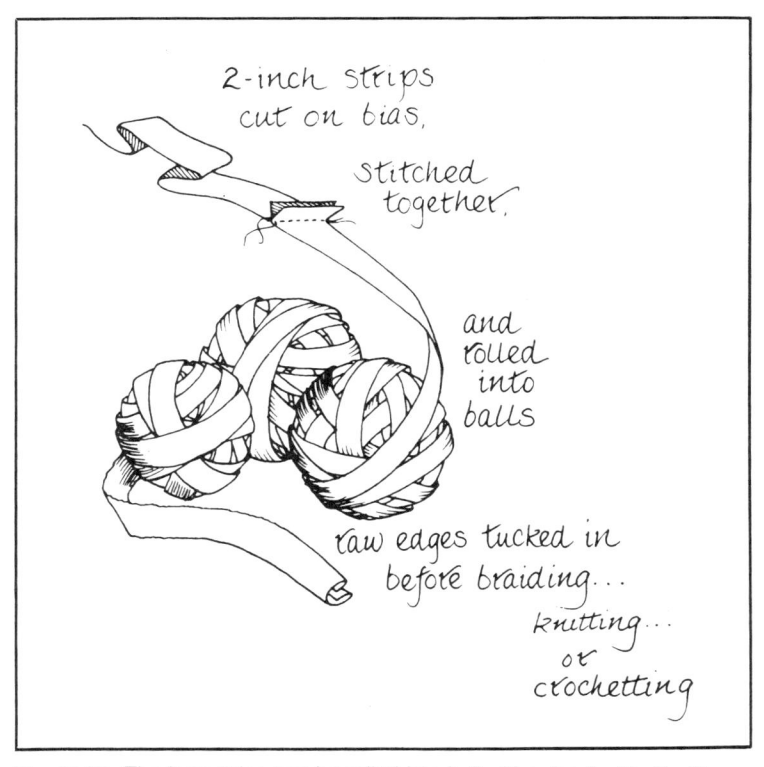

Fig. 11-29. The long strips can be rolled into balls (drawing by Liz Buell).

Before braiding, you must fold the rags so the raw edges are folded in and won't show in the finished rug. The tube thus formed by the folding must be without wrinkles so the finished rug surface will be smooth.

Braided rugs are made by a simple braiding technique. You braid the folded rag strips, right over left, left over right, just as you do when braiding hair.

Once you have made braids from the tubes (folded strips), you start at the center and sew them together to make circular or oval rugs. Use invisible stitches with thread that will match and not show. Use sturdy carpet thread and sew first through the outside of the coiled braid. Then sew through the inner strand of the braid that you're adding. Sew the braids firmly (Fig. 11-30). Be sure you don't sew them so tightly the rug will curl.

Rag or Woven Rugs

Rag or woven rugs were made on a home loom. Although other rugs were made of rags, these woven rugs usually were the only ones referred to as rag rugs. They were woven, using rag strips instead of yarn, and with a heavy linen or cotton warp (Fig. 11-31).

The rags were dyed when possible, and colors often were shaded by twisting two different colored rags together. Sometimes the rugs were planned with certain colors. Other times they were created in hit-and-miss patterns with whatever colors were available. They were serviceable and quite likely may have been the first type of American rug made.

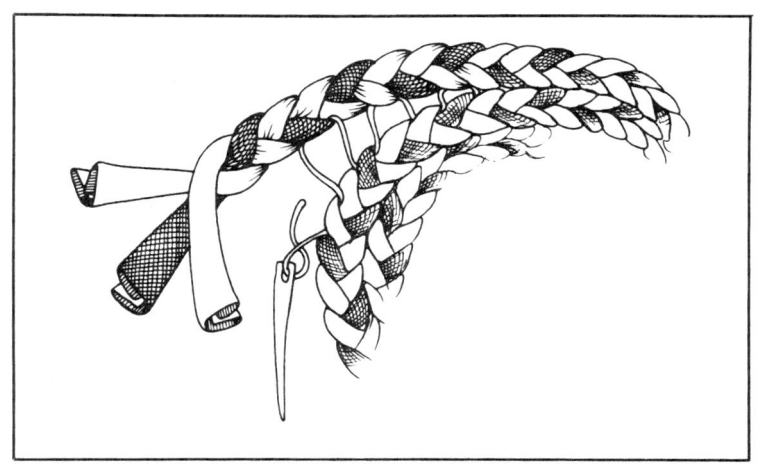

Fig. 11-30. Sew the braided coil firmly but not tightly (drawing by Liz Buell).

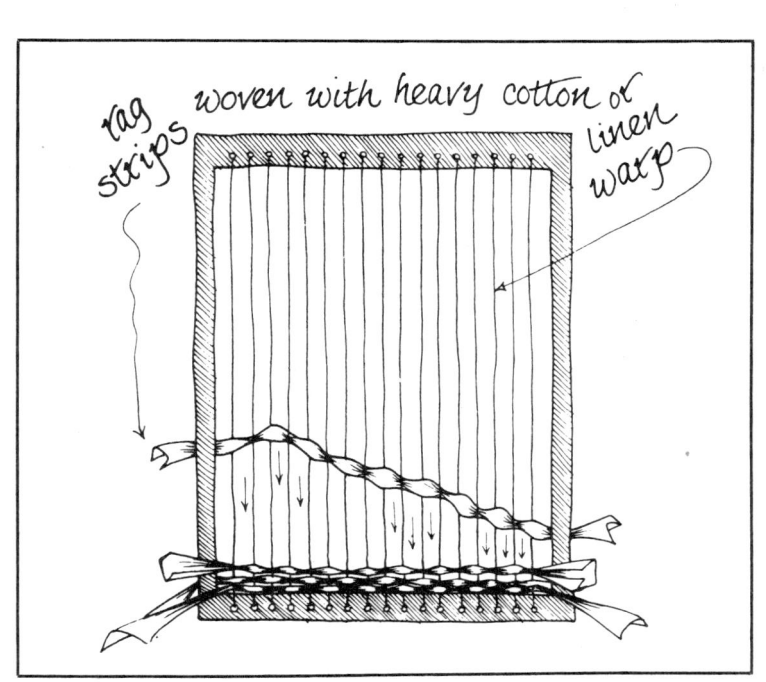

Fig. 11-31. Rag rug made on a home loom (drawing by Liz Buell).

Knitted Rugs

Knitted rugs were made by knitting rags on large wooden needles. Either strips or squares were knitted, then arranged in whatever designs and color combinations were desired, and finally sewn together. These knitted strips could be made into round or oval rugs. Sometimes they were sewn onto a lining. In later years, yarn was used instead of rags for knitting rugs.

When making knitted rugs of rags or heavy yarn, you knit strips or squares (Fig. 11-32). Then you arrange the strips or squares in pleasing combinations and sew them together, using heavy thread. With squares, you can make square or rectangular rugs. With strips, you can make oval, round, or rectangular rugs.

Another type of knitted rug is made with a lining. You knit and purl yarn strips until they are 3 or 4 inches wide and of the length you want the rectangular or square rug you're making. You can make a round rug with these strips, too.

Make your lining for these rugs from burlap or ticking of the size you want your finished rug. Hem it. Then sew both sides of each strip to the lining. If you're using ticking, you can line the knitted strips up along each strip of the ticking.

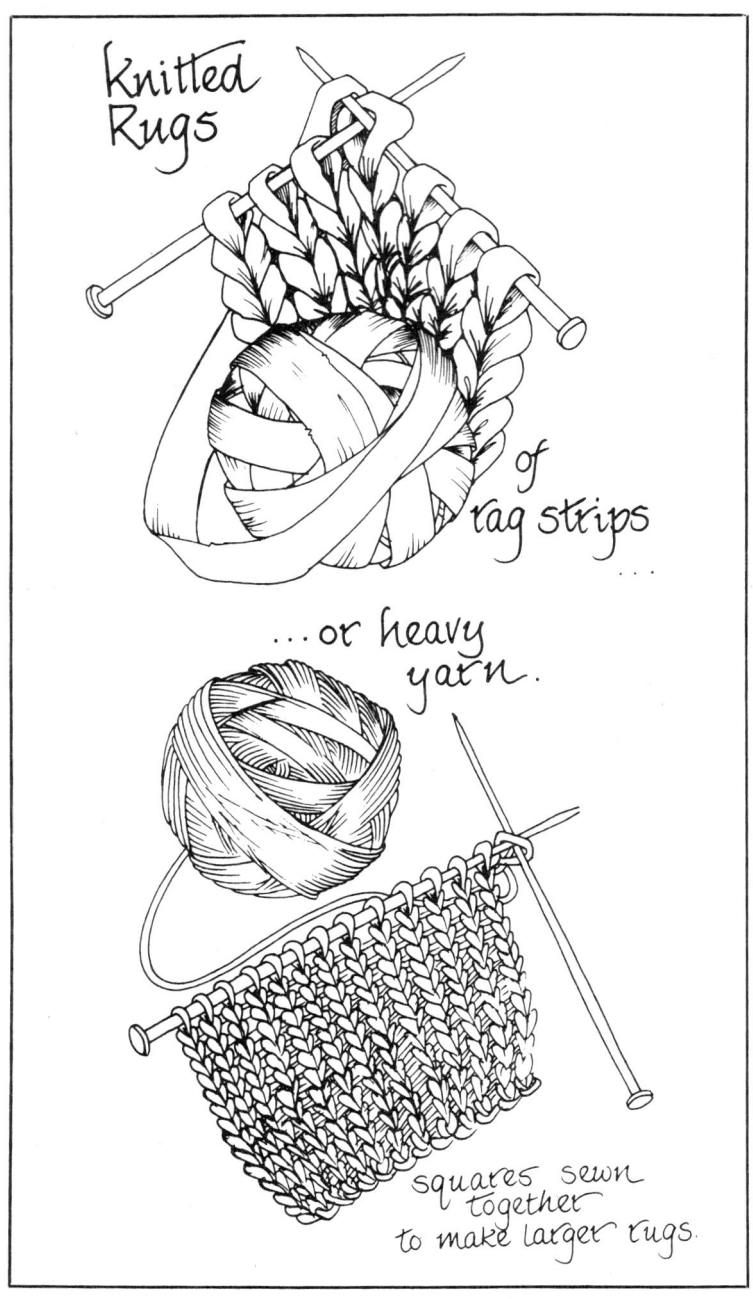

Fig. 11-32. Knit strips or squares when making knitted rugs of rags or heavy yarn (drawing by Liz Buell).

Crocheted Rugs

Crocheted rugs are thought to have originated in the mid-nineteenth century and have been made in many homes since then. The trick in making them is to increase just enough, as one crochets round and round, so that the finished rug will lay flat and not curl up.

Crocheted rugs usually are round. Cut the rags into about 1-inch bias strips and sew the ends together. Then with a large wooden hook, crochet the rug, starting with ch three (Fig. 11-33). Then sl st in first ch. Ch one, two sl st in each ch st and continue sl st round and round. Every so often though, you may have to increase or widen so that the rug will lay flat. You have to use your judgment about this.

Another way to crochet rugs is to use a single crochet stitch (Fig. 11-34). Ch three; then sl st in first ch. Ch one; sc in each stitch, around and around. Increase enough so the rug will lay flat, but do not increase so much that it will ripple instead.

Hooked Rugs

Hooked rugs were made especially throughout New England, from colonial days until the late 1800s when machine-made rugs gained in popularity. This type of rugmaking developed into one of the truly American folk arts.

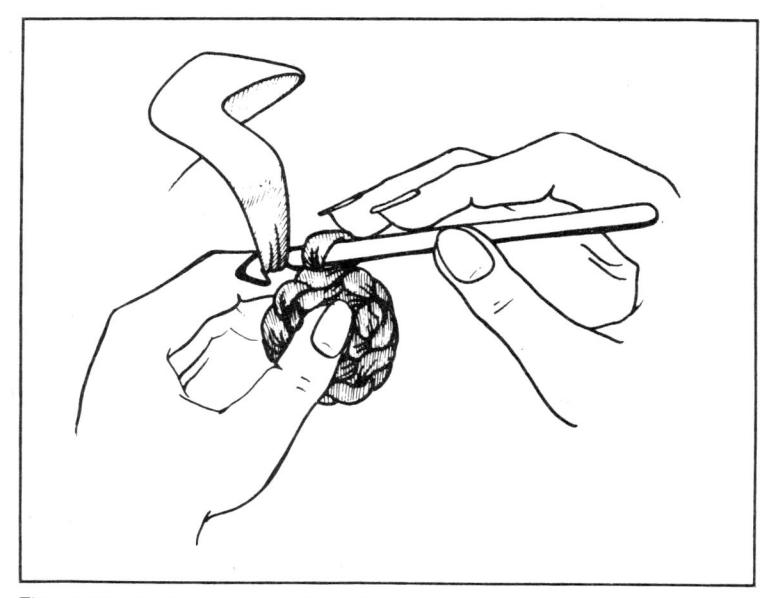

Fig. 11-33. Starting a chain stitch (drawing by Liz Buell).

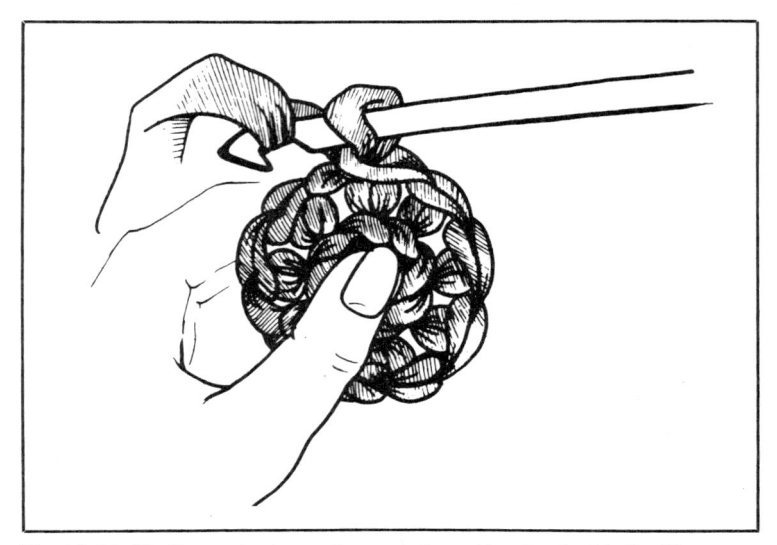

Fig. 11-34. Starting a single crochet round rug (drawing by Liz Buell).

The homemaker hooked thin strips of cloth through burlap or coarse canvas or linen. The early rugmakers even used old sugar and flour sacks for the backing through which they hooked the strips.

These rugs were hooked in various designs, and the creativeness of the woman was truly revealed. The designs usually were simple, but they were spontaneous, colorful, and original. Although they might be crude and primitive, they were created in a sincere attempt to add color to drab homes and cabins. Designs on these rugs would include birds, animals, flowers, scenes, patriotic emblems, and geometric designs.

To make a hooked rug, you need a foundation, a hook, and preferably woolen fabric cut into thin strips. You'll probably want a frame to hold your work as you hook. To hook a rug, you pull narrow woolen strips up through burlap mesh to make loops and the top (Fig. 11-35).

Many burlap backings come with a design already stamped on them. You then decide your color scheme (unless one is given with the backing) and buy wool to match. You can buy wool in graded shades for shading the various parts of your rug.

When starting to hook, though, you may want to use old woolen clothing cut into strips, for new wool gets rather expensive. If you don't have much old wool clothing, look through thrift shops or go to rummage sales where it often can be obtained inexpensively.

Cut your fabric on the straight grain of the goods. If you're using wool flannel, it's a general rule to cut it into strips of ⅛ inches to ¼ inches wide. With heavy fabrics, you cut narrow strips and with lightweight fabrics, wider strips. After hooking awhile, you'll be able to determine the widths of various fabrics that will hook well.

If you're going to do much hooking, it's a good investment to purchase a cutting machine. They cut your fabric quickly by cutting several strips at one time.

Most rug hookers use a hand hook. It looks like a crochet hook with a wooden handle. When using these, you work from the front of the rug.

There are automatic hooks that can be used and usually make the work go faster. With this type of hook, you work from the back of the foundation.

Before you start hooking, machine stitch around the edge of the burlap foundation. Sew about 1 inch beyond the outside edge of your pattern. When doing this, use two rows of straight stitching or one row of zigzag stitching. This keeps the rug from fraying while you're working on it.

Some rug hookers prefer to finish the edges of the rug before they start hooking. Others leave it until they've finished. When

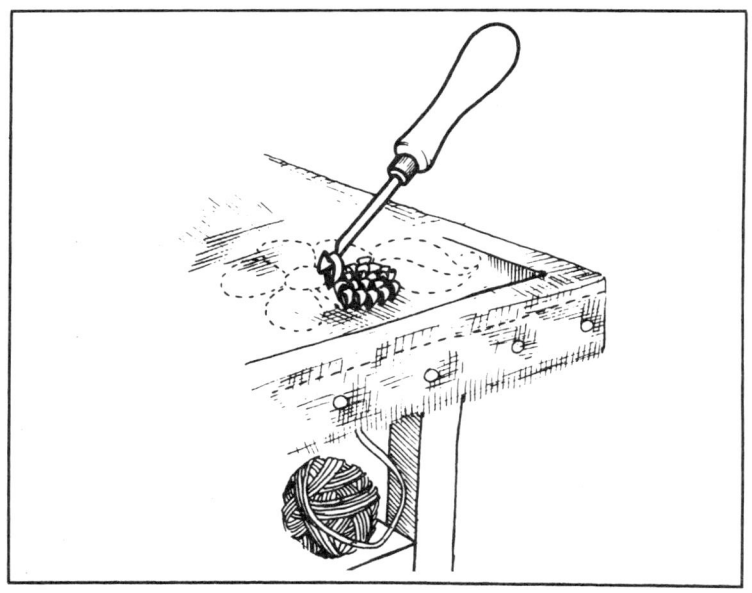

Fig. 11-35. Narrow rag strips or yarn are hooked through burlap on a frame to make a hooked rug (drawing by Liz Buell).

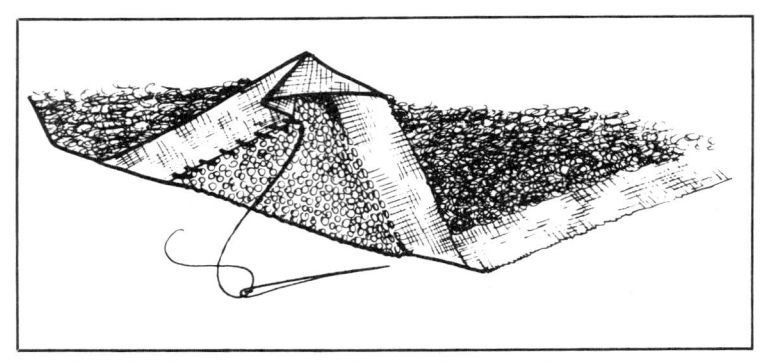

Fig. 11-36. Turning the hem under the rug (drawing by Liz Buell).

finishing before hooking, turn a hem under all the way around (Fig. 11-3). Then sew it securely with a number of rows of basting stitches. If you do it this way, you'll hook your rug to the edge through both thicknesses.

When finishing off the rug after hooking, turn the hem under and sew it into place. With both methods of finishing, you'll probably want to sew rug binding over the hem to finish it more neatly and durably after you've finished your hooking. Finishing the rug off well is important because the edges get a great deal of wear. There are other methods of finishing a hooked rug.

You'll probably want a frame to hold your work firmly while you're hooking, although some rugmakers who use a hand hook work without a frame. Some rug hookers prefer a frame on a stand. Others would rather have one they can use on their lap. If you're doing large rugs, the lap-held frame gets heavy and unwieldy as you get near the end of your work. This method is very good for the smaller hooked pieces you may be working on for chair seats and hangings.

To hook your rug, hold the hook in the right hand (reverse this direction if left-handed). You hold the strip of wool under the foundation (burlap) in your left hand. Insert the hook down through the burlap from the top and draw up a loop of wool to a height of about ⅛ inch. All ends of the wool will be pulled through the front to about 1 inch and then cut off even with the loops.

Put your hook through the next hole and pull up another loop. Keep doing this, working in any direction that seems easy for you. You'll want to skip holes in the burlap frequently so that the loops will not be packed too tightly together. These skips will not show, for the loops will fill in any skip. Do not skip so frequently that you have spaces in your hooking.

Usually you hook the design of the rug first and finish the background last. It is preferable to hook one or two rows of background around a design as soon as you complete one design and before going on to the next. This lets you make sure the edges of the design will show up well, and it will help you preserve the design shapes when you do the background. Some people would rather hook the background as they go along. This can be done.

You can hook your background in curvy lines or straight lines. It is considered easier, though, for beginning rug hookers to use curvy lines. As you get near the edge of your rug, hook two or three close, straight lines. Since the edges of the rug get the most wear, they must be hooked well.

After you've finished your hooked rug, you may want to get it dry cleaned. A friend who hooks many rugs finds that the lighter colors often tend to get slightly soiled from perspiration and oils from her hands as she works. Dry cleaning freshens it up.

You can press it yourself. One way is to use a damp cloth and steam press the rug well on the wrong side. You also can press the rug on the right side using this method. But do it very lightly.

Rugmaking of any kind is a fascinating hobby and art. As you make objects of beauty for your home, you'll be creating works of art that will be lasting American traditions in the years to come. Your rugs will be the ones that reveal to future generations the rugmaking techniques and designs of this era.

Sheepskin Rug

If you've been thinking of trying your hand at working with animal hides, making a sheepskin rug is a good place to start. Because you will probably be wanting a soft rug, you will naturally be keeping the fleece on and can skip all the messy and more difficult steps like scraping, dehairing, and tanning that would be required for making leather. Because the rug will be used on the floor, there's quite a bit of leeway as to how soft the flesh side can be—from nearly as soft as chamois to almost as tough as rawhide. For durability's sake, you may want it on the tougher side. There is no way you can go wrong. If you start with a sheep hide and are willing to do a little work, you're bound to end up with a nice soft sheepskin rug for your efforts.

First, you need a hide from a freshly killed sheep. If you don't know someone who will be butchering a sheep (most people just throw the hide away and you can usually have it for the taking), or if you don't raise sheep yourself, there are other ways of getting a sheep (Fig. 11-37). During the lambing season (late winter through spring) you can ask sheep farmers for a "bummer" lamb (lamb whose mother has died or refused to accept them). Most will gladly give you one free, and then you can raise it up yourself. This will require quite a bit of attention on your part as the lamb will need to be bottle fed three times a day for several weeks, so be sure you will be able to take on the responsibility. Then, when the lamb is about five months old, be sure that you are emotionally able to handle the butchering, and you've got delicious meat for your table as well as your sheepskin pelt. Another way to get a sheep is to buy an aged ewe or ram.

Let's assume you've got your pelt. Now what? The first step is to clean both sides. You'll want to get all the blood and dirt off. If you have a hose, turn that on full blast and really go over the hide well. Streams or any other running water work well, too.

Now comes the only real work—scraping all the meat, fat, and membranes from the flesh side. It's easiest to do this if you stretch the hide out on a flat surface at about waist level. Then do whatever you have to do and use whatever you find easiest to scrape the hide clean. You can use an assortment of old dull knives and files and keep some liquid soap and a nail brush handy to really emulsify and scrub at the fat. Almost any tool with a flat edge will be of help to you since whatever you use, it's really a matter of persistence and how fine a job you want to do. One of the next steps, salting the hide, will help remove most of the membranes that are missed this first time around. Provided you get off the pieces of fat and meat, it really doesn't matter if you aren't able to get the flesh side perfectly clean. If you plan to progress beyond making rugs (to making buckskin, for example), it is something that you have to learn to do well and maybe even enjoy.

After getting the hide scraped as clean as you're willing and able to do, it is time to tack it up for salting. Ideally, the fleece side

Fig. 11-37. Hide from a sheep makes a nice sheepskin rug (drawing by Liz Buell).

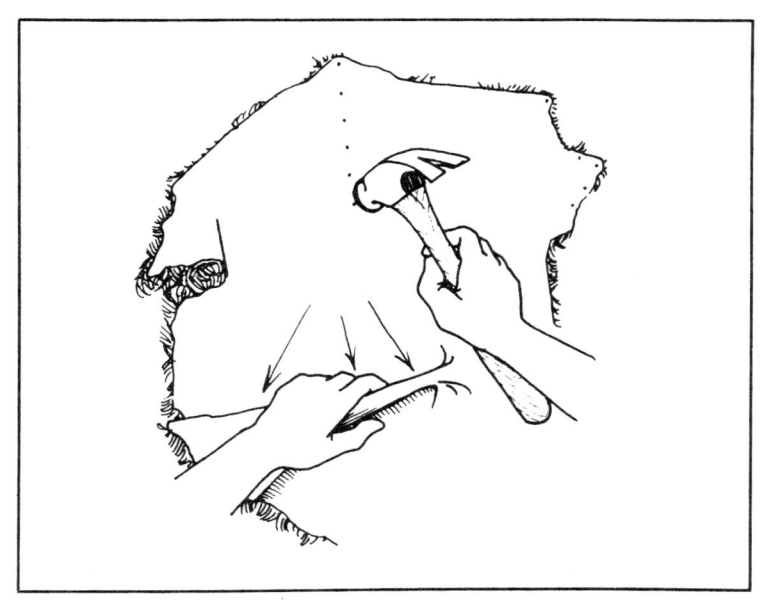

Fig. 11-38. Pull the skin back while nailing (drawing by Liz Buell).

should be close to dry and the flesh side damp enough for salt to adhere to it. If you have a corncrib or some other spot that will allow the fleece side to get some sort of ventilation, you can hang the hide up while both sides are quite wet. If you can't manage this sort of thing, let the fleece side dry and then wet down the flesh side before tacking it up.

Although most books on working with hides say to tack pelts up in a place away from direct sun and heat, you can tack yours up in direct sunlight or even behind the wood cookstove. Make sure the skin will be out of the rain.

When tacking the pelt up, you will want to do it in such a way that the finished rug will lie flat and be as big as possible. The best way to do this is to begin at the neck, and using as small a nail as you can get, hammer a row of nails down the center of what was the critter's back to its tail. Pull the skin back as you go along to prevent wrinkles (Fig. 11-38). Then pull the legs out and tack them, getting both sides to match, and finish it all off by tacking down the rest of the hide. If you keep the nails close to the edge, the nail holes will be less noticeable. If you plan to trim your rug, they'll probably be trimmed off.

Now comes the easy part. Get a bag of salt (not iodized) and cover every part of the flesh side with it. Be especially generous around the edges or any other part where you were unable to scrape the hide completely free of membranes. (If there's any grass or other growing things under the spot where you've tacked up your hide, be sure to cover them before doing the salting.) Wait a couple of days until the salt has thoroughly dried. Then get a wire brush and some sandpaper (a mixture from very coarse to fine is best), and you're ready for the fun part.

Go over the hide with the wire brush to remove the salt, rubbing hardest on the spots where membranes were left adhering (Fig. 11-39). On really stubborn spots, use your coarsest grade of sandpaper. When you've finished, the hide should have a rough suedelike appearance. To get a more chamoislike texture, use the finer grades of sandpaper to remove the rough edges.

When you've got it to your liking, take the hide down and lay it on the ground, flesh side down, to decide whether any of the edges need trimming. If any of them are particularly ragged (if whoever skinned it was new at it, they probably are) or if you want a more finished appearance, now's the time to trim it down. Use a knife for the best results, since scissors will cut the fleece and make your rug look hacked at.

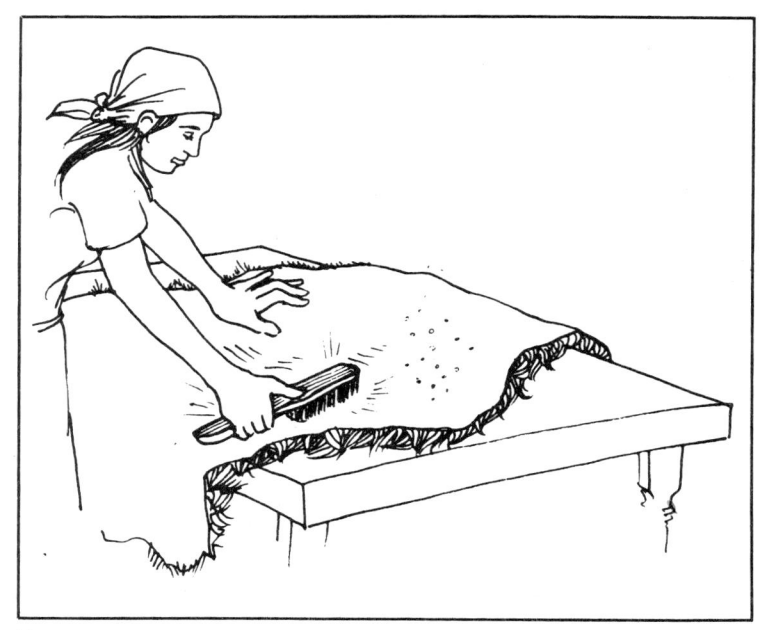

Fig. 11-39. Work dried, salted skin into white leather with a wire brush (drawing by Liz Buell).

If you like the rough appearance of the fleece side, you're finished. If you want to make your rug as soft as it can be, comb it out. You can use a comb, but this is pretty tedious. A rake brush (the kind dog owners use on their long-haired dogs) works best. Don't worry if some of the fleece comes off in your comb or rake as you brush your rug. It's to be expected. Save those bits of fleece, though. Birds love to use them during spring nesting season. If you raise rabbits, the fleece is just the thing for providing extra covering for baby bunnies on cold nights.

Chapter 12

Gardening

What is a garden? Traditionally, the word means a more or less enclosed place in which to grow plants. Although today the word garden has been stretched to mean any place plants are grown, it is well to keep the idea of enclosure in mind when selecting a site and planning the garden. Enclosure may be by a background of shrubs, a vine-covered trellis, a fence, or a wall.

The type of background used will depend a great deal upon the amount of space that can be devoted to it, and the size of the garden to be developed. If you develop a very formal garden, then a rigid formal background is required. Brick walls have been the classic background for most formal garden settings. Since home gardens are generally informal, a greater variety of backgrounds are suitable. If space is limited, a fence or narrow sheared hedge will suffice. With adequate depth, a garden may be developed in front of a large informal shrub planting, or even with the woods as a background.

SPRING AND SUMMER FLOWER GARDENING

Some plants such as irises or peonies look well when grown by themselves in rows. Large irregular masses of several kinds of flowers generally are the most appealing.

The width of the bed or border will determine not only how effectively a garden can be established, but how easily it may be cared for. A 4-foot wide bed is too narrow to include all the desired plants. A 10-foot bed is too wide to work easily unless a patch can be constructed halfway in. A 6 to 8-foot width is ideal.

When using a 6 to 8-foot bed, there is room to plant three or four groups of different flowers from front to back. This will permit planning a perennial garden with plants that bloom at different seasons. It is also more ideal for annuals, for it allows depth enough for large groupings of varying heights.

Plants generally are arranged in a border seen from only one side, with low ones in the foreground and high plants toward the back of the bed. Some departure from this to create irregularity is pleasing. One should not strive for a steplike effect.

Grouping plants of the same kind is better than scattering single plants out along the entire garden. Clumps of three or five delphinium, three or four phlox, etc., will make for impressive groups in the border. Masses all of one color often are more pleasing than a mixture of colors. This is not always possible with all kinds of plants, especially annuals.

Many people say they want a perennial border because they will not have to plant each year, or that it is easier to care for. Although you may not have to replant, there still is considerable work in maintaining an attractive perennial garden. Planning a complete perennial border to have color throughout the season is difficult. The inclusion of annuals with perennials will bring much needed color during midsummer. Many gardens are developed with tall perennials as background and annuals as foreground plants.

You should consider using many of the spring flowering bulbs in the garden. Plan to place these in mass groupings of several bulbs. With a bit of planning, bulbs can be situated so that other plants will cover the ripening foliage during early summer.

Most garden flowers do best when grown in full sun, but many will make fairly satisfactory growth with half-day sun. Gardens located near trees may not only have shading problems, but may receive competition for food and water from the trees.

The flower garden should also be located in a well-drained place. If drainage appears to be a problem, there are two solutions. One is to install drain tiles 18 inches below the surface, leading into a drain or lower part of the yard. If drainage is impossible, a raised bed can be constructed. This may be behind a low retaining wall, or with a soil embankment which will allow excess water to drain or seep out into the surrounding area.

Annuals can at times be grown in poorly prepared soil if enough fertilizer and water are supplied, but perennials seldom survive more than one or two years in poor soil. Beds should be spaded or tilled to a depth of 15 to 18 inches, or about two spade depths. Many soils have hard clay or poor subsoil under the surface. Following house construction, subsoil may have been bulldozed over an area, and only a few inches of topsoil added on which to seed grass. A test hole will quickly reveal what is below the surface.

If the soil is poor, the quickest and most satisfactory way may be to dig out and discard the poor soil, then bring in good topsoil or loam. Most soils, unless they are hard clay, can be conditioned into a favorable garden soil by the addition of varying amounts of organic matter and sand. If there are several inches of good topsoil with poor subsoil, you may remove the topsoil and then condition the subsoil by adding liberal amounts of well-rotted manure, peat moss, leaf mold, or compost.

Most garden soils, unless previously cropped, are very low in fertility and tend to be quite acid (low pH). For a small charge a soil test can be made at state agricultural colleges that will determine what the soil fertility and pH are. A recommendation will be made by a member of the college staff as to what, and how much, fertilizer and lime should be added to grow a satisfactory crop. Samples should be sent as early in the spring as possible. Be sure to indicate the soil is to be used for growing garden flowers. Most garden flowers grow best at a pH between six and seven.

Perennials generally require somewhat higher fertility than annuals, and the plant food should be applied at the time the plants are starting growth in the spring. Garden flowers may be fertilized with either organic or inorganic plant foods. The rates to apply should be based upon a soil test.

If you live in an area with a moderate summer temperature and short growing season, it may become necessary to start many of the plants indoors and set out established seedlings to have flowers by midsummer.

Modern plant breeding and improved selection have results in many new varieties of old-time favorites that offer earlier flowering, a wider range of color, and lower, compact, free-flowering plants. One of the best examples is the large-flowered marigolds. The old African strains were very late and often did not flower until just before frost, but present day varieties begin flowering in midsummer from plants started indoors. They have also developed dwarf, large-flowered types.

When selecting perennials for a particular area, observe what grows well in local gardens. Study several seed and nursery catalogs, consult specialized garden books on the subject, and choose those plants most attractive to you.

Observe the flowering times of perennials in your area. By careful selection it will be possible to choose plants that will flower at different seasons. The vast majority of perennials are spring and early summer flowering. The flowering time may vary greatly between different varieties or species of the same type of plant, such as with phlox, monkshood and day-lilies.

Some perennials may need to be protected with a mulch during the winter to prevent damage. A winter with good snow cover is excellent protection for the perennial border.

Most of the hardy spring flowering bulbs are known as the Dutch bulbs. These include the daffodils, tulips, hyacinths, snowdrops, scilla, crocus, grape-hyacinth, and glory of the snow (Chiondoxa).

Dutch bulbs are planted in clumps in the perennial bed, along the foundation of the house, in front of shrubbery, or in a bed by themselves. Narcissus look well when naturalized (not planted in a formal setting) under deciduous trees or in the grass. When naturalizing, plant in large masses of one color with the bulbs set in an irregular pattern.

EASY-TO-GROW FLOWERS

Although annual flowers are easy to grow and bloom in one season. We recommend perennial or biennial plants as the backbone of the garden. Most will not bloom until the second season, but it seems to us that a homesteader or farmer, by the nature of his/her chosen life-style, must have an ample fund of patience. Most annuals should not be planted until there is no danger of frost and the soil is sufficiently warmed. In the colder regions the soil is not warm enough for planting many annuals until the end of May. Thus, a marigold seed planted in late May will bloom probably in late July-early August. A killing frost may arrive in late August-early September, and your marigold is finished. You've only been able to enjoy its flowers for a month. Use annual plants, particularly if you are the type of person who cannot pass the brightly-colored packets of zinnias and petunias in the supermarket without picking out a few. When many perennials and biennials are finished blooming in late summer, the annuals can take over.

The flowers described below were chosen because they are

Fig. 12-1. The coreopsis plant bears yellow daisylike flowers.

easy to grow, are not plagued by insects or disease, and are essentially maintenance-free. The name listed first is the one by which they are most commonly known.

Malva-mallow (Alcea fastigata). This is a tall (3 to 4 feet) bushy plant that belongs in the back of the bed or border. From early July to frost it is covered with 2-inch rose-lilac colored single flowers. The seeds are large, which makes the planting easy, and germination is rapid (about five days). As these plants are large, seedlings should be thinned to 1 to 1½ feet apart. If the plant begins to crowd other plants, dig it up. Malva-mallow seeds are available from Park Seed Company.

Coreopsis (Tickseed). Like the malva-mallow, coreopsis plants germinate very quickly. These plants are about 2½ feet high and bear yellow daisylike flowers (Fig. 12-1). They enjoy sun and do not require good soil. Coreopsis will bloom from late June to frost.

Foxglove (Digitalis). We have never tried to systematically plant this biennial plant in orderly rows, although we're sure it can be done. When the soil is moist, scatter them thinly over an area and, if time allows, lightly pat the soil where you suspect they might be. They should not be covered. If this method sounds haphazard, it has resulted in foxglove in odd but pleasing places, because the wind has caught and carried the seeds. If little rain has fallen, you might lightly sprinkle the general area of the seeds. Foxglove is an exquisite plant, bearing many bell-shaped flowers on long stems (Fig. 12-2). It is difficult for us to tell you how tall the plants will grow. On the average I would say 3 feet, although we have grown a few that

Fig. 12-2. The foxglove plant bears many bell-shaped flowers on long stems.

were 6 feet. Foxglove plants like moist soil and light shade in the heat of the day.

Sweet William (Dianthus). This was one of the first perennial flowers we attempted that gave us a sweet taste of success. There are many types of perennial, biennial, and annual types available in the seed catalogs. They prefer full sun (Fig. 12-3).

Yarrow or Milfoil (Achillea). The achillea forms mats of flowers on plants about 2 feet high (Fig. 12-4). The seeds are fine and should not be covered, but are easily grown. The plant is in bloom for the whole summer, and the flowers dry nicely for winter arrangements.

Peony. We have not grown these lovely plants from seed, and one source book recommends that the amateur doesn't try (Fig. 12-5). The plants are well worth purchasing and, in fact, will probably still be faithfully blooming when your grandchildren take over the farm. These plants seem indestructible. The only insect that we have seen on them are ants crawling on the unopened buds. They do not harm the flower. One warning about peonies: once they are established, don't transplant them. They may survive, but they'll punish you by not blooming for a few years.

Fig. 12-3. The sweet William plant prefers full sun.

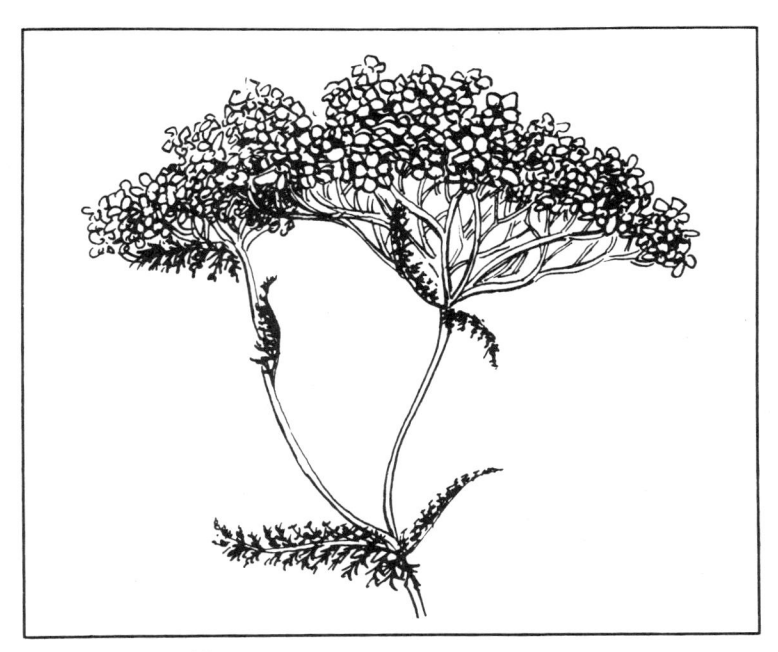

Fig. 12-4. Mats of flowers are on the yarrow plant.

Fig. 12-5. The peony is a lovely plant.

Fig. 12-6. The gloriosa daisy is a perennial.

Fig. 12-7. The shasta daisy is a pretty perennial.

Other perennials that we have grown easily from seed sown directly in the garden include gloriosa daisy (*rudbeckia*), shasta daisy, *anchusa*—variety italica dropmore, and *gaillardia*—variety goblin (Figs. 12-6 and 12-7).

Make sure the seeds do not dry out. One solution for this is to place two flat rocks at either end of your seed row and place a board on them so it covers and shades the row. You'll still have to check for adequate moisture, but not as often. This method also has the advantage of keeping the family cat from digging in the newly planted bed, although it will undoubtedly select the board as a prime basking spot.

GARDEN IN THE PANTRY

Did you know that it is possible to have homegrown, garden-fresh vegetables every month of the year, even if you live in a fifth-floor city apartment? These vegetables can be grown in four to six days on any bit of spare shelf space you might have. Is this the latest miracle of modern biological science? Not at all. It is a miracle indeed, but a simple miracle of nature, known to man for thousands of years.

This miracle is nothing more than the sprouting of a bean or grain seed to create a nutritious and versatile food. Bean sprouts have long been an integral part of Oriental fare, and they have recently gained great popularity among natural food enthusiasts in this country.

Even the United States government has recognized the nutritional and culinary value of sprouts. During World War II, our government tried to encourage their use as a regular part of the American diet. These efforts met with little success. Perhaps sprouts have been relegated by popular opinion to the realm of the food faddists. Whatever the reason, millions of Americans are missing out on a food which is not only delicious, but highly nutritious and economical as well. To top it all off, sprouts are a beautiful idea. One of nature's basic processes, germination, turns a hard, dormant seed into a succulent, deliciously simple natural food. Canned sprouts can be purchased at any supermarket. As with most canned products, though, the flavor and texture undergo a great deal of change in the processing. Canned sprouts are also limited to only one variety—the mung bean.

Growing sprouts in your own home is a simple matter. Mung beans, soybeans, lentils, or other dried beans can be used, as can rye or wheat seeds (Figs. 12-8 and 12-9). The grains will produce a

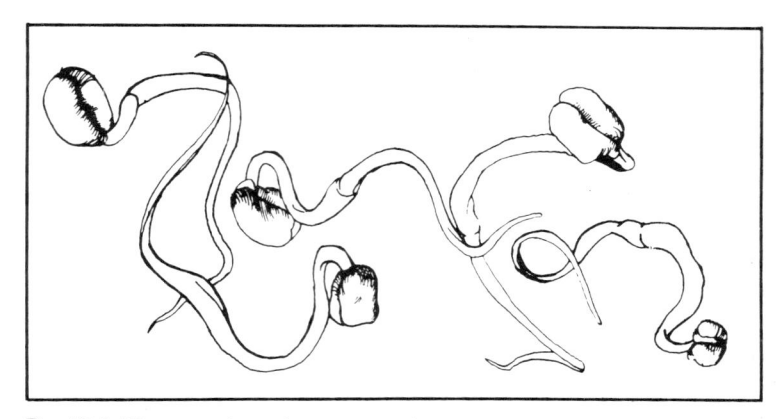

Fig. 12-8. The mung bean is a source of bean sprouts.

sprout with a sweeter, nuttier taste. Seeds bought in the supermarket may sprout, but your best bet is to obtain untreated seeds for sprouting at a health food store.

Germination is a process that involves hundreds of complex changes. Fortunately, nature takes care of the whole thing, without our having to know a single chemical formula. Before a dry seed can sprout, it must absorb a great deal of water. This dissolves the

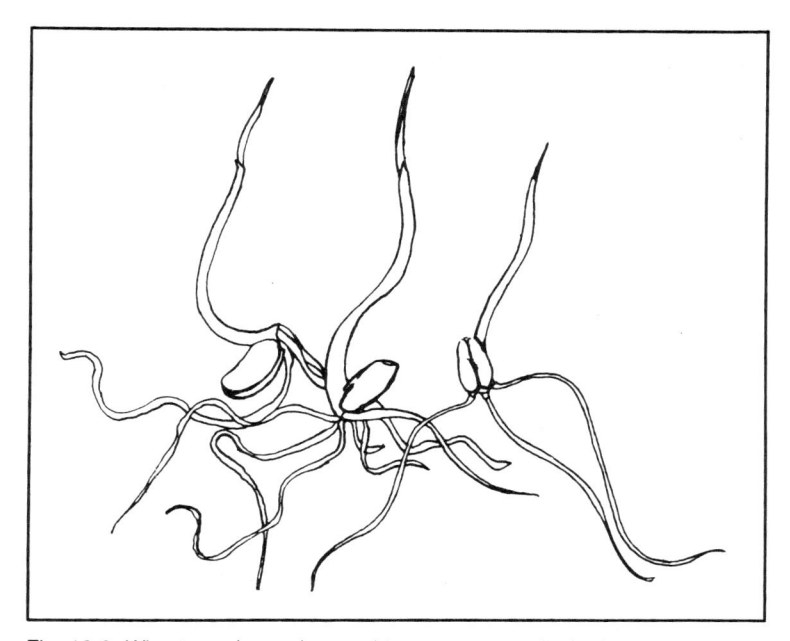

Fig. 12-9. Wheat seeds can be used to grow sprouts in the home.

chemicals in the seed, allowing growth to begin. It also causes the seed to swell to a much larger size. When you start your sprouts, remember that they will increase to as much as 10 times their original volume by the time they are ready to eat.

As the seed germinates and the seedling grows, starches and oils stored in the seed are changed to more digestible sugars, thus improving the flavor of the sprout. Even more important is the seedling's rich production of vitamin C. Beans are a rich source of vegetable protein, making the sprout a highly nutritious vegetable.

To grow your own sprouts, soak a handful of bean, grain, or alfalfa seeds overnight in plain tap water. In the morning, drain them, place them in a clean ceramic or glass bowl, cover with a damp cloth, and put them in a dark place. Keep the sprouts moist, but not wet, by rinsing them with tap water twice a day. This will also prevent mold. In a couple of days the seeds will sprout, and in another two or three, they will be ready to eat. The sprouts should be from 1 to 2 inches long when ready. As with all fresh vegetables, store them in a covered container in the refrigerator.

It is possible to buy commercial sprouting kits. The simplest of these is just a canning jar with a fine mesh screening fitted into the screw-on ring. This makes the daily rinsing of the sprouts more convenient. A homemade version of this device could be made by anyone with a pair of sharp scissors.

What kinds of problems should you expect with your crop? Very few. If your seeds don't sprout, there is a good chance that they have been sterilized by heat treatment or are just too old. Get new seeds and try again. Do not buy seeds intended for planting in the garden, as they may have been treated with toxic chemicals. If your sprouts start to get slimy or moldy, then you are not rinsing and draining them thoroughly or often enough. Otherwise, you should experience no difficulty as a sprout farmer.

INDOOR GARDENING IN WINTER

The major problems you may encounter with gardening indoors in winter are enough light, temperature, soil and nutrients, and bugs. Lighting is often a problem if you live far north, because often there is just not enough of it. Most plants need six to eight hours of light per day, although you can get lettuce, radishes, and some greens with less (Fig. 12-10). The intensity of the light, as well as the lighting time, is important. One way to deal with this is using fluorescent lights.

A grow light will help indoor gardening. The lettuce, greens and

Fig. 12-10. Fresh food can be grown indoors in the winter (photo by Kent Thurston).

radishes will do alright in southern windows without extra light, except for extended periods of cloudy weather. Tomatoes need window light and supplemental light, too. Remember that rest and darkness are also necessary for healthful growth and fruiting.

If you buy a plant light, you will soon learn of the controversy over what bulbs are best for plant growth. Plants need both red light rays and blue light rays for healthy growth. Special plant bulbs, of various brand names, supposedly screen out most of the green-yellow range of the spectrum, thus concentrating on more red and blue rays. Thus, say the manufacturers, these bulbs give more of what the plants need. Other folks swear that they have great luck with regular fluorescent tubes (one cool white tube and one warm white tube). There is a price difference. Regular tubes run $2-$3 each. Grow bulbs are $6-$7 each.

For best results place the grow light between 3 inches and 6 inches above the plant tops. The further away the bulb is, the less the light intensity.

Temperature may be harder for you to deal with than lighting. The lettuces can always be moved to a cooler room (temporarily) to compensate for extra heating, but the tomatoes sure hate that cold. If you have an automatic backup heat system, you won't have the cold problem. Bank the stove well. Insulation helps, too. Beware of drafts. They will kill your plants faster than anything else. Also, plants too close to windows can get very overheated on hot sunny days and frozen at night. Keep all plants 3 inches to 4 inches from glass panes and further away on very cold nights. Plastic on the inside of windows can partially eliminate this problem.

Soil mixtures are important. Plain garden soil gets too packed down and hard. Mix potting soil with well-rotted compost and manure. The well-rotted compost is necessary, or else you will get fungus gnats. Throw in a handful of whatever rock powders you have around and some steamed bone meal.

Each plant will use up its nutrients in 30 to 60 days. Feed them with liquid seaweed and fish emulsion.

Occasionally sprinkle wood ashes around the plants before watering. Do not use ashes that have previously gotten wet. The potash has probably leaked out.

Keep a tin each of compost and manure, brought in in the fall, and add this to the top of the pots throughout the winter. Or you can put both the manure and ashes in a container, cover with water, leave in a relatively warm place for a week or so, and feed the tea to your plants.

Soil depth is another factor. A minimum depth of 8 inches is needed. Lettuce can be grown in 6-inch containers, but it does noticeably better in 8-inch ones. Plants grown in too shallow containers will be stunted, small, and nonproductive if they survive. Use more than 8-inch soil depth for fruiting plants, especially tomatoes, which grow extensive root systems.

Another controversy exists over nonporous (plastic, metal, glazed ceramic) versus porous (clay) containers. The nonporous containers will hold water longer, thus cutting down on your work, but they also can rapidly rot the plants if you overwater or do not provide adequate drainage. If a container does not already have drain holes, either make them or put 1 inch of pebbles in the bottom before adding the soil. Do not count the drainage spaces as part of your soil depth. Nonporous pots also require less fertilization (about half the amount needed for clay pot dwellers).

Bugs and diseases may be more troublesome in an inside garden than in an outside one. Perhaps that artificial environment makes the plants more susceptible. If a plant gets buggy, spray it with soapy (not detergent) water and rinse an hour or two later. This gets rid of many things, but not aphids, and they love peppers. Try dipping a Q-tip in rubbing alcohol and putting this directly on the aphids. If you touch the plant leaves with this, burns can occur. Rinse the plant with clear water.

New plants often bring unwanted bugs that soon make themselves at home wherever they please. Always keep new plants separate for a few days until you are very sure they are pest-free.

Overcrowding the plants will encourage diseases, especially in steamy kitchens. Use only well-cleaned containers. Wash your plants when they get dirty. Clean plants that can breathe are healthier plants. You can wash them in the bath or sink, using one of those rubber spray attachments.

Chapter 13

Food Preservation

One of the major activities of a farmstead (if not the only one) is producing food. When winter approaches, the whole place becomes a food storehouse: house, shed, barn, and the earth itself. Much information has become available on the freezing, canning, drying, pickling, and storing of food.

FOOD STORAGE

In the house, food can be stored from cellar to attic (Fig. 13-1). A cold cellar is quite an asset, and its customary dampness is valued for maintaining proper humidity. Here all the vegetables of the earth can be stored—carrots, parsnips, rutabagas, turnips, and storage-type beets. Expand the variety with the Oriental daikon radishes, cultivated burdock root, and salsify. These root vegetables can be stored, with tops removed, in bins layered with generous sprinklings of sand, leaves (preferably maple but not oak), or sawdust. Cover loosely to maintain moisture or sprinkle occasionally if your cellar is particularly well-ventilated or dry.

An alternative method is to place a moderate amount of vegetables in a plastic bag, throw in a shovelful of sand, and shake to mix. Fasten tightly. To prevent rot, always let root vegetables dry somewhat if they have been pulled from wet ground. Any vegetable that will be stored should be in sound condition.

In separate containers, store apples layered with leaves or sawdust, pears wrapped in tissue paper, and potatoes alone in a

Fig. 13-1. Food can be stored in an attic (drawing by Benjamin Wilcox).

breathable container such as a barrel. Cardboard boxes can be very useful, although they will lose their stiffness eventually due to the moisture. It's a good idea to keep all varieties separate, for convenient access and to minimize spoilage, but especially the carrots, apples, and potatoes because their gases adversely affect each other. Vegetables are not inert when picked and stored; they breathe and change, and storage conditions should be geared to slowing down the latter while allowing the vegetables to respire without losing moisture content.

Peppers, cauliflower, and cabbages can be kept for various lengths of time, wrapped in newspaper. The cabbages can last several months this way, but are best stored outdoors which keeps them just like fresh until May (and also eliminates odors in the house). Chinese cabbage, celery, brussels sprouts, and leeks are excellent stored in the cellar. Pull the entire plants and arrange them close together on the floor with dirt around their roots. Sprinkle roots occasionally to maintain moisture but don't wet the leaves. This method can give you green vegetables for Christmas dinner.

Acorn or table queen is the only variety of squash that likes to be cool and moist, because it is close kin to the more perishable summer squashes. These serving-sized squashes get sweeter as time passes in storage, but eventually dry out and/or mold after about two months. If you have a bumper crop of melons, they will store for a month or so wrapped in newspaper. Crates or net bags are handy for compact storage.

If your cellar is cool enough, sauerkraut can be stored in its crock without the effort of *canning*. All canned goods keep well here, too, as well as a winter's supply of cooking oil. Humidity is not a necessary factor for these sealed containers. Metal cans and components, however, may, must and might be better stored in a drier location.

Each cellar is unique in its temperature and humidity ranges. Thermometers and hygrometers are helpful for accurate information. The ideal conditions are 35 degrees to 40 degrees and 90 percent humidity. If a furnace keeps your cellar too warm and dry, an insulated partition could create a space suitable for the necessary moisture and coolness. Three inches of gravel on the floor can efficiently keep moisture in the air when sprinkled with water. A dry and cool cellar can be appreciated for ideal storage conditions for the other types of vegetables that like to be dry. Moist and cool storage is possible outdoors. There are several possibilities—from individual storage pits in the earth to sinking a truck body into the side of a hill to create a separate underground root cellar building.

Once again, evaluate your own storage resources. You need a dry environment (usually found only inside a house) and one that is not too warm. The squashes could go under the beds (50 degrees to 65 degrees) or in closets or hallways. Perhaps an attic or other uninsulated space is available for the onions. The herbs, grains, etc., can be freezing if necessary, warm if they must, but dryness is essential.

Rodents like to move into the house in cold weather—to store their own food and help themselves to yours. Frequent checks catch mischievous rodents before much damage can be done. Cleanliness in the storage areas is a must, and all should be thoroughly cleaned and aired out in the spring.

Parsnips and carrots can be left outdoors where they grew in the garden. Cover them with hay quite deeply before freezing weather. If there is a good snow cover, they will be in good condition when the frost leaves in the spring, which will prolong your delayed harvest but also make the area unavailable for any early garden work. Kale and collards, leafy members of the cabbage family, can be protected where they grew with insulative bales of hay for a longer harvest of fresh greens.

The principle behind outdoor storage in areas where the frost goes deep is that the vegetable be the kind that will stand being frozen. Care must be taken to provide insulation so that freezing and thawing take place very gradually. Thus, cabbages can be stored in a shed if they are well covered with a blanket of hay or similar material and located in the northern area of the shed away from the sun's warmth. A barrel or tub can be sunk into the ground, filled with root vegetables, then sealed and covered well.

For large quantities of root vegetables and excellent quality cabbage, the trench method is best. Dig a pit up to 3 feet deep and up to 4 feet wide in a well-drained location. Provide a wooden frame around the top to hold back any loose topsoil. Prepare the cabbage by stripping off all loose leaves, but leave the roots attached. Stack upright but not touching, with soil around the roots for moisture and support. Make sure there is an airspace between the tops of the heads and the cover. Use narrow boards across the top frame so that only one slat need be moved for access to the cabbage. This is better than a window or door for a top because the 1½-foot covering of hay piled on top doesn't have to be greatly disturbed. A sheet of plastic covers the hay so it won't get wet and freeze up solid. This is a system that requires a minimum of energy to shovel snow and move coverings—important when your toes and nose are freezing.

Grains, beans, and seeds are the ideal staple foods for energy and warmth and will keep indefinitely when whole, cool, and dry. All provide essential protein, carbohydrates, minerals, and oils.

Whole or ground into flour or cereal, grains can be prepared in many delicious and satisfying ways. Learn how to cook them—wheat, rye, millet, barley, corn, rice, and buckwheat—for variety and nutrition. Beans are important as a complement, and they come in many flavors. The rich oils of sesame seeds, sunflower seeds, nuts, and peanuts are especially needed in the winter for warmth. Ground or whole, seeds and nuts make tasty additions to enrich any dish.

Dried herbs perk up cookery. Dried vegetables, particularly celery leaves, parsley, and carrot tops, give a green flavor to freshen up heavy winter fare.

If you heat with wood, long cooking can be more convenient if you can simmer a pot on a trivet on top of a heater stove. A cookstove is most appreciated in the winter for its warmth and utility. A soapstone (or bricks) in the oven holds the heat long after the fire has gone out, and that's possible also in a gas or electric oven as long as it is heated until the stone is hot. Bring cereal to a boil on top of the stove, then place in a medium hot oven, bank the fire, and the cereal will cook overnight automatically to be ready and steaming hot in the cold winter morning. Cook beans until soft or pressure cook one hour while the stove is hot for breakfast; then place in a crock with seasonings and put in the oven to cook in the residual heat for a delicious dinner, hours later, without the effort of keeping the cookstove fire going.

At winter's end, the diet need not be monotonous if storage and cooking efforts encompass a wide variety of foodstuffs. Early spring is the most difficult time in northern areas. Temperatures get too warm in the storage areas, supplies are exhausted, yet the earth remains brown and bare. Perhaps this is when frozen and canned produce can be most helpful. Yet, if the farmstead has a cold frame or greenhouse, enough fresh produce can be ready now to take over.

If care has been taken to provide for the storage of adequate quantity, quality, and variety, the long winter can be a time of security. One need not be dependent on difficult and costly trips to the supermarket and can be free to enjoy being snowed in. The value of the long winter is its enforced quietude—a time for creative pursuits other than farming, and for social contacts, family togetherness, or contemplative solitude. The security of an excellent food supply can leave one free to explore these other gifts of farmstead life.

STORING FRUITS AND VEGETABLES

Some vegetables and fruits can be stored in home storage areas for use during the winter months. With the higher cost of electricity to run freezers, the unavailability of jar lids when needed, and higher costs for jars, home storage has become more attractive to gardeners. Vegetables that can be stored without processing include beets, cabbage, carrots, parsnips, pumpkins, squash, rutabagas, potatoes, brussels sprouts, celery, onions, and tomatoes. Fruits to store are apples, pears, and plums.

Several factors influence the storage life of fruits and vegetables:

- Suitable stage of maturity.
- Freedom from disease and from insect and mechanical injury.
- Care in handling.
- Rodent control.
- Temperature, humidity, and ventilation.

Fruits and vegetables that are of a size and maturity suitable for table use usually store well. In planning your garden next year, provide for a special planting of such crops as carrots, beets, cabbage, and rutabagas for storage later in the season so they will reach the correct stage of maturity in the fall. Overmature fruits and vegetables are more apt to be woody and will not last as long in storage because of early breakdowns of plant tissue.

Careful handling is a must. Skin injuries, whether caused by insects or rough handling, let disease organisms enter. All bruised fruits and vegetables should be set aside to be used first. Allowing vegetables to dry before storing will help heal many small surface cuts.

Certain fruits and vegetables keep better in particular storage conditions (Fig. 13-2).

Warm Dry Storage (50°-60° F.). *Pumpkins and winter squash* need to be harvested before frost and with a piece of stem left on them. Pumpkins and squash keep better if they are cured for 10 days at 80° - 85° F. An exception to this is acorn squash, which should be stored without curing.

Cool Dry Storage (32°-40° F.). *Onions* have to be dry to store. They can be spread in thin layers in shallow slatted crates or in half full onion bags. *Dry beans* should be treated for bean weevil by putting the shelled beans in a shallow pan in an 180° F. oven for 15 minutes or by refrigerating them below 0° F. for three to four days.

Cool Moist Storage (32°-40°F.). Root crops such as *carrots, beets, rutabagas, potatoes, cabbage,* and *celery* should be stored under these conditions. Cabbage and celery with roots attached should be stored in moist sand or moss.

Moderate Moist Storage (55°-58° F.). *Tomatoes and peppers.* Wash tomatoes, dry them, and remove the stems.

Injuries to Stored Foods

Fruits and vegetables are alive when stored, and they continue to carry on their life processes in storage. They take in oxygen and give off carbon dioxide and heat. Apples, pears, and tomatoes also give off ethylene gas that stimulates ripening of some fruits and

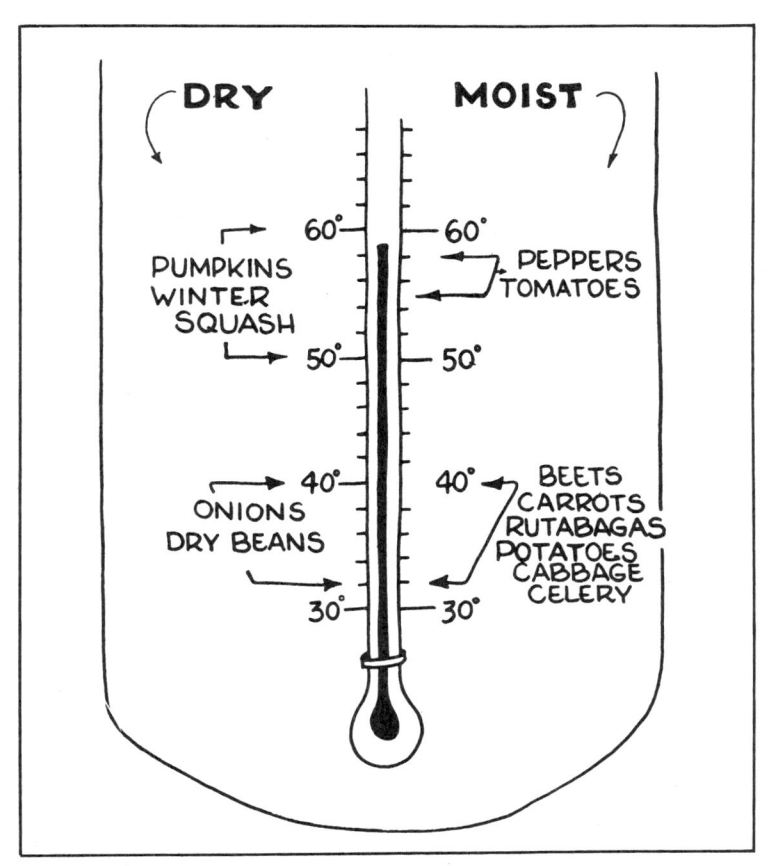

Fig. 13-2. Some fruits and vegetables keep better in particular storage conditions.

vegetables, especially when the temperature is above 32° F. Do not store cucumbers, peppers, and acorn squash with apples, pears, or tomatoes.

There can also be a cross transfer of odors between certain stored crops. Do not store apples or pears with celery, cabbage, carrots, potatoes, or onions. Odors from apples and citrus fruit are readily absorbed by meat, eggs, and dairy products. If the relative humidity is too high, the development of decay is greater.

There are two types of injury to crops in storage when the temperature gets too low. Chilling injury occurs when certain fruits and vegetables are injured by low (35°-50° F.) temperatures even though they do not freeze. Fruits and vegetables that receive chilling injury become weakened because they cannot carry on normal metabolic functions. They often look sound when you remove them from storage, but start to break down shortly after being warmed up. Tomatoes, peppers, squash, and cucumbers are very susceptible to chilling injury. They develop pitting, skin blemishes, and internal discoloration, and fail to ripen.

Freezing injury occurs when tissues of fruits and vegetables, suffering from freezing injury, generally appear water-soaked. They break down quickly when warmed and often are unfit to eat. Different commodities vary widely in their susceptibility to freezing. Some may be frozen and thawed several times without injury; others are destroyed by even slight freezing.

Most fresh fruits and vegetables, when left undisturbed, usually can be cooled one to several degrees below their freezing point before they start to freeze. If they are jarred or moved during this period, freezing starts immediately. Fruits and vegetables are listed in three cold susceptible groups (Table 13-1).

Storage Cellar

Probably the most common home storage area is the house cellar. In the old days when the houses were heated by wood stoves in the rooms, cellars were ideal cool, moist storage areas. Now that most homes are heated with furnaces in the basement, the cellar becomes a dry, fairly high temperature storage area. If your cellar is heated and you need cool moist storage, you can partition off a room in the basement. You will need to insulate it and provide for ventilation. This room should be either on the north or east side of the cellar and should not have hot water pipes or heating ducts running

Table 13-1. Listing of Fruits and Vegetables in Three Cold Susceptible Groups.

Most Susceptible	Moderate	Least Susceptible
apricots	apples	beets
asparagus	broccoli	brussels sprouts
snap beans	cabbage (new)	cabbage (old)
berries (except	carrots	kale
cranberries)	cauliflower	kohlrabi
eggplant	cranberries	parsnips
lettuce	grapes	rutabagas
okra	onions (dry)	turnips
peaches	parsley	
peppers	pears	
plums	peas	
potatoes	radishes	
summer squash	spinach	
tomatoes	winter squash	

through it. If possible, there should be two or more windows in the room. The windows will aid in ventilating the room and in regulating the temperature. The windows should be shaded as some vegetables need a dark storage area. You should equip the room with shelves and a removable slatted floor. By putting a layer of sand or sawdust on the main floor under the slatted one, you can add water to the sand or sawdust to raise the humidity.

Vegetables store better and are more convenient to get at if stored in wood crates or boxes rather than in bins. You can line these containers with perforated polyethylene.

Outdoor storage cellars can be built partly or entirely underground. One completely underground will hold the temperature more uniformly than those above ground. They can be attached to your house, or under an outbuilding, but they should be convenient to reach from the kitchen. The walls and roof of an underground cellar must be strong enough to support the weight of earth over the roof. An air inlet and ventilator are needed for your storage cellar.

Pits are often used for storing potatoes, carrots, beets, turnips, parsnips, and cabbage. The pit may be built on the ground or in a hole 6 to 8 inches deep in a well-drained location. Build your pit as follows:

- Spread a 6-inch layer of straw, leaves, or other bedding material on the ground.
- Stack the vegetables on the bedding in a cone-shaped pile.
- Cover the vegetables with another 6-inch layer of bedding material.
- Cover the entire pile with 4 inches of soil and firm it with the back of your shovel.
- Dig a shallow drainage ditch around the pit.
- On a small pit, if you let some of the bedding material on top extend through the soil, you will get sufficient ventilation.
- Cover the top of the pile with sheet metal or a board held down with a stone.

Another type of small pit can be made with a barrel laid on its side and covered with several layers of straw and earth (Fig. 13-3).

Usually as soon as a pit is opened in the wintertime, all the vegetables should be removed. By making several small pits and storing a variety of vegetables in each, you can open one and use the complete contents before opening another pit.

Keep the storage area clean in all storage conditions. Get rid of fruits and vegetables that show signs of decay. Clean your storage

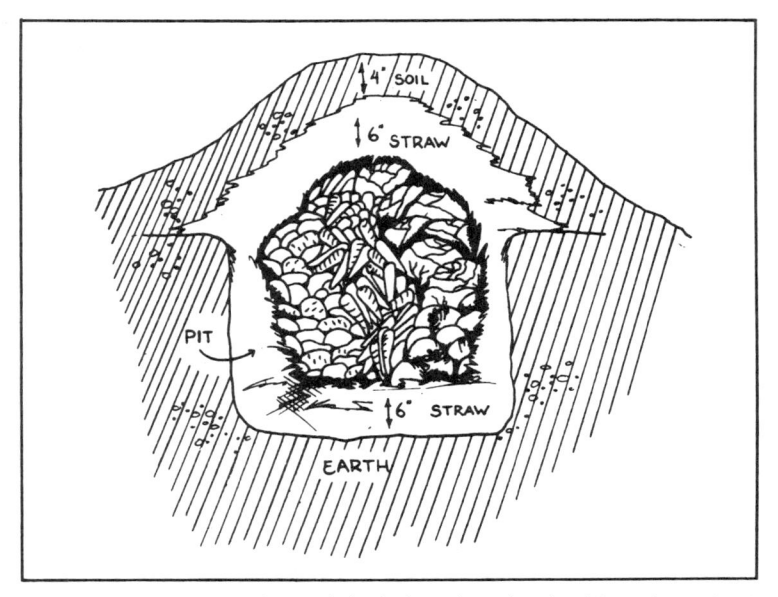

Fig. 13-3. A small pit can be made by laying a barrel on its side and covering it with several layers of straw and earth.

area thoroughly at least once a year. Remove all the boxes and crates and clean and air them in the sun. Wash walls and ceiling in the storage room.

Try to regulate the temperature in your storage cellar by opening or closing windows and doors. Use reliable thermometers inside and outdoors. The outside temperature has to be well below 32° F. Though cooled to 32° F., the temperature will rise again if ventilators are closed because the vegetables and fruit give off some heat. Close the ventilators whenever the outside temperature is higher than you want it inside the cellar.

CANNING FRUITS AND VEGETABLES

With the spiraling cost of food, many people are finding that producing and canning their own food is one way to combat the problem. The whole family can enjoy canning and have the satisfaction of preserving the food they grow. The nutritious, good-tasting fruits and vegetables are available throughout the winter season. Some people do not raise their own food. During the summer months when supplies are plentiful, though, they are able to buy large quantities at a low price and can the food for times when they cannot get fresh fruits and vegetables.

Whether you are an oldtimer at canning or just beginning, the proper canning methods should be followed to prevent food poisoning and spoiled food. There are two types of canners to use. One is a boiling water bath canner, and the other is a steam-pressure canner. All vegetables except tomatoes must be processed in a steam-pressure canner, because they are low acid. Meats, fish, poultry, and dairy products are also low acid and must be processed in a steam-pressure canner if you preserve them by canning. Improper canning of low acid foods may result in botulism food poisoning that may cause death. A temperature of 240° F. is required to kill the toxin-releasing spore produced by *Clostridium botulinum*. In the home the only way this temperature can be obtained is with a steam-pressure canner. At 10 pounds pressure the temperature will be 240° F., which is sufficient to kill the heat-resistant spore. Therefore, if you are canning vegetables, meat, fish, poultry, or dairy products, remember that the steam-pressure canner must be used.

There are several types of food spoilage, but the one that we are most concerned about is botulism. The bacterium *Clostridium botulinum* can produce a lethal toxin. It is imperative that home canners use methods that will destroy bacteria in low acid food.

The boiling water bath canner is used for high acid foods that include all fruits, tomatoes, rhubarb, and pickles. The boiling water temperature of 212° F. is sufficient to kill bacteria that grow in acid foods.

Before you get ready to can, make sure your jars or containers are in good condition (Fig. 13-4). There are several types of jars you can use. One is the old style bailed jar, sometimes called the lightning type. Many people still use the bailed jars. They have two bails, one of which is longer than the other. A jar rubber or a rubber ring is used to cushion the glass top against the lower lip of the jar and produce the seal. Jar rubbers should not be reused. The jar rubber should be placed on the jar away from the bails to prevent breaking the seal. During processing the longer bail is attached to hold the lid in place. Directly after processing, the shorter bail should be clamped down on the shoulder of the jar. This action is referred to as completing the seal.

Another type of jar is the old style *mason jar*. The closure for the old style mason jar, one that is seldom used today, is the porcelain-lined zinc cap. This type of closure is used with a rubber ring to produce the seal and act as a cushion. When using the porcelain-lined zinc caps, the cap is screwed down tightly and then

Fig. 13-4. Make sure canning jars are in good condition.

loosened ¼ inch. The loosened cap allows air to escape from the jar during processing. The lid is tightened completely after processing to complete the seal.

The modern mason jar is sealed with a self-sealing metal lid with the screwband. The seal on this type of closure is at the top rather than around the lip of the jar. The instructions for using self-sealing lids are slightly different. When you put the self-sealing lid and screwband on, the screwband is tightened completely and not screwed back to let out air. The reason for this is that sufficient air will escape without loosening the screwband. The band is not tightened after processing.

The Kerr Glass Manufacturing Corporation issued instructions in 1974 to tighten the screwband prior to processing and also after processing. United States Department of Agriculture (USDA) nutritionists and the Ball Canning Corporation disagreed with these instructions. The accepted instructions are to tighten the screwband before processing, but not after processing. The Kerr Glass Manufacturing Corporation has retracted the 1974 instructions and is following the directions accepted by other companies and agencies. Even though some instructions on lids sold by the Kerr Glass Manufacturing Corporation do have the old directions, the Kerr Glass Manufacturing Corporation is asking everyone to follow the standard procedure of not tightening the band after processing.

After processing and cooling, the screwband is removed from jar for storage. The metal lids can not be reused, although the screwbands can be used for several years.

A new self-sealing lid has recently been manufactured and is available in some stores. This is similar to the two-piece, self-sealing lid in that sealing takes place at the top rim. Instead of having the lid and screwband as two separate pieces, they are one. The directions for using this lid are the same as the old porcelain-lined zinc top. Screw the lid on tightly and then loosen ¼ inch. After processing, the band is tightened to complete the seal.

In the past tin cans have also been used for home canning. To use this method, it is necessary to have a can sealer. It has been very difficult to purchase cans for home canning during the last few years. Some people are able to get cans from canning companies, but there is not a good supply available for the general public.

No matter what type of container you are using, remember to use the size for which you have acceptable canning instructions. Most reliable instructions are for canning in pint or quart containers. Do not experiment with larger or odd size containers. Check all jars and glass tops for cracks or nicks that might cause sealing problems before canning.

If you are purchasing new equipment for this canning season, there are some things to check when buying a boiling water bath canner. The canner needs to be deep enough to be able to have at least 1 to 2 inches of water above the jar, plus room for the water to boil. Many water bath canners are not sufficiently deep to process quart jars and still have the 1 to 2 inches of water above with room for brisk boiling. Most water bath canners have a rack to make it easier to lift the jars from the boiling water and also to divide the jars so they do not touch each other in the canner or fall against the side during processing. It is possible to use the pressure canner for a boiling water bath if it is deep enough so you can allow the 1 or 2 inches of water above the jar. When using the pressure canner as a hot water bath, leave the petcock open. Put the cover on, but do not fasten the cover.

Two different types of pressure canners are on the market today. One type is a weighted gauge that allows you to use 5, 10, or 15 pounds pressure. The other type of gauge is the dial type, which will show actual pressure during processing. When using the dial type gauge pressure canner, it is necessary to allow steam to escape through the open petcock for at least 10 minutes before allowing the pressure to rise. Processing time starts when the dial reaches 10 pounds pressure. The petcock is then tightened, and the pressure starts to rise.

For the weighted gauge pressure canners, steam does not need to be exhausted unless the manufacturer of the pressure canner recommends it. The processing time begins when the weighted gauge begins to rock from one to three times a minute.

If your pressure canner is one you have on hand, check the rubber gasket and the dial gauge at the beginning of the canning season. Remove the rubber gasket in the cover of the canner and check to see if it still has spring and stretch. If it is old and needs to be replaced, replace it before you start canning. If it is satisfactory, wash the gasket with warm, sudsy water, rinse, and replace it. If your pressure canner is of the type that has a dial gauge, the gauge should be tested for accuracy. To get gauges tested, go to your local Cooperative Extension Service office. Most county staffs will test gauges for people who bring in just the gauge and not the cover. The gauge can be removed from the cover of the canner by carefully unscrewing it.

When canning fruits and vegetables, you usually have a choice between doing a hot pack or raw pack. The basic difference is that for the raw pack, fruits or vegetables are packed into the jar without prior cooking. For the hot pack, some cooking is done before placing the food in the jar. For low-density foods such as tomatoes, it may be preferable to use the raw pack. For foods that are high density such as green beans or carrots, you may prefer to use the hot pack. You will be able to have a firmer pack with high-density vegetables if you do use the hot pack. No matter which pack you use, the fruits and vegetables should always be fresh.

The quality of the product you put into the container is what you have after processing. Fruits and vegetables should not be held for long periods of time before canning. If the vegetables have to be stored overnight, make sure it is in a cool temperature. It is preferable to get them directly from the garden and process them. The quality will be better if you can vegetables within two hours after harvesting. Choose only fresh firm fruits and vegetables that are at the peak of ripeness. They should be sorted for size and ripeness for more even cooking. All foods for canning should be washed thoroughly. Inspect your jars. Wash jars, lids, and bands in hot sudsy water; rinse well and then store in hot water for canning. After the beans are cut in uniform pieces, you can choose the raw or hot pack method.

For the hot pack method, the beans should be precooked for five minutes in boiling water. Pack the hot beans loosely to within ½ inch of the top of the jar. If you are using the pint jars, add ½ teaspoon of salt. Use salt without anticaking ingredients to prevent cloudy liquid. For quart jars, use 1 teaspoon of salt. Cover the beans with the boiling hot cooking liquid or boiling water leaving ½-inch space at the top of the jar. Remove any air bubbles by running a table knife or spatula around the inside edge and through the middle of the jar. With a clean, lint-free cloth, wipe the top of the rim to eliminate any grains of salt or small seeds that would prevent sealing.

Place the hot lid on the jar and screw the screwband on firmly. Put the jars in the pressure canner that has at least 2 inches of water. Place the canner cover in position and fasten tightly.

At this time if you are using the dial gauge type pressure canner, the petcock should be open to allow steam to escape. The steam should be exhausted for about 10 minutes prior to closing the petcock. After the petcock is closed, the pressure will start to rise. When the pressure is about 7 pounds, start turning down the heat to allow it to come up to only 10 pounds. When the pressure has risen to 10 pounds, start counting the process time.

If the canner has a weighted gauge, the processing time is counted from the time the gauge rocks one to three times a minute. The processing time for canning green beans is 20 minutes for pint jars and 25 minutes for quart jars at 10 pounds pressure.

After that time is up, remove the canner from the source of heat and allow to set until the gauge is to zero or the weighted gauge no longer releases steam. Wait two minutes before opening the petcock. After the petcock is open, the cover may be removed. Caution should be taken to prevent getting burned with hot steam that is still in the canner. When you take off the cover, back away from the canner rather than putting it to one side.

Remove jars to a folded cloth or a rack. Never set hot jars on a cold surface or in a cool draft. Complete the seal at this time if necessary. Each jar should have enough room around it to let air get to all sides. Do not touch for 24 hours. After 24 hours, test the seal by checking the flat metal lid. Press the center of the lid. If the lid is down and will not move, the jar is sealed. Test the seal on glass jars with porcelain-lined caps or glass lids with rubber rings by turning each jar partly over in your hands to see if the liquid seeps out of the jar or bubbles form at the seal. Each jar should be labeled and stored at a cool temperature until used.

For fruits and high acid tomatoes, use the boiling water bath canner. During processing, water should cover the jar by 1 to 2 inches. Processing time is counted from the time the water boils briskly.

A recent problem in home canning tomatoes has developed because of the acidity variation that affects the safety of the canned product. The problem is associated with a few tomato varieties that are low acid and to some extent the climate and soil in which they are grown. For processing tomatoes, we recommend that if the variety is known to be high acid, follow the directions in USDA's "Home Canning of Fruits and Vegetables." If you do not know the variety of tomatoes you are canning, use the following procedure. Add citric acid in the amount of ¼ teaspoon per pint or ½ teaspoon per quart, being sure to mix well with the tomatoes. Citric acid is a uniform and reliable product for strengthening acidity. You may need to order citric acid from your druggist a few days before you need it.

To can safely remember the following points:

- Don't take shortcuts or experiment in home canning. Use only tested, currently approved methods, such as those described in USDA's *Home Canning of Fruits and Vegetables, Home and Garden Bulletin No. 8.*
- Use only jars, cans, and lids made especially for home canning. Never use ordinary jars such as mayonnaise or coffee jars.
- Do not reuse sealing lids. The rubber ring deteriorates easily and prevents a tight seal. Get new rings for one-piece lids and new metal lids with sealing compound for two-piece lids.

- Do not use overripe food. Products change in chemical composition with age and lose acidity. Make sure the food is of good quality, with no bruises or soft spots.
- Follow exactly the time and temperature specifications for foods and container sizes listed in the instructions. Test the seal according to the instructions.
- Do not use canned foods showing signs of spoilage. Watch for bulging lids, leaks, off-odors, or mold. If in doubt, don't taste. Destroy out of reach of children and pets.
- Boil home canned vegetables covered for at least 10 minutes before serving. For additional information on home canning and food safety, contact the Country Extension Office in your area.

MAKING JAMS AND JELLIES

Homemade jams and jellies taste delicious on hot biscuits or homemade bread on a cold winter morning, but the nutritive value is very limited. About all you get, except for small amounts of some vitamins and minerals, are calories. By commercial standards the weight of jelly is required to be at least 45 percent fruit and 55 percent sugar. The reason the sugar content of the homemade and commercial products is high is not only to make them taste delicious, but because sugar acts as the preservative. The sugar content has to be high enough to prevent the growth of microorganisms during storage. It is possible for mold to grow even in the presence of the extremely high sugar content. If jams and jellies are not sealed properly, mold will form.

A variety of names are given to products of this type—jellies, jams, conserves, marmalades, and preserves. *Jelly* refers to a product made of fruit juice or a combination of juices. A good product is clear, has a tender texture (although firm enough to hold its shape), and has the natural color and flavor of the fruit. *Jam* differs in that it is made of fruit or a combination of fruits that they have been crushed or mashed. Jams do not retain their shape as well as jelly. A *conserve* usually contains citrus fruit and may contain nuts and raisins. *Marmalades* contain small slivers of a citrus fruit or peel throughout a tender jelly product. *Preserves* are slightly gelled and contain more whole or larger pieces of fruit than any of the other classifications.

The four substances needed to make these products are fruit, pectin, acid, and sugar (Fig. 13-5). In order to make good quality products, either the substances must be available in the right pro-

Fig. 13-5. Fruit, pectin, sugar, and acid are needed to make jellies, jams, conserves, marmalades, and preserves (drawing by Nellie Gushee).

portions to each other in the natural fruit, or a commercial pectin can be used. When commercial fruit pectin is used, you are most assured of having a successful product because the guesswork is taken out of the procedure. Commercial fruit pectin comes in the powdered or liquid form in a brand name such as Certo. Some people use the terms Certo and pectin interchangeably; however, there are several brands available. Pectin is a natural substance in fruits and provides a structure to hold sugar after heating. This makes jelly gel. Some fruits contain more pectin than other fruit. The pectin content also changes with the stage of ripeness of the fruit and the variety of fruit. Both unripe and ripe fruit have less pectin than slightly underripe fruit, but the flavor of the underripe fruit is not as good. When making jelly without added commercial pectin, use one-fourth of the quantity of fruit that is slightly underripe and three-fourths ripe fruit. Commercial fruit pectin, whether powdered or liquid, is made from natural fruit that is either apple or citrus. Powdered and liquid pectin can not be used interchangeably as the procedure for using them is different. Both can be successfully used with a recipe developed for the specific type. The powdered form is added and mixed to the unheated fruit or fruit juice. Liquid pectin is added at the time the fruit juice and sugar are boiling.

Many prefer adding pectin for the following reasons. The yield is greater as it requires less boiling time. Fully ripened fruit, which is more flavorful, can be used. The cooking time is standardized, which removes the guesswork. The preparation time is shorter.

Acid is also a necessary ingredient to make jelly gel. If the fruit you are using does not have adequate acid content, and you do not want to add commercial fruit pectin, lemon juice or citric acid may be added. If commercial pectins are used, this is not a concern because commercial pectins have acid added to them.

Sugar is the next essential ingredient needed to make jelly. It helps in the gel formation, but the most important function is preservation. Jellies are preserved by the high concentration of sugar.

As mentioned before, some fruits are more suitable for making jellies without added pectin than others because of the natural acid and pectin content. Pectin and acid content varies with the season, degree of ripeness, and the variety. The fruits that usually have adequate acid and pectin for making jellies are sour apples, blackberries, crab apples, currants, some grape varieties, plums, quince, cranberries, and citrus fruits.

If you choose not to use added pectin, follow a standardized recipe for one of the above fruits. Your local Cooperative Extension Service office has such recipes in a bulletin called *How to Make Jellies, Jams, and Preserves at Home.* These bulletins are free for the asking. Less sugar is used in recipes without added pectin, but the boiling time is longer since it has to be sufficient to concentrate the sugar mixture. In order to tell the precise concentration needed, the mixture can be tested by one of several methods. Temperature method is the most accurate. At 8° F. above the boiling point of water or 220° F., if you live at sea level, the jelly will gel. A candy or deep fat thermometer can be used. Before taking the reading, the mixture should be stirred. Check to see that the bulb is not on the bottom of the kettle. Make sure the bulb is covered with jelly. For jam, the mixture must be cooked to 9° F. above the boiling point or 221° F. The same precautions hold true.

Another method is the spoon or sheet test. This is a practical method when no thermometer is available. Dip a metal spoon into the jelly mixture and raise it out of the steam. Turn the spoon over. When the last two drops run together and slide off the spoon in one sheet, the jelly is at the point it will gel. The spoon test is not accurate for jams and other products.

Another test is the refrigerator method. This is less accurate but can be used. When the jelly or jam nears the end of boiling, remove the kettle from the heat. Place some of the mixture on a cold plate and let it cool in the refrigerator. If the mixture starts to form jelly in a few minutes, the boiling has been sufficient.

The equipment needed for making jellies and jams is not very extensive. A large kettle, 8 to 10 quart size, is needed to boil the jam or jelly mixture. When the mixture comes to full rapid boil, the volume expands greatly requiring a large size kettle. For jelly an apparatus for extracting the juice is needed. If you do not have a regular jelly bag and stand, unbleached muslin or several layers of cheesecloth may be used with a colander in a kettle or large bowl. Other utensils needed are ordinary kitchen utensils that you probably have on hand.

Jars and closures needed for jelly and jam making are sold where canning supplies are available. For jelly and firm jams, any jar that is undamaged and of the size needed for your family may be used. Sealing is done with paraffin and covered with the regular cap. For jams and preserves that are soft, canning jars that seal should be used to prevent contamination and mold developing. The softer products will not retain the seal if only paraffin is used, therefore, these products need containers that can be tightly sealed.

Preparation of containers is the same as for canning. All jars, lids, and screwbands must be washed in hot sudsy water and rinsed in hot water. The jars are stored in hot water until ready to use. The jars must be hot when filled to avoid breakage when the hot jelly or jam liquid is poured. The metal lids with the sealing compound require boiling water poured over them to soften the sealing compound so an adequate seal is assured. Some jelly and jam container manufacturers recommend the jars stand upright for sealing; others recommend the container be turned upside down and then uprighted. The lid will seal when the jar is set upright. Remember to always follow the manufacturer's directions.

Select a recipe best suited for the type of fruit you plan to use for your jams and jellies. Best quality fruit does not have to be used. You may want to use fruit that is small or irregular in shape as the fruit will be crushed and boiled anyway. Make sure it is clean by washing it in cold running water. The fruit should be lifted from the container of cold water and washed in this manner several times, but do not let the fruit soak in water.

The juice of the fruit must be extracted to be used in making jelly. Juice extraction is done differently for different fruits. Soft berries may need only to be crushed. Other harder fruits such as citrus fruits will need to be cooked up to one hour. Water has to be added to the firmer fruit. Strawberries can be crushed and without cooking placed in the damp jelly bag or several layers of cheesecloth. Press or squeeze the bag or cloth in a colander over a bowl. The juice is then poured into a damp bag or cloth for a second straining. The second time the bag should not be pressed. Clear jelly can be made only with clear liquid. Only fully ripe strawberries should be used as this fruit does not contain enough pectin to make jelly without the addition of commercial pectin.

For a fruit like tart apples, a different procedure is used for extracting the juices. The apples selected should be of a tart variety, and one-quarter of them should be underripe if no commercial pectin is to be used. Remove blossom and stem ends and cut into ⅛-inch pieces. Do not bother to peel or core the apples. Add water to prevent burning and to extract the juice needed for jelly. Use 1 cup of water for each pound of apples. Cover the container and bring to a boil. Turn the heat down and simmer for 20 to 25 minutes or until the fruit is tender. The juice is then extracted in the same manner as the strawberry juice. Place in a damp jelly bag or several layers of cheesecloth and press to extract the juice. The second strainer should not be pressed to obtain a clear liquid for making the jelly.

If no added pectin is to be used, a fruit or combination of fruits that have adequate pectin and acid should be prepared and the juices extracted. Cook until the jelly reaches 220° F. or will sheet from a spoon. After cooking time is complete, remove the jelly from the heat and skim the foam from the top. If allowed to set, the jelly may start to gel in the container.

To make the jelly from the extracted juices with added commercial pectin, the procedure depends on the type of pectin. Powdered pectin is added to the juice and then brought to a full boil. The sugar is then added, and the mixture again is brought to a boil that can not be stirred down. The mixture is boiled for one full minute.

When using liquid pectin, the juice and the sugar are combined. The mixture is brought to a full rolling boil that can not be stirred down. The liquid pectin is then added, and the mixture is brought to a full boil again and boiled for one full minute. Remove the foam from the jelly.

When making jams and preserves, the juice does not need to be extracted as these products contain crushed fruit, fruit pulp, or pieces of fruit. During cooking time the mixture has to be stirred continuously to prevent burning or scorching.

There is less concern about the amount of pectin and acid in the fruit because a good quality jam does not have to retain its shape. Recipes are available for making jams with or without added pectin. If commercial fruit pectin is used, add powdered pectin before boiling or liquid pectin after boiling. After cooking, remove the foam.

If commercial canning jars are used, pour jelly and jam into hot jars to 1/8-inch from the top. Wipe the rim and place the sealing lid. Seal according to manufacturer's directions. The fruit in jams has a tendency to float to the top before the gel is formed. To prevent floating fruit when using commercial jars, shake the jar occasionally as the jam cools.

Paraffin may also be used to seal jellies and firm jams. To use paraffin, melt it in a double boiler to keep it liquid and prevent it from reaching the smoking point. Fill hot jars to within 1/2 inch of the rim. Add a thin layer of paraffin and rotate the jar as the paraffin is being poured. One thin (1/8 inch thick) layer of paraffin seals better than one thick layer or two thin layers. For firm jams when sealing with paraffin, do not pour directly into the jars. To prevent the fruit from floating, remove the cooked product from the heat. Stir the mixture at frequent intervals for five minutes. Skim off the foam before each stirring. The jam will then be firm enough to prevent the fruit from floating. Then pour the jam into the hot jars and cover immediately with paraffin.

If air bubbles form, prick them so they will not cause sealing failure later. Let the jellies and jams stand overnight, then cover with metal or other lids. For commercial jars, let set overnight to insure they are properly sealed. Label and date the product and store in a cool dry place.

If you have a lot of fruit on hand and do not have time to make jams or jellies, you can freeze the extracted juice or the fruit and make the jelly and jams as you need them. Remember to label your containers so you know if and how much sugar was added. Commercially canned or frozen concentrated fruit juices made good jelly, too. These canned and frozen juices are made from fully ripened fruit, so choose a recipe that uses added pectin.

When making jams and jellies, make only the amount in the recipe. If you try to double or triple the recipe, you may find your jelly will not gel. If you have questions concerning the preparation of these products, call the Cooperative Extension Service staff in your area for more information.

MAKING LOW-SUGAR JAMS AND JELLIES

You've all seen those pictures of the well-stocked root cellars with row after row of glass jars all filled with the summer's bounty, including little jam pots with pretty labels and paraffin lids. But how can you eat that jam with a clear conscience knowing all the sugar it contains? How many times have you tried to make the jam with less sugar only to find that the Certo or Sure-Jell won't "set" the jam without all that sugar?

It's either the open kettle method with hours of boiling the fruit-sugar mix that can result in a tasteless mush (especially with some fruits, like blueberries), or it's thin, watery jam that tastes good when first made but quickly ferments in storage, because there isn't enough sugar to keep it from spoiling with only a wax seal.

After trying all these methods over the course of several growing seasons and being unhappy with them, we spotted an item in the Walnut Acres (a retail natural foods mail-order store) catalog called L-M (low-methoxyl) pectin. This pectin turned out to be the answer to our searchings. It would make very low-sugar jams or jellies, set properly using a source of calcium ions instead of sugar, and with care in processing would keep in a cool place for a lengthy storage time once sterilized with standard canning techniques. We sent for it and waited impatiently.

When it arrived, we began experimenting with this relatively untested pectin. We found it a very easy material to work with once we were attuned to its basic properties and knew a few ground rules. The following are some of the things we've learned.

Shelf Life

Walnut Acres says the pectin is good for up to a year when stored in the original waxed paper bag. Stored in an airtight glass jar and kept in a cool, dark place, it has worked for us after as long as 24 months after receipt.

Solubility

L-M pectin is not particularly soluble in cold or hot water. You can make up a solution in advance of actual use by putting 4 tablespoons of pectin into a blender containing 1 quart of very hot water (be careful with hot water in a blender—it can be messy and dangerous) on low speed. This solution should be refrigerated and will jell when cold. It can be measured as a solid or remelted and measured as a liquid just before using.

Another method is to mix the dry pectin with the dry sugar thoroughly and then mix this with the simmering fruit mix. This method works very well, but pectin just dumped in alone will lump up in the hot fruit and give poor results.

If you opt to use honey or maple syrup for sweetener instead of sugar, you will find that the dry pectin will dissolve very nicely in warmed liquid honey or a warmed 1/4/2 mix of honey and fruit, even though it stubbornly refuses to go into solution with just water. Your taste will probably tell you to use less honey as it tends to have more sweetness volume for volume when compared with sugar. Honey, having a flavor of its own, can overpower some of the milder fruits like blueberries and raspberries. When the pectin is dissolved completely in the warm honey/fruit mix, the mixture is added to the simmering fruit as in the above method.

Calcium Phosphate

Regular pectins like Certo and Sure-Jell (called high-methoxyl pectins) are made from apples and require large amounts of sugar to thicken. L-M pectin is made from citrus rinds and needs primarily calcium ions to gel and a very small amount of sweetener to give the product an acceptable taste and texture. You may order from Walnut Acres a small jar of dry food-grade dicalcium phosphate along with the pectin. This is the source of calcium ions and has to be liquified before adding to the hot fruit. A saturated solution is made by adding ⅛ teaspoon of the dry calcium phosphate powder to ¼ cup of water. There will be a white sediment on the bottom of the container. This is simply excess dicalcium phosphate that will never dissolve. As long as there is sediment on the bottom, you can be assured that the liquid above it contains all the calcium ions that it can hold. You use 1 teaspoon of this solution, more or less, per cup of fruit mixture. It is added to the hot fruit just after the pectin is. Then all is brought to a boil again.

Both the amount of pectin and the amount of calcium solution affect the thickness of the jelly or jam. An increase in calcium solution seems to make a bigger difference than an increase in pectin. That's nice to know because the pectin is more expensive. If your water is hard, it probably contains some calcium ions. You may need less of the calcium solution to make your jam set.

Storage

Normal jams and jellies inherit good keeping qualities from the large quantities of sugar used. Bacteria and mold don't find it easy to grow in such an environment. This means that high sugar cooks can get away with open kettle canning and wax seals. Not so with this process. We need fairly sterile conditions and a good seal. Follow the steps listed under "Procedure," and you should have no problem.

Once the seal is broken, the jam should be kept cold or at least cool. It should last two weeks if cold, one week if cool. If it goes bad, it simply ferments. If the seal is intact, the jam will keep at least 12 months. We have sometimes found small spots of mold on the surface of the jam, but they did not spread and all was well underneath. This mold spotting happens more frequently if you don't process the jam with enough water to bring the level 2 inches above the jar tops. At any rate, the fear of botulin food poisoning is unwarranted because fruits are sufficiently acid to prevent the growth of the bacteria responsible.

If you have a freezer, you can make this jam up as you need it from frozen fruit and skip the whole canning business. It would take 15 to 30 minutes to make 1 to 2 quarts of jam from thawed fruit. With experience you might make 2 quarts of jam to last two weeks in 10 minutes and dirty one pot.

Advantages

Other than the obvious advantage that your jam has much less sugar and thus costs less and is more healthful, there are other pluses for this L-M method. The jam is brought to a boil only very briefly, thereby using much less fuel than the traditional "boil until thickened" method.

Also, there is less time spent over a stove during the hot summer days. More of the vitamins and flavor are retained during this brief cooking time. Jam made this way tastes as close to fresh fruit as you can get in any canned product. Jams made from frozen fruits and juices taste even better.

Procedure

- Start a water bath canner heating with water sufficient to cover with 2 inches of boiling water the number of jars you intend to use.
- Sort and clean the fruit if necessary.
- Wash jars and lids with very hot, soapy water and rinse in hot water.
- Measure 4 cups of fruit (or multiples of 4 cups—start out small) into a heavy pan (stainless steel if you have it) using just straight fruit or up to 1 cup of water or juice per 4 cups of

fruit as an extender. Apple cider would make a nice extender and flavor enhancer as well.

- Mix 2 teaspoons of dry pectin with 1 cup dry sugar or ½ warmed honey or syrup. You may use more or less of both of these ingredients depending on the thickness and sweetness you desire. If you use the predissolved pectin as mentioned under "Solubility" 1 cup of the jellied pectin/water is equivalent to the 2 teaspoons of dry pectin used above. You may add the predissolved pectin to the fruit mix without first mixing it with the sweetener as we must do with the dry pectin.
- Have ready the jar of dicalcium phosphate solution and some simmering water to warm jars and sterilize lids. When the fruit starts to boil, add the pectin-sweetener mix and stir until all is well dissolved. Bring back to a boil and add 2 teaspoons (for a 4-cup batch) of the dicalcium phosphate solution. Your results will be more consistent if you just use the clear liquid above the sediment. Stir and the jam is done. You may cool a sample on a spoon or in a small dish to check for thickness and taste. If it is too thin, add more pectin or calcium. If it is too thick, add more water, juice, or fruit and bring back to a boil. Retest until you get it the way you want it. Keep track of what and how much you add for future reference on the proportions suited to your taste. If you want to eat it now, put it in a warm jar, cap it and, when cool, place it in a cool or cold place. If you wish to have it for long term storage, go on to the next step.
- Pour near-boiling completed jam into warm, clean jars. Leave ½ to ¼ inch of airspace and seal with sterile lids.
- Process filled jars in boiling water for 10 minutes (start timing when water first comes to a boil) for pints or quarts. This step just sterilizes the surface of the jam and completes the seal on the jar by driving air out. Check the seal when cool.
- Store in cool, dark place.

If it seems like a lot of work now, it won't seem so when those jars of fruit are all ready anytime for yogurt topping, pies, cakes, fruit for the baby, and with peanut butter and toast.

Chapter 14

Cooking

This chapter contains some excellent recipes using apples, honey, parsley, spinach, and beets. It's a homemaker's delight.

APPLE RECIPES

Apples have been around for centuries. The German *apfel*, the Celtic *avlan*, and the Anglo-Saxon *aple* are of common origin. There are now hundreds of different species of apples grown in the United States.

Apples are one of the best foods for our health. They're good eaten fresh or cooked. Apples contain vitamins C and B. A nice, ripe apple is from 8 to 11 percent sugar, and fruit sugar is a good source of energy.

When using apples in cooking, remember they blend well with softer materials like rice or tapioca and other cooked fruits. Apples and doughs make a good combination with a little spice to improve the flavor. Combine apples with foods that do not have a strong flavor of their own, which would conflict or cover the taste of the apple.

Apple Chutney

3 green peppers
1 medium sized onion
12 tart apples

1 1/2 cups seeded raisins
1 tablespoon salt
3 cups vinegar
1 1/2 cups sugar
1 1/2 tablespoons ground ginger
3/4 cup lemon juice
1 1/2 cups tart grape jelly
1 tablespoon grated lemon rind

Peel and core the apples. Put peppers, apples, raisins, and onions through a food chopper. Place in a large saucepan. Add the remaining ingredients and simmer 1 hour or so until thick. Pour into sterilized jars and seal at once. It makes 4 pints.

Apple Cranberry Pie

2 1/2 cups sliced apples
1 1/2 cups halved cranberries
1 cup sugar
1/4 cup water
nutmeg
cinnamon
pie pastry

Cook your apples, cranberries, and sugar together in water over low heat until the fruit is tender. Line a 9-inch pie plate with pastry and fill with cooked fruit. Sprinkle cinnamon and nutmeg on top. Cover with crisscross pastry strips. Bake at 450° F. for 10 to 15 minutes. Reduce heat to 350° F. and bake for 25 to 30 minutes.

Apple Muffins

2 cups sifted flour
2 teaspoons baking powder
1/2 teaspoon salt
1/2 cup sugar
1/2 teaspoon cinnamon
1 egg, beaten
1 cup milk
1 tablespoon melted shortening
1 cup finely chopped raw apples

Sift dry ingredients and moisten with the combined egg, milk, and shortening, stirring only enough to blend thoroughly. Add the chopped apples, turn into well-greased muffin pans, and sprinkle the surface with cinnamon sugar (2 tablespoons of sugar mixed with ½ teaspoon cinnamon). Bake at 350° F. for 25 minutes.

Applesauce Aging Cake

1 teaspoon cinnamon
1/2 teaspoon nutmeg
1 1/4 cups sifted flour
1 teaspoon baking soda
1/2 cup shortening
1 cup brown sugar
1 egg
1 cup tart applesauce
1 cup seedless raisins
1/2 teaspoon ground cloves
1/2 teaspoon salt

Mix first six ingredients. Sift together a few times. Cream shortening with a big spoon. Mix sugar evenly throughout. Add egg and beat until light. Stir in applesauce lightly. Add flour mixture in three stages, beating thoroughly each time. Add raisins. Be careful not to let them bunch up on the bottom of your pan. Pour into greased pan. Bake 350° F. for 30 minutes. Wrap the cake up when cold and eat it a day or two later. The cake gets better in flavor as the days go by. Be sure to put it in a tight box or wax paper to keep it moist.

Fritters

2 fair-sized eating apples
powdered sugar
2 tablespoons flour
1/4 teaspoon baking powder
1 well-beaten egg
1/4 cup milk

Pare your apples and core. Slice them and sprinkle with powdered, sifted sugar. Make the batter with flour, baking powder, egg, and milk (like thick cream). Dip apple slices in your batter and drop into boiling hot fat. Take out as soon as they become dark brown in color. Drain on paper bags and sprinkle with powdered sugar.

Apple Breakfast Cake

1 1/2 cups tepid water
1 cake compressed yeast
1/4 cup sugar
1 1/2 teaspoon salt
3 1/2 cups flour
4 tablespoons melted fat

Dissolve the yeast in the tepid water. Mix and sift the dry ingredients and then add the yeast and water. Mix well. Now add the fat and beat thoroughly. Set the cake in the warming oven (or warm place) to rise. When it has doubled its bulk, stir it well and turn into a shallow, greased baking tin.

Spread the dough evenly all over the pan with hands or spoon. Cover the top with good, firm, tart cooking apples, sliced thin. After your dough has doubled its bulk again from rising, bake it in a moderate oven 380° F. or 400° F. for 45 minutes. About 15 minutes before it is done, remove the cake from the oven and pour over it a syrup made by combining and boiling for 5 minutes:

1 cup brown sugar
1/2 cup water
2 tablespoons butter
1/4 teaspoon nutmeg

Return the cake to the oven and finish baking. Serve hot.

HONEY RECIPES

There simply isn't anything healthful that can be said for sugar. Honey, on the other hand, does have minerals (including iron) and some vitamins. More important, it's a natural, unrefined sweet that can be free of additives and preservatives.

Cookies and cakes baked with honey will stay fresh longer because honey absorbs and retains moisture. This makes honey a wonderful ingredient when cooking for a few days ahead or sending goodies through the mail. Honey holiday treats are practical, too. Baking can be done a few days ahead of time.

Most baking recipes calling for sugar can have a honey substitution. You can use about ⅔ cup of honey for each cup of sugar that the recipe specifies. Other liquids should be reduced at the rate of ¼ cup less for each cup of honey that is used. In baked goods, also add ½ teaspoon baking soda for each cup of honey in the recipe you are improvising.

Baked goods brown faster with honey as an ingredient. This can be both a curse and a blessing. It makes for beautiful crusty brown bread, but possibly an almost burnt appearance in a few long baking recipes. To prevent the latter, most bread, cookies, and cakes are baked at 325° F.

Honey Drops

1 cup shortening
1/3 cup light brown sugar
2/3 cup honey
2 eggs
2 3/4 cups flower (use half all-purpose white and half whole wheat)
1 teaspoon baking soda
1 teaspoon baking powder
1/2 teaspoon ginger
1/4 teaspoon salt
1/2 teaspoon cinnamon
1/4 teaspoon cloves
3/4 cup raisins or nuts

Cream shortening and brown sugar together. Add eggs and honey. Mix well. A somewhat curdled appearance is normal. Mix together flour, salt, baking soda, baking powder, and spices. Add to shortening mixture and mix well. Stir in raisins or nuts. Drop by rounded teaspoons on lightly greased or teflon baking sheet. Bake at 300° F. to 325° F. for 8-12 minutes or until lightly browned. It makes about three to four dozen.

Basic Bread

1 cake or package of yeast
1/2 cup flour
1/2 cup lukewarm water
1/2 tablespoon honey
1/2 cup shortening
2 cups milk (or water)

1 tablespoon salt
1/3 cup honey
2 beaten eggs
6 cups flour (use half all-purpose white flour and half whole wheat flour)

Soften yeast in the ½ cup lukewarm water. Add the ½ cup flour. Set aside. Heat milk gently. Add salt and shortening, stirring well. After shortening is melted, cool slightly. Add ⅓ cup honey. Stir to dissolve. Add beaten eggs, yeast mixture, and the last 6 cups of flour. Mix together and turn onto a floured surface. Knead 5 to 8 minutes or until smooth and satiny. Shape into a ball. Put in a lightly greased bowl and cover it with a lid. Let rise in a warm place (80° F. to 85° F. is best) until double in bulk. This may take about an hour and a half. Punch down and shape into rolls or put in bread pans. If you make bread, fill each pan no more than two-thirds full. Let it rise again. Bake at 325° F. for 25 to 30 minutes or until golden brown.

Honey Snacks

Mix together equal amounts of peanut butter, honey, and dry milk. Any of the following may be added: toasted sesame seeds, coconut, raisins, or nuts. Spread on whole wheat bread.

Slaw

1 cup honey
1 cup vinegar
1/2 cup finely chopped onion
1/2 teaspoon salt
1 medium head of finely chopped cabbage (4 to 6 cups)
1/4 cup diced green pepper
1 cup diced celery

Combine honey with vinegar, onion, and salt. Bring to a boil and simmer for five minutes. Cool. Pour over prepared vegetables and toss lightly. Cover and chill for 12 hours or more to blend flavors. If handy, stir occasionally. It makes 8 to 12 servings. For variety, substitute a little shredded purple cabbage or sweet red pepper.

PARSLEY RECIPES

Parsley is a small green herb that can be used fresh or dried

(Fig. 14-1). It can be frozen for future use. It's good both dried and fresh—in gravies, meat and fish dishes, soups, egg dishes, casseroles, cream and cheese sauces, breads, butters, and vegetables. It's a very versatile herb whose flavor enhances many dishes.

In the summer, plan to freeze and dry some parsley for winter use. One handy way to freeze parsley is to bring in some extra each time you're picking some from the garden to use in current meals. When freezing, wash the parsley thoroughly. Then package it in small plastic bags or plastic containers. When you want to use it in the winter, just take what you need and chop it into meat loaves, casseroles, soups, gravies, etc. You won't be able to use frozen parsley as a garnish, but it's ideal for cooked foods.

To dry parsley, cut the fully grown parsley clusters from the stems. Dry only the leaves. Some authorities recommend that you immerse the parsley leaves into boiling water for 30 seconds and drain well. Others do not recommend this. So you have your choice.

Fig. 14-1. Parsley is a small green herb.

Either way, place the sorted parsley sprigs onto a shallow container such as a pie tin, cookie sheet, or piece of heavy-duty foil. Put this into an oven heated to no more than 200° F. Leave the door open for circulation and dry the parsley until the leaves are crisp. This should take less than 30 minutes. When the parsley crumbles upon being stirred, you'll know it is dry enough. Store the cooled parsley in an airtight container. To save energy, you can simply hang the parsley in a dry, dust-free area for several days until dry.

To have fresh parsley all year round, grow some on your windowsill in the winter. In the late fall, transplant some healthy parsley roots into clay pots. Usually you cut the tops back and let the parsley grow again. Be sure dirt is packed well around the roots. Keep the plants watered and place them on a sunny south windowsill.

Parsley, as well as being so flavorful and easy to grow, is a nutritious herb. It contains vitamins A and C and some iron, too.

There are more than 30 varieties of parsley that are recognized by their leaf shapes. Two kinds of parsley are most common—the flatter leafed parsley, sometimes called *Italian* parsley, and the *curly leafed* parsley.

Parsley Salad

Mix together one or two bunches of washed, chopped parsley (preferably the Italian type), one peeled and diced cucumber, three sliced scallions, and three peeled and diced tomatoes. Chill vegetables until ready to serve. Then beat ½ cup olive oil (less if you desire) with ¼ cup fresh lemon juice. Salt and pepper to taste. Pour the dressing over the salad and toss lightly. You could serve it with some other dressing of your choice. It makes about four servings.

Parsley-Cheese Balls

These parsley-cheese balls can be served as an appetizer or a salad. Blend ½ teaspoon paprika and salt to taste into 8-ounce cream cheese. Roll into small balls. Then roll the balls into finely chopped parsley until they're well covered. Chill and serve with lettuce and tomatoes or on toothpicks as appetizers.

Herb Bread

Slice almost through a loaf of French or Italian bread, leaving slices attached at the bottom. Then cream ½ cup butter with ¼ cup minced parsley. Salt and pepper to taste. Add 3 tablespoons chopped chives. Spread one side of each slice with the butter. Then place the loaf on a baking sheet or wrapped in foil and heat at 375° F. for about 10 minutes or until heated through. Serve this piping hot.

Parsley Dumplings

This is an old-fashioned American recipe. Sift together 2 cups sifted flour, 4 teaspoons baking powder, and 1 teaspoon salt. Add 3 tablespoons finely chopped fresh parsley. Then cut in 2 tablespoons shortening. Break one egg into a measuring cup and beat slightly. Add enough milk to make 1 cup of liquid. Add the milk-egg mixture to the dry ingredients and stir lightly. Drop by spoonfuls into boiling beef or chicken stock. Cover tightly and cook 15 minutes without removing the cover. Serve at once while hot.

SPINACH RECIPES

Since spinach was enjoyed in China as far back as 647 B.C., it seems fitting to give you several of their recipes (Fig. 14-2). They cook spinach only a very short time with hardly any liquid—a good rule to follow.

Spinach Steak

1/4 cup peanut oil
3 cups round steak, cut in slivers, against the grain
1 pound spinach, cut into large pieces
1 minced clove garlic
1 cup shredded onion
1 tablespoon cornstarch
2 tablespoons soy sauce
1 teaspoon salt
1/4 cup water

Heat oil. Sauté beef for 1 minute. Add garlic and onion. Put in spinach. Cook 2 minutes. Blend together cornstarch, soy sauce, salt, and water. Stir several minutes until juice thickens. It serves six.

Spinach Soup

1 pound cut up spinach
1/2 pound diced lean pork
1/2 cup diced onion

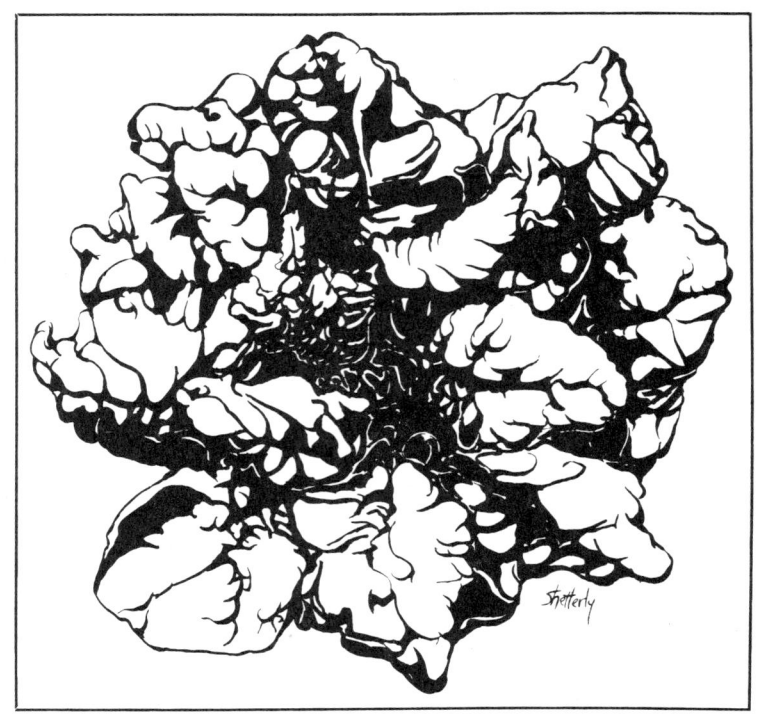

Fig. 14-2. The Chinese enjoyed spinach as far back as 647 B.C.

1/2 cup diced celery
1 1/2 quarts stock (or canned clear chicken broth)
salt to taste

Heat stock in pot. Add all ingredients. Bring to a boil. Cook 10-15 minutes. It serves six.

Fried Spinach Balls

2 cups cooked chopped spinach
2 tablespoons melted butter
2 eggs
1 cup bread crumbs
2 tablespoons grated onion
2 tablespoons grated cheese
1/8 teaspoon allspice
1/4 cup water
bread crumbs

Combine spinach with butter, one beaten egg, crumbs, onion, cheese, and allspice. Mix thoroughly. Let stand for 10 minutes; shape into balls. Combine remaining egg and water and beat together until well blended. Roll spinach balls in crumbs, dip into egg, and again into crumbs. Fry in hot deep fat (375° F.) until brown. Drain on absorbent paper before serving. It serves six.

Spinach-Rice Casserole

1 pound fresh spinach (or 1 package frozen chopped spinach)
1 cup hot cooked rice
1 teaspoon grated onion
1 cup grated cheese
2 tablespoons butter or margarine

Cook spinach. Drain and chop. Mix hot, cooked rice with cheese, onion, and butter so that it blends, then fold in spinach. Bake at 350° F. for 25 minutes. It serves four.

Spinach and Cheese Pie

9-inch unbaked pie crust shell
1 package (10-ounce) frozen chopped spinach, thawed and drained
1 cup shredded Swiss cheese
1/3 cup sliced scallions
1/4 cup grated Parmesan cheese
4 eggs, lightly beaten
1 1/4 cups light cream or milk
4 teaspoons Worcestershire sauce
1/2 teaspoon salt

Prick pie crust with fork. Bake in preheated, 450° F. oven 8 minutes. Layer half the spinach, Swiss cheese, and scallions. Repeat. Combine remaining ingredients. Pour over spinach mixture. Bake 10 minutes. Reduce oven to 325° F; bake until firm, 20 to 25 minutes. Cool five minutes. It makes one 9-inch pie.

Spinach, Tomato, and Cheese Loaf

2 cups cooked, drained spinach
2 1/4 cups canned tomatoes

1/4 cup chili sauce
1/2 pound grated cheese
1 cup cracker crumbs
juice from 1/2 onion
1/4 teaspoon salt
1/4 teaspoon freshly ground pepper

Preheat oven to 350° F. Toss all ingredients in a bowl until they are blended. Place in a general loaf pan and bake for about one hour. If you wish, serve garnished with crisp bacon. It serves eight.

Blender Spinach Souffle

4 slices cubed bacon
1/4 cup cooled bacon drippings
2 cups packed, washed spinach (or 1 16-ounce package frozen spinach)
3/4 cup milk
4 separated eggs
1/4 cup flour
1 thin slice onion
1 teaspoon salt
1/8 teaspoon pepper
1/2 cup diced cheddar cheese

Heat oven to 375° F. Grease a 1-quart casserole. Fry bacon crisp, drain well, and reserve drippings. Set bacon aside. Cook spinach until tender. Drain well. Put all ingredients except bacon and egg whites into blender container. Cover and process at "chop" until smooth. Turn into saucepan and cook over moderate heat until thickened. Add bacon pieces. Cool slightly. Beat egg whites with rotary beater until stiff. Fold spinach mixture into beaten egg whites. Turn into prepared casserole and bake 30 minutes. Serve immediately. It serves six.

BEET RECIPES

Beets are no longer just a seasonable vegetable, although any vegetable tastes best fresh from the garden. If you really like beets, you will probably prefer tender baby beets boiled and buttered or young beet greens, although beets are very compatible with such sweet spices as cinnamon, cloves, and allspice, or celery seed, dill, and horseradish which, according to tradition, was also served with boiled dinners in New England. Oranges, raisins, and apples also have a place in some beet recipes.

Beets are one of the few vegetables whose flavor is not altered perceptibly by canning. Canned beets are inexpensive and are handy for a quick side dish or salad ingredient. A little embellishment makes them very presentable.

Beets in Orange Sauce

1 can (1 pound) sliced beets
juice of 1 large orange, or 8 tablespoons canned or frozen diluted orange juice
1 tablespoon cornstarch
1 tablespoon butter or margarine
1/2 teaspoon cinnamon
1/4 teaspoon ground cloves
1 tablespoon grated orange peel (optional)

Drain beets, reserving liquid. Add beet juice to orange juice to make ¾ cup liquid. Add cornstarch, butter, cinnamon, cloves, and grated orange peel. Cook in saucepan, stirring constantly, until thick. Add beets. Heat to boiling point. It serves four.

Red Flannel Hash

4 tablespoons butter or margarine
1 pound ground chuck steak
3/4 teaspoon salt
freshly ground pepper
1 large potato, boiled and cut into small pieces
4 small finely chopped, cooked beets
1 medium, finely chopped onion
3 tablespoons thick cream

Melt butter or margarine in a skillet over low heat and add ground meat, salt, and pepper. Stir in potato pieces, beets, and onion. Simmer over low heat for 10 minutes, stirring constantly. Add cream and stir through. Cover and simmer for 30 minutes, stirring occasionally. Hash is done when a crust forms on the bottom. Fold in half like an omelet. It serves four.

Beet and Fish Hash

3/4 cup flaked cooked fish

3/4 cup chopped cooked potatoes
2 chopped cooked medium beets
1 tablespoon minced onion
1 tablespoon minced parsley
1/2 teaspoon salt
1/4 teaspoon paprika
1 teaspoon Worcestershire sauce
3 tablespoons cream, evaporated milk, or plain milk
1 1/2 tablespoons fat

Mix first eight ingredients and moisten with cream. Cook in fat, stirring until hot, then pat lightly into a cake and cook until well browned underneath. Fold like an omelet. It serves four to six.

Beet and Cabbage Slaw

1 16-ounce can julienne-style beets
6 cups coarsely shredded red cabbage
1 medium-size thinly sliced onion
1/2 cut vinegar
1/3 cup sugar

Drain beets, reserving 1/2 cup liquid. In a large bowl combine beets, cabbage, and onion. In a saucepan combine vinegar, sugar, and reserved beet juice. Bring to a boil. Pour over vegetables. Toss lightly. Cover and refrigerate several hours, tossing occasionally. It serves eight.

Stuffed Beets

Whole cooked beets
French dressing
Sour cream or cream cheese
Horseradish
Parsley flakes

Marinate small whole cooked beets at least 24 hours in French dressing. Drain and scoop out centers. Fill with a mixture of sour cream seasoned with horseradish to taste, topped with parsley flakes, or fill beets with a mixture of cream cheese thinned with a few drops of orange juice and grated orange rind to taste. Use as an appetizer or buffet vegetable.

Pickled Beets

3 pounds beets
1 stick cinnamon
1 teaspoon whole allspice
6 whole cloves
1 pint vinegar
1/2 cup water
1/2 cup sugar

Cook beets in boiling water until tender and remove skins, roots, and tops. Tie spices in cheesecloth bag. Heat vinegar, water, sugar, and spices to boiling. Add beets whole or sliced and boil 5 minutes. Remove spice bag. Pack beets in sterile jars and fill jars with hot liquid. Seal. It makes about 3 pints.

Orange Marmalade Beets

1 can tiny whole beets, including liquid
1/3 cup orange marmalade
1 pat of butter or margarine
1 teaspoon lemon juice
1/8 teaspoon ground ginger

Add marmalade, butter, lemon juice, and ground ginger to the beets. Heat. Thicken liquid with a little cornstarch, if desired.

Beet and Apple Salad

1/2 cup dairy sour cream
1 tablespoon prepared white horseradish
2 apples cored but unpeeled and cut in julienne strips
1 teaspoon sugar
1 teaspoon chopped chives
1/2 teaspoon salt
1/8 teaspoon pepper
2 cups cooked beets or 1 can (1 pound) whole beets, cut in julienne strips

Blend together first seven ingredients and combine with beets. Chill. It makes six servings.

Beet Salad, Midwest Style

4 fresh washed medium beets
1/3 cup vinegar

1/2 teaspoon caraway seeds
1/2 teaspoon anise
1 tablespoon lemon juice
1/2 cup water
1 tablespoon corn oil

Boil beets in water to cover over moderate heat for about 15 minutes or until tender. Remove beets and discard water. When beets have cooled enough to pare, cut into thin slices. Return beets to saucepan and add all other ingredients. Cook over low heat for 5 minutes. Allow to cool for 10 minutes at room temperature. Place mixture in a bowl. Cover with plastic wrap, sealing all edges. Refrigerate for at least 5 hours. When ready to serve, mix with corn oil. It serves six.

Baked Beet Casserole

4 tablespoons melted butter
4 tablespoons cornstarch
1 cup water
4 tablespoons brown sugar
1/4 teaspoon salt
3 tablespoons horseradish
4 cups cooked beets
1/3 cup dry bread crumbs
3 tablespoons butter or margarine

Blend butter and cornstarch. Add water gradually and cook until mixture begins to thicken, stirring constantly. Add sugar, salt, horseradish, and beets. Pour into greased baking dish. Cover with crumbs. Dot with butter. Bake in a 375° F. oven about 20 minutes or until crumbs are browned. It serves six to eight.

Barbecue Beets

Trim off stem and root ends of young beets. Place five or six on a large square of heavy-duty aluminum foil. Add 2 tablespoons water and a pinch of salt. Seal foil to make a package and place on grate over moderate fire. Cook 50 or 60 minutes. Test for doneness by piercing through foil with a steel tined fork. Serve each person whole beets. Skins will come off easily, and beets will have a rich red color.

If you prefer, peel and slice beets and place on foil with seasonings and a pat of butter or margarine. Seal package and cook on grate about 40 minutes.

Index

A

Achillea, 274
Acorn, 285
Adhesives, 155
American Society of Testing Materials, 62
Amoco gas, 169
Anchusa, 277
Annuals, 269
Apel, Fred, 202
Apple, 140
Apple recipes, 309
    breakfast cake, 312
    chutney, 309
    cranberry pie, 310
    fritters, 311
    muffins, 310
Apple recipes, fritters, 311
Apples, 309
Applique, 233
Ash, 140
Asphalt roofing paper, 145
Auger bits, 153
Ax, 140

B

Babiche, 214
Backhoe, 2
Baer, Steve, 64
Baffle system, 88
Ball Canning Corporation, 295
Bar, hard nose, 170
Bar, roller nose, 170
Bar, sprocket nose, 170
Barbed wire, 194
Barley, 286
Bar oil, 169
Bars, 170
Breadboard, 115
Beetle, 161
Beet recipes, 320
    baked beet casserole, 324
    barbecue beets, 324
    beet and cabbage slaw, 322
    beet and fish hash, 321
    beet salad, Midwest style, 323
    beets in orange sauce, 321
    orange marmalade beets, 323
    pickled beets, 323
    red flannel hash, 321
    stuffed beets, 322
Beets, 288, 320
Berry, Wendell, 55
Birch, 140
Blue Cross and Blue Shield, 13
Bolt wood, 123
Booker, Frank, 175
Bow saw, 18
Braiding, 254
Brussels sprouts, 284
Buckwheat, 286
Bulldozer, 39
Butterick, 225
Buttons, 225

C

Cabbage, 288
Calcium phosphate, 306
Canada, 123
Canning, 285
Carlton Chain Company, 171
Carrots, 288
Cauliflower, 284
Cedar, 190
Celery, 284, 288
Cellar for storage, 290
Cellulose fiber, 117
Certo, 300
Cesspool, 58
Chain, 170
Chain, sharpening, 170
Chain saws, 161
Chain saws, buyer's guide, 162
Chain saws, caring for, 168-172
Chain saws, electric, 166
Chain saws, using, 168-172
Charcoal, 91
Charcoal, making, 91
Chilling injury, 289
Chimney, 77, 177
Chinese cabbage, 284
Chinking, 25
Chisel and punch set, 154
Chisels, wood, 153
Clamps, 155
Clostridium botulinum, 293
Cold frame, 196
Cold frame, calculating the angle of the top, 196
Cold frame, constructing, 199
Cold frame, modular design, 197
Collector, 59
Combination square, 154
Comforter, 240
Compass saw, 152
Condensation, 103
Conserve, 299
Construction projects, 175
Consumer Reports Magazine, 118
Contractors of insulation, 110
Cooking, 309
Cookstoves, 69
Cord, 122
Coreopsis, 272
Corn, 286
Coverages of insurance, 15
Crafts, 224
Craftsman, 150
Crapper, Thomas, 50
Crocus, 271

D

Daffodils, 271
Damper, 84
Davis, 227
Dianthus, 274
Digitalis, 272
Dishwasher, 223
Disston, 150
Distillation, 92
Dow Chemical Company, 115
Dowsing, 31
Draft, 84
Drawknife, 154
Drill, 155
Drill press, 156

E

Earplugs, 171
Elm, 140
Energy, 94
Energy, ideas for saving, 94
Environmental Protection Agency, 49

F

Farm, 14
Farmer's Almanac, 196
Fawcett, 70
Federal Housing Authority, 106
Fence, 190
Files, 154
Fire extinguishers, 89
Fireplaces, 105
Fisher, Susan North, 202
Flax and wool, 247
Flax brake, 249
Floorboards, 83
Flue, 78
Food, 283
Food, preserving, 283
Food, storing, 283
Footprints, 159
Forest, 122
Forest, managing, 121
Forest, types of, 122, 123
Fountain, Harold, 55
Foxglove, 272
Fruits, canning, 292
Fruits, storing, 287
Fuller, 150
Furnace, wood, 74
Furnaces, 74

G

Gaillardia, 277
Gardening, 268

Gardening, spring and summer flower, 268
Gardening, indoors in winter, 279
Garden in the pantry, 277
General Services Administration, 118
Germination, 278
Gloriosa daisy, 277
Grape-hyacinth, 271
Grease gun, 155
Great Lakes, 123
Greenhouse effect, 62

H

Hackling, 249
Hacksaw, 152
Hammer, adze-eye, 158
Hammer, ball peen, 153
Hammer, claw, 153
Hammer, nail, 158
Hammer, sledge, 153
Hammer, tack, 161
Hammer, utility club, 153
Hammer blossom, 159
Hammers, 156
Handsaw, 152
Hand tools, 152
Hardwood, 123
Hardwoods, upland, 124
Hardwoods, wetland, 124
Harrington, Sir John, 50
Hatcheling, 249
Hatchet, 146
Heat flow, 95
Heating, 59
Hetcheling, 249
Hinging, 134
Honey, 312
Honey extractor, 202
Honey recipes, 312
  basic bread, 313
  honey drops, 313
  honey snacks, 314
  slaw, 314
Horses, 150
Hotbed, 199
Howe, 227
Hyacinths, 271
Hydraulic jacks, 155

I

Infiltration, 94, 99
Inland marine floater, 15
Insulation, 100
Insulation, adding, 100
Insulation, fiberglass, 111

Insulation, homesteader's guide to, 105
Insulspray, 116
Insurance, 11
Insurance, auto, 15
Insurance, fire, 13
Insurance, flat rate fire, 14
Insurance, homeowner's, 13
Insurance, liability, 16
Insurance, life, 16
Insurance, major medical, 13
Insurance, medical, 12
Insurance, protection for animals, 16
Iripolymer Foam System, 116
Irises, 268
Ironwood, 140

J

Jams, 299
Jams, making, 299
Jams, making low-sugar, 304
Jams, storing, 306
Jellies, 299
Jellies, making, 299
Jellies, making low-sugar, 304
Jotul, 70

K

Kalwell Corporation, 62
Kerr Glass Manufacturing Corporation, 295
Kettle, 67

L

Land, 1
Land, managing, 4
Land, open, 7
Leeks, 284
Leich, Harold, 55
Lentils, 277
Level, 154
L-M pectin, 305
Log cabin, 18
Log cabin, building, 18
Log cabin, cost per room, 29
Log cabin, door, 22
Log cabin, extra room, 25
Log cabin, floor, 22
Log cabin, foundation, 20
Log cabin, loft, 23
Log cabin, porch, 25
Log cabin, roof, 24
Log cabin, windows, 22
Logs, 21
Logs, first cross, 21

Logs, saw, 123
Logs, sill, 21
Logs, veneer, 123
Lumber, 142
Lumber, recycling, 142

M

Mallet, 159
Malva-mallow, 272
Maple, 140
Marginal savings analysis, 108
Marigolds, 270
Marmalades, 299
Mason jar, 293
Maul, 159
McCall's, 255
McKenna, Helen, 49
McLeod's Island, 18
Melons, 285
Milfoil, 274
Millboard, 82
Millet, 286
Minisaws, 165
Miter saw, 152
Mittens, 251
Montgomery Ward, 227
Mung beans, 277

N

Narcissus, 271
National Bureau of Standards, 107
National Fire Protection Agency (NFPA), 82
New Home, 227
Nicholson, 150
Norway, 50
Nova Scotia, 18

O

Oak, 140
Ohio State University, 113
Oilstone, 154
Onions, 288
Owens Corning, 112

P

Pargeting, 184
Park Seed Company, 272
Parsley, 314
Parsley, curly leafed, 316
Parsley, Italian, 316
Parsley recipes, 314
    dumplings, 317
    herb bread, 316
    parsley-cheese balls, 316
    salad, 316

Patchworks, 233
Pectin, 300
Pectin, L-M, 305
Peen, 158
Peonies, 268
Peony, 274
Peppers, 284, 288
Perennials, 270
Pinking shears, 226
Pits for storage, 291
Pliers, 154
Plumber's snake, 80
Plumbing, 49
Polyethylene sheet plastic, 101
Polystyrene, 116
Polyurethane foam, 116
Pond, 36
Pond, embankment, 36
Pond, excavated, 36
Pond, selecting a site, 37
Posts, 193
Potatoes, 288
Poultry buildings, 144
Power saw, 155
Power tools, 152
Preserves, 299
Pulpwood, 123
Pumpkins, 288

Q

Queen Elizabeth I, 50
Quilt, crazy, 242
Quilt, tube, 242
Quilting, 232
Quilting projects, 238
Quilts, 242
Quoin, 158

R

Radishes, 283
Radishes, Oriental daikon, 283
Rafter square, 154
Rakers, 171
Raking, 2
Rapco Foam, 116
Rasps, 154
Ratchet brace, 153
Rawhide, 214
Rice, 286
Rodents, 8, 285
Rudbeckia, 277
Rugmaking, 251
Rugs, 254
Rugs, braided, 254
Rugs, crocheted, 259
Rugs, hooked, 259

Rugs, knitted, 257
Rugs, rag or woven, 256
Rugs, sheepskin, 263
Rutabagas, 288
R value, 96
Rye, 286

S

Saber saw, 155
Salsify, 283
Sauerkraut, 285
Saw timber, 123
Scilla, 271
Scissors, 226
Screwdrivers, 153
Scutching, 249
Sears, Roebuck and Company, 227
Seedbed, 40
Seedling machine that is electric, 209
Septic tank, 54
Sewing, 224
Sewing machine, 226
Sewing machines, treadle, 226
Shasta daisy, 277
Sheetrock, 148
Shims, 158
Shovels, 172
Shovels, fire, 172
Shovels, round mouth, 172
Shovels, scoop, 174
Shovels, square mouth, 172
Simplicity, 225
Singer, 227
Sledgehammer, 161
Snowdrops, 271
Snowshoes, 212
Snowshoes, making frames for, 213
Socks, 251
Socks, divide for heel, 250
Socks, materials, 250
Socks, toe decrease, 251
Socks, turn heel, 251
Softwood, 123
Soil Conservation Service, 10
Solar heating system, 59
Solar heating system, active, 59
Solar heating system, passive, 61
Soybeans, 277
Spades, 172
Spades, garden, 172
Spades, tile, 174
Spark arrester, 80
Sphagnum moss, 22
Spinach, 317
Spinach recipes, 317
    blender spinach souffle, 320
    fried spinach balls, 318
    spinach and cheese pie, 319
    spinach-rice casserole, 319
    soup, 317
    steak, 317
    spinach, tomato, and cheese loaf, 319
Spokeshave, 154
Spoons for carving, 220
Springhouse, 45
Springs, 41
Sprocket, 170
Sprocket, rim, 170
Sprocket, star, 170
Spud for peeling, 153
Stand, 122
Stanley, 150
Staple gun, 154
Steel, 74
Stepladder, 146
Stove, barrel, 90
Stove, box, 73
Stove, cast-iron, 75
Stove, chamber, 73
Stove, circulator, 74
Stove, cleaning, 87
Stove, combination, 73
Stove, fireplace insert, 74
Stove, freestanding, 73
Stove, Scandinavian, 75
Stove, setup, 81
Stove, wood, 71
Stoveboard, 82
Stovepipe, 84
Stovepipe, cleaning, 87
Stovepipe, connecting, 86
Stoves, 69
Stoves, Ashley, 69
Stoves, Riteway, 69
Stoves, sheet metal, 69
Stoves, Shenandoah, 69
Stoves, Wonderwood, 69
Stumps, 1
Stumps, removing, 1
Styrofoam, 112
Swage, 158
Swales, 6
Sweden, 50
Sweet William, 274

T

Table queen, 285
Tennessee Valley Authority, 118
Thimble, 86
Thompson, Walter, 209
Tickseed, 272

Toilet, automatic slop, 51
Toilet, biological, 54
Toilet, composting, 52
Toilet, oil flush, 52
Toilet, one-piece, 50
Toilet, pressurized flush, 51
Toilet, shallow trap, 50
Toilet, vacuum, 52
Toilet, waste water, 55
Toilets, 49
Tomatoes, 288
Tools, 18, 149
Tools, hand, 152
Tools, power, 155
Treadle sewing machines, 227
Tree, felling, 130
Trees, 18, 125
Trees, access, 125
Trees, criteria for selecting to cut, 126
Trees, growth rate, 125
Trees, site quality, 182
Tulips, 271

U

U-factor, 63
United Parcel Service, 75
U.S. Department of Agriculture, 10

V

VanderZwaag, David, 18
Vapor barrier, 101
Varnish, 217
Vegetables, canning, 292
Vegetables, storing, 287, 288
Vegetables, warm dry storage, 288
Vermiculite, 118
Victorian era, 243

Vise, mechanic's, 154
Vise, woodworking, 154
Vises, 154
Vogue, 225

W

Walnut Acres, 305
Water, 30
Watercourse, 41
Wedge for splitting steel, 153
Wheat, 286
Wheeler, 227
White, 227
Widow-makers, 132
Wildlife, 4
Wildlife and land management, 4
Wilting, 130
Windows, 97
Winter squash, 288
Wood, 67, 121
Wood, drying, 129
Wood, heating with, 67
Wood, splitting, 140
Wood, upland mixed, 124
Wood, wetland mixed, 124
Woodchopper's maul, 153
Woodlands, 6
Woodman, Mary Ann, 244
Woodshed, 175
Wood stove, 71
Wood stove, buying, 71
Wood stove, safety, 77
Workmen's compensation, 12
Wrenches, 154

Y

Yarrow, 274